PERSUASION: Theory and Practice

PERSUASION: Theory

Second Edition

and Practice

KENNETH E. ANDERSEN
University of Illinois

PHILLIPS MEMORIAL
LIBRARY
PROVIDENCE COLLEGE

ALLYN AND BACON, INC.
Boston   London   Sydney   Toronto

BF
637
P4
A53
1978

Copyright © 1978 and 1971 by Allyn and Bacon, Inc., 470 Atlantic Avenue, Boston, Massachusetts 02210.

All rights reserved. Printed in the United States of America. No part of the material protected by this copyright notice may be reproduced or utilized in any form or by any means, electronic or mechanical, including photocopying, recording, or by any information storage and retrieval system, without written permission from the copyright owner.

Photo Credits: United Press International—pp. 2, 136, 168, 308; Elliott J. Echelman—pp. 24, 46, 104, 186, 210, 234, 286, 340, 366, 384; Ellis Herwig—pp. 72, 400.

Library of Congress Cataloging in Publication Data

Andersen, Kenneth E
    Persuasion.
    Bibliography: p.
    Includes index.
    1. Persuasion (Psychology) I. Title.
BF637.P4A53 1978   301.15'4   77-15499
ISBN 0-205-06086-2

To my wife, Mary
To my mother, Anna

Contents

PREFACE		ix
I	**PERSUASION: A JOINT PARTICIPATION**	1
	1 The Nature of Persuasion	3
	2 Persuasion, the Individual, and Society	25
II	**PARTICIPATION AS RECEIVERS**	44
	3 Motivation, Attitudes, and Behavior	47
	4 Receiver and Situation Analysis	73
	5 Attention and Interest	105
III	**CREATION OF MESSAGES**	120
	6 Preparation	123
	7 Content	137
	8 Organization	169
	9 Language and Style	187
	10 Delivery: Bringing the Message into Being	211
IV	**PARTICIPATION AS SOURCES**	232
	11 Ethos: Creation and Effects	235
	12 Persuasion and Effects upon the Source	267
V	**USE OF CHANNELS AND SETTINGS**	284
	13 Relationship of Channel and Setting	287
	14 The Persuasive Campaign: Multiple Channels and Settings	309

VI PERSPECTIVES ON PERSUASION 338
15 Ethics and Persuasion 341
16 Totalitarian Persuasion 367
17 Evaluating Persuasion Effects 385
18 Creating a Response System to Persuasion 401

EPILOGUE 415
SELECTED BIBLIOGRAPHY 417
SUBJECT INDEX 423
AUTHOR INDEX 429

Preface

This edition, like its predecessor, is designed for students in their first persuasion course. Attention is given both to the theory of persuasion as a basis for practice in the classroom setting and, more importantly, in careers and personal lives, and also to the practice of persuasion as a basis for formulating and testing theory. The emphasis throughout is on participation in the persuasion process as users of the process—as persuaders, as potential persuadees—putting persuasion to work to enhance our lives individually and collectively.

The first edition of this book was written in the late 1960s when the field of persuasion was undergoing a transition that incorporated many new emphases. This edition reflects the evolution of interest in persuasion into the late 1970s. Much of the material is new, and some chapters have been totally rewritten. Other chapters remain largely unchanged in structure and content because the material has withstood the test of time, and additional research has served to validate the points made.

Those acquainted with the first edition will find the same emphasis upon a full examination of the persuasion process in terms of the forces involved and the variety of results obtained. The book remains eclectic in approach. With the greater volume of research findings and writing on persuasion, the generalizations offered are less tied to specific research studies since the generalizations can be based upon a greater amount of tested material.

The most obvious change is the effort to ground the persuasion process in a concept of human beings as active agents working through persuasion to control their lives and to establish and test their own life plans. The ethics chapter goes beyond the previous material to provide a more specific statement of a means for resolving the ethical questions which confront us in persuasion.

The effort to treat the material in the book as in invitation to dialogue with the reader is enhanced. The style is more direct and overtly invites the reader into a dialogue on the many issues relative to persuasion theory and practice.

Readers will discover the following presuppositions. First, learning is possible only when there is active involvement on the part of the learner. I ask you to stop reading and to challenge the material by seeking alternative explanations. Although a text cannot replace the vigorous dialogue of the classroom, it can provide a sense of dialogue with the participating reader.

Second, the history of persuasion theory and practice, as well as contemporary theories and practices, have much to contribute to our understanding of persuasion. Contemporary empirical research, descriptive and experimental, similarly has much to contribute. We profit by drawing upon all sources. Our goal is to derive the best understanding of persuasion we can obtain to apply as a persuader, as a consumer of persuasion, and as an informed, participating member of society.

Third, although persuasion is grounded in careful research and analysis, its practice will always remain an art. Persuasion theory draws heavily upon generalizations developed in the speech communication discipline and in fields such as psychology, sociology, philosophy, and logic, but application of the theory always involves unique elements. The skill in moving from theory to wise, sensitive application in specific situations is an art to be cultivated by practice.

Fourth, persuasion is sufficiently complex that we will never understand it fully in the same sense of being able to make precise predictions of the results. But it can be profitably studied. The fact that we do not know everything does not mean that what we know is false. As our understanding of the process grows, we have been able to formulate better and more specific generalizations. Our theory has become more complex, and we have abandoned the simple prescriptions that claimed to yield the easy formula. A more complex theory with a greater number and more specific generalizations is a much more powerful theory.

Fifth, persuasion involves ethical considerations. It is preeminently concerned with the choices made by persuaders and receivers alike. With choice comes the matter of ethical considerations and value judgments. They are of importance in their own right, but the ethical decisions also markedly affect the persuasion process and its outcomes.

Persuasion as a process is central to our existence as individuals and as members of a complex society. Understanding the persuasion process is essential to understanding human behavior. Inevitably the study of persuasion leads us to a deeper examination of ourselves as well as others.

Any author owes debts to many who contribute to the formation of the content and to the production. I remain indebted to my teachers—titled professors, students, and colleagues. I grow more dependent on them every day.

I wish to express appreciation to those who commented upon the first edition—Professors Thorrel Fest, Ted Clevenger, and Ivan Harvey—and to those who reviewed the first edition as a basis for this revision—Professors Jack L. Whitehead, The University of Texas at Austin; Richard Rieke, University of Utah; Richard Ullman, California State University at Fresno; Donald Shields, Indiana State University; and Robert Jeffrey, The University of Texas at Austin—I also appreciate the advice of Professors Richard Rieke and Jack Whitehead, who reviewed this manuscript.

I wish to express appreciation to the University of Illinois, which selected me for the Program of Study in a Second Discipline, which allowed me to spend the fall 1976 semester working in the Department of Philosophy at Illinois under the guidance of B. J. Diggs, professor of moral philosophy and ethics. Professor Diggs encouraged me and both illumined and exemplified many concepts in the area of morals and ethics. Without that study program, this book would have been completed several months earlier—but it would have been a different book.

I wish to express a personal debt to my wife, Mary, who coauthored chapter 15 and assisted in revising it through her continuing interest and study in the area of communication and ethics. I record an obligation to my son, Erik, who respected the need to shut the study door and who too often settled for a hug rather than talk or play. Finally I express my appreciation to Dr. Terry Noonan of Carle Clinic, whose skill as a surgeon made it possible for me to sit long hours at my study desk and the typewriter once again.

Urbana, Illinois
May 1977

PERSUASION: Theory and Practice

1 PERSUASION: A JO

1 The Nature of Persuasion
What Is Persuasion?
A Definition of Persuasion
A Model of Persuasion
  A General Communication Model
  A Persuasion Model
The Study of Persuasion
An Orientation to the Book

NT PARTICIPATION

2   **Persuasion, the Individual, and Society**
    Persuasion and Choice
    Persuasion and the Persuader
        The Decision to Persuade
        Alternative Decisions
    Persuasion and the Receiver
    Persuasion and Society
    Persuasion as a Means to Truth

1 The Nature of Persuasion

Persuasion is a communicative activity that unites people—yet it also permits maximum individual choice. Persuasion is a key to maintaining a complex, voluntary society in which people have the right to their choices and responsibility for them.

At its best, persuasion is a clear statement of mutual respect and of self-respect by the people involved. In being open to persuasion, we express a respect for the right and responsibility of others to influence our beliefs and actions and a respect for ourselves as choice makers. When we are persuaders and ask others to choose a particular action or belief, we express a respect for their right of choice and a respect for our own beliefs and ourselves. Without this respect, persuasion becomes at one extreme a matter of force and coercion and at the other extreme an empty, perhaps harmful, ritual.

If you were to ask a group of people to suggest synonyms for or associations evoked by the terms *persuasion* or *persuading,* you would quickly obtain a wide range of responses: influence, attitude change, propaganda, selling, political campaigning, seduction, action, deceit, information, motivation, manipulation, and so forth.

The connotations that prevail may be positive or neutral (for example, if you ask students in a class with *persuasion* in the title), but for many, persuasion suggests something undesirable, something more or less hidden and unfair, a subtle or not so subtle playing on feelings or a lack of information to manipulate people. It may suggest people doing things to other people without regard for those people, their needs, their integrity. Negative connotations are so linked to the term *persuasion* for some people that these associations become part of the meaning of the word. This view is often associated with the belief that persuasion is so pernicious that most people are powerless to resist. They believe that persuasion is not only bad but also destructive because it is almost irresistible.

We can safely assume, however, that the persuasion process is not so simple or bad that it can be accurately described in such a fashion. Persuaders soon learn that it is impossible to reform the world by a single persuasive effort or even by massive efforts. It is tempting to settle for the false view that those seeking to disrupt and destroy (others) are successful, while those seeking to unify and build (ourselves) are not. But we all know that some attempts at persuasion are highly successful, some partially successful, some have no effect, and some are disastrous failures. Sometimes the skill of those involved makes a difference in the outcome; sometimes it does not. Sometimes the occasion, the means employed, or some accident makes a great deal of difference in the outcome; sometimes it makes no difference.

The practice of persuasion is older than recorded history. The earliest writings contain explicit references to the importance of persuasion activity. In reading this book you will find references to the theory and practice of persuasion, both ancient and contemporary. Many of the problems that the ancients identified are still troubling us today: questions about the role and function of persuasion in society and the lives of individuals, questions of ethics and values, questions related to the effectiveness of particular means of persuasion.

This book should help you to increase your understanding of persuasion. Using it as one part of your effort at understanding, you can know more about the persuasion process as it relates to you and the people around you. The book will not offer you a simple formula for the complete understanding of persuasion. A complete understanding demands a full understanding of both yourself and the other person. Obviously that degree of complete understanding does not exist. But we can understand more than we do about persuasion. And given its central role in our lives, we can hope that we will continue to grow in that understanding throughout our lives.

WHAT IS PERSUASION?

We cannot legislate the meanings of words for people, but it is important for us to develop sufficient common ground that we can communicate with reasonable efficiency. This book provides my definition of persuasion. This section begins by involving us jointly in the process of definition and by laying the groundwork for what follows.

THE NATURE OF PERSUASION

We will begin to formulate a definition of persuasion by asking a few questions about some ordinary situations.

1. "Because I need to find out how well you are understanding the material we have covered this far, we will have an hourly quiz next Monday." Is this a sample of persuasion?

2. "Will you give a dollar to help a child live?" Head down, I walk on into the bank as if I hadn't heard the question. My office partner says, "Ken, they are hitting us for another donation. This one is for kids with muscle diseases." I give five dollars. Is this second message more persuasive? Is it because I am used to "giving at the office"? Why is my officemate successful?

3. The sign on the corner of a rarely traveled residential street says, "Stop." A car goes through without stopping. The next day a police car is sitting empty halfway down the block. The car stops at the sign. Why? Are you sure of your reason?

4. It is late, you are tired, frustrated, and you've made no progress on a speech assignment. Your roommate has been trying to sleep, without much success. "Let's go get a pizza." "Can't." "Come on! Do you good." "Have to get this speech done." "You aren't getting anywhere anyway. We can yak about some ideas over a pizza. I heard a good speech in my class you might do something with." You go. Were you persuaded? By your roommate?

5. "My fellow Americans, if elected I will bring law and order to the city. People will be able to walk down the streets in safety. We will have law and order if I am elected!" Many people vote for the candidate, and he is elected. Did he persuade the majority to vote for him? Or did the majority view on the need for law and order persuade the candidate to stress that issue and take the stand he did so he could be elected? Who persuaded whom and to what?

6. A free sample of Dial Spray Deodorant arrives at my doorstep. Several spot ads on television stress the merits of Dial. There is a big display of Dial Spray Deodorant in the middle of the aisle at the supermarket. I comment to my wife that the stuff smells pretty good. She brings home the economy size for me. She uses it when I do not. Is persuasion involved?

7. Since the 1930s, legislation supporting the idea of government provision of medical care for the needy has been introduced in the U.S. Congress. Socialized medicine is beaten down repeatedly. The ramparts stand. Then in the 1960s Medicare and Medicaid are adopted. Were the persuasion efforts in the 1930s failures?

8. "You shouldn't wear white socks. They don't look good." I wear white socks every day for the next week. Any connection?

9. After extensive discussion, we order an encyclopedia set from a salesman who calls at our home. I mention our purchase to a friend, who says, "I got taken on one of those deals once." An article in the *National Observer* reports the Federal Trade Commission has

6 PERSUASION: A JOINT PARTICIPATION

prohibited certain selling procedures of another encyclopedia company. WILL, the education TV station, carries a brief announcement that people have the right to cancel certain contracts within three days. After another extensive discussion about our finances, we call and cancel the purchase. Are some or all of these happenings part of the persuasion process?

What inferences can be drawn from these situations? Obviously there are many, but we can highlight some that are useful to us at this time.

Persuasion is a complex process. Understanding this process will involve an understanding of the psychology of behavior. We must look outside the narrow specifics of a situation to the forces that bear upon individuals in terms of their past history, the present, and their goals for the future.

Persuasion is integral to much of daily communication. Each of us is the target of massive amounts of persuasion from sources far removed from our daily conversations with family, friends, and associates. But these daily interactions also have much persuasion in them, and often the more important effects on our lives come from these ordinary interactions. Each of us is alternately persuader and persuadee in these daily interactions.

Persuader and persuadee are both responding to forces outside as well as inside themselves. The reasons why a particular persuasive effort is attempted are as much a response to forces outside and inside that individual as are the responses to that particular persuasive attempt by the receiver.

Persuader and persuadee are typically involved in an ongoing system of relationships: one to the other and to the society at large. The temperature setting on your thermostat affects me. Similarly if many of us have insulated our homes to save money on heating and air conditioning, we will be using less energy, which may permit a change in U.S. foreign policy.

A tremendous amount of persuasion goes on between and among people. Much of this influence is unconscious: the persuader has no clear recognition that she is attempting to affect the behavior of another person; the persuadee has no awareness that his behavior is being affected by the other. We are much more aware of persuasion efforts being transmitted through the mass media.

Not all attempts at persuasion are successful. Some are successful for a while and then are reversed. Others are not successful for a long time and then the desired goal is achieved.

People may respond one way in one situation but quite differently in another. What turns a person on one day may turn her off the next.

In the analysis of actual persuasion, it is extremely difficult if not impossible to say accurately, "This persuaded him." "The reason he did this was that I told him the truth." It may equally be untrue to say, "He did it of his own free will. I didn't try to influence him. I told him he could do whatever he wanted and I wouldn't interfere. It was all up to him."

To define the beginning or ending of a persuasive attempt may be exceedingly difficult. The entire previous experience of both the persuader and the persuadee is involved in any persuasive situation. The cumulative effects of a whole lifetime of persuasive attempts may finally result in a dramatic conversion for which the persuader of the moment takes credit.

Labeling a persuasive effort a success or failure is a difficult judgment. An appeal for action may evoke support from a few people, have no effect on most people, make one person so angry she forms a group to fight the proposal. The law may be rejected by the legislature one year, enacted into law the next year, declared unconstitutional five years later, and further efforts at legislation of this type abandoned. Success raises questions as to the basis for assessment. Do we make the judgment from the source's point of view? From the receivers'? A success for one partisan is a failure for another one. Is success to be judged immediately or on a delayed basis? How narrowly shall success be defined? The persuader may achieve her immediate goal but suffer tragic consequences in many other unanticipated respects from achieving that immediate goal.

A DEFINITION OF PERSUASION

It is tempting to define persuasion as *communication in which one person seeks to obtain a desired response from another.* But this statement has at least three major problems. First, it does not exclude the use of force, violence, or coercion as a means of persuasion. Second, it makes persuasion essentially identical with all of communication which seeks the creation of shared meanings. Third, the statement gives no emphasis to the role of symbols, particularly language, in persuasion. A more extensive and precise definition will be of greater use to us: *Persuasion is communication in which the communicator seeks through the use of symbolic agencies, particularly language, to effect a desired, voluntary change in the attitudes and/or actions of the receiver(s).* Examining the key terms in the definition will enable us to share more fully in a common meaning of the term *persuasion.*

I will use *persuasion* only in terms of human activity, specifically to actions chosen from among a range of possible actions by self-conscious choice-making individuals aware of the ethical dimensions of the activity. Two or more individuals must be involved. We are not interested in an individual's study and thinking except as these relate to and are part of a persuasion process. We are interested in the participation of both people in the process and concerned about the effects of the process on each of them and further effects on other people.

Communication is an even more difficult term to define. It is one form of interaction between people. It is a transaction in that both parties must contribute to the process, and a variety of different outcomes are possible. Both act mutually and reciprocally to determine the outcome. Communication is a process that is focused upon achieving a degree of shared understanding, of shared meanings for the symbols used in the transaction. Do not confuse the existence of the process with the question of the degree of success. The process of communication may occur even though the attempt to create a degree of shared meaning fails.

The communicator seeks raises several important issues. When two people engage in communication, they typically interchange roles very quickly as each responds to the other. In fact, during face-to-face conversations, we are usually both sending and receiving messages simultaneously. In many instances each person is trying to persuade the other so each is a communicator for one purpose and the receiver for the other. In many persuasive situations, however, we could all agree upon the individual we would identify as the communicator or persuader and those we would identify as the receivers.

The communicator seeks suggests some degree of conscious intent. Conscious intent becomes a problem in the definition of persuasion. The mind can be viewed as having various levels of conscious awareness. Indeed, it takes a psychiatrist to tell us that we are overeating so we will not have to compete in attracting the opposite sex or that we try to be a Don Juan because we are so insecure about our real sexual abilities. Behavior is the result of both conscious and unconscious forces, at least as we discuss these things in normal terms. Similarly, the decision to persuade may be the result of conscious and unconscious forces, and we may not be consciously aware that we are attempting to persuade. To the degree that persuasion has negative connotations, we may repress the awareness. We should view the effort to persuade as goal-directed behavior that results from some choice on the part of the communicator. It may be instantaneous, automatic, and unthinking. Or it may be the result of a careful, extended thought process with a careful weighing and testing of alternatives.

In studying persuasion, it is useful to focus upon many consciously weighed efforts to persuade so that we can see the workings of the persuasion process most clearly. When we seek to improve our practice of persuasion, we will be working at this process quite consciously. So, without forgetting that persuasion is often undertaken without any real sense of awareness, we will typically be talking about attempts at persuasion in which the persuader and quite often the intended persuadees are well aware that persuasion is taking place.

Through the use of symbolic agencies, particularly language, focuses upon the central role of symbols in the process. Symbols are things that stand in place of or represent something else. Although they exist as things in their own right, their function is representational: they stand in place of, they suggest, they link to some other object or thing. All symbols must exist, but they can represent or stand for things that do not exist. For example, we develop the word *justice* for something we create as a concept just as Tolkien created inhabitants for the Third Age of Middle-earth. In a society so conditioned to words and language as ours is, we naturally think of the symbols we call words as being the primary means of communication. And indeed they are. But almost anything else can be used symbolically. Even the absence of words—silence—can be symbolic.

Symbolic agencies are useful only to the degree that they produce a degree of predictability of meaning. Indeed, if each person had a different response to the symbol, there would be no symbol. Symbols function only as they affect the cognitions, the mental constructions, of others. In a very real sense we can only affect, have an impact on, the cognitions of other people. We do not bring their cognitions into being; only they can do that. Our efforts affect, have an impact on, help to stir up or motivate their cognitions.

Effect a desired, voluntary change indicates that the persuader wishes to bring into being, to determine, a particular change or set of changes in the receiver. But *voluntary* indicates that the receiver must also choose or desire the change. While the persuader wants to bring this change into being through the use of symbols that affect the cognitions of the receiver, the persuader is committed to the necessity of the receiver's choosing to make that change. This phrase shows the mutual respect for each other and for self that must be operative in the persuasion process. A choice implies alternatives, meaningful alternatives from which individuals may choose according to their own judgments.

The word *change* should not mislead you. Changes can be of many sorts. It can be a new action or a decision not to repeat an old action. It may be one of degree and not of kind. I may not be more or less favorable toward the President, but I may be more or less firmly committed to the position I already held. I may have a different reason for an attitude or action. I may do something more or less frequently. I may think of something more or less often. I may think something is more or less important to me or to you. All of these could be *desired, voluntary changes.*

In attitudes and/or actions of the receiver(s) indicates that the change can be one that occurs in a belief, a value, an attitude, or it can be a change in action and behavior. Typically the change a persuader seeks most immediately is some type of mental assent. Perhaps the most significant change occurs when a person is willing to listen to further efforts at persuasion; the exposure may ultimately produce a dramatic change. Obviously changes in beliefs or values are sought because a person's behavior is linked to attitudes held, and eventually the change in a belief, attitude, or value should produce a change in behavior.

Persuasion, then, is a complex, ongoing, interactive process in which a sender and receiver are linked by symbols that provide a means of stirring up meanings in the receiver and by which the sender seeks to influence the response of the receiver in some desired way.

A MODEL OF PERSUASION

Persuasion is a species of the genus communication, which in its broadest sense includes everything from human communication to the IBM computer, the thermostat and furnace in our homes, the honey dance of the bee. If communication is restricted to human communication, we begin to encounter the problem of differentiating persuasion from all of communication. Most definitions of communication focus upon the goal of creating shared meanings. Definitions may range from "any dynamic information-sharing process"[1] to "the form of interpersonal exchange through which, figuratively speaking, persons can come in contact with each other's minds."[2] My definition of persuasion goes beyond the effort to obtain a common meaning of a term to the attempt to gain acceptance of a particular way of viewing the world (an attitude) and to action of a specifically desired sort. The goal of shared meanings common to all communication becomes a means to an end of achieving a change in attitude or action.

The problem of distinguishing persuasion from all of communication is compounded by the growing realization that any communication can influence the participants in many different ways. Adults transmit values, biases, prejudices, and patterns of response all too unconsciously to their

---

[1] Theodore Clevenger, Jr., "What Is Communication?" *Journal of Communication* 9 (1959): 5.

[2] Theodore M. Newcomb, Ralph H. Turner, and Philip E. Converse, *Social Psychology* (New York: Holt, Rinehart and Winston, 1965), p. 219.

children. Teachers think of themselves as presenting information, but they also transmit values, attitudes, and perceptions as well.

Actually, the distinction between communication and persuasion is of limited importance. The dividing line is indistinct. There is no harm if we treat a communication situation largely as one of persuasion. There is a slightly greater risk in assuming persuasion is not involved in communication, since very different perceptions may result when one viewer, receiver, or communicator looks upon the situation as persuasive and the other as nonpersuasive. Distinctions between communication and persuasion can be made in many situations, and it seems useful to do so. In most situations where a clear distinction cannot be made, we can simply accept that fact.

Because of the close relationship of persuasion and communication, it is not surprising that we should begin to build a model of the persuasion process by developing a general communication model.

A General Communication Model

A model is a representation in some transformed way of an object, an idea, a process, or a complex, interactive system. A model is useful because it selects certain aspects of a complex unit or system and presents them in a way that facilitates understanding. The model provides the opportunity to study various factors in greater detail; it permits testing of the interrelationships of the parts. Although useful, a model is not the thing examined. More than one model can be used to represent the same thing or different aspects of the same thing. The model is on paper; persuasion occurs in minds and involves the interaction of many forces. The model is static, and the analysis seems to be linear; persuasion is dynamic, interrelated, multidirectional.

The models that follow are worth close analysis because they form the basis of the remainder of this book. Starting with a simple model of a typical communication in which two people are talking together, jointly participating in the exchange, we build to a more complex and specific representation of the persuasion process. The remaining seventeen chapters flesh out the persuasion model that we are developing in this chapter.

We will begin by building a model that represents the minimum requirements for communication. We need to have two actors or agents who have the potential to communicate with one another. There must be one or more channels available. We must have some situation in which the two persons can participate in the sense of being linked or joined by the message. We need one or more potential messages. (These essentials are represented in figure 1A.)

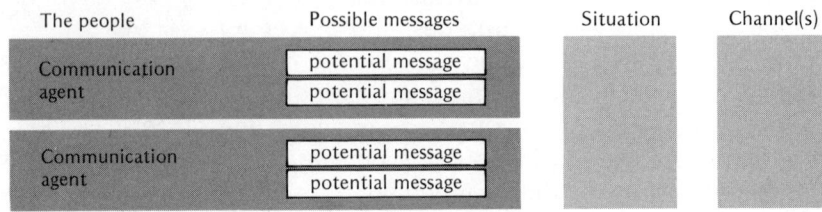

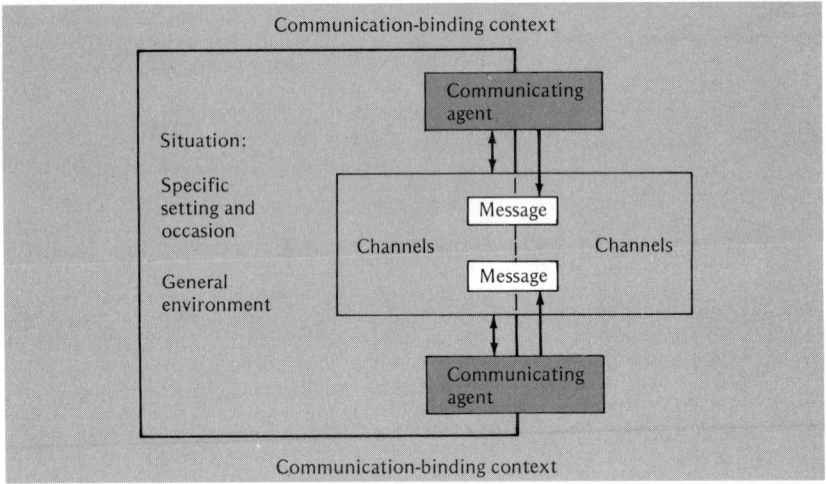

Elements necessary in actual communication

Figure 1. Models of Potential and Actual Communication

But we do not have communication—only the potential for it. These agents, the situation, the channel(s), and the message(s) must become interrelated and joined together in some meaningful sense. The potential must become actual. We can introduce a sixth element to describe the change from the potential relationship of these five different elements to an actual, dynamic interrelationship in which the elements reciprocally affect and to a degree mutually determine one another. The term for this sixth element is the *communication-binding context*.

When communication is actually taking place, we have as a minimum the situation represented in figure 1B. Certain obvious changes have occurred in 1B as contrasted to 1A. Potential messages exist only in the minds of people. In actual communication a message or messages exist as stimuli in one or more channels. These messages exist only because some agent brought them into being. So an arrow links the message to

THE NATURE OF PERSUASION

the person whose activity created that message. Further, messages do not go to other people. People must reach out to messages by using one or more of their five senses to take in some portion of the stimuli available in the channels. The situation directly affects the joint participation of the two agents, helps to determine the channels available, and is a key factor in the responses made by the sources and thus a factor that may strongly affect the message(s) produced. (Of course, people, messages, and channels also help to determine or form the situation.) And, with communication a reality, we now have the communication-binding context that focuses the relationship of these forces one to the other and indicates that a specific reality exists as opposed to all the potential reality that did exist.

Figure 1B represents a typical situation in which two people are communicating. There is no identification or label of source and receiver. There is no identification of the nature of the messages being created in the channels. Perhaps one person is talking, the other nodding her head. Both of these activities are messages; one is not necessarily prior to or more important than the other. The nodding of the head in greeting may produce a spoken response. A particular statement may produce a nod suggesting agreement. You can fill in any of a wide range of specific happenings within this general framework.

Most communication is not quite so simple, of course. Communication may involve a number of people interacting. A variety of communication agents (some you may wish to label agencies) may be present as we watch TV, one person scans a magazine, another reads the paper while we talk. Figure 2 represents one situation. There are four potential agents (or agencies) involved. Perhaps the TV is tuned to the evening news. One roommate is thinking and is oblivious to what is going on. Two roommates are talking about how to judge whether the steak is done enough on one side. The situation is thus strongly controlling the content of their exchange. Change the situation, and the content of the messages would certainly change. The situation does not determine the messages exchanged; the response of the two communicators does.

Since this is a dynamic, interrelated communication situation, any number of possibilities are present. In another instant the roommate who was engrossed in thinking may start listening to the TV. The other two may stop talking about the steak and begin fixing the salad and setting the table. There are hundreds of possibilities for this same situation or for many other situations using these same elements. Remember that a particular point in time suggests a freezing of the activity, whereas communication is really a constant series of linked points in time. To freeze the action misses the motion, the change, the activity.

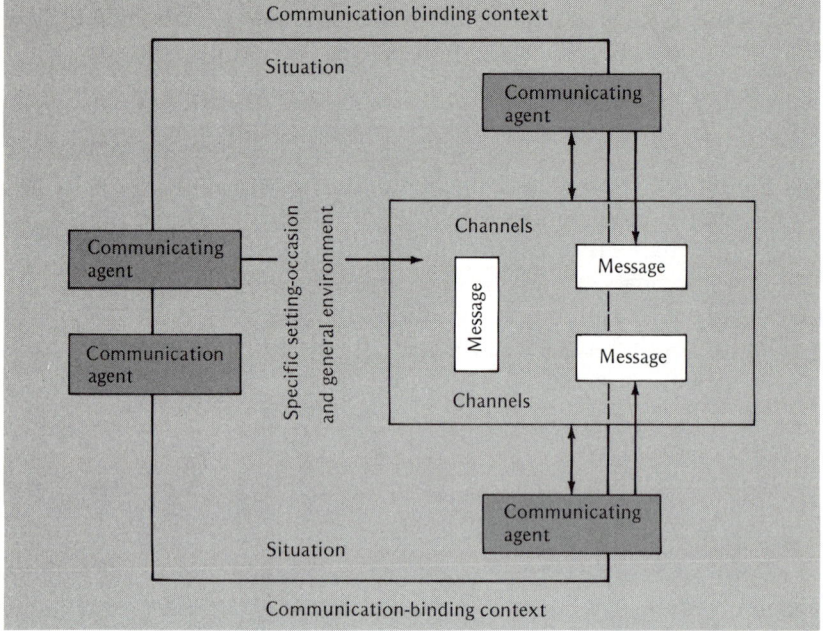

Figure 2. A Transactional Representation of Communication

A Persuasion Model

This general communication model provides the basis for a more developed model focusing specifically upon the persuasion process. The participants are the persuader and the receiver. Of course, there may be many receivers, and each can be a persuader seeking to effect a change in the other. Also, rather than envison that the responses of the receiver necessarily constitute an actual message, we may translate this into a recognition of a potential or an actual message under the label *feedback*. *Feedback* typically describes responses made to a source or individual that in some way provide a basis for estimating effects. For example, the score on a test is feedback; a listing of the right answers for those missed is certainly a greater and more helpful kind of feedback. In face-to-face situations feedback of some sort is readily available. In one-to-one conversations this normally involves a constant interchange of roles as communicator and receiver. With a speaker addressing a large audience, there are feedback cues in the form of facial response, bodily set, and so forth. Often questions may follow during a forum period, or there will be the chance to talk with various people, assess the pledge cards signed, or use some other basis of assessment of impact.

THE NATURE OF PERSUASION

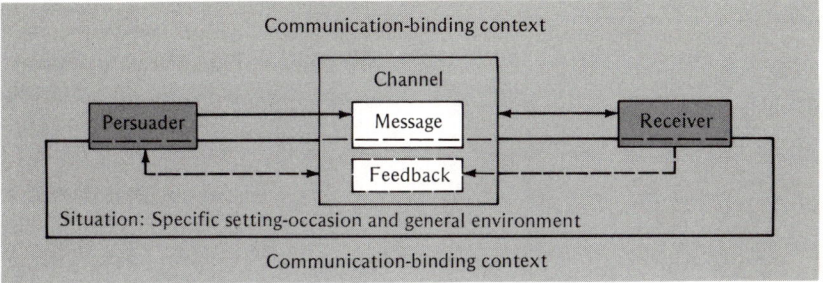

Persuader and Receiver Factors

1. Knowledge, ideas, experiences
2. Attitudes, beliefs, values
3. Needs, wants, goals
4. Interests
5. Group and role memberships
6. Communication abilities
7. Perception of other factors

Channel Elements

1. Nature of media
2. Limits on audience
   a. Target audience
   b. Mass audience
3. Selectivity in transmission of stimuli
   a. Sound
   b. Sight
   c. Others
4. Noise and interference

Communication-Binding Context

1. Interaction of all the elements
2. Effect of time
3. Process nature of communication
4. Complexities due to nature of processes involved in communication
   a. Multiple or institutional sources
   b. Translations or other intermediaries
   c. Mass media

Message Elements

1. Ideas and content
2. Organization
3. Language and style
4. Delivery
   a. Spoken
   b. Written
   c. Others

Situation: Specific Setting-Occasion and General Environment

1. State of things generally
2. State of the topic
3. Immediate environment
4. Audience size
5. Availability of media channels
6. Interaction of other elements affecting setting
7. Public or private

Figure 3. A General Model of Persuasion

In the mass media most feedback is delayed and far more indirect. Changes in the sales of a product may provide a partial indication of effectiveness of a campaign, but since sales are a product of many factors, this feedback is not direct and not easy to interpret.

Rather than suggest the ways in which the model can be redrawn to reflect a specific persuasion situation and ways in which we might more specifically label one or another part of the model in a situation, let us examine the six elements included in the model.

Persuader

The persuader is the source or originator of the persuasion attempt. *Source* may be the better label since the attempt to persuade is often a response to the actions of the receiver, or the persuader is given that task to perform. Thus, labeling the originator of the attempt may raise very complex issues. The source's actions are motivated; actions are the response of the source to some group or complex of forces impinging upon him or her.

A persuader is an active, responsive, and responsible agent, not a passive, impotent being. The source possesses a mind. It has available the totality of the persuader's attitudes, beliefs, information. The mind is able to focus in an anticipatory way upon the potential receiver(s), setting, alternative channels. The persuader can test, alternatively accepting and rejecting a whole series of possible messages without actual delivery of any of them. Obviously the source is limited by what he or she brings to the communication situation. If information is wrong or lacking, decisions will be within what is known. Even if knowledge about the receiver is faulty, the persuader will still act in terms of it. The persuader is free to choose but is bound within the freedom perceived.

The persuader responds to the process of persuasion. During the communication, the source is active both in affecting and in reacting to the situation, the receivers, and the message and in the act of creating the message. The source may be particularly attuned to feedback, which can be interpreted, consciously and unconsciously, to provide additional basis for altering the persuasive effort.

Message

The message is the constellation of stimuli the persuader actually puts into the channel. The message is what we may capture on videotape, or film. The message is the one element in the communication matrix that can be exactly replicated; it can be held constant and reused again and again.

The definition of message in this way is a very crucial point. Whatever the ideas the source may have intended, the message is what is in the channel. Some of what is in the message (a composite of responses of the source that is simultaneously a composite of stimuli to receiver) was put there consciously by the source, but in most instances the vast majority of the elements are unconsciously placed in the message.

It is important to note that the message *is*, but the message does not mean. Meaning is a property of the human mind. Thus, the elements or stimuli that constitute the message have meaning for the person who put them there; they may stir up meanings in the receiver, meanings like or unlike those intended by the source. Further, an observer examin-

THE NATURE OF PERSUASION

ing the process may see quite different meanings from those attached to the stimuli by source and receiver. The concept that the message does not mean but that people have meanings for messages is a critical one. Unless this view is firmly fixed, some parts of this book may appear contradictory.

Channel

The channel is the medium in which the message exists. The channel often is viewed as serving a limiting function: thus, face-to-face communication permits feedback in a direct way that television does not. Television transmits visible as well as audible stimuli. The printed text of the speech is something entirely different from the sounds heard over the radio. Channels have impact in and of themselves. Marshall McLuhan's point that the medium is the message (or the massage) has emphasized this valid point.

Situation: Specific setting-occasion and general environment

Situation refers to both the larger context of what is going on in the world (general environment) and the immediate setting and occasion. The general environment is relevant in that a major news event may prevent the persuader's concern from being noticed. Larger events may be relevant to a specific event in the setting or may be used to stir interest in the receivers by tying to some point in the message. The situation includes past events and those occurring during the transmission of the message. Indeed, it is useful to include the events that follow the message and affect the response to it in the short term.

The situation provides the grounding of many of the other elements in the communication process. But the situation is also affected by the other elements within the communication-binding context. The message helps to shape the nature of the occasion: the serious memorial address alters the situation just as does the humorous parody of the boss. When the boss walks in during the middle of the parody, adding one more receiver, that is part of the setting and certainly affects the responses of all those involved.

Receiver

The receiver is the person (or persons) for whom the communication serves as a stimulus. At times, persuasion will fail because the desired receiver, either by accident or choice, does not pick up the message in the channel. The receiver is an active participant in persuasion. Without the joint participation in using one or more of her or his senses to pick up the stimuli and then interpreting the stimuli and giving them meaning, there would be no persuasion. Accidental or unintended receivers may be of as much interest as those intended by the persuader. Thus, we can limit *receiver* to one receiver or a particular group of receivers, or we can use it to refer to a wide variety of identifiable people and groups.

Communication-binding Context

This combination of words is the least familiar of those employed in the model. One function of this term is to describe the "processness" of the communication event—message, channel, setting, receiver do not mean persuasion until they become intermeshed and related so that each element is, potentially at least, acting upon the other in some sense. The most obvious interaction occurs in the oral face-to-face situation: persuader, conscious of receiver, creates messages that are put in channels to be picked up by the receiver. The receiver's responses may alter succeeding parts of the message markedly from what may have been planned, or the message may cease entirely. One channel may be abandoned, another employed. The source may decide to move to a totally new setting and try a new approach. It is only when all these elements become bound together that the persuasion process is actually occurring in the full sense of the word.

The communication-binding context invites the creation of a whole series of submodels to reflect the complexities of the complete communication process. One may think of Aristotle, perhaps lecturing to his students. The students copy the notes, and these notes form the basis for what we know as Aristotle's *Rhetoric*. We can represent the source, message, channel, setting, and receivers in this way. Many years pass. Lane Cooper decides to translate the *Rhetoric* with particular attention to the needs of the speech field. Again, a model can be supplied for this stage. As part of an assignment, a student reads the Lane Cooper translation in English. Again a model can be detailed. The communication-binding context is designed to invite attention to this potenial multiplicity or layering of processes within the total communication process.

The communication-binding context reminds us that the communication transaction has a finite, limited reality. A communication event one day is different from that of another day. Change any of the elements or any of the interactions in the communication process, and we have a different communication event. The difference may or may not be significant—but the potenial difference is there and must be recognized. Further, while many messages, many receivers, many settngs were possible, the communication-binding context indicates that the actual is caught and bound. The other alternatives are just that: alternatives to what did take place.

If the concept of the communication-binding context serves no other function, it should remind us that after analyzing the separate, discrete parts of the persuasion process, we must bind them together once again and return with greater understanding from the task of analysis. We must undertake a synthesis that yields greater understanding of persuasion.

THE STUDY OF PERSUASION

People study persuasion for many different reasons. The most obvious is to understand the forces that work in our world and to master those forces by understanding, predicting, and controlling them, thus changing what happens. In his discussion of the image of man, Isidor Chein suggests the image that informs the conception of people used as the groundwork for this text:

> . . . [Man is] an active, responsible agent, not simply a helpless, powerless reagent. Man, in the active image, is a being who actively does something with regard to some of the things that happen to him, a being who, for instance, tries to increase the likelihood that some things will happen and that others will not, a being who tries to generate circumstances that are compatible with the execution of his intentions, a being who may try to inject harmony where he finds disharmony or who may sometimes seek to generate disharmony, a being who seeks to shape his environment rather than passively permit himself to be shaped by the latter, a being, in short, who insists on injecting himself into the causal process of the world around him. If man is said to respond to his environment, the word "response" is to be taken in the sense that it has in active dialogue rather than in the sense of an automatic consequence.[3]

So we seek to understand persuasion to predict and control our world. This suggests the concern to master both the theory and the art of putting that theory into practice.

We study persuasion by developing theories about how it may function both from our own past experience and from the experiences of others. There have been and are still many attempts to form a theory of persuasion, but none of these theories yields absolute prediction. There is much about man we do not understand; therefore, there must be much about persuasion that we do not understand. One function of a theory is to provide both an invitation to that test theory and a means to do so.

Thus, you are invited to examine the various theories and approaches to persuasion—both those you hold and those supplied by others—and

---
[3] Isidor Chein, *The Science of Behavior and the Image of Man* (New York: Basic Books, 1972), p. 6.

test them by observation in actual practice. Obviously persuasion cannot be reduced to a formula, not even a complex one. As long as the formulas are general enough, they are helpful, suggestive guides. But when they are applied in a specific situation with a demand that they guarantee success, the formulas fall short. The prescriptive approach has two inherent flaws. (1) Exceptions to the generalizations always occur. Thus, the person who treats the generalization as prescriptive tends to reject what may be a useful generalization. (2) The approach denies the practitioner the opportunity to draw upon the totality of theory and to attempt to generate a unique solution that best fits the particular instance—one that will never again be exactly duplicated.

Assuming the view that persuasion is a complex, interrelated, interactive process means accepting the practice of persuasion as an art calling for insight and judgment in application that cannot be matched by the application of rigid, unvarying approaches and treating persuasion as a fixed process.

In addition to your own experience and that of others and the available writings directly on persuasion, you can use sources from many other fields of knowledge—psychology, sociology, history, logic, philosophy, linguistics.

Perhaps most importantly, you as a student should observe and analyze the many efforts at persuasion in which you are involved. We live in a world of persuasion, and we contribute to that world. Pay attention to the happenings in that world; they are a good check on the theory being taught and the assumptions being made. Practice both in and outside the classroom and in roles as persuader and receiver alike. This will provide a good basis for learning about persuasion *if* you are open to seeing what works (and does not work) in various situations.

AN ORIENTATION TO THE BOOK

As you have already seen, section I introduces you to a point of view about the persuasion process. This has involved defining persuasion and suggesting its relationship to communication generally. We have developed a model that will be the framework for the remainder of this book. The final chapter in this section sketches the role of the persuasion process in our lives as individuals and as a society.

Section II focuses upon the development of a psychology of human behavior. As the views about human nature have changed, so have the persuasion theories. As philosophical views change, so do the theories of persuasion. In many senses your theory of persuasion is the definition of your philosophy of life and your view of the psychology of people. And your practice of persuasion is the operationalization of these views. Often, we infer a person's philosophy or psychology by looking at her or his persuasion practices. Section II treats such matters as attention, interest, motivation, attitudes and values, and analysis of situation and receivers.

Section III discusses the role of messages in communication. The material in this section has comprised the bulk of most other persuasion texts since the traditional emphasis has been upon telling potential communicators (speakers) how to construct messages that were designed to be maximally effective in obtaining the desired audience-response. But messages can be only as effective as permitted by the interaction of all the elements in the persuasive process. So, although central, messages and the factors that contribute to them are not sufficient to provide a complete understanding of persuasion. The value of message elements is determined by the response of the receivers to these elements.

Section IV discusses the role of sources in persuasion. Not only does the source affect the receiver through the messages he or she frames, but also the reputation of the source and the impression that develops in the receivers concerning the source are key elements in determining persuasive impact. This section also stresses the forces that impinge upon the source and reminds us that the source is not a totally free agent but is responding to other factors.

Section V deals with the effects of channel and setting on persuasive outcomes. Particular attention is given to the relationships between channels and settings and the role of mass persuasion campaigns.

Section VI deals with some special problems of interest relative to persuasion: ethical problems in persuasion, including the ethical question involved in the very act of persuasion; the relationship between societal forms and persuasion forms with emphasis upon "totalitarian persuasion"; listening as related to the persuasion process; and the evaluation of persuasion effect.

SUMMARY

Persuasion is a communicative activity that unites people—yet permits maximum choice. Functioning at its best, it both affirms and contributes to the mutual respect and self-respect of those jointly participating in the persuasion process.

Persuasion is interpersonal communication in which the communicator seeks through the use of symbolic agencies, particularly language, to effect a desired, voluntary change in attitudes and/or actions of the receiver(s).

As a general concept, communication may be used so broadly that any response to stimuli becomes an instance of communication. Even restricted to the concept of a dynamic information-sharing process, communication is relevant to machines and animals, as well as humans.

Communication is the preeminent instrumentality by which we affect our world and are affected by it.

The process of persuasion is integral to much of our communication. The relationships are such that a clear distinction is nearly impossible. The distinction adopted in this book stresses that in communication a human agent seeks to create a common understanding or meaning of some idea, whereas in persuasion this goal of creating a shared understanding becomes a means to the goal of changing an attitude or action. It is not simply an understanding of what the communicator means that is desired.

Persuasion is not a new study. From our inception, we have sought to use the power of speech to affect our environment for personal and collective benefit. Thus, persuasion was a subject of concern in the earliest writings. The heritage of persuasion theory and practice is vast and significant. In studying persuasion today, we do not seek to learn the theories of the past or simply to memorize formulas or prescriptions relative to the process. Rather we seek to test theory by observation and practice. We participate in a world of persuasion as both persuader and receiver. We can learn from the study of what happens in these roles.

Six factors are common to all persuasion situations. The dynamic interplay of these factors determines the effects of the persuasive transaction. These factors, persuader, receiver(s), message, channel, situation, and communication-binding context, become the basis for the analysis in the remainder of this book.

DISCUSSION QUESTIONS AND PROJECTS

1. What definitions do members of your class have for the term *communication*? For *persuasion*? What are the differences in emphasis within the definitions? Do these differences form patterns that can be meaningfully differentiated? For additional definitions you may wish to consult Howard H. Martin and Kenneth E. Andersen, *Speech Communication* (Boston: Allyn and Bacon, 1968), pp. 50–53.

2. Do you feel communication is really synonymous with persuasion? What communication that you engage in does not have persuasive elements? What about the simple "Hi! How's it going?" Does this have persuasion implications? If so, what are they?

3. Construct a general communication model. To what degree does this model serve as a model of the persuasion process? Can the persuasion model be made more specific

than the general communication model? You may enjoy comparing your model to the many given in F. Craig Johnson and George R. Klare, "General Models of Communication Research: A Survey of the Developments of a Decade," *Journal of Communication* 11 (1961): 13–26.

4. Suppose you were going to construct a theory of persuasion and did not have access to previous theories. What would be your approach? Observation of others? Your past experience? Experimental studies? Books or ideas supplied by famous practitioners? What would be the strengths and weaknesses of each of these approaches?

5. Analyze a date you had or some other social event. What persuasive strategy did you employ? In dress? In topics of conversation? In response to the conversation of others? To what degree were these adaptations automatic? To what degree conscious or even calculated?

6. Do you dislike being aware of the fact that you are consciously attempting to persuade your parents, roommate, friend? Would you prefer to be unconscious of this desire, even if it is really there? Why? What does this imply about your view of persuasion?

7. In what sense does a sit-in or protest march involve persuasion? What kinds of responses occur? In terms of the participants? The targets? Those not directly involved and the general public? In what sense can such activities become counterpersuasive?

8. This chapter defines the message as something existing in the channel. In what sense does more than one message exist in the channel? Does a message exist in the source? In the receiver?

9. The model presented in this chapter shows persuader, message, channel, and receiver as overlapping with situation. Why? How are these elements distinct from the situation? How are they grounded in or even determined by the situation?

10. In delivering your first persuasive speech, try to analyze the way in which the other communication elements affect your efforts. How free are you as persuader to do anything you wish?

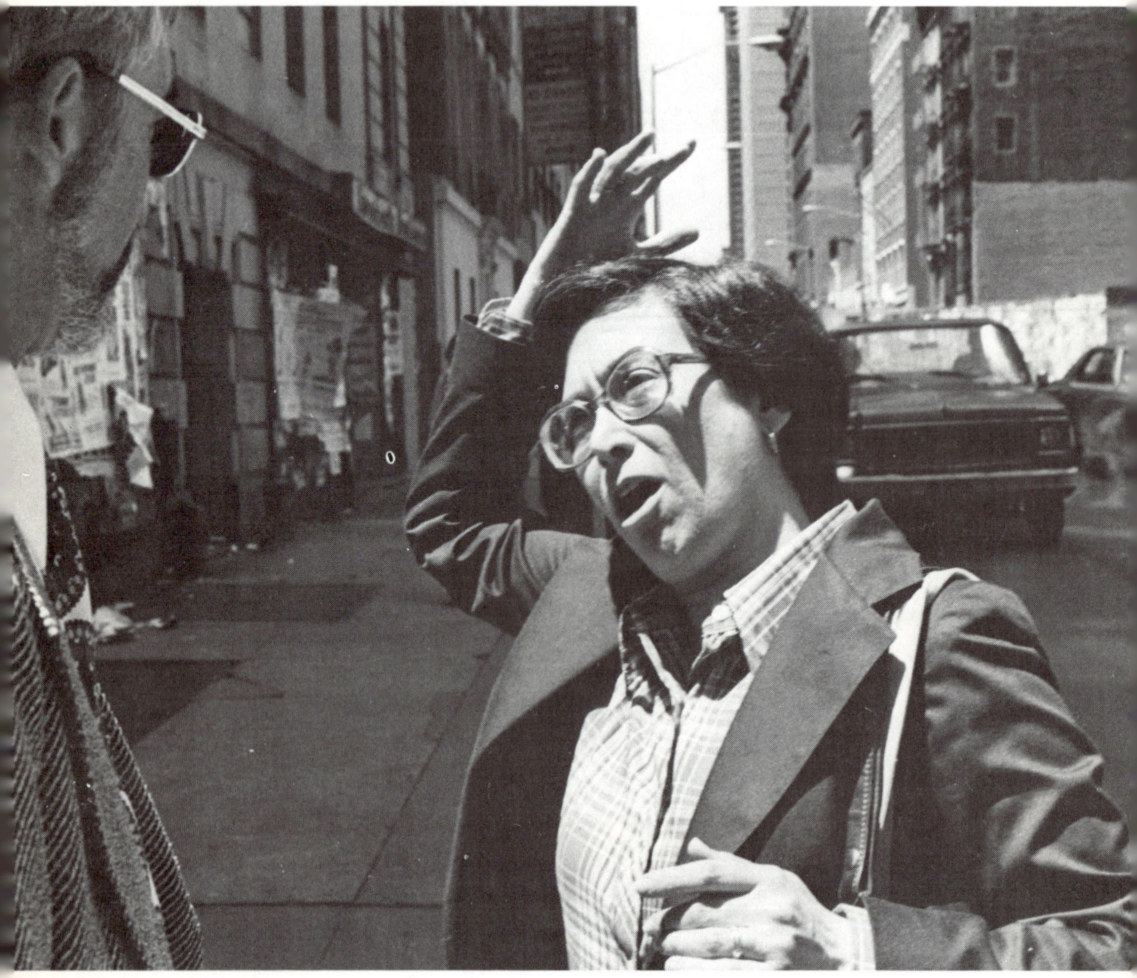

2 Persuasion, the Individual, and Society

The practice of persuasion is as old as the human race. Comments on the theory and practice of persuasion are as old as recorded history. Many of the shapers of Western thought, such as Plato, Aristotle, and Cicero, devoted a share of their writings to discussions of both the theory and practice of persuasion. The importance of persuasion is stressed repeatedly in the *Iliad* and the *Odyssey*. The need to protect the right to persuade has been perceived in all democratic nations. The right to express one's convictions and to influence others is protected by the First Amendment to the United States Constitution and by a long tradition of custom and law in many countries. The need to be able to attempt persuasion is indicated in the protest and agitation for such opportunities where the right is suppressed.

The study and practice of persuasion has a long tradition. But technological progress has so changed communication that there is a threat of a "persuasion overload." The development of the printing press changed the world. But the impact was gradual; only slowly did print become a means of communication of direct use for large numbers of people. Even today many neither read nor write. But the last few decades have brought rapid means of transportation of people and materials, radio, the telephone, television, motion pictures to most of the world's population. In the United States, almost everyone has access to these media of communication—at least as consumers of media.

The amount of persuasion between individuals and within families and primary and secondary groups is not much greater today than it ever was. But the amount of persuasive material being pressed upon us by the various mass communications media threatens to engulf us. Because of this great density of persuasion efforts, those using the media are pushing harder and harder to gain attention. Unlike the electronic media, people cannot significantly increase the number of available communication bands. As the targets of so many persuasion efforts, it is hard for us to reach out to those efforts that will help us as individuals and a society. The din of so much persuasion threatens to deafen us to needed persuasion.

We are concerned with the practice of persuasion in our nation, our work, our daily lives. "Credibility gaps," "Watergate," "I am not a crook!" "I will never lie to you," are suggestive of situations in which we have questioned the truthfulness of those who lead us. We are forced to ask questions about the legitimacy of certain means of influence. We are even asking whether the images of growth, expansion, and progress are meaningful and desirable persuasive appeals or whether we need to develop a new group of persuasive appeals, which emphasize that we are living on a finite planet with very finite resources. We are asking questions about access to communication: should the wealthy, the established corporation, the famous political, business, or entertainment figure have access to such a large audience for their persuasive efforts, while most of us do not? We know that persuasion makes a difference, and we have to be concerned with those differences and the ways in which they are produced.

Although we need to be sensitive to the problems of persuasion in today's society, we also need to note a more positive aspect. For over two thousand years, persuasion was considered the property of the privileged few: the aristocracy, the clergy, the educated, the ruling classes. Persuasion was treated in terms of restricted settings such as the courts, the legislative assembly, the church, and the university. The expansion of education in the last century, the increased emphasis upon self-determination, the concern for the distribution of rights and opportunities and duties to all people have made it inevitable that persuasion be perceived in a broader sense. Persuasion has been liberated; it is now treated as a process involving everyone. And it is not just a matter of decisions about important issues. Persuasion is as much a phenomenon of the breakfast table as the conference table, the bedchamber as the legislative chamber, of the rabble and rebel as the elite and the content.

To the degree that we may be able to make more choices about our personal lives and can make voluntary rather than forced choices about matters related to survival, we may have increased the amount of persuasion taking place in our family and in the groups in which we participate. But the majority of the increase comes from the additional, often trivial, choices about matters outside our immediate concerns for self and survival. Choices are to be made among the products and opportunities offered in a complex, highly developed society. Take soap, for example. Since we no longer make it ourselves, we buy it. And there are hundreds of different kinds for different functions: washing dishes, washing clothes, bathing, and so forth. Further, the cost may range from three or four cents an ounce to several dollars an ounce.

Most of us would be unable to contemplate a life without these opportunities to influence and be influenced in our choices. Although we could do without many of the trivial choices, we want to be able to make these, as well as basic ones. Persuasion is as essential to the lives we lead as breathing. And in many senses persuasion is just as natural and automatic for us as people, as symbol-using animals.

PERSUASION AND CHOICE

The ability to choose is central to the definition of persuasion. The persuader chooses to seek a particular action or attitude by others and chooses the means by which to influence the choice of the receiver. Any action or attitude must be voluntarily chosen by the receivers. Choices are basic to participation in the persuasion process. If there is not a choice among alternatives, there is not an instance of persuasion.

But do we really have choices? How are we to think of people? Are they robots? Perhaps we have an illusion of choice and are misleading ourselves about the degree to which we can make a difference. We all agree that we do not always decide the problems or situations with which we will be confronted: we cannot choose the family in which we are born; we cannot choose the state of the economy at the time we are hunting for a job; we cannot determine the weather.

But we can choose the response we make to situations, at least to a significant degree. And one choice affects the later situation and the choices that will then be made. An infant has little choice about anything. But a year-old child can direct his or her parents in certain ways. As the child grows, the child makes more choices and weighs a greater number of alternatives. One function of parents is to increase the opportunity to make choices and to establish the responsibility upon the child for so doing. So even though we do not choose the family into which we are born, we do begin to act and react in that family. Gradually our previous choices shape the choices available to the family and available to us within the family.

George Kelly, in his work on construct theory, describes people as "scientists." People contemplate in their own ways the events that occur around them and that involve them. They seek to interpret and understand what is happening. People are active, not passive, in the attempt to master their world. Master need not mean power in the traditional sense; it can mean to know, to understand, to predict, and thus to gain some ability to control, to be able to deal with the world in an active, affirmative sense.[1]

Human beings need to understand their world. They want to control what happens to them; they try to become self-determining. There is not one life plan that people must or should follow. Rather people have to evolve their own goals and define their own "good" life. Each individual has the right to his or her own life plan within the stricture of respecting and preserving that same right for others.

The obligation of parents, friends, social institutions, and the society is to give each person the means to develop a life plan and to test it out by trying to live by it. People live with and among people. Others are necessary for the infant to survive. As members of a society, we are interdependent; we need other people to accomplish our goals. We probably could live alone without other people (after a certain age), but our experience in terms of goods and ideas would be drastically curtailed. Our ability to consider alternatives would be limited.

Since we need other people to be able to develop and live our individual life plans, we must make it possible for people to function in ways that will help us. The best way is for others to be accorded the same possibilities that we want for ourselves. The reality of living in a society, of needing other people so that we can develop our own vision of the "good" and pursue it is that we must respect and value the same rights for others. We want the best thinking, the best alternatives, the best persuaders so that we can make the best choice. When other people work for me I want them to do their best work. So I incur a responsibility to them in that I need to universalize what I will for myself as an opportunity. In no sense does my view of the world become one I can or should force upon them. But I can and should indicate its merits to them.

Persuasion is essential to the maintenance of such a view of the relationship of people and the right of choice. To affirm the idea of maximum growth of the individual, the right to self-development, and the fulfillment of our own aspirations, is to affirm the necessity of persuasion. We need to have the information and insights that others bring to us in

---

[1] George A. Kelly, *The Psychology of Personal Constructs* (New York: W. W. Norton, 1955), 1:3–5.

their persuasion and vice versa. We need to find accommodation with others when our wishes conflict. I can shove you out of the way, but you may shove back, and one or the other or both of us (or others who are not directly involved) may get hurt.

We inherit a very complex society, a complex set of social institutions, a culture. But fixed, static laws, institutions, or cultures may not permit us to pursue our individual plans. We must have the opportunity to change what is permitted. But none of us can change social institutions alone; we need others.

At first glance it might seem that a powerful dictator might have the capacity to rule without regard to the wishes of others. But no ruler can survive without the support of others. Such support is always conditional. A leader who demands all the wealth will soon discover that others will join and take it away. The leader needs the support of advisers, soldiers, tax collectors, accountants, cooks, doctors. In short, she or he must persuade a significant number of others to support and accept his or her rule by choosing that rule. The leader must provide opportunity for others to pursue their goals. And in giving such choice, the leader is ultimately served better. Tyranny by one individual is not possible; tyranny by many may be.

We are interdependent. The more technologically advanced the society, the more we depend on one another to enable us to pursue our individual plans. We need some understanding of the rules of the interaction, the rules of the game, and the possible forms and varieties of the game. A common set of rules, expectations, or norms must be shared and accepted to a significant degree by the parties involved in the persuasive transaction. So we develop implicit understandings of what is and is not permitted. We regulate when, how, and to what ends persuasion may be employed. In part, we do this by enacting and enforcing laws. But more importantly and less obviously, we do this through a series of understandings acquired from the culture, from societal institutions, from our interactions with others. Our sensitivity is such that we quite unthinkingly operate with one set of rules with one individual and different sets of rules with another. Of course, there are certain rules that characterize us as individuals in all situations in which we act.

This approach does not deny that there are many societies in which the option of choice about significant aspects of the individual's life is absent. The essentials for survival and the rights and obligations are not equally distributed. The problems of distributive justice are real. Some cannot easily change those who govern. Many cannot substitute a steak for a bowl of rice. Many cannot choose to invest in long-range improvements without risking their own death or those of their children from starvation. In the United States, there are economic, political, social, and individual forces that negate or constrict the fullness of this vision. But, in my view, the weapon of choice in these situations is persuasion.

To stand for human choice and self-determination within the constraint of a meaningful protection of the same right for others is to declare for persuasion. Persuasion has always been one factor influencing our lives. It should be dominant over force, coercion, lack of information, or lack of choice.

PERSUASION AND THE PERSUADER

The people who participate in the persuasion process do so jointly in relating to each other through the activity. Every individual is actively interpreting, acting, and reacting to those things brought to and contained in the communication-binding context. Persuasion is inevitably a joint participation by all involved, although often our role is not conscious on our part. At other times, of course, we are highly sensitive to our role or function. To analyze the process, we need to look at ourselves in terms of the various roles we and the persuasion process may play. We will first examine our role as persuader, both in terms of the decision to persuade and alternative decisions. Then we will examine the relationship of persuasion to us as receivers, as a society, and the relationship of persuasion and truth.

The Decision to Persuade

Beginning with its earliest influences upon us as children, experience teaches that persuasion is generally an acceptable means of influencing those around us—a legitimate means of achieving our multiple goals.

People respond to both external and internal forces. These forces, as interpreted by the individual, may result in an action, which is often an effort to persuade. Although it is customary to view the source of the persuasion stimuli as the instigator—as the agent who decides to originate the persuasion attempt—it is fully as valid to view that effort as the response made by the persuader. Other times we recognize that people are speaking for someone else, often for a fee. Experimenters have often studied the effects of persuasion upon receivers; unfortunately they have rarely examined the influence of the factors that bring the persuader to attempt persuasion or the effects of the persuasion process upon the persuader.

The decision to persuade is a chosen response. The entire process that the persuader follows in preparing and implementing persuasive efforts is an opportunity to study the response of the person to multiple factors. The topics treated, the means employed, the language used are key elements of the behavior of the persuader. We believe we know a person based on our interpretations of her or his actions—especially the persuasive goals that the persuader serves.

To achieve many of our goals and ameliorate many of our needs, we must affect our environment and the forces operating in it. We turn to or become involved in the network of persuasive efforts. Individuals or groups decide to persuade because this is the choice among the alternatives. Some persuasion will be directed toward long-term goals, some toward short-term goals. Every persuasion effort involves some factors related both to short- and long-term goals. Further, each persuasion effort must relate in some degree to other efforts of the individual. We wish to survive as well as win the race. We want an order from the firm next year, as well as this month. We want to enjoy our friendships both tomorrow and today.

There are six reasons why people persuade.

> 1. *To gain a desired decision.* The persuasion process may provide a stimulus for a person or group to reach a decision, be the means by which the decision is reached, or be a factor in the decision. Indeed, the persuasion effort may be the action resulting from a previously reached decision. The decisions may be as mundane as buying a particular brand of toothpaste or detergent; they may be as significant as choosing a job, dropping out of college, choosing not to be married, or deciding to adopt a child. The efforts of a long-forgotten persuader may affect a decision being reached. There seems no way to separate a lifetime of persuasion activity from the specific decision-making process. The intertwined nature of societal decision making and persuasion is immediately apparent. Persuasion involves the communication of information—not just data but interpretations, responses, meanings. The information includes reasoned judgments, feelings, objectives, value positions, and biases. Persuasion is as much a means for assisting two people to reach a collective decision as it is for the society as a whole.
>
> 2. *To maintain continuity and normalcy.* People seek to meet their psychological and physiological needs. They seek to adjust conditions and adjust to conditions so that their needs will continue to be met. Who wants to worry about whether food will be available tomorrow? Businesses seek to maintain a rather constant rate of growth or stability in their sales. The importance of this goal is indicated by consideration of an alternative. Suppose you awoke tomorrow to a totally new world with new laws, new attitudes, new values, new causal connections. How would you feel? How would you cope? Much of persuasion is devoted to the assurance of survival, a degree of control

and security, which yields a sense of well-being. We seek in part to continue the status quo. Persuasion in this sense serves people in a variety of ways as an emotional outlet. Persuasive attempts can provide a catharsis for the individual. They can occupy the time of the bored, and they can serve a variety of relatively transitory needs.

3. *To achieve long-term personal goals.* The status quo may be sufficient for the moment, but we want to evolve new patterns leading to new possibilities. The concept of growth, of striving toward some better future, is a prominent image in literature, psychology, philosophy, and religion. Not all goals involve more status, money, fame, consumption; they often involve more freedom, ability to serve, more fullness and richness in being, not having. Each person defines the goods she or he will pursue.

4. *To fulfill various roles.* Parents have certain responsibilities to children. So they persuade their children in terms of our model or conception of the role of the parent. We accept the obligations of our jobs. More and more people do work that involves persuasion as a partial or even central activity. The surgeon may persuade the reluctant patient to have the needed surgery while dissuading him or her from dangerous, unneeded cosmetic surgery. The waiter, the management consultant, the gas station attendant all serve other people and in so doing use persuasion in some senses. We accept obligations as secretary of our club, as elder in our church, as chair of the rush committee, as solicitor for charitable drives. We may define the responsibilities of the various roles differently, but we are accustomed to taking on such roles and understanding our implicit obligation to discharge them. We recognize that other people will hold us responsible for discharging the obligations of those roles. Responsibility for specific persuasive efforts and the success of those efforts accompanies the roles.

5. *To achieve larger societal goal.* Much persuasion flows from the perception of imperatives placed upon us as individuals by those larger interests with which we identify and are associated. Hence, the U.N. diplomat may become more committed to the goals of the United Nations than to those of her own country. The born-again Christian serves God by communicating the "good news" of the Gospel. We persuade to save the redwoods, our society from the "communist plot" of fluoridation of the water supply and sex education in the schools. Although these actions carry personal rewards, we generally see them as beyond our individual needs and the obligations of any specific role assigned to or accepted by us. The activity is voluntary; it is one of service and altruism. Much of the discussion about politics and social issues is related to this aspect of persuasion.

6. *To affirm and understand ourselves and the world.* The act of persuasion suggests a degree of personal value; it is an expression of self-esteem and an affirmation of self-worth, as well as an expression

of respect for others. It is also a means of testing our ideas and views of the world. The act of attempting persuasion thus is a rewarding activity in itself. To attempt persuasion is to affirm, "I am. I matter. My ideas and opinions matter and can make a difference in your life as well as mine. Further, I am confident enough to try out my ideas, to test them, and possibly to change them."

Alternative Decisions

The decision to persuade is only one of several alternative responses. Differences in perception, comprehension, judgment, past experience, habit, and values all potentially affect the responses made. A person who has been successful in persuasion in the past may try again. But one who rarely succeeds may not view persuasion as a meaningful choice. In the same situation one person may elect to attempt persuasion, another retreat with defeat or apathy, a third to gain an end by force. Some people appear to abandon persuasion as a meaningful way of mediating with their environment. Even in dealing with family or friends, the assumed authority of prescribed roles such as father or boss may produce a reign of force met in turn by counterforce, trickery, and guile. The authoritarian or dictatorial father may be countered by deceit and guile. Further, in our complex society many people feel they are denied access to the society's persuasion marketplace.

When meaningful use of the persuasion process is denied—either access to the process or attention given to the process—alternative means of expression will be found. The instability of some family and personal relationships or the problems of continuity in dictatorships illustrate the use of revolution, escape, or rebellion that results when persuasion cannot be meaningfully employed. Force or threats of force often produce a sullen silence and undoubtedly breed frustration. The controversy over human rights often focuses upon the right to persuade. That people attempt persuasion in the face of threats to life and family is testimony to the desire to persuade.

The prohibition of efforts to persuade relative to certain aspects of a person's life is commonplace. Obvious examples exist in the political life of certain countries, the aspirations for freedom of those held as slaves, the rebellion against parents who will not permit discussion of certain subjects or questions about certain values or who, in contrast, provide nothing to rebel against. But lack of attention to the pleas of groups and individuals can be just as disheartening. Those who give up hope of persuasion, those who have been beaten back in their attempt to use persuasion will ultimately utilize other approaches. Martin Luther King, Jr., gave a voice to many who were being denied a hearing. Sit-ins, marches, and other forms of nonviolent protest became powerful persuasive tools to restore a recognition of and a voice for those who were being denied meaningful access to persuasion. Obviously certain kinds of actions will provoke powerful reaction and overt hostility, as well as the more traditional efforts at counterpersuasion. But the alternatives of loss of contribution and participation by those shut out and the increasingly probability of even more disastrous eruptions must be considered.

Those who live at or under the poverty line, those who do not have adequate diets, those whose survival is a matter over which they seem to have little control are unlikely to turn to persuasion to meet their needs. Persuasion tends to be a lengthy process and solutions are often slow. But the lack of the essentials of life so destroys our conception of what people should be able to do that some obligation exists to bring the individual to the point where participation in the persuasion process as persuader (and receiver) is meaningful.

Some people do not turn to persuasion as a means of attempting influence. In general when they do not habitually consider persuasion as a means of achieving their goals, they are in some sense not fully human. Being human in the fullest sense means the use of persuasion. People may turn to force either as a habitual pattern or in a sudden eruption of destruction either for self or others. Those who cannot persuade openly might turn to deceit, trickery, or guile. Sometimes people violate the social and legal norms in a frustrated response. Or they may lapse into a kind of indifference, cease to participate in the society, and appear to yield up control over their own lives. Any system that denies people a reasonable degree of control over themselves through the opportunity to influence decisions relative to their lives should be seen as malformed, malign, and sick.

We have focused on the positive ends and effects of persuasion. But persuasive techniques are available for any purpose. The persuader may seek to destroy the freedom of others or trick a store clerk out of an extra dime or dollar. The persuader may seek to destroy a friendship or disrupt a marriage. Persuasion may be used to spread societal malaise, and with particular effectiveness in a time of rapid change or stress. (Chapter 16, "Totalitarian Persuasion," focuses upon destructive uses of persuasion.)

But even persuasion that seeks bad ends by using harmful means is presumed to be a better alternative for the society and individual than force or withdrawal. For meaningful persuasion to exist, everyone must have some opportunity for access to and freedom in choice of response. The interaction of force, persuasion, and apathy in all societies and groups is obvious. The balance of these factors in a society is a complex, delicate process. Ideally, decisions to use force or to withdraw will be temporary and will themselves be decided as a result of a persuasive process. One person running amok cannot be allowed to destroy the fabric of a society while we try to reason with him. There is no justification for a certified lunatic to run free, harming self and others. But the decision to restrict his freedom must be one upon which others can agree, as well as the procedures for determining when restraints shall be applied. And the decision is never ultimately decided, only provisionally so.

PERSUASION AND THE RECEIVER

Usually when people are asked why they are involved in persuasion, they respond with statements such as "To get what I want"; "Keep a good job"; "Helps me get what I need"; "That's how I make my living." Rarely do they talk about the function that persuasion may be serving for them as potential persuadees.

We are constant recipients of attempts at persuasion. We are bombarded with advertisements, billboards, advice and argument from friends, associates, spouses, children. Much of what is news is deliberate persuasion. The mayor's statement that the tragic death rate will be curbed by greater use of policemen, stiff sentences, and the addition of thirty more police officers patrolling for speedsters on the major roads is news *and* conscious persuasion. The mass media have come under fire for making news of groups who march, sit in, or attack the status quo. "Why give attention to the 3 percent who are malcontents? Publicize the 97 percent going to class and doing their work!"

Persuasion is a tool for the receiver: it may serve or it may destroy. What can persuasion do for the receiver? At the most basic level, it aids in the decision-making process; it puts others to work for our benefit. How does the persuader serve the receiver?

1. The persuader can sound the cry of alarm, arousing us to face a problem, often a problem that we were not aware existed.

2. The persuader can provide us with information about causes, about solutions, about reasons for us to act. If the problem is significant, competing streams of persuasion will evolve. These will, with little effort on the receiver's part, provide information, alternative lines of analysis, discussion of solutions.

3. The persuader may rouse us to persuasion, to take up the cause or to move to counter persuasion.

4. The persuader may cause us to test our habits. Our mental world tends to become ordered, balanced, congruent. We see things as we think they are; we stop seeing what we look at. We may

suddenly discover a new toothpaste that claims to "fight cavities 59 percent better," and we buy it. Who cares about toothpaste? It is not worth a year's research, but we all do care at one level. The persuader can lead us to check to see if the world has changed, if yesterday's solution, yesterday's tax payment, yesterday's ideal is still functional. The persuader may inoculate us by testing the rusty tool, the unused idea.

5. The persuader may enable us to succeed in our work, in attaining our goals, both personal and public. We cannot know, we cannot have time to gather all the information we need. But the role of persuasion is to bring us these materials so we can make reasoned, informed decisions. A persuader works for us.

The higher a person rises in terms of decision-making responsibilities, the more essential persuasion becomes to him, particularly as receiver. He becomes increasingly dependent upon others to provide relevant materials: information, analysis, solutions. His task is to absorb all that he can and then make the best judgment. He thus puts all the others to work for him, but he is heavily dependent upon their work.

Of course, the persuader can affect us negatively. We can be confirmed in our idiocy. We can be persuaded to "buy the Brooklyn Bridge." We can be persuaded to take out an insurance policy on our daughter, an endowment that will mature in eighteen years to provide $5,000 for college. We may not know that regular life insurance for a similar cost on both parents would provide $50,000 for the daughter's education if either parent died. Further, if the parents live, their earnings are likely to provide sufficient aid; certainly more than the $5,000 guaranteed—but not guaranteed to balance the rise in tuition and cost of living.

The days of "preserving the Aryan race" or "keeping the bloodlines pure" are not past. People are being persuaded to yield their freedom to avoid responsibility. Persuasion is a powerful instrumentality. People in responding may make their lives richer, more meaningful, and more useful or they can destroy the richness of their own lives and quite possibly our life as well. The role of persuadee is an active one: the results of that activity are our responsibility both jointly and individually.

PERSUASION AND SOCIETY

Humanity can be viewed as an aggregate of distinct individuals. But people can also be viewed in terms of relationships to other people, in terms of a society or groups within the society. Initially we looked at persuasion as related to individuals. Even in that context we were forced to see individuals as part of larger systems. What is the role of persuasion for the society?

If a society is to remain viable, it must provide for its own maintenance. This means meeting the needs of its people. To talk of the United States is not to talk of one entity but to talk of numbers of people involved in multiple interactions of many sorts and types—socially, politically, economically, morally. All of us play many parts.

For a society to exist, the people within it must accommodate themselves to one another and must have a means to reach collective decisions. Persuasion is the coin of interaction. Individual decisions typically involve other individuals. One woman trying to save the Great Lakes from pollution is powerless if she acts alone. But when other members of the society must become involved, she can turn to persuasion to accomplish her goal. It is for very few things in our lives that we, ourselves, are the sufficient means. Most goals involve the use of resources beyond our own. Hence, we turn to the groups and institutions of the society.

The organizations that we use (and are used by) may be large or small. They may relate to a single issue or to multiple ones; the organization may be constituted for a matter of an hour, a day, a year, or centuries. One person belongs to many of these organizations.

A company is an organization; "Save the Redwoods" is an organization; the executive branch is an organization; the ad hoc committee on constitutional revision is an organization. Within each of these are many subsystems. Hence, persuasion will function at and between many levels, as well as between and among various organizations. In these organizations, persuasion will be directed both internally and externally.

These organizational systems provide opportunities for decisions on developing a product, merchandising the product, selling a service, establishing a national policy, voting an appropriation, developing a campaign to gain greater support.

In a complex society it is difficult for the individual to perceive how she affects the destiny of a society. Some people view society as outside any control. The state becomes an abstraction without relationship to its constituents. Yet it is said that a few men persuaded President Franklin Roosevelt to develop the atomic bomb. An aroused public opinion was a key factor in persuading Lyndon Johnson to abandon his effort at reelection. President Nixon persuaded the American public to elect him to the presidency, and then public opinion persuaded him to resign the office. A failure of diplomatic persuasion may lose the peace for all of us, and we cannot directly control the outcome. Yet the success or failure of a nation and the establishment of national policy depend on mobilizing the support of the people.

Persuasion certainly determines the course of a society. But to attempt to trace this process and evaluate the influence of one or more parts of it is an overwhelming challenge. Think of the effort required to examine a single election campaign. How do we analyze a presidential campaign? Do we focus upon the candidates, the advisers, the precinct workers, the straw hats, the billboards, the issues, the voting records of the last twenty-five years, the conversations at the corner bar and on the assembly line? All these and much, much more are involved in the campaign. The complexities are glimpsed but not untangled; the portion of the process that is visible is a small percentage of the totality.

We should not neglect the role of persuasion in the sense of the numbers of people who are employed in some portion of the persuasion process. We are moving from a nation of people who grow or make things to people working with words in a service economy. People function increasingly as decision makers, as interactive links in a complex system.

The mass media in the United States are largely dependent upon commercial advertising for the revenue that supports their communication of the news, entertainment, and so forth. Salesmen have graduated from selling anvils (never on credit) to leasing IBM machines available with a complete package of installation and service. Many traveling salesmen have traded in the week-long railroad or car odyssey for jetting coast-to-coast while dictating orders into a portable recorder. The communication-persuasion business is a larger percentage of our work force. And this does not include those who work for companies and groups that are dependent upon the results of persuasion for their existence.

We elect legislators, governors, and the President to be persuaders. We seek leaders. We may complain about the expenditure of taxes and money, but we want the information about improving our crops, we want the air we breathe monitored, we want to have the alternatives explained to us. We want our police to be concerned about our rights and to perceive their role as one of service. In brief, we pick our leadership to be good persuaders, to so influence us or attempt to influence us that in the pull of contrary strains of persuasion influence, we will find solutions for our problems.

Often we decry the failure of people to accept the obvious solution. We are troubled that so many people don't have an opinion about an urgent topic—indeed, don't even know it is an urgent topic. We bemoan the waste of time spent in trying to reach these people and the years it sometimes takes to get action. Yet this inertia is a safety feature in a society. A society that leaps from one viewpoint to another would be unstable and dangerous. The difficulty of "dragging people kicking and screaming" to what is good for them and society is counterbalanced by the fact that the delay provides a test of importance, of validity, of usefulness. A delay permits accommodation to change on the part of those who might resist. Persuasion permits the various points of view to be heard and all to feel they had the opportunity to participate or indeed did participate even if their goal was not achieved. People accept change, even change they oppose, if they feel consulted and given an involvement in the process that brought the change about. So the delay may be an important safety valve.

Persuasion is not a sufficient explanation of change or the lack of it. But the process of persuasion is a tool of the individual and of the group to affect the collective decisions of a society. The persuasion process is not a sufficient explanation of the totality of societal processes, but try to explain a society without consideration of the process.

PERSUASION AS A MEANS TO TRUTH

The argument about what is truth is probably matched in urgency only by the question of how to know the truth when it is found. How does persuasion relate to truth and to the discovery and recognition of truth? Or does persuasion relate to particular types or classes of "truth" or "truth claims"?

The answer to these questions is partially one of personal values. An answer is implicit in the material that has already appeared and the material that follows. Let us consider four ways in which persuasion and the use of persuasion relate to truth.

First, people use persuasion to communicate their truth. While it is often assumed that truth has some innate, automatic appeal to people, rarely have we been content to rely upon this assumption. For whatever reason, man seems to treasure his fallen state. Thus, the church needs the minister to preach the word of God, the candidate needs her workers, the true believers must be ever ready to take up arms against the mass of the mistaken.

An individual who believes she or he has found a truth feels a concomitant responsibility to share it with others, even those who resist it. The more certain we are of the truth and the more urgent that truth is in terms of the fate of humanity, the more the need to communicate it.

But one person's truth may be another's fatal fallacy. Is the world better off if we wait for complete certainty? Only idiots are completely certain about many basic things. And if we wait for all to agree, there is no need to communicate. Each of us needs to accept the necessity of acting upon a truth, of persuading as effectively and appropriately as we can, while admitting that tomorrow we may realize we were in error.

Second, people use persuasion to reach accommodation. To discuss the "true" solution to the Arab-Israeli conflict seems an exercise in nonsense. Yet some types of peace are judged to be better than some wars, although some wars are judged to be better than some types of peace. What is the alternative to some accommodation reached through the peacemaking—persuasive—efforts of involved people of involved nations, Arab, Israel, and others? The process of accommodation can let two opposing parties find some acceptable answers. This ability for both to survive and for both to feel they have benefited seems to be a "truth."

Third, persuasion may provide the opportunity for individuals to evolve a best solution or choice by drawing upon the mass of persuasion efforts directed toward a problem area. Although not a perfect tool, persuasion in action is a marketplace of ideas in which we as individuals and a society can seek the best buy available. And we can buy a portion from one and then the other. It would be nice in one sense to rely upon some final authority who could direct us to the truth. But can we be sure we interpret the directions accurately and that the authority can be trusted for tomorrow as well as today?

Perhaps we should simply make the correct, logical decision. But how? Does the truth speak for itself? What I believe to be logical may be demonstrated even to me to be stupid by counterargument. The persuasion process makes available to us decision-making materials that are far beyond our personal ability to generate. What is correct or reasonable involves more than formal validity. What faith commitments should we make? Are slaves natural, normal, ordained by necessity, by God, or natural law? Perhaps it is logical to kill all the defective human beings so that their genes cannot be transmitted. There are only limited resources of food and energy. Granted, defectives will still be born, but the law of averages operates with altered odds.

Persuasion as a process brings to us diverse sources of information, motivation, analysis, understanding. We draw upon these to develop our best judgment. Persuasion as a process can no more guarantee freedom from erroneous judgment than can we as individuals. But the diverse materials provide the possibility of the sifting and winnowing that is basic to good decisions. At least some of the bad may be driven out by the good. Collective analysis may balance some of the idiosyncrasies of individual judgments.

Finally, persuasion means that people have the opportunity to affect others: through our actions, we can alter the environment, we can alter our life space. Persuasion provides a means to act. In the search for meaning of existence this opportunity to realize existence by acting is also a "truth."

SUMMARY

Persuasion is central to the activity of the individual, the group, the society, and the world. It is a means to balance the needs and goals of individuals who need one another to maximize the possibility of choosing their own good life and leading it. Persuasion thus is an expression of self-respect and respect for the other. It commits the joint participants to choice—both the freedom to choose and the responsibility of choice and the obligations that follow from having chosen.

There are alternatives to persuasion—force, anarchy, random response, withdrawal. Failure of the persuasion process often leads to one or more of these alternatives. But a sense of fair distribution of rights and responsibilities, duties, and obligations suggests that every person must be given meaningful access to the use of the persuasion process.

The decision to persuade arises out of many forces and should be seen as a choice, a response made. Such a response aids us in reaching decisions, in seeking both short- and long-term goals, in discharging the obligations of various roles that we perform, in influencing others to share in our commitments to various points of view, and such a response affirms self-worth.

In our role as receiver, the persuasion process also serves many functions. It alerts us to potential problems, it tests our habits, it gives us new information and new points of view.

Persuasion is the mortar between the blocks of a society. It is the means of reaching solutions to problems confronting a society. The complexity of a modern society demands interrelated systems of persuasion both within and among smaller units of the society. The systems range from the buying habits of one family to the antitrust case filed by the government against a conglomerate.

The persuasion process does not guarantee the best solution or finding the truth. But it seems to provide the best mechanism available to approach truths while balancing the tensions among individuals and groups. The alternatives of force and authority, of anarchy, of withdrawal seem less and less feasible as an answer to the twenty-first century, unless the failure of the twentieth makes the twenty-first a different reality from any we can yet conceive.

As an instrumentality, persuasion serves individuals, groups, and society. It can serve badly or well. The greater the understanding of the process and the realization of its potential and limitations, the more effectively it may serve us.

DISCUSSION QUESTIONS AND PROJECTS

1. Persuasion clearly provides a means to affect the behavior of others. To what degree is the availability of persuasion a safety valve for the individual? To the society? Why must this channel of communication be open?

2. What is the responsibility of a person to act if he or she "knows" an urgent truth? What are the limits on this necessity to act? How do we respect the "rights" of others if we "know the answer and the answer means survival"?

3. What is the relationship between force and persuasion in a democratic society? In a totalitarian society? Are the differences of degree rather than type?

4. The late 1960s and early 1970s saw a rash of violence, particularly on campuses and in cities, when people believed they were not having a voice. How much is this a failure of the persuasion process? How much is this a failure of the individuals to accept results of the persuasion process?

5. Does every person have access to the persuasion process? Can an individual affect society, or is this limited to certain people?

6. People are fond of quoting the statement, "What is good for General Motors is good for society." Is it true that what is good for the individual person or group or company is good for society? How does access to persuasion by all and the frequent necessity to persuade others to obtain the individual good protect the society and the individuals in it?

II PARTICIPATION A:

3 **Motivation, Attitudes, and Behavior**
The Concept of Motivation
Attitudes, Beliefs, and Values
Attitudes and Behavior
Motivational Theories
    Drive-Motive Theories
    Cognitive Models
    Learning Theory
The Matrix of Motivational Forces

4 **Receiver and Situation Analysis**
Value of Receiver Analysis
Process of Receiver and Situation Analysis

Prior Analysis
Immediate Analysis
Concurrent Analysis
Postanalysis
Receiver Classifications and Response Tendencies
Variability of Response

5 **Attention and Interest**
The Nature of Attention
Interest and Attention
Selectivity of Attention and Perception
Suggestion
Implications for Persuasion

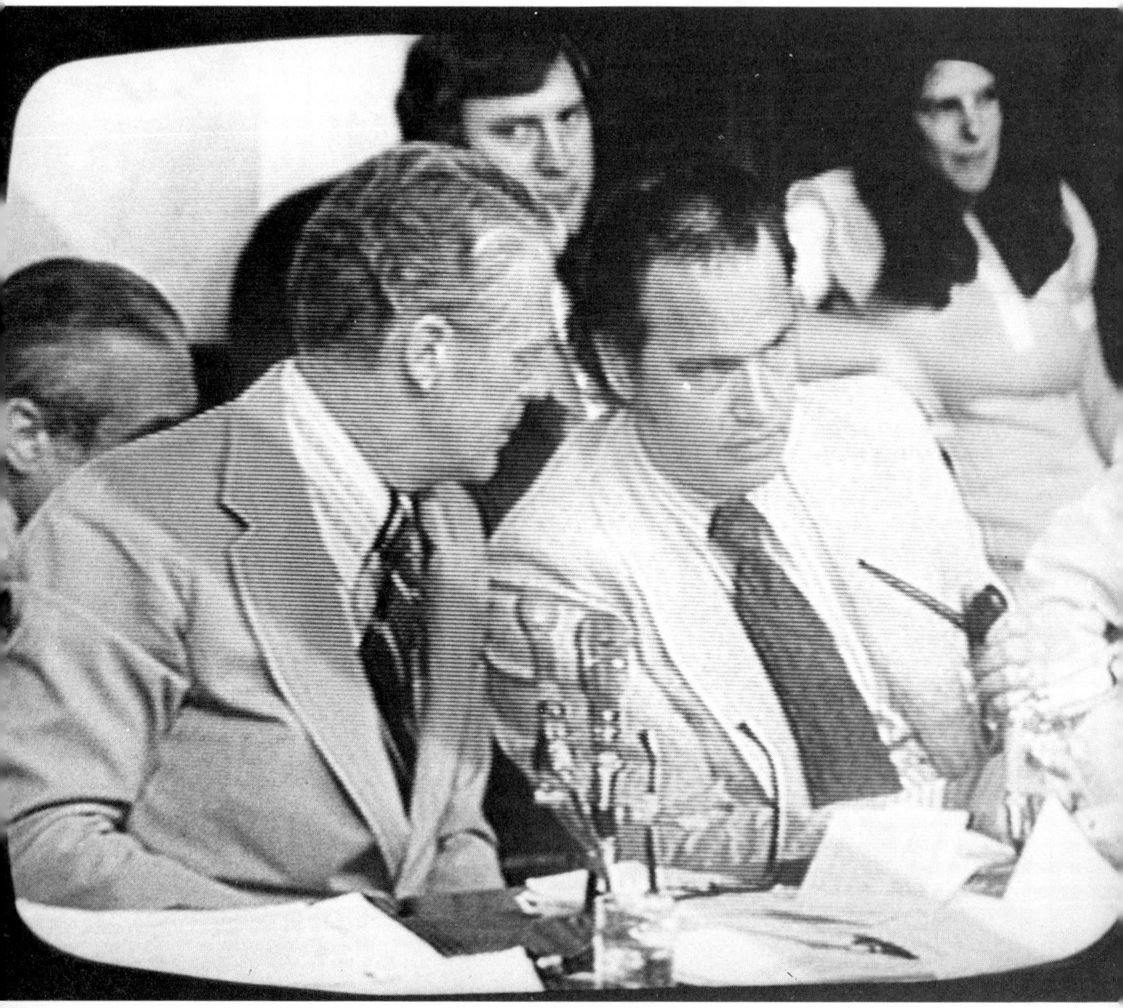

3 Motivation, Attitudes, and Behavior

The science of persuasion is the science of motivation; the art of persuasion is the art of motivation. The persuasion process is one in which the communicator seeks to utilize, marshal, modify, adust, refocus, and redirect the motivational forces impinging upon the receiver(s) so as to adjust and alter their behavior or potential for response.

THE CONCEPT OF MOTIVATION

Motivation is a central concept in psychology. It has been studied in every context: animal psychology, human psychology, social psychology, physiological psychology. It is studied in learning, attention, political attitudes, group processes, marriage, divorce, criminology, artistic endeavor, and so forth. Whatever the emphasis of a chapter or a work in psychology, the study of behavior and, hence, motivation, is ultimately a concern.

Broadly defined, motivation is the process of arousing, sustaining, or altering behavior. This process includes both unconscious and conscious forces. The relationship of conscious and unconscious forces in motivation may be likened to an iceberg appearing at sea: at any moment only a small portion of the iceberg shows above the surface. But other parts of the iceberg do exist; they can be investigated; and different portions of the iceberg may be visible at different times.

Motivation is concerned with the process by which behavior is energized and directed. We must look to motivation for the energy that prompts and directs activity. Motivation involves stimuli that are both external and internal to the organism, and responses to the motivation involve both internal and external elements.

The relationship between the learning process and the motivational process is marked. We are motivated to learn; motivation affects learning, but learning also affects motivation. Through trial and error and through the impact of forces in our environment, both human and nonhuman, we learn successful and unsuccessful ways of accommodating ourselves to the limits of the world and to the imperatives of the forces impelling the individual. This refinement and interaction with motivational forces involves maturation, innate potential, and the unique experiences of individuals with a culture, family, and friends.

Although we do not learn the physiological motivations with which we are born, we do learn the methods by which these drives are met. Further, we acquire (learn) all kinds of goals, all types of attitudes, beliefs, and values. We acquire perceptual categories to deal with experience; we acquire a language. Communication functions in terms of these learned factors and the channeling of basic motivational forces.

This chapter focuses upon four topics of particular importance to persuasion: the nature of and centrality to persuasion of the concepts of attitudes, beliefs, and values; the relationship of these to behavior; some motivational theories with high potential for yielding insight concerning the persuasion process; and, finally, the interrelationship of motivational forces. As a preface to this material, four points about motivation provide a framework for understanding.

1. The process of motivation involves consideration of both general forces and specific factors. It is not enough to know that people are motivated by hunger. Why does one person turn to raw fish, another to burned sirloin? Broad, energized motivational forces are focused and channeled by a variety of specific factors. Each individual is a unique being and unique in terms of the internal, mental reality brought to any situation.

2. Behavior is ongoing, and motivation is a continuous ongoing process as well. People are constantly acting and responding to motivational forces over time. It is therefore impossible to set a beginning and an end to a unit of motivation. An organism is not a motor waiting to be turned on; it is running at some speed, and change means alteration in degree or in direction.

3. To name behavior or a cause for behavior is not to explain behavior. Some approaches to motivational theory seem to consist largely of the creation of a taxonomy to use in describing-naming behavior. For example, instinct theorists developed an expansive catalog of instincts. A new pattern of behavior was identified, seen as repeated and generaliz-

able, then named. An activity might be seen as a result of the "nesting-building" instinct. But this does not explain why one chooses a ranch style house, another a New England saltbox. It does not explain why one father relates to a child in one way and another in quite a different way.

In today's psychologically (or pseudopsychologically) oriented world, everyone has the tendency to play the game of "to name is to explain." A pattern of deviant behavior is explained as adolescent rebellion. But further analysis is needed to determine why one boy steals purses, another smokes marijuana, a third joins a hippie movement, a fourth comes in five minutes past the deadline from a date, a fifth gets all A's. Names are useful only to the degree that they provide insight and understanding, which suggests the ability to identify, predict, and possibly control.

4. In the context of the study of communication, the way in which a constellation of motivational factors came to be is less important than what they are at a point in time. Within the limits of individual, inherited differences, every person at birth has potential to develop in many different ways. One culture may teach that dancing is evil; another may consider dancing the ultimate rite in the worship of the deity. One child may learn to speak French, another German, another Swahili. Any language is learned as naturally as any other one; yet after a time, any other language becomes strangely unnatural. It is important to understand that much of human behavior is no more natural than the opposite human behavior. For purposes of communication, it is more practical to focus upon the motivation that is, and accept it as it is, rather than unduly attempt to understand the complexities of the process by which all the things that were potential became the more limited reality of what is.

This is not to suggest that the persuader is indifferent to differences in people or that the evolution within environment and culture is unimportant. The essential focus on motivation in a specific setting is what is the reality of motivation, not how it came to be. Often, of course, a look at the forces that shaped an individual is the most effective means of predicting what motivational forces and factors will be relevant.

ATTITUDES, BELIEFS, AND VALUES

Historically much of the research and theory relative to motivation has worked with a model of S-R relationship. A stimulus (hunger) produced a response (activity). This response might consist of random behavior (the animal becomes extremely active in its cage until it accidentally presses a bar and discovers the available food) or the behavior could be very specific (the rat immediately presses a bar and goes to the food tray to await the arrival of the food). Behavioristic psychology markedly influenced theoretical models and research activities in the direction of the simple S-R pattern.

Undoubtedly the behavioristic influence was and is a useful approach. Historically it served as a corrective for an excess of assumptions about the nature of mental processes, the role of instinct, and "conscious" reports through a process of introspection of what occurred inside. Further, this effort to avoid easy explanations by inserting all kinds of processes or factors into the human mind as the complete and sufficient explanation of behavior serves as a constant check on today's psychological research and theory.

Much current research and theory, however, centers around an enlargement of the S-R model with an emphasis upon the organism that mediates between the stimulus and the response: the S-O-R model. This general pattern has been refined, modified, and emphasized in many different ways. The S-O-R model offers great utility in examining communication phenomena, and the models that are discussed under the heading of motivational theories are developed in this framework.

The S-O-R model invites attention to the mediational processes—to the activities of the organism that go between the stimulus and the response. The concept of attitude has gained great prominence as one of the mediators between stimulus and response. Attitudes have become a central concern of communication in that the persuasion process is viewed as seeking some modification in attitude, per se, or in the activity linked to an attitude.

Attitude Defined

An attitude is a learned, relatively stable set involving a tendency to respond in predetermined ways toward specific objects or general classes. This definition is closely related to one Gordon Allport postulated in 1935: "An attitude is a mental and neural state of readiness, organized through experience, exerting a directive or dynamic influence upon the individual's response to all objects and situations to which it is related."[1] These definitions contain elements that benefit from further exposition.

Attitudes are "learned," "organized through experience." They are acquired in the same ways that other knowledge is acquired. Attitudes represent a summation and generalization of past experiences, both direct and indirect. Since attitudes are learned, an alternative or contra-

---

[1] Gordon W. Allport, "Attitudes," in *Handbook of Social Psychology*, ed. C. A. Murchinson (Worcester: Clark University Press, 1935), p. 810.

dictory position could also have been learned if the proper forces had been operative.

It should not be assumed that attitudes are the result of direct personal experience. Attitudes are transmitted and conditioned by the cultures, groups, subgroups, and individuals with whom a person comes into contact, as well as by the communications media. We acquire attitudes toward objects and classes with which we have had absolutely no direct experience. Often we adopt the norms or standards of the group with which we are or wish to be associated.

The importance of referential groups is hard to overestimate. Children adopt quite unconsciously the attitudes, beliefs, and values of their primary groups (initially the family). Gradually the maturing individual moves into other primary groupings, into increasing association with more tangential secondary groups, and into the possibility of exposure to a wide variety of ideas from a multitude of sources. The power of these early referential groups has been frequently demonstrated: the shift from one attitudinal system to another may call for rather dramatic reorientation, involving strong conflicts, with guilt, anxiety, and rebellion as manifestations of the conflict.

In areas where we do not hold a prior attitude, it is likely that we will almost unconsciously adopt the norm or standard of the group. The firmness with which the group standard is anchored will vary in terms of the importance of the group to the individual, reinforcement from other groups, and so forth.

The referential group may supply a norm or an attitudinal position, or it may serve to reinforce a preexisting attitude. Often the validity of an attitude—the knowledge it represents—may seem questionable, and the person seeks assurance and support. In committing himself as a member of these groups, he can derive support of his attitudinal position. An individual may identify with a group to which he does not belong but aspires to membership. Thus, reference groups serve to instill attitudes, to reinforce them, and to provide a defense against alteration.

An attitude involves a generalization. The variety of experiences with a class or object will vary. Some of the experiences will likely be positive, some negative; yet the dynamics of attitude formation are such that some relatively consistent and ordered view is established. (Perhaps this ordering consists in the view that the object in question is highly variable.) The attitude offers a generalization abstracted from reality—a reasonably consistent, ordered picture of that reality. The way in which the generalization simplifies and abstracts from reality can be seen easily in the operation of our own attitudes as they relate to our experience. For example, we may think Danes and people of Danish descent are people unduly proud of their heritage, tight with their money. If we have an extremely close friend who is a Dane, she is treated as the exception. Indeed, she in a sense stops being identified as a Dane and becomes our friend, a "special" Dane.

"Relatively stable" indicates that attitudes tend to persist over time but that they can be changed. Certain attitudes may be easy to change; others may be totally resistant. Rokeach, in developing a classification of attitudes, notes that some concepts, which he labels "primitive beliefs," are central and basic to a person's conceptual framework and almost impossible to change, whereas others, labeled "inconsequential beliefs," are easily changed.[2] Since the persuader typically seeks an attitude change, the very existence of the persuasion concept testifies to the possibility of alteration of attitudes. But clearly the possibility of change is greater for some attitudes than for others.

Attitudes are defined as "sets involving a tendency to respond in predetermined ways," as "mental and neural states of readiness." These sets may be specific to one object: often when one object bulks large in life, we may have very specific attitudes toward it. Classes or objects that are less important will involve more general orientations, less specific to members of the class, and less sharply and often less consciously defined attitudinal positions.

These attitudinal sets provide us with expectations that affect the responses of attention, perception, meaning, and interpretation. Furthermore, attitudes are sets to action—responses of a more overt nature.

Since attitudes set response tendencies, we expect a pattern of directed, predictable response. Allport's definition, which notes "directive or dynamic influence," may sharpen this point. Attitudes may serve a motivational function and provide energy for action, but they are also directive; they channel that action. An attitude may be the direct cause of action and/or a channel that directs or affects the action.

Attitudes are "valenced": that is, we respond positively or negatively to objects or classes. Attitudes can, and often do, involve powerful emotional components. We become involved with our activities. We gain powerful attitudes toward our country, which become associated with symbols such as the flag. For someone to walk on a piece of dyed cloth, available for a dollar at the K-Mart, may result in fine and imprisonment when that cloth is the American flag.

The valenced nature and the importance of this valencing are shown in the research of Osgood, Suci, and Tannenbaum, who attempted to explore the connotative dimensions of meanings of words by considering the responses of many individuals to a wide variety of concepts on many bipolar adjectives. When they factor analyzed and interpreted

[2] Milton Rokeach, *Beliefs, Attitudes, and Values* (San Francisco: Jossey-Bass, 1968).

these responses, the most consistent dimension to emerge—and that dimension that accounted for the greatest percentage of variation in meanings—was the evaluative one. The key set of terms in the evaluative dimension is *good-bad*.[3]

The final portion of Allport's definition, "response to all objects and situations to which it is related," may need clarification. Some attitudes are general; they are potentially relevant to large numbers of situations, and they may apply to many different, even apparently diverse, objects or situations. Thus an attitude (perhaps this could be termed a "value") associated with urban living may be relevant to what jobs we take, how we behave in the city, what we teach our children. Other attitudes may be specific to one class or object. (I like Crest but not mint-flavored.)

Further, situations may and usually do call forth more than one attitude or even clusters of related attitudes. An individual who rings someone's doorbell and asks for an opinion about low-cost housing may well tap an attitude related to that person's feelings toward blacks, Jews, Japanese-Americans, or Puerto Ricans, depending upon specific conditions. Or she may tap feelings toward the poor, welfare, government activity, or a general liberal orientation. She may touch upon ego needs. If the questioner is a friend with known attitudes, this relationship may affect the response. If the questioner is black, or poor, or a Gallup pollster, the response may differ. Thus, no one attitude or attitudinal cluster is necessarily aroused; many different attitudes may be referenced, and the response will be a result of these several forces.

The individual may or may not relate any one or all of these potential attitudes at a given point in time to a situation. Many apparent changes in behavior, many apparent successes in persuasion, can more likely be explained as a shift in the attitude that was seen as *relevant to* the situation rather than a change in the attitudinal structures of the individual. The meaning an individual gives to a situation will determine which attitudes are likely to become relevant.

Measurement of Attitudes

The term *attitude* has been labeled a "hypothetical mediational construct." No one has ever gone inside the brain and weighed an attitude. But the concept of an attitude is useful because it explains and integrates many phenomena. We have "identified" an attitude when knowledge of that "attitude" makes behavior relatively predictable and understandable.

[3] Charles Osgood, George Suci, and Percy Tannenbaum, *The Measurement of Meaning* (Urbana: University of Illinois Press, 1957).

Since an attitude is manifested in behavior, behavior becomes the means of measuring an attitude. Perhaps the most typical way is to use verbal behavior in the form of an opinion. An opinion is a statement made about something; on the basis of this and possibly several opinion statements, we estimate the attitude. The typical attitude test is simply a means of collecting a number of opinion statements. Like all other means of measurement this approach involves a number of problems in terms of its reliability and validity.

Attitudes are approached in terms of a continuum with the effort to identify the degree of more or less on this continuum. An attitude thus becomes meaningful as one compares the behavior or reactions of one individual to those of another. Repeated experience with a particular measure of an attitude gives a context and a perspective within which the measure takes on value. We gain norms or standards, which help us to understand a response to the test. A person who argues that all believers in capital punishment ought to be executed is presumably more opposed to capital punishment (whatever his consistency) than is a person who argues that it ought to apply only to treason in time of war. Hence, persons who venture opinions become comparable even if these opinions are expressed in response to an attitude test.

No one could argue that any one attitude, let alone all the possible attitudes, is capable of being measured accurately in every instance for every person. However, attitude tests have been useful predictors of action. Unfortunately the results of such tests are subject to tremendous amounts of misinterpretation, especially by those unsophisticated in measurement theory or in an understanding of the way in which attitudes relate to behavior. Attitude tests will continue to be much used in experimental studies in persuasion and are key factors that determine what can be done in such research. As better techniques of attitude measurement become available, persuasion may become a more exact science.

Beliefs

It might not be necessary to separate the concepts of belief and value from the concept of attitude. In many senses the separation of beliefs and values from the concept of attitude is merely a means of discriminating among attitudes in terms of one dimension—specificity. Further, beliefs and values are established in ways that are analogous to attitudes. Provided the reader is sensitive to the fact that writers differentiate among attitudes, beliefs, and values in different ways and that not all writers make such differentiations, or that some may fail to maintain them, no real difficulty should ensue from discussion.

A belief is defined as "an accepted datum about the world." Thus a belief is more specific and limited than an attitude. An attitude is presumably related to and based upon a constellation of beliefs about an object or a class. If an attitude toward Danes is summarized as "Danes are bad news," a number of specific beliefs would need to articulate with that attitude. A change in beliefs or in the importance of certain beliefs may produce a change in attitude.

Clearly a belief may be true or false as related to facts in a real world. But not all beliefs are descriptive of facts in the real world. Some beliefs are concerned with value judgments: "Vanilla is better than chocolate." Some are higher levels of abstractions. The key point is to remember that the belief is accepted by the individual holder as a datum about reality, about the world. True or false, capable of empirical demonstration or not, it is believed.

Beliefs, like attitudes, can be incompatible with one another. But this incompatibility while only potential would seem to pose no problem for the holder of the beliefs. When beliefs come into conflict with one another or they are seen to be inconsistent with an attitude to which they are clearly related, a potential pressure for adjustment is present.

Values

Values are attitudinal configurations that have become integrated, inclusive, and dominant over other attitudes so that they constitute referential cores basic to the person's actions—especially to conscious judgmental actions. A person's values are the reference points for the operationalized philosophy of life of the individual.

Values are important because they are influences on almost every behavior (at least potentially), and, in one sense, the goals of an individual are linked to the values held. Thus, a person who might make the acquisition of money a central value in life will behave both specifically and generally in ways that are congruent with this value. (Actually this is worded more as a goal than a value, although the value may be both acquisition and money.) Presumably this value exerts weight in the ongoing behavior of the individual and cuts across the whole of activity. In this sense, values become important elements in persuasion in terms of both source and receiver.

ATTITUDES AND BEHAVIOR

Attitudes are important because they predict behavior. Yet each of us can recall many instances in which we believed one thing and did another, and many studies have shown that people hold one attitude but act in ways that are inconsistent with that attitude. The validity of the definition of an attitude as exerting a directive influence, as being a motivation to action, seems to be challenged by our experience and some research findings.

But why should we assume that a single attitude would determine action? We must consider the total motivational field that may be operating. Let us assume you like your roommate. On a particular Sunday afternoon, you are tired and more than a little upset about a date the previous evening. You have a paper due tomorrow morning. Your pattern is to need a long block of time with full concentration in order to get a paper written. Two people have called, one twice, trying to locate your roommate, who left for the afternoon to give you a chance to work on the paper. Three people stopped by, including the landlord, who is trying to collect the rent owed by an ex-roommate you didn't like anyway. At 5:15 someone calls to declare you the "winner" of a free 8 x 10 colored photograph if you will come in this next week for a sitting. About then the roommate walks in and says, "About done? Let's go get some pizza. I'm hungry!" If you explode at your roommate and scream about insensitive clods, is your behavior inconsistent with your liking your roommate? Yes and no. The other factors are strong enough to overshadow the liking for the roommate temporarily. Further, one good thing about friends and roommates is that you can blow off steam by yelling at them and apologize later.

To expect every behavior to which an attitude may be linked to be controlled always or even generally by that attitude alone is silly.

Obviously, if a meaningful attitude exists it must at some time make a difference in behavior. The person with one attitude will differ in behavior to some degree in some situations at some times from a person who does not hold that attitude or who holds a different one. One attitude is dominant at one time, but not at another. Some attitudes are salient to a particular person and not to another. We are unfair to those we like one day; we overcompensate the next day. Neither action is a precise representation of our feeling, but if we take the average of our actions over time, we may see that the attitude does guide behavior.

Hence, we need to remember that the relationship between a particular attitude, belief, or value and a particular behavior is complex. Other characteristics of the individual must be considered—other attitudes, values, beliefs, motives, habits, patterns of expression—as well as characteristics of the situation, such as the norms of behavior, presence of reference groups, expectations of others, anticipated consequences. Martin Fishbein and his associates have developed attitude scales that attempt to measure attitudes in terms of such factors as behavioral intentions, perceived desirability of acts, our view of the behavior expected by others, and our desire to comply with those expectations.[4] Given all the factors to be considered, it is surprising that we can predict behavior from attitudes as often or as well as we do. Behavior can also influence and determine attitudes. Often we change an attitude to match behavior rather than change behavior to match an attitude. Sometimes a change in attitude produces a later change in behavior; sometimes a change in behavior produces a later change in attitude. Both changes are important in persuasion, and the changes can occur in either or both the persuader and the target of the persuasion effort.

MOTIVATIONAL THEORIES

Many theories of motivation could be explored. We shall examine three categories of motivational theories relevant to communication: drive-motive theories, which link innate physiological-psychological tensions to behavior acquired to mediate these tensions and hence to learned social motivations; cognitive models, which focus upon the mental processes involved in making adjustments between and among cognitions; and the relationship of learning-theory models to motivation models.

To study communication we must formulate a psychology of human behavior. People normally approach communication in terms of their psychological orientation. Persuasion techniques employed reflect the persuader's perception of human nature generally and the nature of the particular receivers. To the degree that the psychology is valid, the desired predicted results are more probable; to the degree that it is invalid, there is less likelihood of success. Researchers and writers in communication approach the process in terms of one or more psychological theories. Even the understanding or acceptance of theory or research conclusions may depend upon adherence to a particular psychological viewpoint.

Drive-Motive Theories

This approach treats motivation as a problem of discovering the physiological-psychological imperatives common to all people. These imperatives are presumably innate but are modified by experience. Although certain drives come with birth as givens, these forces are not sufficient to explain behavior. Born into a social environment, inherited

---

[4] Martin Fishbein, "Attitude and the Prediction of Behavior," in Martin Fishbein, ed., *Readings in Attitude Theory and Measurement* (New York: John Wiley, 1967), pp. 477–92; I. Ajzen and M. Fishbein, "The Prediction of Behavior from Attitudinal and Normative Variables," *Journal of Experimental Social Psychology* 6 (1970): 466–87.

givens and potentialities are modified by circumstances of environment and experience.

Many variations of this same approach could be described. Let us first look at a rather general explanation of this theory of motivation.

A person is moved to action by certain physiological imperatives, called drives, which involve internal stimuli: hunger, thirst, sex needs, temperature regulation, fatigue, freedom from restraint, and (potentially at least) emotional responses to the environment. A drive is a persistent internal stimulus that causes activity until the tension or the conditions constituting the stimulus are met or modified. Since behavior is ongoing, the power of a drive may show in a change in degree, source, or direction of energy.

Drives can be primary (natural innate ones) or secondary (acquired). They can be described in terms of appetites, which involve activity toward something, or aversions, which prompt avoidance. Drive strength can vary; often for purposes of definition, drive strength is defined in terms of length of deprivation. Thus, someone who has not eaten for twenty-four hours is presumed to have a stronger hunger drive than one who has not eaten for four hours.[5]

A motive is a learned pattern of behavior that is associated with the amelioration of the tension of the drive state. Hunger is a drive; the specific patterns (motives) by which this drive is met are the result of learning. These motives channel a drive but also develop motivational properties in themselves.

It is a major step from discussion of the hunger drive to the explanation of very complex and interrelated behaviors that characterize the adult in the society. Indeed, contradictory elements seem to emerge. Presumably one of our drives is survival; yet at times we proudly give our lives. Tracing the complex evolution from the initial bodily based needs to complex social motivations is beyond the scope of this text. However, the basic lines for such an explanation have already been suggested. Drives generate behavior; through a learning process, including trial and error, we acquire motives—patterns by which these drives can be satisfied. In later life as well as at birth, we depend upon others in meeting basic innate needs. Thus, society teaches us what patterns are acceptable. We develop patterns of social-psychological needs. Smiles, kind words, praise, which were originally associated with rewards that met bodily needs, become rewards themselves. We learn that praise for being thin is worth more than the joy of food and being fat. We

---

[5] It is perhaps unfortunate that we tend to think of drive states as measured by deprivation states, a rather negative pressure. Motivation can also be approached in terms of goal-directed behavior; the anticipated reward or reinforcement may be the energizing force.

acquire habits that acquire motivational properties. Placed in a strange environment, an animal will seek to become acquainted with his immediate surroundings. So, too, through education we become acquainted with our surroundings and learn values, attitudes, and beliefs almost as painlessly as learning to prefer steak to wieners.

The degree to which needs are innate or acquired and the methods by which needs are transformed into patterns of behavior by maturation, learning, and socialization are subject to continuing debate.[6] But we certainly acquire patterns of response in mediating with the motivations that impinge upon us. Some patterns are so general they almost characterize mankind; others typify a given culture or subgroup. The total constellation is unique to each person.

However derived and shaped, the patterns of behavior acquired in dealing with innate and learned needs are powerful forces that must be taken into account to understand the success and failure of persuasion efforts.

Variants on the Approach

Many psychological theories could be explored that follow the pattern of identifying innate imperatives and then tracing the multiplication of these few imperatives into the motivational complexities of the adult. Only two such approaches will be mentioned: one linked to adjustment theories and one to growth motivation theories.

All of us are familiar with the concepts of Freudian psychology. Freud posited a motivational force (libido) common to all human beings. This force may be directed into sexual activity (viewed in a wide context of alternative means of expression), sublimated into desirable, socially approved activities, or repressed and manifested in personally and socially undesirable ways. Although Freud focused narrowly upon one motivational force, the pattern of this drive's being modified by experience into a variety of patterns and motivational factors is analogous to the pattern described above.

Freud's followers soon moved beyond the narrowness of the original emphasis into behavior theories, which centered upon personal adjustment and used such terms as anxiety, projection, aggression, and unconscious motivation.

A different approach views certain social motivations—and what might be termed more "altruistic" or healthy or humane motivations—as also innate. Maslow, for example, has postulated two general motivational

---

[6] Such books as Robert Ardrey, *The Territorial Imperative* (New York: Dell, 1966), Konrad Lorenz, *On Aggression* (New York: Harcourt, Brace, and World, 1966), and Desmond Morris, *The Naked Ape* (New York: McGraw-Hill, 1967), stress innate mechanisms as accounting for what many psychologists see as more the result of conditioning experiences.

forces: "deficiency and growth." Maslow links his work to many important writers, including Horney, Jung, Fromm, Rogers, and Allport. Maslow views man as born with certain needs, which exist in a hierarchical relationship. Once a person has largely met deficiency motivations (safety, love, self-esteem), she or he will be motivated primarily by growth, self-actualization, or self-realization. Self-actualizing motivation will be most pronounced and obvious in those who have fulfilled the deficiency motivations, but it is present in all. Maslow, as do Rogers and others, perceives the self-actualizer as a healthy, more desirable individual growing toward his unique self: "self-actualization (defined as ongoing actualization of potentials, capacities and talents, as fulfillment of mission [or call, fate, destiny, or vocation], as a fuller knowledge of, and acceptance of the person's own intrinsic nature, as an unceasing trend toward unity, integration or synergy within the person)."[7]

Growth theorists like Maslow perceive drives toward growth, self-actualization, an answer to the search for meaning, as innate rather than as the result of the socialization of primitive bodily based drives.[8] Whatever position an individual may take about the degree to which such altruistic or growth motivations are innate versus acquired, these motivations are powerful forces in the actions of people, and their effect cannot be discounted in communication.

Cognitive Models

Although some psychologists prefer to omit the concept of mind in the analysis of behavior, most focus upon the mind as the mediator between stimulus and response. Indeed, the mind as the shaper and holder of experience in the form of remembered experience, beliefs, attitudes, values, habits, and as interpreter of the present situation has become the key element in modern approaches to persuasion. Hence cognitive models are extremely relevant in the implications they hold for persuasion theory and attitude change.

Many theories of attitude change revolve around some variation of balance or consistency theory, which looks to the relationship among cognitions in the mind for the factors that energize change.[9] The assumption basic to all cognitive consistency models is that thoughts, new cognitions as well as the totality held in the mind from the past, tend to

[7] Abraham H. Maslow, *Toward a Psychology of Being* (Princeton: D. Van Nostrand, 1962), p. 23.

[8] You might enjoy reading some of Carl Rogers's books, such as *On Becoming a Person* (Boston: Houghton Mifflin, 1961).

[9] For example, examine the various approaches to attitude change treated in Chester A. Insko, *Theories of Attitude Change* (New York: Appleton-Century-Crofts, 1967).

organize themselves in meaningful ways. As long as a new cognition does not disturb the current balance, no change is predicted unless it is one of further strengthening and reinforcement. However, if the new cognition is discrepant—does not fit—in some way with the reality previously held, a pressure for adjustment exists. This basic assumption is common to concepts of balance, strain toward symmetry, congruity, and dissonance.

Consistency theories do not assume that all cognitions are actually consistent or that consistency among cognitions or the means to consistency will fit the tests of logic. Wide "potential" discrepancies are tolerated among attitudes, beliefs, values, specific information, and behavior as long as these are not perceived as inconsistent. Without the perception of inconsistency, cognitions are homeostatic, in balance, as far as the individual is concerned.

Balance theories begin by postulating for purposes of analysis an individual as being in a homeostatic condition; cognitions are organized into a relatively consistent structure as perceived by the holder of the cognitions. Then something occurs; some new information or factor is introduced, which disrupts the condition of balance.

Various sorts of information could yield disruption: conflicting orientations, approaches, views, or information offered by friends, referential groups, or authorities. To the degree that these sources are perceived as attractive, knowledgeable, or acceptable, information from such sources could cause imbalance. Actual experience could yield discrepant perceptions; failure or something contrary to expectation could produce the imbalance. Information could be drawn from a variety of media sources. A communication could provide an assertion or some stimulus that linked existing cognitions, which as a result of the linkage could be perceived as imbalanced, discrepant. Behavior, either as the result of free choice or under a degree of duress, even forced compliance, could also create conditions of imbalance.

Four rather general sources of imbalance are conflicting approaches of other persons or sources valued as referential points; conflict between experience and expectation; new associations, which reveal conflicts either within a person's cognitions or between behavior and cognitions (presumably these were always potential); and forced compliance in some behavior.

Once the congruence of the cognitions has been disturbed, the organism is motivated to regain balance. This is a mental operation but could involve overt action as well, either as a means to balance or as the result of new balance. The balance that is achieved may be a restoration of previous conditions by some mechanism or the evolution of a new condition of balance.

The formulations of balance theory have differed in terms of focus, terminology, and both the degree to which specific predictions of behavior can be offered and the degree to which the theory yields empirical verification. Three major approaches will be discussed briefly below.[10]

Balance-Symmetry Models

The term *balance* was initially associated with Fritz Heider. This approach focuses upon the desire of people to have congruent beliefs and feelings about an object or event. An attitude is presumed to contain both affective (feeling) and belief (cognition) elements. When these elements are reasonably consistent, the attitude is stable. But when the individual's tolerance limit (which will vary with individuals) is reached, an attitude becomes unstable. Thus, a change in attitude may occur as a result of either changing cognitions or changing feelings. One who feels slighted and hurt because a friend fails to meet an expectation may soon find that certain cognitions about the person change (for example, he becomes cooler in the relationship and finds reasons for it). Presumably one could render an attitude unstable either by affecting the feeling dimension or the belief dimension.

Newcomb's postulated "strain toward symmetry" is a refinement of the general balance approach. Newcomb focuses upon the orientations (attractions) between communicators and orientations toward objects or events (attitudes). If two people are positively attracted toward one another and they share similar attitudes toward an object, the relationship is balanced. However, if attitudes differ but attraction is high, the situation is unbalanced and there will be a strain toward symmetry.

Unfortunately, balance models and strain toward symmetry approaches have not always yielded precise predictions of the mechanism by which adjustments will be made; further, the problem of measurement of degree and intensity of orientation still remains.

Congruity Model

The congruity model of Osgood, Suci, and Tannenbaum is similar to the balance model and is a special application of it. Osgood and his associates developed a semantic differential as a technique for measuring the connotative aspects of meaning of concepts. The dimension of meaning that explains the greatest proportion of the variation among judgments of people lies in what is termed the evaluative dimension—the good-bad continuum.[11] The empirical derivation of the evalu-

---

[10] Chapters 5 through 8 in Arthur R. Cohen, *Attitude Change and Social Influence* (New York: Basic Books, 1964), contain good expository materials on these approaches and are relatively intelligible upon first reading.

[11] Osgood et al., *Measurement of Meaning*.

ative dimension lends support to the view that attitudes are marked by an evaluative component, which is an extremely dominant dimension of the attitude.

Use of the semantic differential permits measurement of two or more objects or events, or of an object and a communicator, in terms of their position on the evaluative continuum of the differential.[12] Once the two concepts have been linked by an assertion, the resultant change in valuation of the two can be examined utilizing the differential.

Osgood postulated a congruity hypothesis: when two concepts (people and/or objects or constructs) are associated, they exert influence one upon the other and tend to become more congruent. Thus a well-liked communicator who endorses a relatively disliked position presumably improves the disliked position but also decreases his own position in terms of the evaluative continuum. Concepts that are more polarized in terms of the end of the continuum presumably exert stronger pulls than do those toward the middle. It is also possible to introduce an incredulity effect, where the assertion that links two concepts is simply not accepted by the individual being studied. Thus, "No! There is some mistake. He would never say that." No change in positions of the two concepts—the object of the statement and the maker of the statement—would be predicted.

The congruity model has been usefully employed in predicting changes in perception of sources and constructs. A refinement of the model that took into account not only source and concept but compositional and delivery elements permitted more accurate predictions than the predictions for oral messages, which took into account only source and message.[13]

Cognitive Dissonance Model

The preeminent name associated with cognitive dissonance is Leon Festinger. Festinger focused upon the conditions operative after a decision has been reached. This model thus is concerned not with the processes involved in reaching the decision but with what occurs after the

---

[12] Later researchers have argued that the other dimensions of meaning that have been isolated, such as dynamism, should also be included. The potency dimension, for example, may provide a means of refining the prediction of the degree of movement of two concepts. Placement on the evaluative dimension may not be a sufficient indicator of predicted response.

[13] Compare the results of David Berlo and Halbert Gulley, "Some Determinants of the Effect of Oral Communication in Producing Attitude Change and Learning," *Speech Monographs* 24 (1957): 10–20, using two elements, with Erwin Bettinghaus, "The Operation of Congruity in an Oral Communication Situation" (Ph.D. diss., University of Illinois, 1959).

decision is reached. Suppose that a person has to choose among several alternatives, each of which contains some degree of desirability. Once the decision has been made, the elements rejected still exert a potential attraction for the individual. This creates a condition of cognitive dissonance, a presumed drive state, in which the tension motivates the person to action until the dissonance is resolved. One key mechanism of alleviating this dissonance is to change attitudes. Thus, the rejected alternatives become less desirable, less attractive; the accepted alternatives become more desirable, more attractive.

This theory is interesting for the predictions it makes that at first seem contrary to expectations. For example, assume that a person is hired to present a point of view that is opposed to the one she actually holds. If she is paid $500,000, she presumably endures no dissonance. But if she agrees to do it for $3.95, she may well feel a good deal of dissonance. Hence, to alleviate the dissonance she may change her attitude, finding that the position to which she verbally committed herself really does have more merit. The closer the person is to the point between agreeing and not agreeing to make the statement, the more likely her change in attitude becomes. Similar experiments have been conducted with forced compliance in which persons are forced to choose a less desired alternative.

Different people respond differently in dissonance situations. Some appear to have a much higher level of tolerance for dissonance than do others. Further, a change in attitude may not be the only means of resolving the tension. Very real difficulties have been encountered in attempts to measure operationally the drive state that Festinger postulates exists. Too, some of the predictions can be explained by other theories, and not all of the individuals used in experiments seem to respond in the manner predicted by the hypothesis, perhaps because the situation produced no dissonance for them.

Learning Theory

Learning theory has relevance to persuasion theory in two contexts: (1) learning is centrally involved in the process by which the infant grows to become the complex individual who comes to communication with attitudes, information, language, and so on; (2) learning theory can be used to explain the creation of new attitudes or behavior where none previously existed or to explain changes in previous attitudes or previous behavior patterns.

The relevance of learning theory to the development of an individual is unchallenged. An individual acquires a language with all the richness of denotation and connotation that a language possesses. He learns attitudes, he learns behavior patterns, he develops response patterns that become habituated. Learning theory can be used to explain how two potentially identical people become totally opposite beings.

When an individual possesses no information about an object or event, when he has no prior attitude, no prior experience, he is in a learning situation. In the absence of competing stimuli, an individual can learn whatever is being offered. Thus, when we have no prior attitude concerning a person, a situation, or an event, we can rapidly learn about it. We may not be at all resistant to learning that a problem exists or incorporating materials that fill a vacant spot in our world view.

But a learning model could also be used to explain the change within an attitudinal structure. Learning theory could explain not only how an attitude comes to be but also how it is changed. Certainly learning experiments have focused upon the matter of acquisition of new patterns, the extinction of old patterns, and the replacement of one pattern with another. It is highly feasible to use a learning-theory orientation as the approach to persuasion. Attitude change and the relationship of mental constructs to actual behavior then become a specialized aspect of the more general learning theory.

Much of learning theory and attitude-change theory contains no inherent contradictions. Both are problems of motivation since acquisition and modification of all behavior is presumed to be motivated. Further, the concepts of readiness, habit strength, discrimination, generalization, reinforcement all seem clearly relevant to attitudes and the relationship of attitudes to behavior.

Learning Defined

Learning is a process by which a relatively permanent change in an organism's behavior results from an interaction with the environment—a change that cannot be explained by maturation and is not an innate response or the result of temporary factors (such as fatigue or accident).

The potential and previous learning of an organism limit what can be learned and how rapidly and easily.

Approaches to Learning [14]

Two major approaches to learning govern much of the research and theory in the field. One approach, association theory, ana-

[14] A useful general source on learning theory is Ernest R. Hilgard and Gordon H. Bower, *Theories of Learning* (New York: Appleton-Century-Crofts, 1966).

lyzes behavior in terms of elements, studies the operation of these elements, and attempts to formulate laws of behavior. This approach stresses the importance of stimulus-response connections, reinforcement, past experience, and history. The other general approach, field theory, focuses upon the total configuration of parts existent at any point in time. Past experience and the operation of specific stimuli and specific responses are less emphasized. Rather, response is held to be the resultant of a host of factors operating upon the individual, which can be studied only in terms of the total matrix, not as isolated items.

The association approaches, dominated by Thorndike's connectionism, are most often used to explain acquisition of language and specific behavior patterns. The field theories seem more useful in explaining problem solving—more elaborate and complex behavioral outcomes where individual stimulus-response patterns are resistant to isolation.

B. F. Skinner has influenced learning theory greatly. Of great value is his differentiation of two kinds of learning models: type S and type R. Type S learning corresponds to classical Pavlovian conditioning, in which one stimulus for eliciting a response is substituted for another. Type R, or operant conditioning, according to Skinner, is far more important. In operant conditioning a stimulus is presented; when the appropriate or correct response is made, it is rewarded or reinforced. Over a period of time the responses become habitual, relatively automatic, noncritical. Then we can say that an individual has learned a response.

Applications of Learning Theory

Many applications of learning theory are possible. Each of the laws and generalizations relative to learning could be subjected to extended discussion with profit; however, a brief list of some generalizations derived from learning theory should provide some suggestions of applications possible for persuasion.

    1. Learning must be motivated. (a) Excessive motivation can retard learning. (b) Individuals differ in motivation to learn.
    2. Learning involves the habituation of response.
    3. Individuals differ in terms of ability to respond.
    4. Simpler elements are more easily learned; elements that involve less effort are more easily learned and retained.
    5. Curves of forgetting are very marked at first, gradual at later stages.
    6. Learning demands reward; items that receive positive reinforcement will be retained; those that receive negative reinforcement will be extinguished.

MOTIVATION, ATTITUDES, AND BEHAVIOR

7. Meaningful items are learned more easily than are meaningless items.

8. Frequency of reward, specificity of reward, and immediacy of reward will affect learning.

9. Feedback (information about the response) improves learning.

10. Learning tends to generalize from a specific situation to situations perceived as related; the degree of perceived relationship affects the degree of generalization.

11. Learning involves problems in the transfer of learning; material acquired in one situation may not transfer to another.

THE MATRIX OF MOTIVATIONAL FORCES

Because learning complex structures requires greater effort than learning simple ones, we often seek the easy explanation for behavior rather than a more complex, but accurate, one. It is easy to accept the view that everyone is motivated by power, love of money, or selfishness, or that everyone naturally seeks love, development, goodness, or God. Whatever the validity of such general orientations, they can never explain the specific, complex patterns of behavior of individuals or society as a whole.

Although it is useful to look for general motivational factors, we must examine the specific motivational elements in each situation if we are to understand behavior. This demands hard work, but it yields understanding. We must translate the insights of general theories of motivation into understandings of particular situations. Persuasion operates with particular individuals in particular settings at particular times.

A person at any moment is the center of many forces affecting motivation and activity. According to the theories we have examined, motivation must be studied in terms of an individual's responding to external and internal forces. External forces are only potentially motivating; they take on meaning only in terms of the individual. A stimulus that induces strong reaction in one receiver may have absolutely no effect upon another. Anything outside an individual is only a potential source of motivation: the receiver must perceive, interpret, and thus decide whether and how to think or act.

Succeeding chapters examine the sources of motivation relevant to persuasion in terms of the model of the persuasion process described in chapter 1. Motivations may exist clustered around the communication source. Certainly the message contains great potential for motivational factors. The channels employed and the situation may have powerful impact. We may be strongly influenced by other people. And each person brings preexisting motivational factors to the communication situation, and interprets and responds to all the other factors of the communication-binding context.

In thinking about persuasion, people too often look to the message and the source as the primary or only sources of motivation. We must remember that all the elements of the persuasion process interact. And the message is simply a set of stimuli that must be interpreted and given meaning by the people involved. Motivational forces operate on the source as well as on the receiver. And the two motivational fields are not the same. Since the two are unique individuals, each may respond quite differently to the same stimulus just as they may respond similarly.

Behavior is the result of a multiplicity of factors. Can we understand our own motivations and those of others? Can we as persuaders create and direct motivational forces so as to influence others? The answer to both questions is: "Yes—to a degree."

At birth we can no more choose our motivations than we can control our responses. However, in time we learn patterns of response and gain a repertory of possible responses. We can then make a variety of responses to the same stimulus, and we have acquired bases for choosing among alternatives. So we obtain a degree of control over our lives. The extent of this control certainly varies with circumstances and individuals and the degree to which we believe we can exert such control and are willing to put forth the effort.

As persuaders we seek to affect the motivations of others to elicit a desired response. The persuader evolves a psychology of human behavior. If this psychology is accurate and the persuader can take the perspective of those to be persuaded and thus properly assess potential sources of motivation and their probable effectiveness, the persuader can effectively motivate others. This potential does not suggest the ability to gain complete control over the other person. We cannot know fully the motivations that influence our own actions. We cannot be so effective in taking the perspective of the other person that we understand all that might motivate and what would follow from each motivation. Further, the number of potential influences that may direct behavior is so great we cannot expect to know (let alone control) all of them. Accident and circumstances beyond our control play a greater role in our successes and failures in communication than we like to admit.

So complete control is not possible; the matrix of motivational forces is too complex and diverse. But we can understand and direct our own motivations and those of others to a useful degree. The sounder our psychology, the more skilled we become in observing and analyzing ourselves and others, the more effective we become in taking the perspective of others, the greater ability we will have to understand and control motivation.

SUMMARY

Behavior is motivated. Hence, the student of persuasion is a student of motivation. We are concerned not only with the forces that energize behavior but also with determining how behavior is directed as a result of these forces.

The concept of attitude plays a central role in persuasion. An attitude is a learned, relatively stable set involving a tendency to respond in predetermined ways toward specific objects or general classes. An attitude thus is a generalization about something and is associated with a number of beliefs, specific data accepted as facts. Some attitudes become so integrated, inclusive, and dominant over other attitudes that they constitute key referential cores, which are linked, at least potentially, to many different attitudes and actions. These core attitudes we call values.

A change in a belief or in a relatively peripheral, unimportant attitude may have little impact upon a person's thinking or behavior. Such peripheral, unimportant beliefs or attitudes are often easy to change. But a change in a relatively central, dominant attitude or value may cause a basic change in thinking and behavior.

Single beliefs, attitudes, or even values rarely determine an action by themselves. Usually many attitudes and other factors related to the individual and the situation are involved in determining what action will result. Yet attitudes are a useful concept; properly applied, they can help us understand and predict behavior.

The human being is a complex organism. The physiological and psychological imperatives are so shaped by experience that as humans grow they become highly individual beings. We all hunger but not for the same things. In persuasion the concern with motivation becomes specified in terms of a matrix or field of forces. General motivation theories are of limited value in specific persuasion interactions. Rather, the constellation of specific forces must be analyzed to see what is actually and potentially motivating behavior. The ways in which these energizing forces may be channeled to direct behavior is of key concern.

A variety of approaches to motivation—drive-motives, cognitive balance, learning theory—applied in specific persuasion efforts may yield a similar approach. Cognitive models take people as they are. The drive-motive models spend more time focusing on how we came to be as we are. Learning models often reinforce the other attitude-change models and are useful as explanations for how attitudes are acquired and changed. Two people may start with different theories but agree on the same approach.

The forces that motivate people are so numerous and diverse that we cannot recognize them all. Thus, no one should expect to control the motivations of another. We can try to understand the motivations and potential motivations of others and attempt to influence them through using or rechanneling one or more of these motivational sources.

DISCUSSION QUESTIONS AND PROJECTS

1. Describe the major factors in your theory of motivation. To the degree that the members of your class are willing to share their theories, discuss, compare, and contrast them.

2. Try to create a hierarchical list of motives that determine your actions. How many of these motives are goals you are striving for? How many the results of forces pushing you? How would a list of ideal motivations differ from a list of actual motivations?

3. In what sense is it meaningful to talk about "proper" or "natural" behavior if almost any pattern of behavior can be "learned" by an individual and thus seem correct?

4. John Foster Dulles has been quoted (not necessarily accurately) as urging the Arabs and Israelis to settle their disputes in a "Christian fashion." What does this say about the problem of persuasion involving different cultures?

5. How much are attitudes inevitably culturally bound? How is one "helped" if her or his attitudes reflect the prevailing assumptions and values of the society? How is one harmed? As a persuader? As a person?

6. What attitudes or beliefs have you held in the absence of factual experience with the object of those attitudes? Can you recall instances of some dramatic changes in attitude when you actually gained experience with the object, be it person, class, or event?

7. What motivated you to enter college? What motivations are keeping you in college? What is the balance of immediate versus delayed reward that is operative?

8. If motivation is so complex and the potential factors operating on individuals so diverse, how can a persuader ever hope to evolve a strategy to motivate an audience?

MOTIVATION, ATTITUDES, AND BEHAVIOR

9. List all the beliefs (facts and opinions) you have about some person or thing that is important to you. How consistent are these beliefs with one another? How consistent are they with your attitudes and actions toward the person or thing?

10. Under what circumstances can you argue that a person's behavior really does contradict that person's attitude?

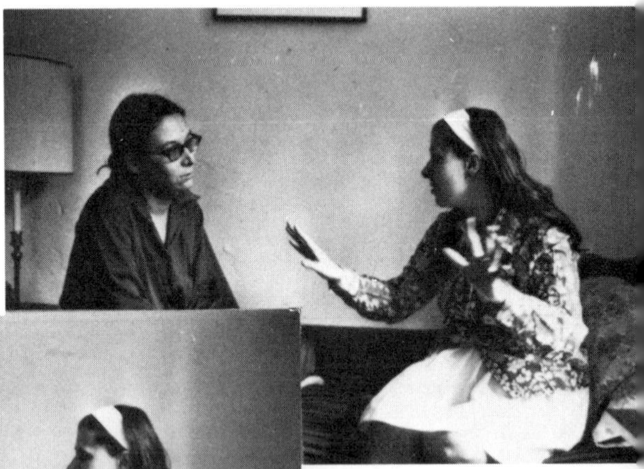
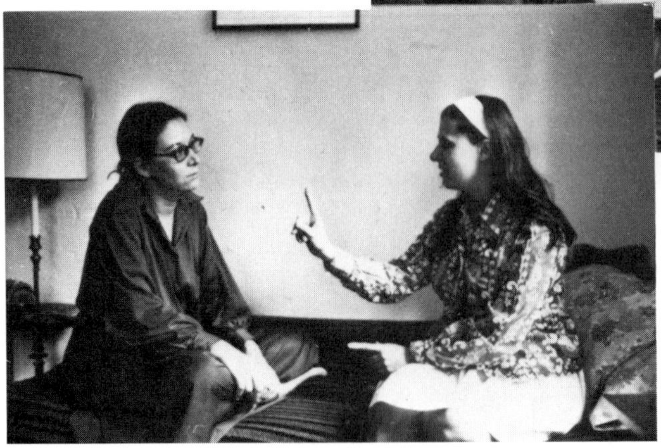

4 Receiver and Situation Analysis

The study of persuasion necessitates a study of the receivers. In many situations both the source and the receivers would label the receivers as the audience. In other instances (such as two roommates talking together), neither one would use the labels *source* and *receiver*. The effects of the persuasion process on receivers are the normal concern of most people. But the persuasion process also has many effects upon the source and people other than the immediate receivers. Hence, the effects on immediate receivers are not the only ones of importance. (These other effects will be highlighted in later chapters.) Since every receiver and every audience is unique to some degree, the ability to estimate persuasion effects in terms of that unique audience is basic to the persuader, the critic, and the study of persuasion and often of interest to the receiver. Because the situation (including the occasion, the setting, the general condition of things) directly affects receivers, we will combine the discussion of receiver and situation analysis in this chapter.[1]

VALUE OF RECEIVER ANALYSIS

If people were not unique, if a person communicated repeatedly to the identical audience, or if the variability of receivers had no impact upon response, audience analysis would be unimportant because receiver analysis would be a limited, one-time matter of careful research.

[1] Further discussion of the effects of occasions, settings, and channels will be found in section V.

The variability of response is one of the frustrations and delights in studying persuasion. A group of receivers subjected to one experience cannot be programmed to forget that experience, return to their original set, and then respond to a different experience without any effect from the first one. In attempting to evaluate the effects of different patterns of organization (in a class, for example), a researcher may be forced to weigh the effects of such things as interest in the subject matter, different experiences, time of day, class size, attitude toward the teacher, and the degree to which the students in a sample are representative of people generally.

A class in engineering English differs from a class in English literature. The Rotary differs from the group assembled for the PTA meeting. Republicans can be differentiated from both Democrats and Independents. The readers of *The Atlantic* differ in certain ways from the viewers of the "Tonight Show." This is not to say that people in these groups are largely different or even importantly so in many respects.

While the uniqueness of each communication event seems a sound generalization, communicators implicitly and, at times, explicitly challenge the generalization in two contexts: in the daily, repetitive, ongoing interaction of one-to-one and small-group settings and in mass-communication settings. This failure to recognize the significant uniqueness of the audience in these or other settings may limit the effectiveness of all communication efforts, including persuasive ones.

In what sense can any communication act be thought to be unique as compared with thousands of other apparently similar acts? One approach is to examine a specific instance. A couple married twelve years with two children are talking over the dinner table. What can be unique about this act that has occurred literally thousands of times before? There are always unique features in every event. Perhaps the wife is tired from the long day, the husband has lost a sale, or perhaps one suddenly feels the urge to visit friends. Or possibly this is the day that the wife decides it is time to get a job outside the home: bridge is boring, the PTA is frustrating, the kids are both in school. But the husband does not wish his wife to work. So the dispute spills over into tension with the children. A sudden overreaction to a small item produces a hurt, sullen silence.

An extreme case? Yes, in one sense, but not in another. What about the effects of day-to-day events upon all of us? There are days when we are gloomy. Is there any college student who fails to ask one day, "What am I doing here?" One roommate forgets to dump the garbage when it is his turn. The pattern prevails for almost a semester and then suddenly his roommates make a running, slashing attack on his total personality. In shock he responds, "But you never complained before!"

The effects of such day-to-day changes are not confined to groups in which interpersonal relationships are the dominant element. These same factors operate in groups in the workaday world. A group meeting to discuss a policy change brings with it the impressions of the last meeting. The slight that one member felt when another laughed at his idea may be a significant item on the hidden agenda for this meeting. The mood of the members will vary; the problems they discuss will change; the alliances will shift. The majority who voted in favor of one proposal will fractionate, and a new majority will be formed for the new proposal.

Perhaps the only constant of these ongoing relationships and interactions is change. Obviously many of these changes are nonsignificant. Day-to-day changes are a constant of life that we all accept and are presumably aware of in our adjustments to one another. Yet it is disturbingly easy to become locked into the habitual pattern, the stereotyped response, the pictures valid of yesterday and inaccurate of today. Thus, the mother of fifty reminds the son of thirty to "put on your overshoes, dear, it may rain today"—advice that the son had given in almost identical tones to his daughter as she set off to school that morning.

The assumption that one continues to deal with identical, unchanged receivers is dangerous. If the communicator is having any effect, she has already been instrumental in changing the nature of her receivers. Day-to-day changes may make no difference, but we should be sensitive to the differences they can make. To be fully effective, the communicator must guard against the tendency to make a habitual response to a fixed view of her receivers. Everyone tends to become caught in the pattern of what was and to structure the present in terms of perceptions in the past.

Individuals change, and when the persuader is dealing with small numbers, she can adjust and thus perhaps markedly alter her effectiveness. But many think that a mass audience is so large that it is undifferentiated; one must deal with the "average." One cannot adjust to the specific audience with television, movies, radio, or in advertising.

We must examine two assumptions: mass audiences cannot be usefully differentiated one from another, and the actual mass audience is best viewed in terms of average characteristics of the entire potential audience.

1. *Can one mass audience be differentiated from another one?* Certainly. Because potential receivers select among the available communications, different audiences emerge. Different interests, habits, cultural patterns, occupations, needs, and many other factors determine what we expose ourselves to, and this yields a differentiation of audience. The reality of selective attention and perception is too well documented to challenge. The audience for "Happy Days" is not the same as that for

"Wall Street Week"; the audience at a folk-rock concert is not the same as that for the Metropolitan Opera. During the 1930s audience researchers noted that proportionally more Republicans than Democrats listened to FDR's speeches over radio. Apparently this disproportionate reaction was because people who labeled themselves Republicans also responded to other factors, such as the desire to appear well informed, habit patterns concerning exposure to public affairs, and probably the fact they owned more radios than did Democrats.

Not every advertiser seeks the largest possible audience in a numbers sense. Hallmark sponsors many operas and dramas on TV and seems quite content with smaller audiences than many advertisers would accept. Why? Hallmark believes it is reaching exactly those people who are most likely to buy Hallmark cards, party favors, napkins. Advertisements of the program reach those who do not watch it, thus furthering the image of Hallmark as a prestige, quality line "when you want the very best." Even NBC receives image value as a network for carrying Hallmark programs.

In some instances the advertiser may be content with the size of the audience, but the network may feel that the effect on the total impact of the network is harmful. It is dangerous for networks to give up the larger audience to another network since viewers develop patterns of exposure to particular networks.

Thus, even the mass media, which theoretically fight for a portion of the entire audience, clearly recognize the fact that audiences select among programs. Radio stations now often deliberately program to certain portions of the market: some emphasize news, others program the top fifty records, some carry soul music or program in Spanish. Relatively few readers of this text subscribe to *The Farm Journal*. Most have not read a single issue of *The Million Dollar Farmer* nor recall many advertisements for five-bottom plows.

The mass media, aware of the selective audience that they reach, sell to advertisers accordingly. Some advertisers seek a large, broadly based audience. Thus they may seek the maximum number of viewers in terms of cost-per-thousand of viewers reached. Preempting a popular program to carry a special or to present live television from the moon may result in thousands of irate phone calls to a local station within the hour. Two years later the popular program may not be available even in reruns.

2. *Should the mass audience be viewed in terms of an average and the communication directed to that average?* Can a communication be directed to the "average" of the actual audience? One test is easy to conduct. Take a magazine and go through it reading, skimming, looking as you choose. Have another person do the same. Will you recall the same articles, the same advertisements? Will you, perhaps even more im-

portantly, recall the same things about the articles and the advertisements? Obviously it is meaningful for the communicator to select a medium that will get to the appropriate set of receivers, but even then only some of the potential receivers will be reached. Second, an advertisement, a program, a movie can contain many levels of appeal. Even a thirty-second spot commercial can have a variety of appeals. And in the 30 minutes of a TV program, 111 minutes of a movie, 156 pages of a magazine, there is the potential to adapt to many different receivers and offer many different bases of response.

The very concept of average can mislead. The average American is slightly more female than male, if married has fewer than 2.2 children, was becoming younger all the time and is now becoming older but can still expect to live to an older age. Such an American seems an odd target for persuasion.

Functions of Receiver and Situation Analysis

Stated most simply, the goal of audience and situation analysis is to provide maximum understanding of the receiver(s) and the situation as these affect the persuasion process. *Situation* is used to include four closely related but separable elements: the specific occasion, the specific setting, the immediate conditions in terms of the people involved and the topic at issue, and the general environment, which includes all the factors not specifically and directly involved but which potentially could have an effect.

While the persuader, the receiver, the critic, and the person seeking to understand the persuasion process may all want to understand the nature of the receivers and the situation, the use to which that understanding may be put will vary.

The Persuader

Planning and preparation increase the chances for success, so the persuader needs to estimate the nature of the audience and situation as a guide to preparation. Not all persuasion is planned; much of it occurs on the spur of the moment without specific advance preparation. To the degree that the persuader can change or adjust to various conditions, the persuader may gain maximum effect.

An analysis of the potential receivers and the situation enables the persuader to maximize the value of preparation. Further analysis just prior to the actual persuasion effort enables the persuader to adjust plans immediately before and during the communication act itself. A continued analysis of the receivers enables the persuader to judge the effect, any need for further action, the reasons for success or failure.

The Receiver

It is easy to understand why others might be interested in analyzing the receiver and the situation as it relates to the receiver. But why would a receiver be interested in a "self-analysis" or analysis of other receivers? In most situations the receiver may make a judgment of the source and evaluate the message but would not think about evaluating his or her role in the persuasion activity. This is a mistake.

What does the receiver gain from a self-analysis? The receiver may identify particular needs, goals, and motivational forces that are influencing behavior. The situation can be producing certain forces that may unduly influence behavior. If the situation or the persuader seem to highlight certain needs or actions, self-awareness may suggest equally pressing needs or actions that may not be served or that could be harmed by a particular proposal. Self-awareness may protect against making a mistake. Further, the conscious awareness of self may aid in the accurate interpretation of the elements of the persuasion interchange.

Second, the behavior of other receivers can have important impact upon an individual. People often follow along, laugh with the group, accept what everyone else is accepting, donate money if everyone is donating. In ambiguous situations, we look to the behavior of people around us to determine the norms that are operating. And many of us conform to those norms. Awareness of the reactions of others and the possible diversity in those reactions may be of value to the individual receiver.

The receiver should be conscious of the voluntary nature of participation in persuasion. The receiver may ask why she or he is involved. What goal is being sought? How do I want to use this interchange? What function can or should it serve for me? The receiver has as much right as the persuader to seek his or her individual goals in the persuasion process.

Obviously the means by which one conducts a self-analysis are not the same as those of an outsider trying to conduct a similar analysis. Obviously, too, the perspective is very different.

It should be noted that we do not always see ourselves accurately. The current emphases in consumer education and the protections being established in revocable contracts are efforts to permit the receiver to do some delayed analysis and alter a decision that looks wrong in retrospect.

The popular books on assertiveness training, self-development, and learning to say no are presumably offering help to those seeking to resist the influence attempts of others. Part of this effort involves self-analysis and the identification of situations and activities in which we are excessively influenced. Then, we try to modify our behavior through conscious effort.

The Critic

Much of persuasion is relevant to general society. During a political campaign, commentators and the public generally discuss and evaluate the efforts of the candidates. We are sensitive to the possibility of overstatement or misleading, deceitful practices in advertising. Hence, the persuasion process is often subjected to criticism of a variety of sorts from a variety of positions. Even the persuasion that occurs between two people is related to general practices in persuasion.

If the critic is to make judgments about what is happening and interpret the persuasion activity and its implications, the critic needs an awareness of the elements involved in the total situation and a perspective on the persuader and the receivers. To offer useful commentary about the interplay of forces in persuasion, critics need a lively sense of those involved in the process and need to be able to distinguish their own values and responses from those of other receivers. They need to be sensitive to the public in all its aspects. The critic needs to be aware there are many different publics. A sense of different audiences and differential responses by those audiences would improve much of the commentary about public affairs and persuasion in its various services to individuals and society.

The Student of Persuasion

The study of persuasion in terms of the communicator, the message, the audience, a social movement, or a campaign has a long academic history. Hundreds of doctoral dissertations have studied persuaders from ancient Greece to contemporary times; persuasion in the pulpit; the legislature; inaugural addresses; the Lincoln-Douglas, Kennedy-Nixon, and Ford-Carter debates; on stage; in nonviolent protests; in the United Nations; and in the courtroom. These studies have attempted a judgment of the effectiveness and quality of the persuasion not only in assessing immediate effects but also making judgments as to alternatives and long-term effects.

As contemporary researchers have sought to develop careful, precise observation and measurement procedures, the importance of all the variables in the persuasion process has become clearer. The role of the audience has been a major focus of study. The research has shown most vividly the need to consider the total system, all the factors caught and held together by the communication-binding context.

PARTICIPATION AS RECEIVERS

We all remain students of the persuasion process as practitioners, as receivers, as observers and participants in our world. To remain aware of the uniqueness of the receiver and the communication event is to enrich our ability to understand what we see and hear. The ability to estimate the variables relevant to response is essential to understanding persuasion.

PROCESS OF RECEIVER AND SITUATION ANALYSIS

This section is written from the point of view of the persuader who is seeking to analyze the receivers and the situation. The process of audience and situation analysis is one that should be continued through the entire process of preparation, actual presentation, and later reflection on a persuasive effort. For convenience we will talk in terms of a single persuasion effort. (We will discuss the more complicated problems of the sustained campaign in chapter 14.) The analysis of situation and receivers can be discussed in terms of four stages; prior analysis, which takes place during the advance planning; immediate analysis, which takes place just before the actual communication activity; concurrent analysis, which takes place during the communication activity itself; and postanalysis, which takes place after the specific communication actively and closely associated activity are completed.

The concerns in the analysis vary with the individual communication event as well as the progress from initial preparation to completion of the communication act. However, answers to certain general questions are relevant at every stage of the process. The information available as a basis for inferring the answers to these questions will change just as the appropriate verb tense for the question will shift.

1. What is the attitude of the receivers toward the goal of the persuader?
2. What is the attitude of the receivers toward the source?
3. What is the importance of the issue to the audience? What is the saliency or relevancy of the topic and materials that might be employed?
4. What is the knowledge and understanding (true or false) of the receivers relevant to the issues and available material?
5. What motivational forces are operating upon the receivers? What are the potential sources for motivation?
6. Is this a homogeneous or heterogeneous audience in their attitude toward the topic and other relevant variables?
7. What strategies and tactics are likely to be markedly effective or ineffective with a body of receivers?

8. What expectations do the receivers hold as a result of occasion, speaker, topic, experience, and so forth?
9. What unique considerations apply?

Prior Analysis

In many instances the communicator will have a good knowledge of audience, occasion, and setting. Target receivers may be well known and the occasion part of the routine of daily life. In these cases the persuader has so much potential information available that he probably cannot digest it all. He can only hope that he remains sensitive to changes and to the shifting elements in terms of their importance. Further, the accessibility of his targets may enable him to sound out these people in advance, to send up a trial balloon, or otherwise conduct information gathering of his choice. (And it should be remembered these are the most typical of the persuasion conditions in which we operate.)

But there are important instances in which the receivers and the nature of the setting are far less well known. Certain general questions may form a pattern for analysis in these conditions.

Situation

1. What is the occasion that calls forth the persuasive effort?
2. What requirements does the occasion appear to impose?
3. What is the specific setting(s) in which the persuasion activity will take place?
4. How do the occasion and setting serve to select the audience?
5. What channels are available for use?
6. To what degree is there an opportunity to manipulate the occasion, setting, or channels to help the persuader?
7. Under what auspices does the communicator appear?
8. How did the source become the persuasion agent? Is this a function of role? Assignment by someone? Self-selected?
9. What is the status of the subject matter being treated?
10. What significant forces may be operating caused by the impact of events and forces outside the immediate communication activity?

Some of these questions are important to planning the persuasion effort itself. Others will be helpful in making predictions about the nature of the receivers and their probable responses. The questions that follow focus upon the receivers.

Receivers

A variety of questions may be posed about the receivers. These factors are interrelated and some serve causally to produce other factors.

Demographic Factors:

1. Age.
2. Sex.
3. Race, nationality, religion.
4. Geographical uniqueness.

A person cannot choose to be twenty-one, forty-three, or seventy-eight; to be male or female; to be born red, white, yellow, or black; to be born in Scotland, Lapland, or Cameroon. Yet to neglect the importance of these factors is dangerous. Students find it hard to understand the sense of relief that swept many in the United States after the atomic bomb fell on Japan, the elation of "this ends the war; it has to end now; my sons will live; I won't have to fight in Japan." To be born and raised in one time, one culture, one religion is to be exposed to influences not present in another.

Choice Factors:

5. Education.
6. Occupation.
7. Income level.
8. Primary roles.
9. Voluntary group affiliations.
10. Interests, commitments.
11. Experiences, social-cultural milieu.

Certainly these factors are not unrelated to items discussed above. But within limits one can choose education, occupation, income level, whether to be married or single. We can join the JC's, the SDS, the film club, or a meditation group. We can go to Hope College, Illinois, or get a job. These are not totally free-choice situations. We are properly concerned about the degree to which some of these factors cannot be chosen by certain individuals. It is not that all would want the same thing; it is that all should have the opportunity to choose them within limits of native ability and interests.

To the degree that people choose these conditions, to the degree that they voluntarily associate themselves with certain groups and employ the standards of selected groups or individuals—these factors are key guides in the analysis of an audience.

Unique factors:

12. Audience size.
13. Reasons for this audience forming.
14. Particular goals, values, desires.

15. Relevant referential groups.
16. Interrelationships of members.
17. Relationship to and knowledge of source.

In addition to examining the general characteristics of the audience, the communicator may profit from considering the forces that produced this audience. Only certain people elect to attend a lecture on bird watching. A protest meeting on busing carries inherently unique factors that shape the people who attend. Churchgoers act differently and in accord with different standards on Sunday than they do on Thursday afternoon.

When little else is known about the potential audience, analysis of the probable audience in terms of the unique factors that bring them into this communication setting may be extremely productive. Even if one plans to start speaking about conservation on a local street corner, one has some basis for generating a picture of the receivers. The possible auditors at 8:00 a.m. will differ from those at 12:00 noon, at 2:15, at 5:15, or at midnight. Even the same auditor is likely to respond differently at these various times.

A brief period of careful thought should provide any communicator with some useful indication of the nature of the potential audience. The value and worth of extended analysis of the audience will vary. There is also a point of diminishing returns, but it is difficult to calculate that point in advance.

Commercial persuaders often employ elaborate means of audience analysis. Even the local political candidate seems to need a poll to identify public sentiment or to define the relevant issues in a campaign. A manufacturing firm may test its advertising or its product in a selected area. A communications medium may conduct a careful analysis of its receivers and then make its findings available to potential advertisers. *Business Week* solicits subscriptions only from those in management and business. Students have polled fellow students and used that information both for audience analysis and for data in speeches. Even for an individual, capital is not usually the limiting factor in prior audience analysis.

Immediate Analysis

Immediate analysis is meaningful when the source and receiver are brought into proximity immediately before the actual communication act. Even in the non-face-to-face setting communicators will attempt to remain sensitive to any changes that might alter planning. Immediate analysis provides the opportunity to validate or correct prior analysis and thus adjust planned procedures. Further, opportunity for additional new information exists.

Situation

The actual environment of the communication event can now be observed. Problems in acoustics, missing lecterns, lack of a public address system, or extreme noise can all be estimated and perhaps remedied.

The nature of the occasion can now be estimated in terms of the behavior of the receivers. The college professor who came to the sales meeting to present an hour lecture on the latest research in cognitive structuring may revise her approach as she becomes aware the audience perceives the occasion as "our night to howl." As a second martini is forced upon her by a man who has just had five, the professor may be forced to revise her presentation.

The student who has prepared a superficial analysis of the cold war may suddenly confront a new situation as he hears the previous speaker give a far more penetrating analysis.

Audience

The immediate situation provides rich opportunities for audience analysis. One can directly estimate age, sex, or audience size. Dress and topics, content, and manner of interactions can all be noted. The speaker can talk with some of the audience members. He can lay the groundwork with the chairman for the statements to be made in his introduction. The speaker can pick up bits of information to adapt his speech particularly and directly to his audience.

Many communicators neglect the fact that they are simultaneously being evaluated and analyzed by their receivers. Caught in the ongoing nature of the factors that affect communication, the communicator has already begun his communication.

Concurrrent Analysis

Concurrent analysis describes the opportunities for evaluating the audience and situation during the actual process of delivering the communication. Some of this analysis process is conscious, but presumably much more of it is unconscious. Of course, the receivers are also engaged in analysis of the speaker and the message. The communication of the actual message gives the communicator maximum opportunity to control the stimuli that impact upon the receivers. The situation provides the maximum opportunity to gauge the nature and the response of the receivers themselves.

Situation

In one sense the occasion is set. The larger influences operating upon the receivers are now determined; the occasion and environment are now exerting active influence upon the communication effect. The source and his communication have now become part of the occasion, and they give it shape, substance, and tone. Indeed, the nature of the communication may now be the key factor determining the nature of the occasion.

Audience

In face-to-face oral communication the source and receiver are now linked. They affect one another reciprocally—that is, they interact to yield effects that cannot be explained by either of them acting independently. The communication-binding context is clearly operating.

The process of communication is now very much a two-way process. The audience is analyzing the source and message; the source is analyzing the message, the audience, and the response to the message. The opportunities for feedback from the receivers to the source are enormous.

Broadly defined, *feedback* is any response that the receivers make to the source or the message. But the source cannot possibly perceive all of these responses or necessarily interpret them correctly. Thus, we should distinguish between the potential feedback available, the feedback actually perceived by the communicator, and the interpretation or meaning given to that perceived feedback.

What is the nature of the available feedback? In some communication situations—especially in settings not recognized as formal speech situations—communicator and communicatee may interchange roles rapidly and with no sense of constraint. The receiver may become a questioner, begin a long tirade, divert the entire stream of thought, or walk away. She may make some responses deliberately disruptive to the persuader's goal; some receivers may attempt to attack or counteract.

In many instances the feedback is not verbal and not overt. The communicator may need to interpret facial expressions, the careful gesture with which a cigarette is extinguished, the meaning of posture, yawns, or eye contact.

In some instances the effective persuader may deliberately elicit feedback, either for the information it provides or as a persuasive technique. She may ask rhetorical questions, ask for a show of hands, conduct a forum period, or make a deliberate attempt to provoke argument.

The most important element in discussing feedback is not to describe the variety of responses possible or to attempt to provide a guide for interpreting such responses. Rather, the communicator must be sensitive to the rich potential afforded by feedback, as well as the danger of misinterpretation.

1. The source must focus and draw upon the potential feedback available. Sources often become so concerned with messages or with their own reactions to the communication situation that they seem incapable of even perceiving they have receivers, let alone focusing upon subtle or not so subtle responses of those receivers. The human mind is quite capable of forming the 150 to 200 words a minute that go into a message, monitoring that message in terms of all kinds of criteria, and simultaneously observing and interpreting vast amounts of receiver response.

The potential information to be derived still bears upon the larger questions noted at the start of this section on audience analysis. The source is concerned with the attitudes of the audience toward the topic, himself, and the various strategic devices that are being employed. But now that the communication *is*—it exists—the source has cues to reaction, not in terms of predicted response but in response to various elements of the message itself. The speaker can attempt to adjust if he notices the audience is bored. If the people in the audience appear confused, he can clarify the content or emphasize the appeals to which they appear to be responding while minimizing those that seem to be producing negative response.

2. The source, perceiving feedback, must interpret it. What does it mean if the audience is looking at the speaker? If the audience laughs at the jokes, are they necessarily getting the message? The source may be "telling it like it is" but the audience may be perceiving it "like it isn't." The member of the audience who appears to close off the communicator and her message may be falling asleep or shutting out unwanted material. Or he may be reasoning himself into agreement with the source, perhaps for reasons totally unlike those being offered by that source. The problems of interpreting feedback are immense. Further, previous error may intensify error. Thus, a source who analyzed an audience incorrectly may continue and be confirmed even more in that misanalysis during the presentation. "But I thought they were laughing with me!"

The speaker must guard against becoming a captive of the feedback. This danger is not as pronounced (at least in the short range) for the written or mass media as it is in face-to-face communication. In the desire to reassure herself that the audience is with her, the speaker may become more entertainer than purposive communicator seeking a predetermined goal.

The danger of this effect is very real. The story of the psychology professor who was manipulated by students is appealing because it could be true. These students decided to give their psychology professor maximum reinforcement whenever he lectured from one corner of the room. Otherwise they gave him negative reinforcement by talking, sleeping, and taking no notes. The first day the instructor was very upset since he never lectured from the corner and thus received only negative reinforcement. The next day the students took notes and gave rapt attention whenever he moved toward the corner. By the end of the hour he was firmly ensconced in the corner, lecturing away fervently. When asked why he was in the corner, he could give no reason.

Postanalysis

Many persuaders unwisely neglect this stage of analysis.

Situation

The original situation no longer plays an active role in one sense. However, some effort should be made to assess the contribution of situational factors to the total persuasion process. The persuader may focus upon the degree to which prior analysis of the situation was accurate, where mistakes occurred, and how such mistakes may be avoided in the future. But most importantly, the persuader must try to assess the new situation that was brought about in part because of the persuasion effort.

Audience

The main concern of analysis at this point is to determine what happened and why. The actual effects of any persuasion effort are often small or even nonexistent. Some effects may persist for a short time and then fade in a matter of hours or days. Many effects, highly important ones at that, are not directly observable. If effects can be estimated, the question of how or why these effects were produced can be attempted. This is an even more difficult question to answer than the one about effects. While the persuader is likely to be most concerned about the question of whether progress was made toward her or his goal, many other effects are also relevant. A particularly important question may be the attitude that the receivers now hold toward the source. Even if the audience did not accept the proposition urged, the image of the source has important implications for the future. Also, the persuader should be concerned about the probable future response of the audience to attempts to persuade on this same topic. Will they be bored and uninterested? Will they avoid any exposure to the topic? Or will they be open to and even interested in further information, discussion, and dialogue on the topic?

These questions bear not only upon assessing the immediate persuasion effect but also upon future efforts at persuasion. The persuader often continues persuasion over extended periods of time. Hence, she needs as much insight into current attitudes and reactions as she can gain. Also, judgment of the comparative effectiveness of appeals may help to determine future strategy.

The bases for analysis at this stage are varied. Some insights can be gained from the immediate response of the receivers. Comments made to the communicator, questions posed, and interactions of various sorts may provide insight. Indeed the communicator may continue her efforts, shifting from persuasion directed at a group to persuasion directed at one member who has a specific question or misunderstanding.

Members of the audience may be asked to comment upon the effect of the communicator, or other forms of feedback may be relevant. In some instances press coverage may provide evidence as well as spread the possible impact of the persuasive effort. The actual behavior of the audience either in terms of immediate action requested by the source or in delayed response may provide helpful insights.

In postanalysis the problem of interpretation of response is very real. The person who comments, "Great speech!" may be absolutely unchanged in attitude; the person who goes away muttering may be the one who is most affected.

Relatively few of us have the opportunity to use the carefully developed and structured measuring instruments of the experimentalist as he seeks to refine communication theory. The judgments of audience response should be properly tentative and as soundly based on data as possible. But that the attempt should be made cannot be challenged.

The persuader should cease analysis only after she has made some assessment of her probable effect, some judgment of the next step in her persuasion campaign, and some estimate of the effectiveness of various elements in her persuasion strategy. Indeed, she should concern herself with the accuracy of her prior analysis in order to learn to estimate her potential receivers in future communication situations more accurately.

RECEIVER CLASSIFICATIONS AND RESPONSE TENDENCIES

In persuasion, only two people or thousands or hundreds of thousands of individuals may be interacting. If we are dealing with one individual—perhaps a close friend, a parent, or a spouse—it is rare that we go to a very elaborate, conscious process of analysis and interpretation. But if the issue is vital, complex, and difficult, we may plan for days and carefully weigh all the alternatives so as to maximize the chances for success. The following discussion will focus on receivers who range in numbers from eight or ten to fifty, one hundred or perhaps four hundred or five hundred in rare instances (although many of the items can be applied to larger or smaller groups).

Any factor relevant to the audience may affect audience response. An audience is a group of individuals in a temporary grouping. We cannot deal with each receiver fully as a unique being in larger groups and in groups where the individuals are not well known to the persuader. So we must settle for some estimates of general tendencies, such as the average, and some estimates of the diversity among them. In some instances audiences can be seen most helpfully as composed of two, three, or four subgroups with particular, important differences among them.

One method of picturing an audience is to distribute the audience along certain continua. Since position on some continua correlates with predictions of audience response, the material that follows will examine some potentially useful continua and predictions concerning response that have been derived from empirical research.

Attitude toward Purpose-Topic-Speaker

The attitude of the audience toward the general topic, specific purpose, and speaker is important to the persuasion effect. Perhaps it is sufficient to discuss the potential for analysis in terms of audience response to the specific purpose, and the reader can then generalize to other lines of analysis.

Conventionally, attitudes are represented in terms of a continuum. This is true of linear rating scales, Thurstone and Likert Attitude Instruments, and the dimensions of the semantic differential. Extremities of the continuum represent highly favorable or unfavorable responses, shading into more neutral ranges toward the middle (see figure 4).

Two individuals may fall at the same point on an attitudinal continuum but for totally different reasons. Furthermore, one person may be extremely tenacious in holding a position; another may shift easily.

A persuader is interested in describing the varying conditions relative to a person's position on the attitudinal continuum. Certainly it is useful to discriminate among receivers in terms of the degree to which the audi-

Figure 4.

Favorable			Neutral			Unfavorable
Highly	Moderately	Slightly		Slightly	Moderately	Highly
1	2	3	4	5	6	7

A Con   Neutral   Pro
A heterogeneous audience

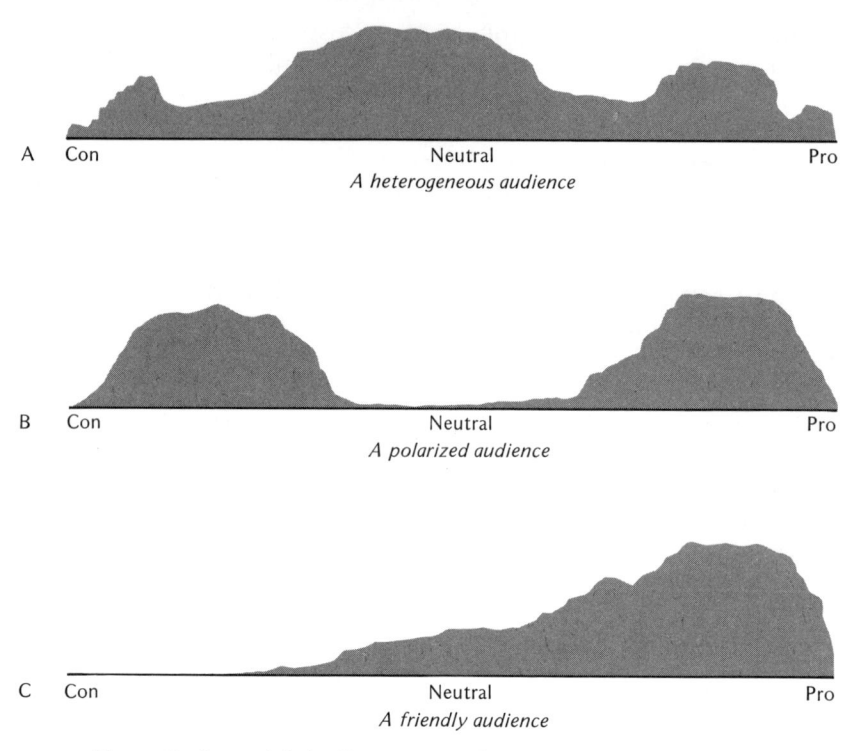

B Con   Neutral   Pro
A polarized audience

C Con   Neutral   Pro
A friendly audience

Figure 5. Potential Audience Attitude Patterns

ence is partially or totally friendly, hostile, or neutral (figure 5). One audience may be quite homogeneous; another may possess every shade of opinion possible.

Audiences can be differentiated on many bases, as in figure 6. The individuals who fall within the "aware-judicial" groups are those who hold a position that involves judgment on their part. This means that the issue has sufficient import to these individuals that they develop some type of cognitive structure to undergird their position. This does not imply that the reasons these people find logical for holding the position would be judged logical by others. Nor are the positions held purely, or

Figure 6.

Pro	Neutral	Con
Aware-judicial	Aware-judicial	Aware-judicial
Habitual	Don't know	Habitual
Self-interest	Don't care	Self-interest
	Self-interest	

even basically, for logical reasons. Many forces may have brought them to this position, and the cognitive structures that exist to defend the position may be totally post hoc, rationalistic, and used to justify a previously held position. The existence of these arguments and awareness of the issue often makes individuals more resistant to persuasion.[2]

People who hold a position from habit may well be less sensitive to the issue and less concerned with reasons to justify their position. Often attitudes supported on a habitual basis are configurations adopted from parents or from prior learning, but are not "involving" to the individual. These people are often vulnerable to persuasive efforts and may make marked shifts.

Self-interest suggests that forces acting upon the person place him in an attitudinal position. A person caught in a crossfire of persuasive efforts may refuse to commit himself. Politicians often stress neutrality on intraparty matters. People with low incomes may favor increasing the amount for personal exemptions allowed on the federal income tax. Potentially conflicting information may not be considered relevant to the attitude.

The "don't know" group are those who are not aware there is an issue or a problem. A persuader often fails to understand that vast numbers of a potential audience may have absolutely no perception that any problem exists. The "don't care" group presumably are aware that some people perceive a problem—but it is a problem that they think isn't relevant to them, does not affect their interests, or is something they should not or could not have anything to do with. "Terrible! I saw this robbery last night and everybody stood there. Nobody even called the police. What is the world coming to?" Apparently this person knew there was a problem but did not perceive the possibility of calling the police.

Attitudes as a Range—Not a Point

The writings of Muzafer Sherif and associates have attacked the view of treating a person's attitude as a point in an attitudinal continuum.[3] They suggest attitudes can be more usefully defined in terms of latitudes of acceptance, rejection, and noncommitment. This technique works as follows: a series of statements concerning a topic or

---

[2] See William J. McGuire, "The Effectiveness of Supportive and Refutational Defenses in Immunizing and Restoring Beliefs against Persuasion," *Sociometry* 24 (1961): 479–89; William J. McGuire and Demetrios Papageorgis, "The Relative Efficacy of Various Types of Prior Belief—Defense in Producing Immunity against Persuasion," *Journal of Abnormal and Social Psychology* 62 (1961): 327–37.

[3] See Muzafer Sherif and Carl I. Hovland, *Social Judgment*. Yale Studies in Attitude and Communication, vol. 4 (New Haven: Yale University Press, 1961); Carolyn Sherif, Muzafer Sherif, and Roger Nebergall, *Attitude and Attitude Change* (Philadelphia: W. B. Saunders, 1965).

proposition is presented. Respondents are asked to indicate all the statements they accept as descriptive of their position, then to indicate all the statements they reject. Statements that they neither accept nor reject fall into the latitude of noncommitment.

This approach to measuring attitudes does result in a different picture. Some individuals have a rather wide latitude of acceptance and can accept several statements as representative of their attitude. (See figure 7A.) Others have a relatively narrow latitude of acceptance—perhaps an extremely small latitude of noncommitment and wide latitudes of rejection. (See figure 7B.)

A frequent pattern is for people who are committed to one extreme end of the continuum to have a rather narrow latitude of acceptance and wide latitudes of rejection. Personality types as well as commitment on a specific issue are presumably relevant here. People may show a wider range of acceptance on one issue, a much narrower one on another.

This technique of attitude measurement highlights an interesting phenomenon. When persons are asked to judge persons or positions on the attitudinal continuum that are either closely approximate to or far removed from their own position, the judgments display assimilation and contrast effects. People tend to displace positions or people close to their own position by judging them as closer to their own position than they really are. This is assimilation. In dealing with points further removed from their attitudinal position, a contrast effect sets in. Individuals and positions more removed are perceived as being even further away; they are displaced by contrasting them even further from the position.

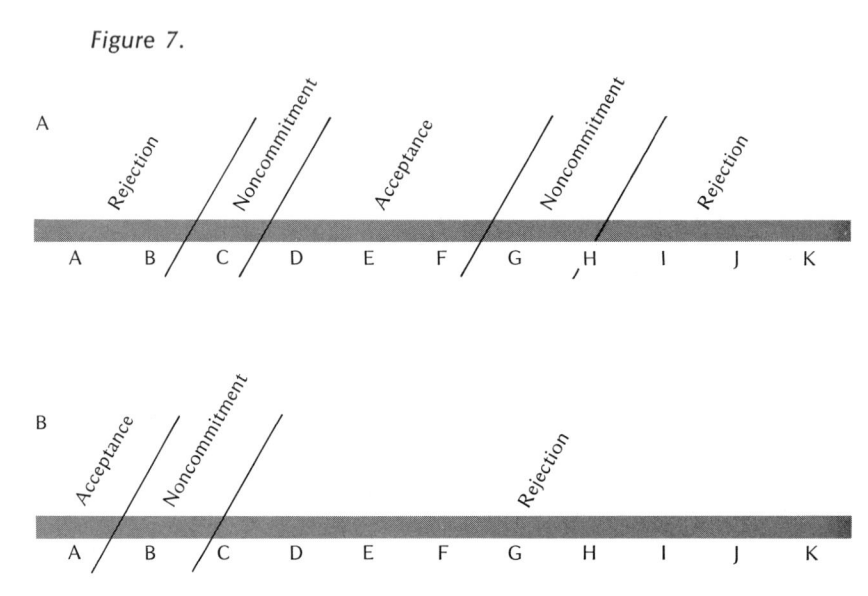

Figure 7.

Thus, a zealot may well perceive a neutral person as being actively opposed to his program. Often, people who are more neutral or who hold wider latitudes of acceptance and noncommitment are more accurate in placement of other positions and people than are those who are strongly committed and who have narrow latitudes of acceptance.

The persuader may fail to perceive his audience and their position accurately because of the operation of this phenomenon. Or his position may be distorted by partisans. Thus, the mediator is frequently accused "most righteously" by both sides as favoring the opposition. Each side apparently believes the other side is making a similar accusation to cover the dishonesty involved.

Personality Variables

A number of personality variables might be assumed on a priori grounds to be relevant to persuasion effects. These personality variables as measured by introspection, paper and pencil test, or projective responses evaluated by experts take on meaning in terms of continua ranging from extroverted to introverted, high to low in self-esteem, open- to closed-minded, and so forth. The personality structure of an individual is intrarelated and some personality characteristics cluster: characteristics as measured by one test predict at useful levels responses on other tests or placement on other continua. There are some particularly useful continua relevant to persuasion effects.

Persuasibility

Many writers have postulated that certain persons are more persuasible than other persons. That is, without regard to topic or situation these people will manifest a greater tendency to shift attitudes than other people will.

This personality characteristic has been investigated by Hovland and his associates: "Results support the hypothesis of a general factor in persuasibility and indicate that the predisposition to change opinions is not wholly specific to the topic or subject matter of the communication."[4]

Self-esteem

Individuals vary in the degree to which they manifest self-esteem, a respect for and valuing of themselves and their opinions. Self-esteem seems to have a relationship to the decision to accept or reject persuasive efforts. Initial generalizations based on empirical research suggested that those with high self-esteem were resistant to persuasion influence, while those with low self-esteem were compara-

---

[4] Carl I. Hovland and Irving Janis, eds., *Personality and Persuasibility,* Yale Studies in Attitude and Communication, vol. 2 (New Haven: Yale University Press, 1959), pp. 226–27.

tively more accepting. But later research has produced important qualifications of this generalization. (Obviously self-esteem and all the other personality variables noted here do not act in isolation.) People with very low self-esteem often do not expose themselves to or become involved in persuasion efforts. They don't see themselves as making a difference, and they do not respond. Those who are relatively high in self-esteem have sufficient trust in themselves and confidence that they are quite willing to expose themselves to persuasion. And often, because they are confident, they are willing to accept a new view and to change behavior. But for a large range of people—those who fall above the minimum on the measure of self-respect to those who fall fairly high on the measure—the initial generalization is still useful. Those with lower self-esteem are more likely to shift in a direction urged by a persuader.

Dogmatism

The concept of dogmatism does not seem as unitary a characteristic as self-esteem. Indeed, it seems to have been approched by psychologists in many different ways. One approach, following the lines of Adorno's thinking, has attacked dogmatism through the concept of authoritarianism. Authoritarian personalities tend to follow rather rigid patterns of thinking. They tend to judge items in terms of referential values determined by groups or people, which are accepted as defining standards. Thus, the authoritarian personality is very concerned with power and power relationships in the hierarchy and comes to act in terms of "might makes right."

Individuals who test as authoritarian in personality on measures such as the F scale tend to be heavily influenced by "authorities" they accept. They tend to respond somewhat less to the ideas and information presented than to the "authorities" presented.[5]

Rokeach has approached the study of dogmatism through a concept called "open-mindedness." Rokeach visualizes the individual as having a complex system of beliefs. Beliefs may be differentiated as being *primitive*—central beliefs relative to physical reality, social reality, and self; *intermediate*—like primitive beliefs but concerned with what one sets as his goals, limitations and self-definition based on experience; *authority*—beliefs as to what authorities we can and cannot trust; *peripheral*—beliefs derived from those we accept as authorities; and, finally, *inconsequential*—beliefs that make no basic difference to the individual.[6]

[5] For example, Frederic A. Powell, "Open- and Closed-Mindedness and the Ability to Differentiate Sources and Message," *Journal of Abnormal and Social Psychology* 65 (1962): 61–64.

[6] Milton Rokeach, "Images of the Consumer's Mind on and off Madison Avenue," *ETC.: A Review of General Semantics* 21 (1964).

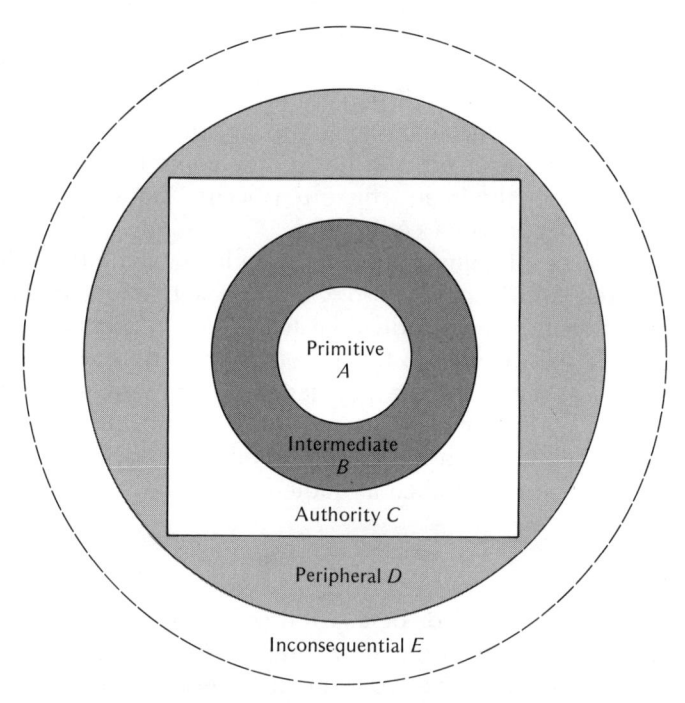

[Figure 8: concentric diagram with labels Primitive A, Intermediate B, Authority C, Peripheral D, Inconsequential E]

Figure 8.

How central these belief systems are to an individual is pictured in figure 8. The more central the belief in this system, the more difficult it is to change; if it is changed, the more it alters or affects the person. Inconsequential beliefs are the easiest to change but the least important if they are changed, since the change is not central to the person. Thus, a switch in toothpaste is easier for a person to make than a shift in religious values, because other actions need not change.

How much and in what manner these beliefs may be changed depends upon how much the person manifests open- as opposed to closed-mindedness as a general personality characteristic. The open-minded individual will tend to compare her belief systems for compatibility; she will tend to respond more to information. The closed-minded individual will rely more upon authority and will tend to trust the status quo more than changed systems.

Saliency

Topics will vary according to the significance they hold for receivers. People find certain attitudes and issues more important and more involving than others. Thus, it is useful to define an audience in terms of the comparative saliency of a topic for that audience.

A number of factors may contribute to this saliency. The degree to which a topic is relevant to self-perception clearly is a factor. A value or a belief that comes under attack may also become more salient for that reason. One important effect of a persuasive communication may be to affect the saliency of the issue. This often occurs though no shift in attitudinal position occurs on a continuum.

A higher degree of saliency seems to indicate that the attitude becomes more resistant to persuasion. Greater saliency would also suggest a greater propensity for the individual to receive information and to be exposed to materials relative to the attitude in question. Hence, the exact implications of saliency for the persuader in terms of its effect in the communication matrix must await further research. But saliency seems to have high potential as an important dimension affecting response and therefore is of great importance in audience analysis.

Sex

The relationship of persuasion impact to sex—a dichotomous variable—is one of the very few demographically related factors in audience analysis to be extensively examined by experimentalists. The ease with which persuasive effects for men and women can be contrasted makes the variable easy to investigate.

The relationship between the sex variable and persuasibility has not been consistent. Many studies have shown no significant difference in persuasibility, but many others have. When differences are found, women are almost universally more persuasible than men. In a study designed to test the importance of the sex variable, Scheidel found that women were significantly more persuasible than men; women tended to transfer the persuasion to other items more fully and rapidly and to retain less of the speech content than did men.[7]

Unfortunately the Scheidel study represents one of the few attempts to focus specifically upon the differential effects of persuasive appeals on the sexes. Additional studies are needed to clarify the impact of this variable. Saliency may be the key to the results obtained. People for whom a topic was salient were described above as probably more resistant to persuasion but also more likely to expose themselves to information concerning the salient topic.

The majority of speech topics employed in these studies have been sociopolitical. Scheidel used the topic of federal power in areas of health and education; others have employed voting rights, possibility of war,

---

[7] Thomas Scheidel, "Sex and Persuasibility," *Speech Monographs* 30 (1963): 357.

and the draft. By cultural conditioning and relevance to personal goals and values, these topics appear more salient to men than women. Hence, it is quite possible that the saliency of the topics chosen aligns itself along the sex variable, and salience—not the sex variable—is the determining factor. The problem of differential effects in retention could follow the same line of explanation.

It would be interesting to see if topics markedly salient for women but unsalient for men might not produce quite different patterns, with men being more persuasible than women. The emphasis upon the women's movement and equality of treatment that marked the mid-1970s and continues to affect our society provides a significant opportunity to discover if this movement has also changed the results of studies that replicate those with significant findings in the past.

The assumption that women are more persuasible than men is not supported by many experimental studies. Further, the degree to which sex differences are the direct cause of the different persuasive impacts needs further investigation. Women do appear more persuasible than men on some topics. The reason why is still in doubt.

VARIABILITY OF RESPONSE

Response to communication varies because people vary. Since the mediational factors such as attitudes, habits, information, personality, and motivations that intervene between stimuli and response differ, responses will naturally differ.

Nevertheless, one of the greatest shocks to many persuaders is the diversity of response that a persuasive communication engenders. "But I never said that." "How could he have gotten that?" "She thought I was the best speaker, yet she only gave me a lousy B. He thought I was about average and rated me B+." "He said I had way too much information and statistics." "She said I left out lots of important information."

Variability of response is one of the few "laws" of persuasion. Previous material has suggested that differences in response may correlate with certain personality characteristics and factors, such as age or gender. Other characteristic audience reactions may give additional insights about what to expect in audience response.

Prior Attitude and Response

The prior attitude of the receivers is a useful predictor of response to persuasion efforts. Similarly the basis for that attitude also relates to response to persuasion efforts.

Many targets of persuasion efforts have no particular interest in and concern about the subject matter. In fact, when people are asked questions on many issues, they will frequently respond, "Oh, I don't know." Often the way a question is asked can cause people to react positively or negatively. Many tests of public opinion have been found to be defective because they unknowingly or in some cases deliberately bias the response patterns. A safe way to interpret this pattern is to say that many people do not have any attitude toward the issue in question. They are not neutral between two points because they do not fall on the attitudinal continuum at any spot; they don't have an attitude. To be asked a question is to be put on the attitude scale at a neutral point. Indeed, the biggest difference among people is often between those who have an attitude about the subject and those who don't. People who are highly pro or con may be closer together and more like each other than those who do not have an opinion. Attitude measurement techniques that work in three dimensions rather than the conventional two dimensions often show that the distance is greater between those with no opinion than between those who are extremely partisan on opposite sides. But the conventional measure of attitudes on one dimension from pro to con gives us a bell-shaped curve in which most people fall at the middle.

One major problem in persuasion is to gain the attention and interest of people who are not involved with the subject and with the persuader's purpose. In the classroom, the receivers will give some degree of attention even if the topic has no interest value for them. But in most communication situations, there are simply too many competing demands for attention. Most people will not be involved unless they already have a prior interest in the subject or are caught by circumstances in such a way that they cannot avoid attention to the persuasion effort. Thus, a major and tremendously important outcome of a persuasion effort is to make the topic one of interest to the receiver. If the receiver truly sees the problem as something about which she does have an attitude, a tremendous change has occurred.

A typical experiment would show a variety of attitudes on some issue with the majority of those attitudes concentrated about neutral ("don't know"). There would be a range of attitudes pro and con and possibly a few committed partisans. Following a persuasion attempt the pattern will typically look quite different. Many of the neutrals will have shifted—typically most of these in the direction urged by the persuasive message but a few in the opposite direction. Most of the favorable people will become more favorable. A few of the hostile people may become more favorable, but some of the extreme partisans on each side may shift quite significantly. Typically those who shift positively will outweigh those who shift negatively as defined by the persuader's intent and so the effort was a success.

But wait a minute! This is not a typical situation since these people were in a situation where a degree of attention to the persuasive effort was required. Further, the testing itself tends to influence response. At least after the fact, the people involved realize that their opinion is important, their attitudes and or intended actions are being probed. Thus they tend to become self-conscious and aware that this is an unusual situation. So the reactions may be unusual. At least in retrospect, they will think more carefully about the persuasion effort. Some may figure out the response that they think is wanted and either try to give that response or quite deliberately give a different one. So the observation-experimental situation causes a change from typical conditions. And these changes often (if not always) influence response.

We need to interpret these results as we generalize to more typical persuasion situations. In typical persuasion situations people who are not interested in the issues being treated probably will not expose themselves to the persuasion material—or if they do, they will largely ignore it. So we expect no change here. But a few may become involved and either accept a position or at least be open to further material on the topic. People friendly to the viewpoint of the persuader will tend to be reinforced. They may become more resistant to efforts at counterpersuasion. They may try to influence others by similar arguments or statements of approval for the position. They may be moved to greater activity.

Those initially hostile to the persuader's intent present an interest problem to the persuader and various possibilities of response. Often those who are hostile will consciously expose themselves to the persuasion effort, knowing that it is presenting an opposing point of view. They do this because they are interested in the topic, because they want to learn more about the topic, or because they want to monitor (and perhaps correct) the persuader's efforts if necessary. Persuasion is not likely to convert the opposition. Indeed, it may arouse them to reaction and persuasion efforts of their own. But in some instances opposition will soften; new information may produce a change in emphasis or interpretation of a problem. Many of the opposition who have held a position without much testing of that viewpoint may shift, perhaps dramatically. McGuire's study of inoculation effects suggests that people who have not had attitudes tested and do not hold a series of beliefs that support the attitude will often change dramatically in the face of a single persuasion effort.

Extreme partisans sometimes make surprising changes in their attitudes. Rather than weaken a position, they will sometimes jump from one end of the continuum to the other. This dramatic conversion can be seen on religious issues, smoking habits, or life goals. Some studies have shown that almost the entire effect of a message was to move a few extremists from one side to the other. A variety of explanations can be offered for this tendency of the extremely committed to make dramatic shifts. Some personalities do not seem to take middle-of-the-road positions; their response style is to take highly committed stands. In contrast, others will never take an extreme stand on any issue. Often dogmatic or closed-minded individuals hold extreme positions. A shift in an authority figure or a change on the part of the authority figure or reference group can produce a similar but more intense change by the highly dogmatic individual. Research also suggests that highly committed people are more suggestible, more persuasible. Occasionally a persuasive effort will cause an already highly favorable person to shift dramatically to an opposed view because of a failure to honor the partisan's viewpoints and actions or to advocate too moderate a stand.

Negative Persuasion

In thinking about persuasion we normally focus upon the positive results: others adopting a desired attitude or action. But persuasion efforts typically produce some degree of negative persuasion; that is, after the persuasion attempt, some people are almost always less favorable or less likely to perform the desired action. Why? A few of those who shift negatively probably do so in response to a personality characteristic. Some people are negatively suggestive: when one thing is suggested, they are prone to resist or do the opposite. All of us display this trait at times, and some people's behavior is characterized by such action. But most of the negative shift will be linked to specific factors in the persuasion effort. The various factors may strike receivers in ways that were not intended or perceived by the persuader. A motivation offered may create a contrary motivation or be channeled in a direction other than that desired by the persuader. Sometimes the negative shifts are caused by the failure of the persuader to direct behavior clearly to the desired outcome. Persuaders seeking to be ironic or to use negative suggestion may be misunderstood, and thus the audience moves in the wrong direction. Excessive attacks and unwarranted accusations often arouse a sympathetic response on behalf of those attacked or challenged.

There will be some degree of negative persuasion with almost any audience. If the majority of the receivers are negatively persuaded, the persuader should examine her or his efforts at audience analysis and other factors for an explanation, and come up with some basis for avoiding this effect in the future.

Immediate and Delayed Changes

Many measures of persuasion effectiveness are taken immediately at the close of the persuasion attempt (for example, after giving a speech, we tend to look toward the immediate response and then decide whether we were a success or failure). But many important effects occur over time. Characteristically people who change from an initial position return to their original position in a short period of time. The return shift is most rapid in the first few days immediately after the persuasion effort and then becomes more gradual. Although some changes have been shown to persist for as long as five months after a single persuasion effort, most studies show a return to the original position quite quickly. These returns parallel our pattern in forgetting material that we have learned.

This tendency to return to the original position suggests the need for repeated persuasion efforts and follow-up of any changes if they are to stick. If the change in attitude can be reinforced in some way or if actions follow that are in accord with the new attitude, the change will tend to persist and may become permanent. If the new attitude is not rewarded, the probability of its being maintained is very low.

Sometimes people whose attitudes do not appear to change immediately will exhibit a change later. Perhaps this is the result of additional information being obtained from other sources, perhaps it is a gradual adjustment to a new idea, perhaps it is a result of sensitivity to the matter as a result of interest.

Some people who resist persuasion efforts appear to accept the position urged after the influence effort is forgotten. In some cases the negative impression of the source may retard acceptance of ideas put forth by that source. After a period of time in which the ideas are no longer associated with the source, acceptance may occur.

But it is wise to remember that, in the absence of further persuasion efforts to reinforce a change, attitudes tend to return to their original position as old habits in thinking and action reassert themselves.

SUMMARY

The process of situation and receiver analysis is essential to understanding persuasion. The persuader, the receiver, the critic, and the person studying persuasion all must grapple with this problem although from different perspectives and for different purposes. Since all audiences are unique in some sense and since this uniqueness has potentially significant effects, through analysis we seek to identify the relevant dimensions. The ability to utilize these insights to the maximum degree will vary according to the persuader.

As an important part of preparation, the persuader seeks to analyze his audience in terms of their probable reaction to his goal, himself, matters relevant to the topic, and the various possible strategic devices that could be employed. Often the persuader has a rich store of personal experience and direct personal interaction to call upon. In other instances he must attempt to derive estimations from data that may be readily available in some cases and almost impossible to find in other cases.

The process of audience and situation analysis should continue throughout the preparatory, implementative, and evaluative stages of a communicative act. Adjustment to continuing sources of information appears imperative if the communicator is to maximize effectiveness. This is especially true in terms of the richness of material available immediately prior to and during actual face-to-face communication.

The analysis of the impact of a communication and the attempt to judge the relative effectiveness of various elements controlled by the source and adjustments made to other variables that could not be controlled are important parts of postanalysis.

Continued development in understanding the persuasion process, both for the discipline and for the individual practitioner, depends upon full awareness of the importance of and the growth in ability in audience analysis.

When dealing with larger groups of potential receivers, it is useful to describe the audience in terms of general characteristics, being sensitive both to estimates of central tendency and to variability of the group. Some audiences may be homogeneous in terms of one or more characteristics; others may be markedly heterogeneous.

It is helpful to picture an audience in terms of its position on an attitude continuum ranging from extremely pro to extremely con. Further, it is wise to estimate some of the factors that contribute to this position. Personality characteristics, which also may be represented in terms of continua, are known to affect persuasive outcomes. Such analyses suggest strategies concerning use of such materials as information, authoritative citation, and motivational appeals.

The concept of saliency—the degree to which an issue or question is seen as proximate—is an important element in audience analysis. Saliency is related to propensity to shift in response to persuasive efforts; it is correlated with the accessibility of the individual to persuasive communications. The apparent differential in the persuasiveness of the sexes may be linked to saliency.

Perhaps the universal law concerning audiences is the variability of responses. Since members of the audience differ in prior attitudes, characteristics linked to persuasibility, variability in response is inevitable. Almost every persuasion effort yields some negative persuasion. Often the neutrals in attitude disappear, becoming partisan. But in the absence of further reinforcement, the audience members tend to regress to their original position. After four or six weeks a significant change usually vanishes. Studies have, however, shown significant persuasion effects persisting for longer than six weeks.

RECEIVER AND SITUATION ANALYSIS

DISCUSSION QUESTIONS AND PROJECTS

1. Try to develop a model that will provide a good representation of alternative audience configurations.

2. During a round of speeches by members of your class, discuss the degree to which the speeches adapted directly to the actual audience. To what degree were the speeches delivered as if to some general audience with no specific recognition of the real audience? Which speeches were most effective and why?

3. What general patterns would you predict for audiences who are essentially teenagers, in their late thirties and early forties, or newly retired? What appeals, what attitudes, what interests, what type of material would reach them? How much of this estimation is really a reflection of your own stereotypes? Can you think of given situations where your estimation would be accurate? Are you sure?

4. Ratings of a round of speeches by all class members can be tallied by the instructor. Reproduction of the scores with the speakers' ratings as the rows and the reactors' ratings kept as columns provides a basis for extended discussion of variability of audience response. Ratings for factors such as content, language, and delivery can be included.

5. For one speech during the term, develop a paper that presents a careful analysis of audience. Include predictions of attitude toward topic, speaker, and materials. Predict response. After the speech test the adequacy of this analysis either through rating instruments or discussion.

6. For a speech round, the class may wish to use an attitude-change measuring device. These changes can be tabulated, maintaining anonymity. Showing shifts for speakers in rows and shifts for receivers in columns will provide an interesting discussion comparing and contrasting diversity of reactions as well as apparent differences in propensity of shift, and so forth.

7. Discuss the problem in deriving an accurate picture of a potential audience by relying upon the statements of the program chairman for the group.

8. What implications do assimilation and contrast effects as described by Sherif and associates hold for a person dealing with a partisan audience and trying for accurate perception of position?

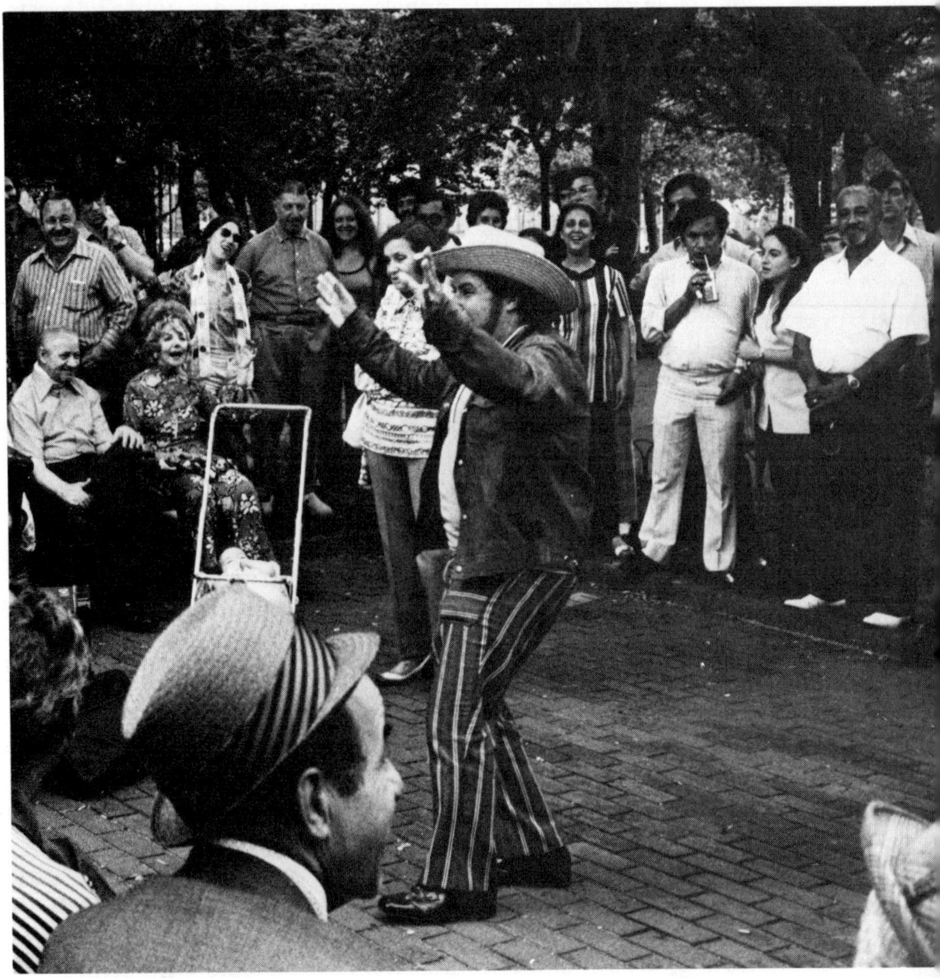

5 Attention and Interest

A Missouri farmer once sold a mule to his Iowa neighbor. The mule was described as extremely responsive and a good worker: "Just treat him kindly, tell him what to do, and you will never have a problem." The Iowan harnessed the mule to the plow, and grasping the reins said, "Giddiup." No response. The farmer jiggled the reins and called loudly, "Git along now." No response. The farmer became increasingly angry, uttered several variations of the command, and slapped the mule with the ends of the reins. The mule appeared to sleep. In high color the farmer rushed to his Missouri neighbor and complained of the transaction, the seller, and the similarity of the seller to the mule. The seller calmly remarked that the Iowan must not have been treating the mule properly or he would have responded to the commands. To show his faith in the mule, the Missourian returned to the field with the Iowan. The mule stood patiently in place. The seller looked about, fetched up a stout two-by-four and hit the mule squarely across the head. The mule shook his head slightly and then in response to a mild "Now, git along please," set to work with good speed. In departing the seller simply said, "You have to get his attention first."

THE NATURE OF ATTENTION

We are all familiar with the effect of attention on our daily lives. We find it easy to work on one assignment, difficult to keep our attention on another. We fall asleep during the lecture but manage to recount in great detail the entire outfit worn by the fellow with the long hair.

The competition for our attention is manifested in the varied stimuli that assault our ears, eyes, noses, sense of touch, and taste buds. To flip through a magazine exposes one to hundreds of efforts to attract attention. The number of conscious attempts made to gain and hold our attention in a single day is fantastic. But the number of potential items to which we may give our attention in any one day is beyond counting.

In one hour of a speech class you may be asked to concentrate on how to dribble a basketball, fight pollution, clean up the student newspaper, get culture, and learn to smile. Meanwhile, your speech is being crowded out by the people running overtime; you now realize you forgot to eat lunch; you lack a date; your foot itches; it looks like snow outside; the instructor looks more bored than the students; and at least six other students look asleep even before you begin your speech. All these perceptions as well as the many more that impinge upon you during the hour are the result of your paying some degree of attention to these particular stimuli and not to others.

Attention Defined

Attention is the mental process by which some stimulus or constellation of stimuli becomes sharper, more distinct, more vivid in consciousness while other stimuli tend to recede. Although this definition focuses upon the result of the process of attention, it would be equally valid to define the process as the behavioral means by which this end result is obtained. Attention then becomes a process in which a relatively unified set involving mental processes, muscles, and sense organs is brought to bear upon a source or sources of stimuli. Attention is a process of selection, a set toward something in the perceptual field, a readiness to respond to particular stimuli.

Without this ability to select stimuli and blot out other stimuli through the process of attention, the senses and the mind would be buried by stimuli. The stimuli would be rendered meaningless and valueless by their profusion.

At any moment an individual is exposed to a vast number of potential stimuli. If the stimuli are not noticed—if they exert no effect upon the person—they are not stimuli in the sense of a stimulus-response pattern. Hence, attention is a process by which we select among potential stimuli.

Think of the stimuli potential in this situation. Probably most of you are reading these pages while sitting down. Have you noticed the pressure of your body on the chair? Do your eyes burn a bit? Is there noise in the background? Have you wondered if you really need to finish reading this now? Have you been conscious of the amount of white space between the lines on this page? Why does the author keep addressing you directly (have you wondered about that)? Has it irritated you? Did you notice if "addressing" had been mispelled? (Presumably you did notice "mispelled.")

Probably the last paragraph took a greater amount of time to read than did other paragraphs of comparable length. Your attention was repeatedly directed away from the flow of ideas in the paragraph to potential sources of stimuli that might now be brought into conscious focus and thus take attention away from the paragraph itself.

Potential stimuli may be differentiated in terms of two fields: external and internal. The sense organs are the agencies that receive external stimuli. Internal stimuli may be viewed in terms of the operations of the mind. Internal stimuli are factors that occur within the mind seemingly of its own accord. Thus, worries, interests, needs, and values may all become the focus of our attention at any moment and block any attention to external stimuli. For our purposes a pain in the toe is external; it involves a response to a stimulus originating outside the mind.

Actually, of course, the distinction between external and internal stimuli is arbitrary. Attention as a mental process involves the mediational activity of the mind, which selects and channels attention. Often we shift from an external to an internal stimulus or an internal stimulus causes us to direct our attention toward an external one. Analysis may separate stimuli, but in reality the process is a synthesis of interactions.

Attention is not a dichotomous matter of either attention or inattention. Rather it is a matter of degree. Concentrated, concerted attention may be given for a moment to one stimulus, somewhat less attention given to the same stimulus the next moment, then perhaps rather diffuse attention to several items followed by stronger attention to a new stimulus that compels adjustments in body and posture. Attention as a bodily set should be assessed comparatively, in terms of relative intensity.

Attention may differ not only in terms of the intensity of the set but also in terms of the extensiveness of items receiving attention. We may focus upon a very limited field or stimulus, or somewhat generally and broadly upon a wider range or span of items. Indeed, we may deliberately include more peripheral items. This shifting from the whole to parts is illustrated in the manner in which we study a picture. We see the whole, we look at elements and parts, and we then look back to a larger unit until we have seen the picture to our satisfaction.

An implicit concept in the previous items is that attention is not something that starts or stops; it is a continuous process. In a sense, a stimulus does not ask for attention; it asks that attention be given to it rather than to something else. The potential stimuli are in competition for attention.

PARTICIPATION AS RECEIVERS

To speak of fading attention or lack of attention really suggests that something else is gaining attention or is now the focus of attention, or that the intensity of the bodily set is being attenuated.

Factors Affecting Attention

Since attention is a process involving the human organism, factors related to that organism will affect attention. Thus, the general state of the organism affects attention. When we are extremely fatigued, attention (which demands energy) tends to be difficult to maintain. We can consciously force attention. But this forcing requires increasing effort and becomes tiring and difficult to maintain. Thus, stimuli that fail to develop some degree of intrinsic interest lose attention, often against the best will of the individual.

Typically factors related to attention are discussed in terms of natural or unlearned factors and acquired or learned factors. Since the latter will be discussed under the heading of interest, only the unlearned factors will be noted at this moment.

Various features seem to serve as selectors of attention in rather automatic ways. Stimuli that are intense (comparatively) gain attention. Stimuli that have a particularly striking quality in terms of volume or brilliance or uniqueness may select attention. Stimuli that are repeated or that persist for longer durations of time may gain attention. Larger objects have more probability of being noticed than do small ones.

The most important natural factor of attention seems to be that of change or variety. Any stimulus becomes tiring after a time, and thus other stimuli become attention getters. Change attracts attention. Thus a sudden quiet in a room attracts attention. Persons may literally wake up because a clock stops ticking; the silence wakes them.

These natural factors of attention—intensity, striking quality or uniqueness, repetition or persistence, size, and variety—are potential in almost any stimulus.[1] Thus, a small object among many large ones receives attention because of its uniqueness. A stimulus that falls below the limen of perception may gain attention through a summation effect. Too intense stimuli can rapidly become tiring and cause attention to shift.

The complexities of the attention process are such that assumptions about what will command attention are extremely dangerous. With the number of elements in any situation that could command attention, there are no formulas for holding attention.

---

[1] The terms employed to describe the natural factors of attention are arbitrary. *Novelty* might be used instead of *uniqueness,* for example. Or *movement* might be used with *change* or as a substitute for it.

INTEREST AND ATTENTION

Certainly the unlearned factors of attention are related to many communication effects. Further, general factors such as fatigue levels, state of the organism, and innate sensitivity of the sense organs affect attention. But the learned or acquired elements associated with attention are basic in understanding communication.

Since attention is an aspect of human response, it must be motivated. Some forces affecting attention, such as the fact that any unchanging stimulus becomes boring and tiring after a time and competing stimuli gain attention, are essentially laws of the attention process. These laws must be kept in mind or forgotten to the peril of effectiveness. But attention becomes linked to our experiences, our learned interests, enthusiasms, values, needs, and desires.

An interest may be defined as some strong, relatively persistent motive that compels observation, involvement, or knowledge about something. All of us are aware of the role that interests play in determining our behavior and how we spend our time. An opera buff may treasure lists of pirated recordings of operas and assiduously read articles and entire magazines that most of us do not know exist. He may engage in extended discussion of the merits of two conductors or two opera stars and find much pleasure in pointing up the fudged high note of the popular prima donna.

Interests suggest relatively enduring patterns that guide and condition response. However, an interest can also be thought of as being relatively short term. Sometimes we are quite interested in passing fancies. A topic may develop a good deal of interest because of the presentation of relatively new information, a unique way of handling the material, or an exciting method of presentation. The interest may dissipate rapidly, however.

The interests and enthusiasms that an individual acquires are key factors directing her attention. And since these interests lead to associations in groups—bridge clubs or bird watchers—and to selective exposure to communication, they are important factors in communication.

But we also acquire certain general reaction patterns that enable some factors of attention to be learned. They must be defined from the point of view of each individual. What I consider basic to my role as father may be seen as meaningless activity by my neighbor. What is old hat to you may be shocking information to me.

1. The vital—materials or issues that can be linked to things that are important to an individual. References to one's life, death, children—things that are central to one's life—fall within this category and clearly command attention. Indeed, the sudden mention of your

name in a crowd commands your attention when other words and other names uttered under identical conditions would not be perceived.

2. The concrete—the specific; vague, diffused, amorphous things are opposite to the concrete. To know that you owe a lot of money is not the same as knowing that you owe exactly the total of your next twenty-one paychecks before taxes. The national debt is almost incomprehensible except when described in terms of our share.

3. Reality—the specifics of what is real as opposed to the hypothetical or possible command attention. This factor of reality is closely linked to, and may be a result of, other factors of attention.

4. Suspense—uncertainty of outcome, the delight or tension of not knowing the alternatives can hold attention.

5. Conflict—wars of words or people hold attention. The massive public commitment to sports, increasingly professional rather than amateur and scholastic, evidences the attention-holding nature of conflict. Even the creation of imaginary enemies can do much to lend interest to a proposition. If you cannot succeed any other way, get arrested and have a confrontation with the enemies of freedom, liberty, and justice.

6. Familiarity—we are often attracted toward the familiar, comfortable, known.

7. Novel—we are also drawn to the unusual, unexpected, different. Many of the effects of style depend upon novelty in language ordering.

8. Proximity—fires in one's home town are somehow more shocking and more involving than fires that occur in the next state. Midwesterners read about the rains and the deaths and the houses ruined because of mudslides in California but spend more energy and generate more excitement about the floods that washed out several roads in the next county.

9. Humor—is there any doubt that humor commands attention? (It also serves other functions as well.)

Several of these learned factors and the whole matter of interests and concerns relate to the concept of saliency. Some interests involve us to a degree, but they are not central to our scheme of things. We can take them or leave them alone. Other areas seem more important to us. If we make a choice in our attention, we presumably select the stimulus that is more salient.

Salience might be thought of as one dimension of an attitude that we hold about things. While we have attitudes toward many things, not all of these things involve us personally. But attitudes of greater moment to us are salient. If a topic relates to a salient attitude, materials relevant to that topic will command more attention both in terms of intensity of set and frequency of attention than do less salient topics.

SELECTIVITY OF ATTENTION AND PERCEPTION

The selective nature of the process of attention has been noted. However, particular implications of this selectivity need further exposition, especially in terms of perception.

Clearly attention is meaningfully linked to perception. As we give our attention to something, we see it more fully, more clearly, more vividly. As they grow, children develop the ability to make discriminations they could not previously make. The process of education helps to develop the ability to discriminate, to see things we did not see before. In a sense education develops our ability to use attention in ways that serve us better.

Previous experience emerges as a factor controlling perception just as it controls or affects attention. People who have been trained to make finer discriminations see things that others do not see. A person who has studied and been interested in the persuasion process should perceive a multitude of elements that another person with less interest and experience and training will not perceive.

But we see what we expect to see; we perceive what we expect to perceive. Multiple experiments on perception have demonstrated this fact.[2] Allport's famous studies on rumor exemplify this tendency for perception and cognition to support expectation.[3] Set or expectation enables us to make a more rapid perception: we not only see it but see it more quickly. An individual who knows a sign is in a certain place on the highway will see that sign at night at almost twice as great a distance as the person does who does not know the sign is there.

The motivational forces impinging upon an individual and the interests and saliency of various matters will affect attention. They will clearly affect perception as well. A hungry person is likely to notice advertisements for restaurants or for food. Supporters of the home team are more likely to see fouls not called by referees on the opposition teams than those not called on the home team. Individuals who disagree with a point of view are likely to see more fallacies in an argument than will those who agree. Clearly we see what we want to see, even without a conscious awareness of this tendency.

Although this characteristic may operate at the unconscious level, once we are exposed to material, it also operates to determine initial exposure. We tend to expose ourselves to material that is in consonance with our views and not to expose ourselves to material adverse to our views. This tendency is not complete and is not capable of being completely

---

[2] See M. D. Vernon, *The Psychology of Perception* (Baltimore: Penguin Books, 1962).
[3] Gordon W. Allport and Leo Postman, *The Psychology of Rumor* (New York: Holt, 1947).

implemented if it were. Republicans tend to watch and listen to communications from Republicans. People who do not like the viewpoint of *Time* magazine typically do not read it. If someone does not agree with your viewpoint on a subject, she may refrain from discussing it rather than argue the point. Our habits lead us to talk with certain people, read certain publications, talk about interests with those who share our interests. We may not consciously avoid conflicting points of view, but our habits may be such that we will not frequently come in contact with those views.

In essence, then, we not only operate selectively in terms of attention and perception in the situation but habitually expose or do not expose ourselves to situations and material as well. Thus, we insulate ourselves in many ways: we are prone to perceive things selectively and perceive them in accordance with our experience, values, interests; we may defend ourselves against adverse stimuli by not perceiving them or by misperceiving them. We may withdraw our attention once it is gained, and we may not be exposed to potentially aversive materials.

SUGGESTION

The process of suggestion is linked to attention. Suggestion is a mental process in which the stimuli operate in the periphery of the field of attention and consciousness, and materials, ideas, or actions tend to be accepted in an uncritical fashion. The process demands both the noncentrality of the phenomenon in attention and relatively uncritical acceptance. Much of the suggestion process operates below or just at the threshold of conscious attention and perception and yields its effects through summation or habitual patterns of response. The success of the suggestion process is determined by the stimulus and the internal conditions of the organism operating together.

Suggestion is often classified in terms of patterns or types. Thus, suggestion can be direct or indirect, positive or negative. It may arise from the individual—autosuggestion—or from other sources—prestige suggestion. Countersuggestivity arises when people do the opposite of what they are told to do.

The effectiveness of suggestion will vary with the total situation and the state of the receiver. An American flag, massed banks of flowers, and formal robes may enhance the responsiveness of the audience to certain stimuli. The architecture of a church is planned to reinforce worship. Doing things as a unit (such as singing anthems) heightens suggestivity. The receiver who is under sway of strong emotion may be highly suggestible. A person who is very tired may be suggestible. Perhaps a person under hypnosis represents the ultimate in suggestibility by seeing, feeling, and reacting under the suggestions of the hypnotist.

ATTENTION AND INTEREST 113

We have all attempted to make conscious use of suggestion—a yawn to indicate the hour is late, the statement that one must get back to studying soon, the candlelight dinner with wine and soft music that has become a trite representation of the seduction scene. The gas station attendant who remarks, "Fill it up!" does sell more gas.

The operation of suggestion has been extensively studied in psychology, but its application to communication poses difficulties. Certainly the suggestion process operates in communication. But the degree to which a communicator can consciously plan and implement a process of suggestion seems unclear. Everything, from manner of dress, charisma of the source, nature of the setting, audience size, interaction among the audience members, to language and delivery and any of the message elements, may operate suggestively. In some sense this process can be used as a convenient explanation for communication effects not easily explained by identifiable factors. The suggestion process involves a number of factors that have not yet been treated. The impact of language, prestige of source, emotional appeals, setting and circumstances, and medium will be discussed in later chapters.

It seems impossible to differentiate between the direct effects of these stimuli and that portion of the effect that results from less direct operation of these stimuli in actual communication. Under controlled laboratory conditions and with carefully controlled procedures, it may be possible. If we drive into a gas station and habitually fill the tank the attendant's "Fill 'r up?" simply accomplishes what we had already decided to do. The degree of critical judgment necessary seems a meaningless question. In the total complex of stimuli operative in any communication situation, what operates suggestively for one person may have no impact upon another and may be subjected to critical analysis by a third.

Advertisers using the mass media seem particularly conscious of the power of suggestion, and suggestion plays a prominent role in much advertising. Careful use of color, backgrounds, the right movie or athletic star, music, lighting, the scene or situation photographed or dramatized often places more emphasis upon a suggestive linkage of the product with some image than it does upon any quality of the product. The same advertisement is repeated frequently or is put in a pattern that reinforces the suggested associations. A portion of the money for the advertising campaign is poured into research on the desired image for the product, and additional money is spent in pilot testing varying advertisements and advertisers for success in creating the desired image.

Such techniques seem particularly useful in selling products where the actual difference in performance is minimal or nonexistent. Indeed, poorer-quality products often attain higher sales than better-quality products because the consumer buys the image and can live with the reality. Such campaigns may be less effective with many matters of public policy. As persuaders we will rarely be involved in campaigns so elaborate and expensive as commercial advertisers develop. However, we do function as consumers and thus need to be sensitive to the role of suggestion in determining our consumption habits. Are we more masculine or feminine or free or happy because we smoke one cigarette or another? Is our window cleaner because of the lemon smell in the cleaning product? Why can't the Marlboro man smoke Virginia Slims? It is not the product that makes the difference in this case; it is the advertising.

Suggestion is a powerful tool, with other factors. Commercial advertisers may be forced to have suggestion carry the burden of the persuasive effort for some products. In dealing with our personal problems, in public controversy we can use suggestion and not be dependent on it.

IMPLICATIONS FOR PERSUASION

A communicator seeks to serve as the selector of the attention of her receivers. This does not mean that she can or should completely dominate the attention of her receivers or that she will be able to focus their attention at will upon herself at one moment and upon her ideas at another. Since attention fluctuates among the multiplicity of potential stimuli to which the individual is subject, and since any one unchanging stimulus becomes tiring, attention will fluctuate in degree and direction. A communicator needs not only to win but also to rewin attention. Further, the realistic communicator understands that some items are basic to understanding and acceptance, so she seeks to draw maximum attention to these items while permitting others to operate with less intensity.

Attention can be divided into three types: involuntary, voluntary, and nonvoluntary. Involuntary attention is the result of stimuli of such magnitude or impact that a person automatically and uncritically gives attention. Thus a gunshot, scream, flash of light, or other sudden change may gain involuntary attention. Such responses are usually related to survival.

Voluntary attention is forced attention. Situations often demand that a person consciously force attention on a stimulus. This type of attention involves effort—an awareness of work—and thus becomes self-defeating as the effort detracts from the fullness of attention on the desired stimulus source and the tiring causes attention to become more difficult to maintain.

Nonvoluntary attention is given without a sense of effort to something that attracts the attention because of interaction of the perceiver and the perceived. Involuntary attention is really determined by the nature of the stimulus. Voluntary attention is determined by the effort and con-

ATTENTION AND INTEREST

scious desire of the person to focus on a stimulus. Nonvoluntary attention is a result of the person's interest and involvement in the stimulus. A speaker can use involuntary attention only for highly limited purposes; an audience may give voluntary attention, but the effort and the self-defeating nature of this effort render it suspect. What the communicator is seeking is nonvoluntary attention.

To gain nonvoluntary attention, the speaker or writer needs to find either materials that appeal to the receiver's motivations and interests or materials that can be treated to develop such appeal. Certainly she can use factors, learned and unlearned, that stimulate attention. Rather than add these or embellish the communication with specific attempts to use one or more of the factors, the communicator should attempt to find topics, materials, ideas that have natural interest and attention value for the receivers. The selectivity of attention and perception, the degree of control an individual exercises in exposing himself to materials, the competition between external and internal fields of stimuli, and the number of potential stimuli suggest the problem faced by a communicator who seeks to create new interests and to involve receivers in materials initially perceived as irrelevant and meaningless.

Attention is not a value in itself. It is a value to the degree that it provides the opportunity for the communicator to affect perception, comprehension of materials, and acceptance. Communicators can confuse the need to direct attention with the need to dominate by demanding complete attention at every moment. Clearly this is a psychological impossibility and must be self-defeating.

Furthermore, although involuntary attention can be used by a communicator, it often is unplanned and is more intrusive than helpful. A chair that suddenly falls apart at the moment of the speaker's climactic appeal is likely to produce a marked shift of attention, laughter, or other mechanisms to release the tension created by the incident.

While auditors may force attention to the speaker out of courtesy, they are unlikely to continue unless they hear something rewarding. Forced attention will detract from the auditors' ability to focus upon the ideas of the speaker and prove very tiring.

The communicator seeks to use the process of attention, then, to aid in the accomplishment of his purpose; however, he must be very careful that he does not use it negatively. In one recent class a student speaker who had just been introduced paused to adjust his tie and then fired three quick shots point-blank at the first row with a handgun loaded with blanks. He then proceeded to give an extended speech loaded with statistics, facts, and testimony of authorities and concluded by asking if gun legislation could increase the probability of what could have happened in that classroom.

Much of the speech was totally lost. The first instinct of many was to dive under chairs when the shots were fired. The instructor thought wildly, "It has happened; I've got a tripper; he has really blown his mind." This involuntary attention may not have destroyed the speaker's purpose, but it did make the remainder of his speech irrelevant. When I read the outline later, I realized I had not retained any of the content.

Often the communicator builds excessive distractions into his communication. The person who figures that a snappy joke every three minutes will wake up his audience may well be right. But if the joke is irrelevant to his purpose and to the process by which he is seeking to lead his receivers to acceptance, the jokes are defeating because *they* get the attention. Too many speakers who are not paid to be entertainers send away an audience in possession of two or three new stories and nothing else.

The communicator must attempt to integrate attention factors with the texture and fabric of his communication. Good motivational appeals, sound logic, specific supporting materials, sound acceptable authorities, and an alert, responsive, flexible delivery will encourage favorable attention. If the other elements of the speech are well planned, attention often follows naturally. However, the communicator should always be sensitive to the problem of gaining and maintaining attention.

Lack of attention is often erroneously blamed for a failure in communication. It is unfortunate that when one thing starts to go wrong with a communication, many other things start to go wrong. Thus, a person who uses poor logic is often going to have rather vague language. The audience will become confused; in the attempt to understand the argument being made, the audience will tune out and attempt to wrestle through the idea. If reading, the receiver may stop and reread it again or continue on. But the communicator may have lost vital ground she will never regain. Thus the communicator has poor logic and vague language, loses attention, and fails. It seems as if everything has gone wrong when one problem really produced all these outcomes. Similarly, when a speech works, everything seems to go right even though some individual items were potentially bad.

Often a speaker will pick a particularly interesting topic of significant concern to his audience. Because of their concern, the receivers manifest great attention; they follow the communication carefully; they become involved; the communication succeeds. Judged in terms of persuasive tactics, strategy, and implementation, the speech may be far poorer than another one that deals with a less interesting topic. The second speaker may strive harder and receive less attention.

One final point needs to be made about attention and its relationship to communication. An audience tends to identify with the communicator, particularly in an oral situation. In a classroom with a friendly audience—indeed, in most situations—the audience feels some sense of rapport with the communicator. If the communicator gets into trouble, shows she is extremely nervous, makes a few slips, or forgets the words she memorized the night before, the audience will normally pretend that their attention is not drawn to these problems. But they may become so involved that they feel something akin to the speaker's rising tension. They will begin to pull with the speaker; they will give attention to what comes next; they will almost literally heave a sigh of relief as the speaker concludes. Unfortunately, here again the attention of the audience has been directed to the wrong things (the speaker and her problems) and not to the message the speaker sought to communicate. To the degree that the speaker wishes her message to be the central focus, she must direct attention to the message and not to things that detract from it.

Although this example deals with the speaker who is in trouble because of poor performance skills, the same process can operate in reverse. Many people love to perform as communicators. They dress to the hilt; they use their voices as if they were organs; they affect the manner of William Jennings Bryan with a touch of FDR. They gain rewards from the act of performance and from the skill with which they control attention—they play the auditors. Such communicators often do gain attention—but to themselves, their skills, their performance. Too many auditors go away saying, "I just loved your voice. I could listen to you all day. You could read the telephone book and I'd listen." But what happened to the message?

Clearly, the key canon by which the communicator tests the attention gained from the audience is "Did it aid in the accomplishment of my purpose?" But what test should the receiver employ? Receivers should use the same test applied from their point of view. Receivers may well wish to control their attention by mentally testing ideas, raising alternative issues, and otherwise controlling their attention. This is particularly easy with written material, but it is also possible with speech and film. The rate of presentation and the amount of repetition is such that the individual can think beyond the material being presented and still comprehend the material being presented.

SUMMARY

Attention is a process in which a particular stimulus or set of stimuli becomes more vivid in the consciousness than others. This effect is produced by a relatively unified set of the body involving mind, muscles, and sense organs. It constitutes a set of readiness to respond to a given set or classification of stimuli.

PARTICIPATION AS RECEIVERS

Attention is a key process in all of communication since it determines what is perceived with fullness and clarity. Attention is basic to but not sufficient for successful persuasion.

Attention is affected by both learned and unlearned factors. Of particular importance to communicators are those acquired interests, commitments, and attitudes that control not only what we give our attention to but also affect the perceptions that are derived. We modify our actions so as to increase exposure to desired stimuli and to decrease exposure to undesired stimulation.

The communicator seeks to be the selector for audience attention. While not able to dominate attention completely, even for short periods of time, the communicator nevertheless seeks to channel attention in ways that contribute to the goal. Forces both inside and outside the receiver will affect the degree to which attention will be commanded. The communicator can utilize learned or unlearned attention factors, can seek to develop messages, manipulate settings, and utilize techniques of suggestion, but the receiver is the ultimate controller of attention. Thus, the communicator seeks to gain the involvement and interest of the receiver, which in turn makes attention easy and natural. And the attention given to the material being communicated becomes rewarding to the giver.

DISCUSSION QUESTIONS AND PROJECTS

1. Discuss how much the topic determines attention.

2. In your next outline identify the elements that serve as attention selectors.

3. Should a student who picks a topic that has high interest value and commands strong attention be thought a better persuader than a student who picks a dull topic and by great effort makes it moderately interesting? What difference, if any, should exist between a classroom evaluation and the reality of actual persuasion in the "real world"?

4. In an experiment a number of women were asked to judge the quality of four sets of hose. All the stockings were identical and packaged in identical boxes. Three pairs had perfume in the box; one did not. Not surprisingly, only a small percentage of the women found the hose without perfume to be of good quality. What implications does this finding have for restaurants, stores, and those who sell to the public?

ATTENTION AND INTEREST

5. Make a special effort to note attempts at suggestion by salesclerks, gas station attendants, and others in two or three instances. How many would you have noted if you had not been watching for them? Did your conscious attention to these efforts alter your responses?

6. During a church service a bird flew into an open window and swooped around the church. Finally the bird alighted at the altar and pecked at the collection plate. The minister addressed the bird, "I know you are one of God's creations, but I wish you would leave because you are making me a nervous wreck." Considering this situation from the point of view of attention, was this a good procedure? What other approaches might the minister have taken?

7. Discuss the impact of efforts at involuntary attention: (1) as a deliberate device for an introduction, (2) in the body of a speech, (3) in the conclusion, and (4) as external distractions that should be treated by a speaker.

8. Why do you think expressions like "therefore," "next," "in summary," "the second point is," "going on to," "the cause is" gain attention? Do such words draw attention because of natural attention factors? Because of learned attention factors? Why do you think the use of internal summaries and transitions gains greater comprehension and retention of content?

9. Collect a series of advertisements either for the same product or for different products that compete for sales with each other. What is the relationship between the medium, the probable audience, the appeals used, and the differences among the advertisements? What attention devices can you identify? What efforts at suggestion?

III CREATION OF M

6 Preparation
Selecting the Specific Persuasive Goal
Processes of Message Preparation
Delivery: The Message Comes into Being in a Channel

7 Content
The Message as a Matrix
The Nature of Proof
Logical Appeals
Motivational Appeals
Use of Data
Interrelationship of Methods of Yielding Proof

8 Organization
Patterns of Organization
Process of Organization

SSAGES

Application in Outlines

9 Language and Style
The Nature and Function of Language
The Nature and Function of Style
Analysis of Language and Style
Language and Style in Persuasion
   Attention
   Comprehension
   Acceptance

10 Delivery: Bringing the Message Into Being
Nonverbal Communication
Speech
   Visual Stimuli
   Audible Stimuli
Comparative Effectiveness

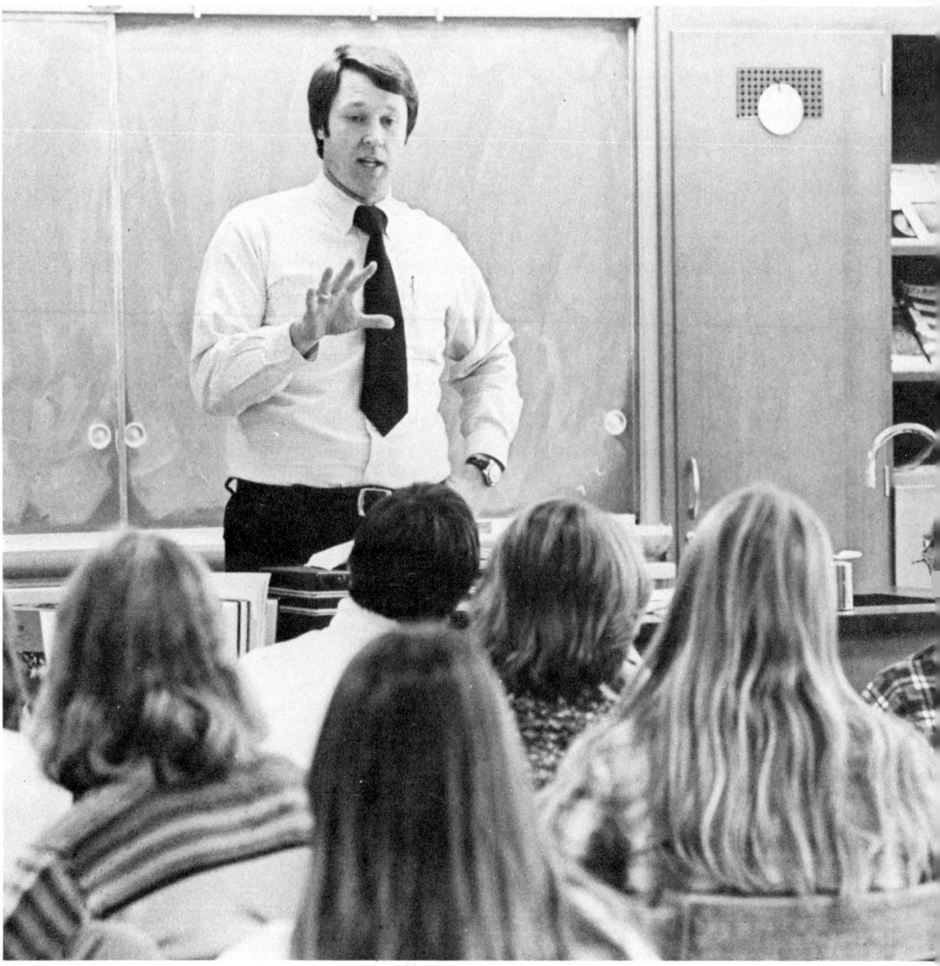

6 Preparation

This chapter serves as an introduction to section III, which deals with the processes involved in creating messages. Succeeding chapters in this section focus upon effects linked to various message factors. They draw upon theory, practice, and data derived from observation and experimentation. Since the communication process is so complex, we deal in generalizations, not universal laws. Judgments based on theory and observation constitute a needed complement to experimental data.

This chapter surveys the process that a persuader follows in preparing a message and stresses the elements relating to developing a clear goal or purpose for the persuasion attempt. The process of preparation is traced from the point of view of the persuader. Many of our persuasive efforts begin as an instantaneous reaction to something. In these instances any planning is done in at most a few minutes and at the least in a fraction of a second. For purposes of this chapter, we will talk about a more elaborate, formal process of planning, one that could stretch over hours or days and that permits careful reflection.

To impose a temporal sequence and logical progression on the interrelated process of preparation steps distorts what really happens and ignores the instantaneous nature of so much of persuasion. To sequence the steps and order them logically, however, is to enable us to study the preparation process and to gain an understanding that can improve our persuasive abilities significantly. Much of the persuasion we do can be preplanned and improved significantly by doing so. Indeed, we can not only plan our strategy but ask others to give us advice. In many campaigns nearly as much time and perhaps more talent goes into planning the persuasion campaign than in executing it. Sensitivity to the steps in good preparation may improve the instantaneous persuasion efforts significantly.

SELECTING THE SPECIFIC PERSUASIVE GOAL

The failure to derive a good, realistic, specific persuasion goal and purpose statement and then to relate and test what one does in terms of that statement is the most significant reason why many persuasion efforts fail. A sound purpose is based upon good audience and situation analysis, careful selection of material in terms of that analysis, and proper implementation through effective communication techniques.

Influences on the Specific Purpose

A persuasive act takes place in terms of a specific receiver or receivers in a specific situation and with some particular topic and purpose. The specific purpose or goal of the individual persuasion act must tie to these specifics as well as the general reasons why we persuade that were discussed in chapter 2.

A specific persuasion goal often arises when the persuader responds to a highly specific need: "I want a date for Friday night." Or the persuasive effort may be a response to the efforts of others. We are sometimes pushed into persuasion as a response to the actions of others. Often we compete with another persuader trying to influence the same group or receivers. My family often becomes a three-way persuasive struggle as each of us tries to win the others over to a particular restaurant on our night to eat out.

The persuasion effort may be the result of an assumed or assigned task. If you volunteer to go door-to-door in the march on birth defects, the purpose has been set. When we persuade as part of our job or in groups, we are normally one person working in an interrelated system that joins the efforts of many people. The role of the individual is often specifically defined by the job held, the expectations of others, one's own perception of responsibilities.

The knowledge, understanding, and abilities of the persuader structure the purpose. A persuader cannot present information that she or he does not have; we cannot seek to accomplish a persuasive purpose that we do not perceive as a possibility. What we know, think, and can do are particularly powerful limitations since we are unaware of them in most cases. Furthermore we have other goals, values, and commitments, which shape the specific goals we formulate in any situation. We may have no objection to earning a million dollars but would object if we had to rob a bank, defraud the government, or encourage a war to get it.

The receivers may determine the specific purpose. A persuader often takes on that role at the direct request of the receivers: the audience in effect asks someone to be the persuader and dictates the topic and the purpose. When we visit a used car lot and want to buy a car we ask the dealer to function as a persuader. Even if the audience does not determine the purpose directly, it will cause the persuader to adjust, discard, or reshape and refine the general goal being sought in terms of a specific purpose tied to this audience.

Finally, other forces in the world may shape the specific purpose that we formulate. Events may cause us to abandon certain topics or certain approaches in treating a topic.

Selecting the Specific Purpose

Whatever the forces or needs that move a person to persuasion there is usually some sense of a subject matter area, a general or specific purpose, and a target audience.[1] No persuader should assume that the specific persuasion purpose is totally predetermined. The persuader should follow a pattern of analysis that provides for maximum adjustment of the purpose to the imperatives of the receivers, the subject matter, and self.

If a person begins with the general idea of urging the receivers to support higher education, we might label this a general purpose or goal. But whether the person has ten minutes, ten hours, or ten years in which to persuade, the general purpose is so broad and can be approached in so many ways that it is in no sense a guide to what should be included in the message. The persuader needs to translate this general purpose into a specific one that reflects the realities of the subject matter, the audience, and self. Throughout the preparation process the communicator should maintain a lively sense of each of these elements.

The Nature of the Audience

An extended period of audience analysis is essential at this stage of the process. The persuader could simply ignore the audience and fire away at a purpose without adjusting to the receivers. But the persuasion efforts would be totally irrelevant to anything except the noise level of the society. One audience may oppose a proposition for

---

[1] Students in a class are in a unique situation; this is one of the few times in your life that the subject matter is not largely dictated by the factors that impel you into the persuasion situation. Enjoy the freedom despite the trauma of wondering what you should talk about. Rarely will you ever have such freedom again.

one reason, another for a different reason, and a third audience may favor it. Some auditors may be concerned with taxes, others with services. The persuader must decide where her audience is in terms of attitude and actions and then discern some means of achieving her goals.

The best advice concerning accommodation to an audience is to *take an audience where it is and move in the direction you want it to go.* A reasonable purpose in one instance may be to create an awareness of a problem; in another, to open an audience to further information; in a third, to implement a belief in overt action; in a fourth, to reinforce opinion in the face of counterpersuasion.

If the audience is heterogeneous, with a wide range of receivers in terms of attitudes toward the topic, interests, personality characteristics, and predispositions, the communicator should make adjustments. But typically an audience is homogeneous in terms of at least a few variables. Defining these similarities and planning strategy in terms of them can pay significant returns.

The persuader may find it possible to describe the receivers as partisans strongly favoring his viewpoint and simply needing advice or help in putting their principles into action. In some instances the audience may be largely hostile or largely disinterested in the topic. At times the persuader would be wise to divide the audience into different subgroups. And, of course, the analysis should relate not only to attitude toward the persuasive purpose but also to such questions as knowledge of the subject matter, interest in or importance of the topic for the receivers, or possibly attitude toward the persuader.

Some situations may warrant an attempt to move an audience radically from one point of view or one action to another. Apparently radical changes can be obtained when action initially linked to one attitudinal position or value is linked to a quite different one. A person may suddenly evidence a complete transformation. However, the extremity of the change urged may be counterproductive. The auditors may feel too threatened, and they may shut out the persuasive stimuli, attack the source, or mount strong counterpersuasion efforts. Often a new movement is crushed because it arouses strong opposition too quickly. Further, the opportunity to select tactics that will initiate the process of change may be totally lost in the focus upon massive upheavals. How many times have you totally altered behavior or belief in response to one persuasive effort?

The persuader may have repeated opportunity to continue and reinforce persuasion efforts; other people and other factors in society will typically operate to bring parallel persuasive efforts to bear on the same audience.

Although it cannot be demonstrated that one should set a modest goal for all situations, it seems valid to assume that success is most probable when one sets an achievable specific purpose—one that has reality for the specific audience. To ignore this limitation may result in unwise planning, irrelevant efforts, or even the creation of forces that directly conflict with the goal of the persuader.

The Subject Matter

The realities of the topic area condition the purpose. The material that can be found, the data available, the issues that have been developed, the status of the problem, the total world—all have an impact.

Self

We are rarely able to function like the chameleon, putting on colors, ideas, and values for the moment only. A person commits himself to persuasion because it is instrumental to his goals; total change of purpose to fit the audience's view means he has abandoned his stake in the proceedings. Why persuade in opposition to one's desires? (Granted, a person may change, and hence his persuasion efforts may change.)

It is difficult to settle for a limited persuasive goal such as opening an audience to further information when the persuader really wants to "take them all the way by telling how it really is"! But if such an attempt is more likely to freeze the audience in their current attitude or even to intensify their current condition, we must be realistic. Many are the "hotheads" who undermine the possibility of persuasion for others. They typically think they have been more virtuous and honest for telling those "fat cats just where the truth lies." But is it more ethical to confirm these people in their current status and to lessen the probabilities for success of other "truth tellers"?

In essence, the idea of taking an audience from where it is and moving it in the direction you want it to go with a potentially obtainable goal is a sound standard. The direction is defined by the individual; the realities of subject matter, audience, and skill of the communicator will define the potential degree of change.

Framing a Specific Purpose Statement

Although much persuasion has been and will be attempted without a consciously formed and carefully drawn statement of purpose, the persuader can profit from the effort. The following criteria are suggested as a means of judging the viability of a specific statement:

1. Is the purpose clear, meaningful, and precise?
2. Is the desired goal clearly identified? Is the goal one of persuasive nature, not merely information transmission, entertainment, or some other nonpersuasive one?
3. Does the purpose reflect the realities of audience, subject matter, and the communicator?
4. Does the specific purpose have a reasonable potential of being accomplished? We have sought to achieve perfection in goodness or evil since recorded history. We have not yet achieved it. Rare is the persuader who can do it in five minutes.
5. Is the purpose essentially singular? Seeking to accomplish two or three major purposes is dangerous. Some mediational goals may be noted as steps to a more ultimate goal, but purpose statements that combine two or three coordinate ends are likely to result in unfocused, potentially meaningless persuasion attempts.
6. Is the purpose free from the confusion of means and ends? It is proper to focus upon the means to be employed and to designate a major appeal or key motivational force, but these elements should not be confused with the goal.
7. Is the purpose statement adequately refined and modified as the thinking and analysis of the persuader change during the preparatory process? It seems naive to assume that a purpose statement once framed may not need refinement as the preparation process continues. Indeed, the purpose may change as the actual communication is under way. Clearly a purpose found untenable through further work should be altered.

PROCESSES OF MESSAGE PREPARATION

Having refined the impulse to persuade into a relatively specific purpose statement, the persuader moves to the next stage—planning the message. In the preparatory stage the persuader must assemble, test, and select from among the possible means of achieving his purpose.

The remainder of this chapter discusses message elements. This emphasis on message is not meant to be misleading; persuaders must assess the degree to which they can shape or alter any of the forces contributing to potential persuasion outcomes. We may try to adjust the specific environment or alter the medium to be employed. We may attempt to manipulate the audience in ways unrelated to the message, perhaps by crowding the audience or by increasing the temperature in the room. But the message is the preeminent means the persuader has to control the stimuli that impinge upon the receiver. The persuader may not be able to control events, but can control the explanation given of them, the decision to mention or not to mention them, and the time and manner of their presentation.

The process of message preparation and implementation has been described often by communication theorists. The classical pattern divided the process into four steps: invention—finding the proofs and selecting among them; disposition—organizing the material; elocution—wording and styling of the material; pronunciation—delivering the message into a channel.

This pattern describes the evolving process of preparation quite well. When one first decides to persuade, there is almost an infinity of possible topics and means. As she pursues the topic area, even more possibilities tend to emerge. Then, as the persuader refines purposes and selects material in terms of the audience, the subject matter, and self, she sets limits and qualifications upon the process. Having decided what material to use, the persuader structures it first in terms of large units and relationships of ideas, then more carefully until she is polishing the specific phrase to achieve a desired image. But at the moment of delivery the persuader returns to a larger range of choices. Presumably if she has been an effective planner, the persuasion message may be much like that preplanned, and the skills of delivery will translate the plans into reality. But the multiplicity of variables—new factors, feedback from receivers—is such that much freedom of choice is again available.

Actually, freedom of choice exists throughout the planning process. As the persuader is organizing her material, she may decide she lacks information or that a given appeal will not be functional, so she returns to the process of discovering and selecting material.

This concentration upon various elements at different stages reflects prior decisions and has a sense of sequential value. One can simultaneously do all the things necessary in the formulation of a message. Communicators do simultaneously invent, organize, style, and deliver messages in many communication settings. Such communication reflects more of the habitual responses of the communicator and less of choice, discretion, and control. When the potential of the communication act is sufficiently great and when it can be anticipated in advance, careful preparation is possible and should produce more effective persuasion.

Selection and Development of Material

The process of the development and selection of material actually begins in the early stages of audience and subject analysis essential to the derivation of the specific purpose statement. However, the analysis of audience and subject continues during the accumulation and selection of materials.

Audience analysis must also be continued. The persuader must hold a clear perception of the nature of her receivers in order to provide a basis for choosing among various materials. She should be concerned not only with their general attitudes toward subject, purpose, and source but also with how to project their response toward given appeals, given pieces of evidence, and alternative methods of development. She must estimate the need for attention devices, motivational appeals, evidence, and even the proper delivery techniques.

Subject analysis must be expanded. The persuader must develop an understanding of the subject matter materials sufficient to provide a proper basis for preparation. Obviously a persuader who is hunting for material just sufficient to fill time limits is not ready to begin constructing a message. The persuader needs to assure a sufficiency of material so that she can weigh choices and select among the possible rather than be forced to incorporate everything she has available.

This stage of subject analysis usually involves some research not limited to library resources. Research may involve a good deal of thinking about one's own resources, knowledge, and experiences. It may involve tapping the resources of others through interaction, discussion, or direct questioning. In large persuasion campaigns several people will function entirely as researchers.

During the effort to organize material or in later stages of preparation, a communicator will undertake additional research to find a specific piece of evidence. Research becomes easier and more meaningful when the researcher has a sense of direction and knowledge of exactly what she needs.

Clearly the potential persuader will wish to know more than one point of view relative to a problem area. The persuader usually ensures that she has been exposed to the ideas of those who oppose the view she is advocating. This should enable her to plan more effectively and select material of potentially greater utility. Even the persuader who is seeking to reinforce the views that she shares with a friendly audience will often find it valuable to use material that refutes and counteracts some of the opposing viewpoint. In this way she protects her audience to some degree from future counterpersuasion and provides arguments for them to use in their turn as persuaders.

As part of this process of obtaining and selecting materials for the message, the persuader will need to determine strategy and plan tactics for its implementation. What major motivational appeals and methods will be employed? What subsidiary motives? Should the purpose be revealed? What sorts of evidence, data, and support forms will be employed? What problems in attention will be encountered, and how can these be met? Are there specific adjustments to be made to elements of the setting, the medium, the audience? If not already determined, what media will be employed; what target audience will be involved; what time, place, and specific environment will be utilized?

Organization and Structure

Techniques of organization may be employed very early in the process of invention. It is helpful to set down a preliminary listing of what is known on the topic, the issues involved, and the points of view available. During the research process and in the selection of material, persuaders will often work with outlines as organizational patterns. Analysis and synthesis are complementary processes. The persuader is concerned both with the analysis of the subject, audience, and setting and with the synthesis of a message resulting from his best estimate of what will be most effective in terms of these forces.

Many communicators consciously make decisions about items such as support forms and appeals only as the potential communication is being organized either mentally or on paper in an outline.

The outlining process is a critical stage in the development of an effective message. The discipline of an outline forces one not only to examine the gross structure but also to highlight the relationship among the smaller points. To the degree that it successfully provides a means to test what the communicator plans to do, an outline enables him to examine different choices. An outline should represent the best preparation possible for a communication up to the moment of an actual delivery. The final outline generally is complete. It indicates the title, purpose, introductory elements, the major points and subpoints within the body of the message, the conclusion, and bibliographical sources. Thus it provides a means of judging the appeals being used, the attention elements being employed, and the amount of evidence and reasoning contained in the message. Even the language and style may be assessed in terms of the language employed in the outline.

Frequently persons who are not adept in using the outline refuse to use one. They prefer to write out a complete manuscript. Then they make the even more tragic attempt to memorize and deliver the exact manuscript or to tinker with the wording before printing it. Unfortunately, the complete manuscript does not carefully highlight the relationship of points; it does not enable one to examine as conveniently and critically the various factors being blended into the communication. Seeing on paper words such as "From this it follows that . . ." seems to relieve the communicator of the responsibility to ensure that it does indeed follow from this.

There are, of course, all types of outlines and all types of uses for them. However, the outline is the discipline of the process of organization and structure and, as in other things, such disciplining usually pays.

Language and Style

Whatever a persuader's thoughts, language is usually the preeminent means by which these thoughts must be communicated. Vague, imprecise language often means vague, imprecise thoughts. Obscure references, a concatenation of mellifluous phrases may indicate more polish than insight. The perfecting of language and style is often the means to perfecting thought.

Rarely is it wise to attempt to polish the style and language while working with the selection of material or organizing this material on a gross level. Only after these decisions have been made should the persuader shift to the careful selection of language units and the polishing of style.

Style can be defined in many ways. In one sense it is the characteristic patterns of behavior that denote one person. In this sense communication style includes topics, methods of appeals, language, and manner of delivery. More typically, style is restricted to the form and order of language elements. In this book, *style* is typically employed in the latter sense.

When a thought is expressed in words, it is difficult to separate the effects of style from the effects of the material. To change the style is to alter the material in some way, subtly or not so subtly. Hence, it is very difficult to estimate the effects of good language and style on communication. Although this question will be discussed in greater detail in chapter 9, it may serve for the moment to note that people who have good language choice and style are generally more effective persuaders than those who do not. Even if the perfecting of style is only the perfecting of thought, the persuasive impact should still be heightened.

Often style is confused with the idea of ornateness—being grand, novel, unusual, or cute. Such styles are employed but often with negative impact. Every communication has a style; we all have personal style, and we are all capable of variation in terms of the style we employ in adjusting to different audiences, subjects, situations, moods, purposes. The test of a good style is its functionality, which is certainly not the same thing as elegance.

DELIVERY: THE MESSAGE COMES INTO BEING IN A CHANNEL

The delivery process—pronunciation—has traditionally been viewed as the final stage in the process of preparation. But since in many ways it is not part of the preparation process but is a process that follows the series described above, it seems preferable to treat it as a distinct process in its own right. Of course, many communicators do preplan and practice the delivery of a communication; hence, this could be viewed as part of the preparation process. Many writers work with a series of preliminary drafts much as a speaker may try out alternate ways of expressing ideas or practice a speech with a tape recorder.

The actual process of putting messages into channels involves the results of the preparation process, as well as other forces now operative upon the communicator. In many situations the receivers act as a direct influence upon the communicator, especially through feedback in the oral situation. The realities of the setting may dictate change. Further, the act of finally "communicating" the message often involves a heightened state of awareness on the part of the communicator. She typically modifies some of what she had planned to say, responding to her feelings of the moment with "oops, must get this in"; "must give that more emphasis."

Hence, this moment of delivery in a sense returns the communicator to her original position as she began the process of invention. Persuasive forces are still operating; her own unique qualities are still exerting an effect; the potential audience is now actual; the subject matter elements are still having an effect. The preparatory process certainly is a major influence upon the communicator in this setting, but it is only one of the operative forces. Clearly the communicator is free to make adaptations to the totality of the forces now operative.

SUMMARY

This chapter began the consideration of the role of message elements in persuasion. Since the creation of the message is an act by a source, the persuader, this chapter approaches the task of message creation from the point of view of the persuader.

Specific forces shape the translation of general purposes into a specific goal and purpose statement appropriate to a particular communication effort. The general impulse to persuade must be translated into a specific purpose in terms of the interaction of the purposes of the communicator, the nature of the audience, the possibilities in terms of the subject matter and in the context of the total situation.

Once the specific purpose has been set, the remainder of the preparation process should be devoted to accomplishing that purpose. Whether in the act of deriving materials and selecting elements for the message, or organizing, styling, or finally creating the actual message in a channel, the persuader should rigorously test whether his or her actions are the most effective for achieving the established purpose.

DISCUSSION QUESTIONS AND PROJECTS

1. Discuss the validity of these two claims. (1) The better persuader is more likely to end up following the preplanned persuasive pattern. (2) The better persuader is more capable of adjusting to changing circumstances but less likely to need to do so.

2. Discuss the degree to which the process of preparing speeches and writing papers is linear in the sense of moving sequentially from one stage to the next. How accurate are the stages described in this chapter in tracing your patterns of preparation?

3. Discuss the various patterns the members of your class use in preparing speeches. How do these patterns differ from those used in writing papers?

4. For a round of speeches, have each class member write down the specific purpose of each speech. Talk about the similarity or differences among the various perceptions of the members of the class. What does your discussion suggest about the effectiveness of the various persuasion efforts? Can you correlate the success of the speaker with the unanimity of agreement on purpose?

5. As part of a critique, have each person reveal the specific purpose of an attempt at persuasion. Then as a class discuss ways in which the specific purpose might have been altered to be more effective for this group.

PREPARATION

6. Individually or as a group, select a general persuasive goal that you might wish to accomplish. Then think of many existing groups that you might attempt to persuade. What specific goals would you establish with each of them? Justify the differences in your purpose statements. In addition to thinking of groups that already exist, think of audiences that you might reach through one or another of the local media or through a publicly announced lecture. How would the specific purpose change for these respective audiences?

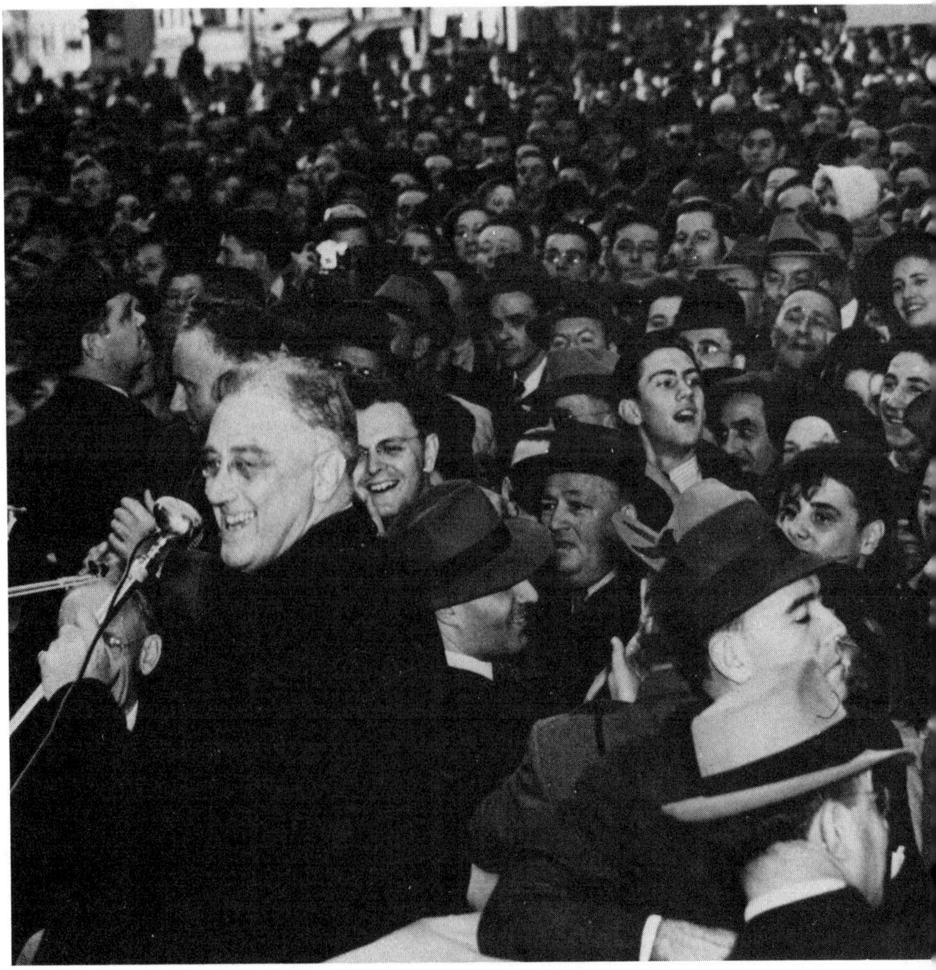

7 Content

The message is the element most under the persuader's control in communication. The message is the product of the source responding to the persuader's perceptions of all the factors involved. The message is the primary means by which the persuader seeks to affect the behavior or thinking of others. A message may be the direct cause of an effect; it may be a contributing cause; it may serve a mediational function; or it may have no effect.

The way people generally talk about communication leaves two false impressions: that messages say something and that messages determine what happens in communication. The first impression is false because messages do not mean; rather, people give meaning to messages. The second impression is false because any or all of the factors in communication, not just the stimuli that constitute the message, may determine the response. For ease and brevity in communication I must depend on you to remember that messages mean and gain any effects only in terms of the interpretive activities of our minds. Further, although we may focus on one factor in the process, all the factors must be considered both individually and in their complex interactions. One element may be the dominant factor in some case, but it is impossible to determine this fact for sure. This element would be dominant only because other elements did not operate with greater power. You may, for example, be the only person talking to the group, but in one sense this is because the others are not choosing to talk at this moment.

In many instances the message is only mediational in its function. It simply sets the scene for a predetermined response; the audience is waiting for a signal to do something. Or the message can function to link a source and her prestige to an idea. The source's prestige may be the factor producing the effect, and the message serves only to transmit the claim, to channel the action. The persuasive impact of an order is not normally caused by elements within the message but to the prestige or relationship of the source to the receiver. A message may be ritualistic in function, and the act of repeating the message or hearing it may be the source of the effect. A familiar prayer repeated in time of stress or a jingle or nursery rhyme may function in this way.

Many messages essentially produce no effect at all, although it would be untrue to say that a message has no effect. It takes some of its creator's time; it may affect him. It occupies some attention from the audience; it may produce a sound sleep or strong but transitory emotional impact. But in terms of the goal set by the originator, a communication may produce no effect in altering the status of an attitude or action. In general, the message is most realistically seen as a contributor to the effects involved and not the sole cause.

There are a number of alternative responses to any situation. Similarly there are many alternative messages that can be framed. Even within a message there is a practical infinity of possibilities in alternative organizational patterns, examples and illustrations, emphases, appeals, and words that could be used to communicate the same basic message. Different choices could yield different effects (some markedly, even traumatically different), but some would produce no difference at all. Ultimately the task of making the optimal choice becomes the test of the communicator's effectiveness.

THE MESSAGE AS A MATRIX

The result of a complex set of stimuli, the message itself is also a complex of stimuli. We tend to think of the symbols, particularly words, present in the channel as being the message. But these symbols function as stimuli; they have meaning in terms of the responses humans make to them. These symbols exist in themselves; they can be counted, measured, calculated. But by definition as symbols, they function to represent something beyond their own reality. Reactions to symbols will be affected by the variety of factors in the total communication process—factors related to source, setting, channel, and the receivers themselves.

The understanding of persuasion effects is hampered by the assumption that stimuli can be classified in terms of labels that meaningfully indicate response. Such classifications are meaningful at some level and to some degree, but to assume that a communication stimulus will elicit a single, invariable response in every situation is nonsense. Responses by the same person at different times or by different people at the same time may contrast sharply. Further, to suggest that the responses produced will be similar in degree or intensity is also nonsense. To concentrate on stimuli rather than the response of receivers to stimuli limits the understanding of message effects in persuasion.

Words in a message carry information about objects, things, being, or reactions to objects, things, being. Words simultaneously provide a basis for critical evaluation of content, emotional response, judgment about the communicator, an aesthetic response to style, a judgment of the locality where the speaker or writer was born and raised. The gestalt that is the response to the message may result from many parts.

There are multiple response dimensions possible for every word. Multiply this word by the totality of stimuli of a speech, an hour of television, a book, or a movie, and the variety of stimuli and their potentiality to engender multitudinous, diverse response becomes incalculable. A sentence may cause one receiver to lose interest, another to develop it. A paragraph drawing upon a noted authority may make one person respond more favorably to the ideas in the remainder of the communication, while another is lost in the memory of his previous connections with the authority cited. One person responds with tears to a simple statement about the futility of war. (Perhaps a son was killed.) Three others conclude the speaker is a "bleeding heart." A fifth agrees that war is futile.

Two basic points implicit in the previous discussion need clear statement: (1) the message contains a variety of complex stimuli that interact in numerous and complex ways, and (2) stimuli do not have a single or a universal effect upon receivers. No message, even a word, is ever a simple thing. A message is a complex matrix.

A matrix is analyzed by extracting the roots—those forces or factors that operate to produce the values that make up the matrix. The intent of section III, therefore, is to analyze the matrix we call the message. No single factor will suffice to explain the effect of a message.

This chapter will focus upon the stimuli in a message in order to extract the roots of both the logical and the affective or emotional impact of a message and to determine how they operate to produce belief. The two cannot be separated in actual communication either on the basis of intent of source, classification of stimuli, or response of receivers. Later chapters will attempt to extract other roots.

Recall that message is defined as that which exists in the channel, placed there by the source whether intentionally or not. Other things may be present in the channel and add or detract from the message.

THE NATURE OF PROOF

Aristotle's *Rhetoric* describes proof as "a kind of demonstration; for we entertain the strongest conviction of a thing if we believe that it has been 'demonstrated.' Rhetorical proof, however (is not scientific demonstration)."[1] Aristotle describes three kinds of proof as supplied by the speech: ethos, pathos, logos. And near the end of the vital introductory section he notes, " 'Persuasive' means persuasive to a person."[2]

Contemporary speech texts, particularly those in argumentation, are likely to define proof as the result of reasoning applied to evidence. In this restricted use, proof is linked to logical demonstration and excludes demonstrations on the basis of emotional appeals or the credibility of the source.

What constitutes proof? Should proof be limited to belief induced by logical arguments? Since this is a matter of definition, we can arbitrarily define it as we wish. However, an examination of the various ways in which proof is employed serves to introduce the role of logic as an appeal or proof in persuasion.

One answer is to differentiate between proof and acceptance.[3] Acceptance is contrasted to proof by linking acceptance to desire, wish, or feeling; proof results from a proposition or assertion being stated with reasons to justify this assertion. Therefore a rational (logical) connection should exist between the elements. But what constitutes a rational connection? This involves moving from an accepted truth to derive a new probable, hence accepted, truth. Such a move involves the mental process of inference going from the known to new knowns and implications—the logical relation that holds when inferences are valid. In deduction this involves questions of both the formal validity of the system and the truth of the premises employed.

Philosophers seem to focus upon methods to objectify the reasoning system apart from the wishes of the user. Schematic devices for testing validity such as the diagrams much used for syllogisms and the rules concerning syllogisms are illustrations of this effort. The problems of the truth of the premises in deduction and the adequacy of the observations in inference cannot be solved by such schematic devices.

---

[1] Lane Cooper, *The Rhetoric of Aristotle* (New York: Appleton-Century-Crofts, 1932), p. 5.
[2] Ibid., p. 11.
[3] The following is based in part upon ideas from Jack Ray and Harry Zavos, "Reasoning and Argument—Deduction and Induction," in *"Perspectives on Argumentation,* ed. Gerald R. Miller and Thomas R. Nilsen (Chicago: Scott, Foresman, 1966), pp. 50–54. This book has much of value to the student interested in the nature of evidence, reasoning, and argument.

For convenience, *acceptance* and *belief* are used to suggest the desired goal in persuasion. This avoids confusion with the restricted use of the term *proof* that some people employ. But it must be realized that whatever the basis for belief, people like to believe that the matter has been demonstrated. Research in cognitive balance suggests that once an attitude is changed, new perceptions and new beliefs will follow to justify attitudinal structure. The process of rationalization, broadly defined as supplying good reasons for what we want, clearly suggests this process. One appeal frequently employed is "Let us be logical." In persuasion there is no real way to know whether it is the logic that persuaded or the use of the logic as an appeal that persuaded or the credibility of the source induced by the use of logic that persuaded.

The communicator seeks to induce belief. An audience may well accept a proposition for reasons that are logical, partially logical, or essentially illogical. If we define proof from the viewpoint of the receiver, proof occurs when something has been demonstrated to his satisfaction (whatever that means). Defined on the basis of message elements, proof results when reason is utilized to move validly from accepted truths to new truths. This, of course, poses problems of determining the accepted truths initially, which seems a receiver-dependent element in much of communication. For example, one may well deal with an accepted body of truths in physics (although some of these may be overturned tomorrow) and thus build from accepted to new truths. But what are the accepted truths about the reasons for poverty, U.S. involvement in Vietnam, or the animosity between Arabs and Israelis in the Middle East?

While this book talks of the forces that induce belief and acceptance and avoids the term *proof* for the most part, we must remember that most people will talk of things being proved to them, although this proof may not meet criteria set forth in an argumentation text or by the philosopher. All of us may face situations in which the proof needed to persuade must meet rigid standards of logical adequacy. In law courts and scientific papers, arguments made to experts in their field of competency need to meet these standards. But in general the persuader is showing the probability of something to a less specialized audience; hence, the demonstrations may be more varied and in the realm of probable rather than total demonstration. A completely rational demonstration may, for a variety of reasons, be impossible.

LOGICAL APPEALS

Appeals to our ability to make rational choices are important aspects of persuasion. The effects that logical appeals produce in persuasion are yet to be fully explored, but consideration of their direct and indirect role is essential. The difficulty of analysis and testing should not limit appreciation of their value. Nor should the tendency of some to worship at the shrine of logic as the only basis on which people should act and then constantly bemoan our failure to do so, thus suggesting we never use logic, cloud our perception of the value of logic analysis and logical appeals as one factor governing action.

Definition

The use of logical appeals is linked to the use of reasoned discourse and the process called *argumentation*. The distinction between argumentation and persuasion is confusing because of the plethora of definitions employed. Argumentation may be best understood as a specialized instance of persuasion. As a species of the genus persuasion, it is distinguished by the degree to which the invitation to reasoned discourse becomes the process by which the "demonstrating" to the receiver is managed. The emotional and ethical appeals become ancillary and less dominant in emphasis. But clearly they still exist and are contributory. Argumentation is a form of discourse that emphasizes the process of reasoning. But this process of reasoning is also used in thinking and appears in most discourse. So the separation of argumentation from the rest of persuasion is based on emphasis. Some critics, with a very narrow view, might find little they would term argumentation in the persuasion in our society; others viewing the matter more broadly might classify large segments of public discourse as argumentation.

The term *logical appeal*, not argumentation, was used as the label for this section. Why? First, because the use of logical appeals is possible in discourse that would not be classified as argumentation by most observers. Furthermore, the use of evidence, with inferences being left to the receiver, and the appearance of empty or invalid logical forms fall within the purview of logical appeals.

Logic should not be allowed to limit the concept of logical appeal unduly. Logic may be defined as "the systematic study of the structure of propositions and of the general conditions of valid inference by a method which abstracts from the content or *matter* of the propositions and deals only with their logical *form*."[4] Logic is concerned with validity, with relationships within a formal structure. In committing oneself to a system of formal language in order to talk about matters of validity, one commits oneself to a system of logical analysis.

Used in the restricted sense of a study of structure, logic becomes the study of formal validity, not truth. But logic is an important tool that we

---

[4] "Logic," *Encyclopaedia Britannica* (1959), 14: 305.

utilize to improve our decision making. Although questions of validity are not a sufficient test of truth, they are an important part. And analysis through such formal structures can often yield understandings that are not readily apparent upon first inspection.

The relationship of truth and validity may be illustrated in two simple syllogisms:

(1)	(2)
All dogs are cats.	Some dogs are cats.
All cats are animals.	All cats are animals.
Thus, all dogs are animals.	Thus, all dogs are animals.

The first syllogism is formally correct. It meets all the requirements established for a categorical syllogism as far as formal validity is concerned. The conclusion is true and so is the second premise; the first premise is untrue. The second syllogism violates the rules of formal validity for the categorical syllogism. Although the conclusion happens to be true, the structure is such that the conclusion is not warranted by the claims made, regardless of the truth of those initial claims. Thus, while formal validity does not guarantee the truth of premises nor does lack of validity guarantee that the conclusion is false, validity tests do enable us to examine the conclusiveness of at least one dimension of the truth claim process.

We use reasoning and powers of observation to yield understanding and knowledge of the world. The relationship between evidence and reasoning is an extremely close one, as will be seen in the discussion of proof.

Evidence is usually defined as the body of available fact and opinion. But both facts and opinion often represent the fruits of a long chain of reasoning built on facts and previous conclusions. No fact, no observation speaks for itself; someone must speak for it. Smoking, particularly cigarette smoking, is injurious to health. But this fact is a conclusion drawn from many other facts and reasoning chains. Indeed, some still protest that it is not a fact.

The room in which I sit is ten feet high. But this fact is not announced by the room. It is announced by me. Do you accept it? If you knew that I simply estimated this as I sat at my typewriter, you might be less sure of the accuracy of the claim. If you thought I obtained it from architectural drawings, you might be more sure that your measurement would agree with mine. But it is my understanding that architects derive room heights on the basis of measures taken from midway between the floor and ceiling of one room and the floor and ceiling of the next. Otherwise, the sum of internal heights of buildings would be several feet shorter than external heights. Further, this is an old building, and a new drop ceiling was installed a few years ago. To prevent injury the old plaster was knocked off the ceiling, leaving bare laths exposed. What is the height of the room? If measured at the east wall of the room, the height is different than at the west wall. Indeed, the height varies along the west wall. Is a statement about the height of this room anything other than a claim for belief?

Clearly any piece of evidence, fact or opinion, or reasoning chain is a claim for belief. It may be accepted and neither source nor receiver may perceive it as a claim for belief, but it is that, at least potentially. In reasoning we move from known or accepted things—whether facts, beliefs, values, world views, or any other form or presupposition—to new known or accepted things. Both the original knowns and the new knowns may be false.

Perhaps now the nature of logical appeal can be meaningfully stated. Logical appeals are involved when the unit of discourse invites acceptance on the basis of a judgment of the demonstration of the reliability and validity and the "truthfulness" of the claim in terms of "reality." In effect, a logical appeal invites the receiver, "Come, reason and examine along with me, judge the claims for belief made, whether in evidence or reasoning." The invitation may not be accepted, or its operation may be more indirect in inducing belief than direct.[5]

When there is a claim for belief, whether through evidence or reasoning, whether overt or covert, whether actual or potential, we approach the requirements for an "argument." In order to examine the junctions at which a belief claim invites or has the potential for challenge, let us examine a Toulminian layout for argument.

Stephen Toulmin's *The Uses of Arguments* provides a schematic layout for the examination of arguments.[6] This is not a new reasoning system or a new logical system, but it is a significant variation on the more traditional schematic devices used for laying out arguments.

The minimum for an argument is a datum that is offered as leading to or yielding some claim. A claim alone is merely an assertion; there is no

---

[5] This is the closest I can come to defining a logical appeal as something in a message. At best it is only potential because the receiver may not treat it as logical or respond to it with any evidence of testing, reasoning, or challenging the demonstration of its probability or correspondence to reality. Remembering that proof is proof to a person as far as persuasion is concerned, a persuader is not, at this juncture, concerned with what a critic or anyone else could cast into a logical scheme and test.

[6] Stephen Toulmin, *The Uses of Argument* (New York: Cambridge University Press, 1958). The introduction and essays I, II, and III are particularly valuable for purposes of this chapter.

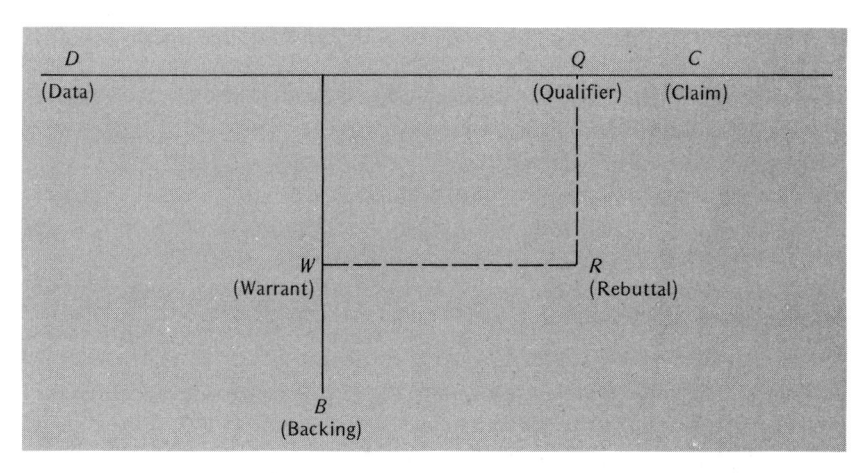

Figure 9. A Toulminian Layout of Argument.

argument until support is offered. The datum may be an observation, the opinion of some individual, any of a variety of things. More than one piece of data may be offered. If in an argument we raise questions about the data, corrections, and the validity of reporting, the data become claims for belief, and a new layout would be constructed with the data taking the place of the claim and new elements supplied to support the claim.

In many instances the attention goes not to the data but to the principle that legitimates the move from data to the claim. Toulmin calls this legitimating element a warrant, since it "warrants" the move from data to claim. An attack may be made on the relationship by arguing that the warrant does not legitimate the move from data to claim.

Since very few things that we deal with in the everyday world are completely universal, Toulmin provides for a qualifier, a force term. This indicates the degree of certainty or probability that the claim has. Although the criteria for determining the qualifier may vary in terms of the field or the problem area in which the argument is operating, the force is invariant in the sense that a good experiment in physics should have the same meaning in terms of qualification as a good experiment in communication.

The qualifier is based upon the rebuttals that can be offered to the claim in terms of specific exceptions or factors that affect the operation of the warrant. These rebuttals suggest the exceptions, restrictions, and cases in which the warrant does not serve to legitimate the move from data to claim.

Finally, the validity of the warrant may be challenged. Backing must then be supplied for the warrant. To see this operation clearly, envision the warrant as the claim with a new system constructed with data, warrant, qualifiers, and so forth. Backing serves a "warrant-establishing" function.

These, then, are the areas that may be questioned concerning an argument: data, warrant, qualifier, rebuttal, backing. As Toulmin notes, if people fail to agree upon some warrant at some point in moving through a series of warrant-establishing activities, no rational assessment of argument is possible. If two people in a disagreement cannot agree on some standard or some presupposition at a warrant level, they will be unable to offer "logical" reasons to one another, although they will have "logical" reasons for their own beliefs.

Form of Logical Appeals

Logical appeals take many forms: evidential claims, reasoning patterns, presentational systems. The following is not an exhaustive enumeration of the forms they may take, but it suggests the variety and nature of logical appeals.

Evidence

Whether fact or opinion, evidence constitutes one form in which a logical appeal may be made. The specification of the exact cost per square inch, meticulous documentation of material, validation of the source as expert, clarification of the procedures in observation, and reinforcement of the evidence by providing several sources all saying the same thing are illustrations of the logical appeals made by presenting evidence. "Here are the facts," "This is a knowledgeable expert who knows" are logical appeals. Clearly these have appeal beyond the directly logical and may not even have impact as logical appeals.

We are more accustomed to thinking of chains of reasoning that the speaker constructs or quotes from others as being logical appeals. These chains may be a mixture of reasoning patterns.

Deduction

The movement from a generalization to application in a specific case is a basic reasoning pattern. In some instances the generalization may be developed and supported in an earlier part of the communication and later utilized as the basis for application. Or the basic generalization may be assumed as supplied by the audience and the conclusion drawn. For example, "No wonder he is a juvenile delinquent; look at the home he comes from. The poor kid didn't have a chance." In this case the receiver supplies the generalization that bad homes produce juvenile delinquents.

Syllogisms, an important tool for the analysis of deduction, focus upon "allness" terms: all, none; either, or; if, then. The majority of arguments that utilize deductions are more likely to deal with generalizations at a variety of levels of probability or universality than with absolute certainty. Aristotle made enthymemes—which deal with probabilities rather than certainties—the key to persuasion.

Induction
Whereas deduction moves from the general to the specific, the inductive pattern moves from specifics to formulation of a generalization. This, then, is a process in which individual cases are investigated, analyzed, and enumerated to establish some generalization. This is the method of scientific investigation.

Analogy
Analogy is based upon the assumption that two things that are alike in certain key aspects will be alike in other respects not known. The tests of analogy depend upon the degrees of similarity and the degree to which the things unknown are likely to be linked to known patterns. Analogy is also a form of exposition used in making material clear and vivid. Thus, analogical forms may or may not be essentially logical appeals. The form may vary little; in fact, it may clarify for some receivers while functioning as a reasoning pattern for others. Many of the guilt-by-association techniques and propagandistic techniques use analogy, metaphors, or similes as logical appeals.

Sign
Sign reasoning is essentially reasoning by correlation. "That lightning is very close; the thunder will wake the baby," is a sample of sign reasoning involving a two-step correlation.

Authority
Many writers urge that argument from authority is not a reasoning process. Whatever the answer, offering authorities as support is clearly within the realm of logical appeals. Many people do accept the judgment of others—experts, friends, or majority of a group—as offering a logical reason for belief. In arguing one side or the other, writers and speakers often evaluate the qualifications of the authorities and then argue that one side or the other is correct because an authority supported it.

Causal

Causal arguments are based upon the assumption of a cause-and-effect world. For every event there are one or more causes; for every cause there may be one or more effects. Reasoning chains may move from cause to effect, from effect to cause, or in an extended chain of cause to effect, which in turn causes another effect, which in turn causes another effect, and so forth.

If demonstrated, causal arguments are a kind of ultimate argument to many people since deduction, induction, sign, analogy, and even authority are ultimately dependent upon either definition or the causal nature of the real world in yielding valid inferences. With mathematical systems and other formally valid systems, causal reasoning is not significant. Thus 1 plus 1 equals 2 because we define it to do so. But it is the assumptions of cause and effect and the regularity of the world that are basic to reasoning about the "real world."

The next group of items is essentially patterns of presentation but they have impact as logical appeals.

Method of Residues

There are a number of variations of this approach, but all follow the pattern of creating a number of alternatives and then working through to leave only one remaining possibility. The person who finds alternatives other than those originally listed by the source may not be strongly convinced by this procedure. The dilemma and trilemma are specific instances of this approach. Establishing straw men and then destroying them with vigor and vehemence is an old technique. Despite the ethical implications, it can be a powerful appeal.

Problem-Solution

This is classified as a pattern of logical appeal since it normally demonstrates that a problem exists, gives some analysis of the problem, and then accepts or rejects solutions in terms of this analysis.

Two-sided Presentation

The willingness to consider both sides operates as a logical appeal. The appearance of candor is also an added appeal, but the very act of appearing to refute the opposing arguments by their mention has dimensions of logical appeal.

Effect of Logical Appeals

Experimental studies have generally not examined the question of the degree to which logical appeals are or are not persuasive. Rather, the studies have compared the efficacy of logical proofs with other types of appeals, particularly emotional ones.

In summarizing seven experiments on emotional and logical speeches and speaking, Paulson found no clear pattern. In three instances the differences were nonsignificant; contradictory findings emerged in other studies.[7] Certainly these studies provide no basis for the assumption that logical appeals are more powerful sources of persuasion than other forms of appeal.

In a particularly interesting field study, Hartmann found that emotional leaflets were more effective in winning votes than were rational leaflets. But the rational leaflets won adherents, since people who received them gave more votes to the party in question than did those who received no leaflets at all.[8]

Studies face the problem of operationalizing "rational" or "logical" and "emotional" appeals. How does one assure that the logic or emotion is safely independent of a tinge of the alternative appeal? Further, how does one assure that the appeals, although qualitatively different, are of the same quantitative impact? One should not compare a bad logical speech with a good emotional speech and then declare emotion is more powerful than logic in persuasion.

Evidence and Documentation

The adequacy, quality, and degree of documentation of evidence is a factor related to logical proof. Cathcart found in a survey that audiences believed a speaker should present evidence. His study, which used four forms of a speech, found that one form that supported assertions but did not document evidence and one that supported assertions and documented and qualified the sources were significantly more effective than a form that contained only assertions. But the form that supported assertions and documented the source without qualification as expert was not significantly more effective.[9]

Smith found that merely labeling statements alternatively as fact or rumor affected the acceptability of the statement. This acceptability was also limited by other factors such as degree of initial plausibility.[10]

---

[7] Stanley F. Paulson, "Social Values and Experimental Research in Speech," *Western Speech* 26 (1962): 133–39.

[8] George W. Hartmann, "A Field Experiment on the Comparative Effectiveness of 'Emotional' and 'Rational' Political Leaflets in Determining Election Results," *Journal of Abnormal and Social Psychology* 31 (1936–37): 99–114.

[9] Robert S. Cathcart, "An Experimental Study of the Relative Effectiveness of Four Methods of Presenting Evidence," *Speech Monographs* 22 (1955): 227–33.

[10] George H. Smith, "Belief in Statements Labeled Fact and Rumor," *Journal of Abnormal and Social Psychology* 42 (1947): 80–90.

In a study of evidence Dresser found that quality of evidence did not significantly influence attitudes and that listeners tended not to perceive weaknesses in evidence.[11]

Perceptions of Valid Logic

Studies in psychology reveal that the judgment of the validity of logical patterns is influenced by factors other than formal validity or truthfulness.

Morgan and Morton tested students in an identification of syllogisms. They concluded that a person is likely to accept a conclusion that expresses his or her conviction with little regard to the validity of the inferences involved.[12] Similarly Lefford concluded that attitudes, beliefs, and feelings influence reasoning in the direction of the convictions.[13] Shenfield found that people characterized by tolerant or intolerant attitudes tend to distort the validity of syllogisms, at least in some topic areas, in the direction of their biases.[14] Of course there are studies that indicate that attitudes and values do not necessarily influence ability in reasoning.

Clearly, then, an individual's logical reasoning abilities, even dealing with something as structured as formal syllogisms, are influenced by factors such as emotions, attitudes, and set. And it must be stressed that in these instances the people believed they were completing the assigned task; finding correct and proper logical inferences. Thus the materials yielded proof to them.

Two-sided Presentations

The most researched area of investigation in logical appeals is the matter of one-sided versus two-sided presentation.

The seminal study in this area is that of Hovland, Lumsdaine, and Sheffield.[15] Their study tested the effectiveness of one versus both sides

---

[11] William R. Dresser, "Effects of 'Satisfactory' and 'Unsatisfactory' Evidence in a Speech of Advocacy," *Speech Monographs* 30 (1963): 302–306. A host of experimental studies has failed to demonstrate the value of evidence inclusion. See James C McCroskey, "A Summary of Experimental Research on the Effects of Evidence in Persuasive Communication," *Quarterly Journal of Speech* 55 (1969): 169–76.

[12] J. Morgan and J. Morton, "The Distortion of Syllogistic Reasoning Produced by Personal Convictions, *Journal of Social Psychology* 20 (1944): 39–59.

[13] Arthur Lefford, "The Influence of Emotional Subject Matter on Logical Reasoning," *Journal of General Psychology* 34 (1946): 127–51.

[14] Nathan Shenfield, "Tolerant and Intolerant Attitudes and Logical Thinking," *Dissertations Abstracts* 18 (1958): 2240; also see Donald L. Thistlewaite, "Attitude and Structure as Factors in the Distortion of Reasoning," *Journal of Abnormal and Social Psychology* 65 (1950): 14–25.

[15] Carl I. Hovland, Arthur A. Lumsdaine, and Fred D. Sheffield, "The Effects of Presenting 'One Side' Versus 'Both Sides' in Changing Opinions on a Controversial

presentation when the weight of evidence supported the main thesis. Presenting both sides was significantly more effective for members of the audience with more than a high school diploma. The one-side presentation was significantly more effective for those with less than a high school education and for those who favored the side presented.

Later research on sidedness has been limited to audiences with less variability than those used in the above study. Paulson found no difference in opinion shifts resulting from speeches in which the opposing side was barely mentioned versus those in which it was not mentioned.[16] Shanck and Goodman found no difference in effectiveness.[17]

Hovland, Lumsdaine, and Sheffield noted that omission of an argument that a person knew and favored was particularly detrimental to persuasion in the both-sides version. The failure to do more than mention opposing arguments may account for findings such as those of Paulson. This suggests that two-sided presentations demand at least the appearance of a rebuttal.

Strategy in Use of Logical Appeals

The studies on logical appeals are too incomplete to provide a complete theory on which to base strategy and tactics. However, the following generalizations seem warranted as basic guidelines for strategy and tactics (although specific circumstances might dictate sharp deviation from these indications):

> 1. Audiences expect the use of evidence and logical appeals in situations that they identify as formal attempts at influence. When audiences are set for the appearance of logical materials, the apparent use of such materials seems essential to avoid some degree of negative response.
> 2. Some receivers tend to be relatively open to information and reasoning materials and are likely to be influenced by them. Others (close-minded) seem less influenced by information and reasoning and are more effectively reached by other appeals or by authority citations.
> 3. Situations exist that call for a maximum of logical appeals. This

---

Subject," *Readings in Social Psychology* (New York: Henry Holt, 1947), pp. 566–77. The material under the same title appears as chapter 8 by the same authors in *Experiments on Mass Communication* (Princeton: Princeton University Press, 1949), pp. 201–27.

[16] Stanley Paulson, "Experimental Study of Spoken Communications: The Effects of Prestige of the Speaker and Acknowledgement of Opposing Arguments on Audience Retention and Shift of Opinion," *Speech Monographs* 21 (1954): 267–71.

[17] C. Shanck and Charles Goodman, "Reactions to Propaganda on Both Sides of a Controversial Issue," *Public Opinion Quarterly* 3 (1930): 107–12.

seems to be true of certain settings—experts presenting a truth claim to other experts, lawyers arguing before the Supreme Court, the content of a treatise in a scientific journal.

4. Since people typically desire to appear logical, the presence of logic is often seen as a mark of respect to them and serves as a motivational appeal apart from any logical impact.

5. Logical proofs may significantly enhance the credibility of a source.

6. Evidence and documentation can improve persuasiveness as contrasted to repeated assertions without support.

7. Evidence may be particularly useful in enhancing the persuasiveness of a message whose source is seen as not having much prestige.

8. Logical appeals may not be perceived as such by receivers.

9. Receivers often, but not always, judge validity and acceptability of logical appeals at least in part in terms of prior set, attitudes, and convictions.

10. Two-sided presentations seem warranted when dealing with hostile audiences, with relatively well-educated groups, and probably when dealing with persons more interested in the topic or with greater information on the topic.

11. Logical proofs are not necessarily more effective than emotional or ethical appeals, but often they are as effective and in some instances may be more effective.

12. Logical appeals are likely to have a high degree of acceptance for friendly audiences. (a) They may make a friendly audience more resistant to counterpersuasion. (b) They may provide them with arguments to use on others, thus spreading impact. (c) Often a friendly audience is seeking to rationalize, to find good reasons for that which they already believe; thus, they seek logical support for their position.

13. A hostile audience may respond favorably to logical appeals. (a) Both sides' presentations may be effective. (b) A sleeper effect may occur in which evidence and lines of argument are retained and over time may affect the attitude in question.

14. Audiences need to be motivated to use logic and to make the effort necessary to make a rational choice.

Ultimately the persuader may ask, "Why use logical appeals? Why not just hit them with a sure-fire emotional appeal and be done with it?" The most important answer is that logic can be effective; indeed, in certain instances it is the most effective means to persuasion. Emotional appeals are no more sure-fire than logical ones. In some instances emotional appeals, and certainly badly chosen ones, could be disastrous to the persuader. Normally the most effective persuasion will demand a fusion of various appeals.

Another answer lies in an ethical dimension. While people may be motivated to act for a variety of reasons, many communicators wish to offer the receivers a reason for belief, a ground for action. Although the communicator cannot offer all the reasons for belief because of limitations, such as time, understanding of the receivers, or interest, he can offer some. Logic and reasoning are useful tools for making the correct decision. Perhaps the ability to make informed choices must grow with use. Politicians who give the voter no basis on which to make a rational choice have not served the voter or their country in the long run. Many people accept the philosophy that an individual given the information and the alternatives will make sound choices.

Although it has not been fully demonstrated, logical appeals seem to have a more lasting effect than emotional and ethical appeals. Logical materials also make a person more resistant to counterpersuasion. The heightened effects of emotion wear off, but the information and conclusions presented as logical appeals are often retained, and acceptance may even grow over time.

In the use of logical appeals three cautions regarding strategy should be offered. Reasoning, making hard choices, and weighing alternatives are work. We must be motivated to work; therefore, we will make the effort only if motivated to do so. Either we must be motivated by the communication or the material must be linked to active motivational forces that the receiver brings to the communication. To succeed, the persuader must motivate attention, comprehension, and acceptance.

The second caution is that the evidence, reasoning, and logical appeals must be directed to the receiver. Many communicators do an excellent job of showing why they personally believe or accept the proposition, but they fail to show why the receivers should believe or accept it. The communicator must identify evidence and reasoning with the frame of reference of the receiver. To show why I benefit from your buying a set of dishes is not to show why you benefit. A communicator will want to assure herself that she can justify that which she recommends, but she must demonstrate to others that they too should accept the conclusion. This is the goal of communication and not (basically, at least) self-persuasion.

The third caution is linked to the second. A communicator cannot build a complete logical system in five, ten, or five hundred minutes of communication. She must omit some steps in the process and most of the available evidence in the face of realities of time and interest. Therefore, the communicator must select among the available appeals. This means she will usually supply what is needed and utilize the beliefs, the presuppositions, and assumptions of the audience to supply the pieces. Most persuasive communications are not exercises in logical demonstration. Thus, the communicator seeks the delicate balance between too much and too little logical appeal and the most effective choices to use.

MOTIVATIONAL APPEALS

The term *motivational appeals* is linked to the classical term *pathos,* although contemporary sources would tend to use *emotional appeals* as the rubric.

Definition

Motivational appeals are stimuli designed to create a tension, to elicit a feeling or affective response from a receiver. Motivational appeals are directed to the wishes, wants, desires, goals, and needs of the person. These needs and wants are not necessarily logical, or necessarily illogical; rather, they exist either as the result of inherent predispositions or the conditioning of the self by the society and one's experiences. Appeals to emotions are clearly one part of this area of motivational appeals.

Without making the distinction sharper than it is, motivational appeals may be contrasted to logical appeals. Logical appeals essentially present the situation, the alternatives, the set of probabilities. Motivational appeals present how we want it to be, feel it to be. One function of logical appeals is to serve as the means through which we can choose among alternatives in satisfying wishes and the goals that motivate us.

The chapter on motivation discussed the forces that direct and channel human behavior. Now we must consider the way in which message elements tap these forces for persuasive ends.

Form of Motivational Appeals

Motivational appeals can be classified in terms of many dichotomies: overt versus covert, altruistic versus base, pleasure versus pain, strong versus weak, reward versus punishment, natural versus learned, direct versus indirect. For purposes of examination let us treat motivational appeals as engendering approach or avoidance behavior. Some goals, objects, or wants are things we seek to approach. We seek to obtain them, to continue them. In contrast, other things are marked by avoidance: we avoid punishment; we plan to avoid hunger; we use deodorant to avoid "B.O." Avoidance is associated in a real sense with fear. Those things we fear serve as negative goals.

Motivational appeals may be manifested in almost any aspect of a communication. The elements of setting may well contribute. Contrast the situation when Franklin D. Roosevelt delivered his declaration of war message to Congress after Pearl Harbor with that of Woodrow Wilson asking a very divided Congress and nation for a declaration of war. A church, a funeral, a wedding—all have emotional overtones that few can ignore.

The topic itself and the materials used in developing the topic contain strong opportunities for motivational appeal. The language and style may have strong impact. The manner of delivery, particularly in oral media with the voice and visual elements, may create strong emotion. Even the source may create great emotion. Douglas MacArthur's "Old Soldiers Never Die" speech to Congress created an immediate impact that is lost upon those who read the speech today.

In essence, motivational appeals are potential in almost any factor of the communication process. This potential impact becomes realized only in terms of how and to what the receivers respond. In some ways the diversity of response to motivational appeals is greater than that to logical appeals.

Effect of Motivational Appeals

The power of motivation was described in chapter 3. Since behavior is determined by motivational factors and since motivational appeals are designed to stir up, create, or tap these motivational forces, these appeals can have strong impact. The research cited on the relationship of logical versus emotional appeals suggests that emotional appeals can be as powerful as and at times more powerful than logical appeals.

Avoidance Motivation

The tension aroused in many situations is one of avoidance. We may become frustrated in trying to obtain a desired goal. Initially we may respond with greater efforts to reach our goal, but if the frustration persists our behavior becomes less adaptive and we may revert to earlier patterns that are rigid and nonadaptive. In certain instances we may abandon the goal entirely to avoid the frustration. The strength of the tendency to retreat and to resist rises sharply as we approach the negative goal we are trying to avoid.

Repressed motives may well be attributed to others. This may explain a good deal of the projection tendency of certain people to see all manner of evil that others do not perceive in the communicator and communication of such programs as sex education.

The tension associated with avoidance responses may be described under a number of terms. A typical one used in communication research is fear. The most quoted study in the area of fear appeals in communication is by Janis and Feshback.[18] Working with high school students and the topic of tooth decay, the researchers found low fear appeals to be more persuasive. Apparently the high fear produced an avoidance response that negated the persuasive effort. The higher the degree of fear, the greater the anxiety produced in the subjects. When anxiety exceeds a certain level, apparently a defensive avoidance reaction negates the effect of the communication.[19]

These initial studies have been supplemented and quantified by the work of later researchers. Hewgill and Miller found that a high credibility source can use strong fear appeals successfully.[20] Goldstein found that acceptance of fear appeals varies with personality types. "Copers"—those who related to and recognized their own needs and emotions—were contrasted to "avoiders"—those who failed to recognize personal implications in sexual and aggressive sentence items. The copers were able to handle stronger levels of fear appeals while minimal fear appeals received greater acceptance among the avoiders.[21]

Colburn found that the persuasive effect of fear appeals is a function of the relationship between level of fear and importance of the topic.[22] As the importance of the topic as judged by receivers increases, the level of fear-arousing materials may also be increased to achieve higher levels of persuasion.

In summarizing research on fear, Leventhal reported that increases in fear generally increase persuasion, but there are obviously circumstances in which this is not so. If a person feels inadequate to cope with the danger, fear appeals are often not persuasive. A variety of complex internal and external factors relate to the impact of fear appears.[23]

---

[18] Irving L. Janis and Seymour Feshback, "Effects of Fear-Arousing Communications," *The Journal of Abnormal and Social Psychology* 47 (1953): 78–92.

[19] David Haeffner, "Some Effects of Guilt-Arousing and Fear-Arousing Persuasive Communications on Opinion Change (Ph.D. diss., University of Rochester, 1956); Irving L. Janis and Robert F. Terwilliger, "An Experimental Study of Psychological Resistance to Fear-Arousing Communications," *The Journal of Abnormal and Social Psychology* 65 (1962): 403–10.

[20] Murray A. Hewgill and Gerald R. Miller, "Source Credibility and Response to Fear-Arousing Communications," *Speech Monographs* 32 (1965): 95.

[21] Michael J. Goldstein, "The Relationship Between Coping and Avoiding Behavior and Response to Fear-Arousing Propaganda," *The Journal of Abnormal and Social Psychology* 59 (1959): 252.

[22] William Colburn, "Fear Arousing Appeals," in *Speech Communication*, eds. Howard H. Martin and Kenneth E. Andersen (Boston: Allyn and Bacon, 1968), pp. 214–23.

[23] Howard Leventhal, "Findings and Theory in the Study of Fear Communications," in *Advances in Experimental Social Psychology*, ed. Leonard Berkowitz (1970), 5: 120–86.

Approach Motivation

The role of approach or reward appeals has not been investigated intensively in terms of persuasion. Common sense suggests that people do work for rewards. Learning theory has repeatedly validated the positive effects of reward. Studies of goal-directed behavior in small groups clearly indicate the power of approach motivations.

The paucity of approach motivation research in persuasive settings is probable because of the very real difficulty in operationalizing the variable. Deprivation can be measured in terms of time. But striving toward long-range goals or toward altruistic ends poses greater problems in quantification.

The person who doubts the strength of approach motivations need only examine the commitment some people make to long-range goals. Parents naturally and healthily give up personal freedom and a measure of economic freedom to enjoy children. People willingly risk their lives for purposes beyond their own gratifications.

Strategy in Use

Motivational appeals are one of the most important areas of decision in persuasion strategy. Since attention, comprehension, and acceptance must be motivated, either the receiver must bring sufficient motivations to the communication situation or these motivations must be aroused or created by forces operative in the communication situation.

1. Communicators cannot assume that receivers bring with them the motivational forces necessary to insure attention, comprehension, or acceptance. In fact, receivers' motivations may frequently be contradictory to those necessary for accomplishing the persuader's purpose. They are for the most part simply irrelevant to the persuader's task.
2. All elements in the communication process have a potential for motivational impact. To the degree that the communicator can manipulate these elements, the potential impact may be heightened. This may range from manipulation of the setting to efforts to heighten suggestivity by audience participation and interaction.
3. There may be motivational forces that are not manifested in overt or emotional responses.
4. Motivational appeals should be proportional to the worth of the idea and the importance of the issue. Research in fear appeals shows that the level of fear should be proportional to the significance of the topic. The same appears to hold for reward approaches. Excessive and unwarranted appeals can prove sharply counterproduc-

tive. Indeed, an excess of emotional response can be sharply disruptive to the communicator's purposes.

5. Motivational forces affect attention and perception.

6. Motivational appeals can be relatively overt with friendly audiences. (a) A friendly audience is favorably disposed toward the topic and purpose and may share many of the motivations of the communicator. (b) Many friendly audiences need vitalization, restimulation, and the motivation to turn mental assent or belief into overt action. This can demand strong motivational appeals. (c) Group facilitation and group identification are useful techniques with the friendly audience.

7. Motivational appeals should generally be more covert with hostile audiences. (a) Since motivation is the key to human activity, the hostile audience must be motivated. (b) Being hostile, the audience may be particularly prepared to reject the excess of emotion, the blatant appeal. These audiences can be very sensitive in detecting such appeals. (c) With hostile audiences motivational appeals may need to seek common ground and common referential points from which the communicator and communicatees can operate.

8. Some settings justify a level of motivational appeal that other settings will not permit.

9. The concept of appropriateness seems particularly relevant to decisions in the use of motivational appeals. This also provides guidelines for questions in style, delivery, or materials selected.

10. Different cultures and subcultures have different standards concerning the proper kind and degree of emotional and motivational factors.

11. Motivational appeals should normally be blended with logical ones so that the two reinforce one another and so the motivational appeals do not seem tacked on. To the degree that motivational appeals appear intrinsic to the material, they tend to be more effective.

12. Consonant and mutually reinforcing motivational appeals seem more effective than appeals that "shotgun" the entire range of possible appeals. Subsidiary appeals should be used that reinforce the dominant appeal.

13. Motivational appeals need to be distributed throughout the communication rather than concentrated solely in the opening. However, motivational appeals should be emphasized early in the communication.

USE OF DATA

Claims or assertions form the major headings of a speech. Research suggests that it is the major headings and major ideas that are retained both on an immediate and on a delayed basis. Belief and acceptance of these headings is determined by the support offered. One does not simply make a logical or an emotional appeal. One must largely develop it out of materials used to support and develop the assertions although the assertions may contain some degree of appeal per se. To illustrate how supporting materials function to yield appeals, let us briefly examine the ways in which material can be presented.

To Clarify

One important function of supporting material is to clarify the meaning of the communicator. Three forms of support serve primarily this function.

Explanation

Explanation is probably the most used support form. An effective means of increasing understanding is to explain: tell how something works, tell what happened, tell the sequential procedure to be followed. Explanation serves the function of "telling it like it is," and it seems to suggest less bias by the "reporter" than some other support forms.

One particularly useful form of explanation is definition. You can attempt to deal in that which you wish to include and deal out that which you wish to exclude. A receiver who does not understand what is being communicated is unlikely to accept it. When he and the communicator are operating with different frames of reference, communication must be impaired. Definitions through restatement, context, or illustration may clarify without appearing to tell the receiver what he presumably ought to know.

Comparison and Contrast

Analogy is one form of reasoning. But comparisons and contrasts (analogies) also make things distinct. The metaphor, the simile, and other techniques gain much of their impact through analogy. Sharp differentiation between two things, even relatively similar things, can be obtained through the use of contrast. Contrast offers the opportunity for a subtle and not so subtle polarization of audiences by magnifying differences and sharpening antagonisms. Stress upon similarities may be used to reverse the process and yield identification.

Some comparisons and contrasts are literal and direct in a one-to-one sense and yield a greater sense of proof. Other analogies are hypothetical and yield more of their impact in terms of humor, appeal, suggestiveness, intensity.

Illustrations

Illustrations are relatively developed or extended examples. As such they provide maximum opportunity to use many of the factors of attention: reality, proximity, the vital, humor. Illustrations are particularly effective means of developing motivational appeals. For these reasons illustrations are often used to introduce material. Statistics and other generalizations are frequently coupled with illustrations to heighten impact.

Making a point clearer and increasing the impact serve to prove in a very real sense. So, to the degree that materials are emotionally powerful and maximize comprehension, they do contribute to belief.

To Prove

Although the following forms of support also clarify and increase impact, their major function is to obtain belief for the assertion by providing support for an argument.

Specific Instances

Specific instances are relatively undeveloped examples. They are often used to achieve the effect of piling up data by suggesting that one case is not an isolated example but is representative and typical. Thus, specific instances are often coupled with an illustration as a basis for induction.

Specific instances are often used as a means of reinforcement. Instance piled upon instance seems to become overpowering in the absence of negative instances. This technique is often employed in the propaganda technique of building the "yes-yes" response.

Statistics

Statistics are mathematical summations or condensations of one or more characteristics of possible examples. Counting all the people who died of cancer in the United States last year will yield a descriptive statistic. A statistic can be used to compare the percentage of deaths caused by cancer versus highway accidents. Statistics are also used in far more elaborate ways, for example, to test for the significance of experimental findings or as summations of complex data gathered through elaborate sampling procedures and extrapolated to describe American public opinion.

Statistics are extremely useful, for they offer great power in their capacity to summarize and to yield strong predictions. But they can also conceal and mislead. They are only as valid as the methodology used in deriving them and their interpretation within the limits which that methodology sets for inductions derived from them. Many communicators, deliberately or not, distort the statistic that was validly derived by claiming it proves something that it does not.

Statistics seem to have persuasive appeal to many people, perhaps because people assume that one cannot argue with figures, that it is difficult to assess the validity of many statistical claims, or because they sense the precision that appeals to the myth of "science knows." Whatever the basis, statistics seem to have a unique appeal. Some people will accept a conclusion simply because of the appearance of statistical data even if the data are not significantly related to the conclusion.

Testimony

Statements by people, expert or lay, or the personal testimony of the source can have high probative value. These authorities present their claim in any of the forms suggested above, as well as in blanket assertions. Thus, a unit of material may be both an authoritative opinion and a statistical claim coupled with an illustration to suggest the importance of the statistic.

The role of testimony as a support for belief on the basis of the authority making the claim is discussed in section V. Sometimes testimony is used for the claim for belief contained within the material cited; at other times it is used for the probative value of the person offering the testimony. In many instances both elements contribute to the proof offered by the testimony.

To Improve Retention

Two final forms of presenting material seem largely designed to maximize retention although they serve functions of clarification and proof as well.

Repetition and Restatement

Repetition involves repeating material exactly as originally stated. Restatement means a degree of alteration but with the same essential point being made. The value of these techniques has already been suggested in the treatment of learning theory. Certainly we are all familiar with the use advertising makes of this technique. Repetition and restatement characterize summaries, transitions, and conclusions. Their demonstrated importance further substantiates the value of these procedures.

Restatement appears to be an effective technique to encourage generalization of learning and appeals to an informed and intelligent audience who might resent repetition. Alternatively, repetition seems warranted for less-informed or less-intelligent audiences. In some instances the technique of repetition is deliberately used to arouse irritation—to so saturate the person that he or she must respond.

Supplemental Media Aids

This method of presenting material is not distinct from those discussed above. Rather, media aids are involved when material is transformed in some way from its original form into a new one. Most of us are familiar with audiovisual aids. Statistics can be presented in the form of a graph or other visual display. Sound can be used to supplement or reinforce the visual, which itself can be used to supplement sound. Working models can be employed as a means of demonstration. Various training procedures incorporate a series of interrelated audio and visual elements together with practice.

Although we tend to think of support materials as appealing to either the sense of sight and/or sound, this is clearly too limited. For example, printed advertisements can incorporate three-dimensional effects. Materials to be touched and felt may be included. Perfumes are advertised with special inserts that when scratched release the perfume scent. Thus, the advertiser has available a wide range of supplementary media aids (at some expense) beyond the visual associated with printed advertising.

Commercial persuaders appear to be making greater use of these supplemental media aids. The popularity of multimedia presentations in entertainment and in educational settings suggests the potential of these aids. The potential of multimedia presentations in persuasion has only begun to be explored.

Although the above forms for presenting supporting material are not mutually exclusive, the categories suggest ways in which material can be presented with consequent effects upon persuasiveness. Failure to exploit the variety of support forms available may detract from attention levels (because of a lack of variety) and from persuasiveness, in that each form has limitations as well as strengths. A variety of well-chosen support forms is often conducive to greater persuasiveness.

INTERRELATIONSHIP OF METHODS OF YIELDING PROOF

A historic tendency in the analysis of communication has been to categorize stimuli in mutually exclusive categories. For example, in such a taxonomy an item might be considered a factor of attention or a motivational appeal, or an attempt at establishing source credibility but not as serving all of these functions at the same time. This tendency to label stimuli in separate, mutually exclusive categories is clearly seen in the treatment of logical and emotional appeals under the rubrics of conviction and persuasion.

The application of this approach and the indication of its weakness are illustrated in a study by Ruechelle. [24] Ruechelle asked students, adults with no background in speech, and speech teachers to rate both the degree of emotional appeal and the degree of intellectual appeal in short, two-minute speeches. He found that the speeches could not be separated as emotional or intellectual; different individuals responded differently to similar materials. Further, the expert speech teachers were little better able to differentiate consistently than were the adult and student raters. Ruechelle was working with complete short speeches, fairly large units of materials. Different results might have been obtained if he had used shorter units of materials, such as sentences or paragraphs.

Closely linked to the view that various proofs can be classified in separate categories is the attempt to place them on a continuum. As applied to the relationship of motivational and logical appeals, this suggests that as the degree of logical appeal increases, the motivational appeal decreases. The continuum method seems to yield no significant improvement over the complete separation in different categories. (See figure 10A.)

A better representation in terms of the two dimensions would be to treat them as separate, independent dimensions. Thus, the degree of logical appeal is evaluated on one dimension and the degree of motivational appeal on another, with the unit of material being evaluated plotted in the proper position in terms of these two reference axes. As figure 10B suggests, good persuasive speeches are rarely completely emotional or completely logical; the most effective speeches probably manifest a high degree of appeal in terms of both dimensions.

But the treatment in figure 10B is restricted to only two dimensions and does not suggest the interaction of the two dimensions. Units of material may involve effects in terms of more than these two dimensions. A more effective representation would be a matrix of factor loadings. As represented in figure 10C, the various mediational factors that affect persuasion (such as attention, comprehension, and belief) are listed, and stimuli are evaluated in terms of the impact they have. To complete the matrix with numerical values is impossible in the abstract and exceeds the level of present knowledge in actual communication. But reasonable inferences of weight can be drawn. The approach represents a useful solution to the problem of representing the various forces without distorting beyond reason the relationship of stimuli to these factors.

Analysis of a message according to the pattern suggested in figure 10C involves both the identification of mediational factors through which

---

[24] Randall C. Ruechelle, "An Experimental Study of Audience Recognition of Emotional and Intellectual Appeals in Persuasion," *Speech Monographs* 25 (1958): 49–58.

164 CREATION OF MESSAGES

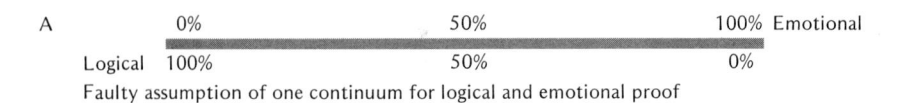

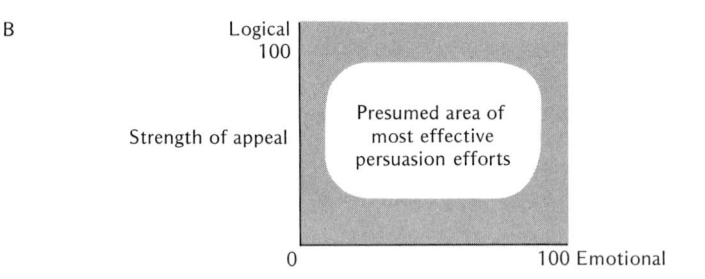

A 0% 50% 100% Emotional
Logical 100% 50% 0%
Faulty assumption of one continuum for logical and emotional proof

B Logical 100
Strength of appeal — Presumed area of most effective persuasion efforts
0   100 Emotional

An improved view: A two dimensional representation

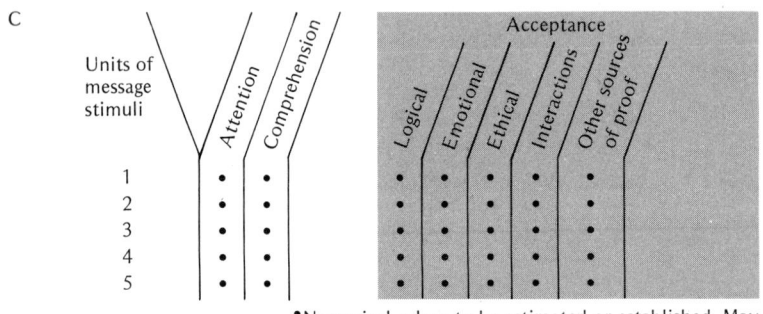

C Units of message stimuli / Attention / Comprehension / Acceptance (Logical, Emotional, Ethical, Interactions, Other sources of proof)

1
2
3
4
5

*Numerical values to be estimated or established. May be positive or negative as well as zero weight.

A more comprehensive multidimension representation utilizing a matrix

Figure 10. Representations of Methods of Proof.

messages create effects and the identification of the impact of given units of stimuli in terms of these factors. A complete analysis would include not only the content of the message, factors related to organization, language and style, and delivery, but also factors outside the message.

In large part we have talked about stimuli in terms of the direct effect produced. That is, we have discussed the degree of logical appeal or motivational appeal that units of discourse contain. But, in addition to these direct appeals, stimuli interact in producing effects and serve mediational or facilitating functions one for the other to yield effects. A high level of motivational appeal might not be acceptable unless it came from a highly creditable source. Accurate data being reported may not be given attention unless the degree of motivation is high enough to command attention. Thus, the data may prove only if the motivational appeal is sufficient to cause them to be heard.

A communication is validly treated as a gestalt. The totality of the communication is more than the individual units added together. The totality of effect involves complex interactions and interrelationships—the direct effects, the interactive effects, the facilitating effects.

Despite the complexity of this approach, it is a valid one at this stage in the development of the field of persuasion. Through this approach, as applied in terms of analysis of response of an individual or the average response of individuals, the following points are recognized:

1. The same stimulus produces different effects with different people at the same time.
2. The same stimulus produces different effects with the same person at different times.
3. Response to stimuli is complex and multiple, not singular and univariate.
4. Stimuli may have direct effects; they also interact with other stimuli to produce effects.
5. Stimuli may serve a facilitation function, making possible an effect by other stimuli. However, the stimuli cannot produce the effect directly by themselves, as the effect is not possible without the presence of the facilitating stimuli.
6. Stimuli should be evaluated in terms of the multiple impact they may have rather than in separate, distinct categories.

SUMMARY

The message is a complex of stimuli consciously and unconsciously placed by a source in a channel or channels to be picked up by receivers. Messages occupy central attention in persuasion because they are the element in the communication process that is most under control of the source. The message that the source frames provides his maximum control over what stimuli will be brought to the receivers.

It is valuable for analysis to separate the various processes that occur in persuasion, the various elements that are involved, and the various ways in which messages operate to produce effects. But in so doing we must remember that the effect is ultimately a gestalt result of the totality of these forces operating in direct and interactive ways to produce effects within the communication-binding context.

Logical appeals are powerful forces in persuasion. But logic alone is rarely sufficient to yield persuasion. Nor is the logic that proves to individual receivers necessarily valid when tested according to traditional patterns of analysis. Desires and wishes of receivers affect and determine what they accept as logical demonstration. Thus it is possible for one person to report she is convinced by the logic while another person remains horrified at the lack of logical structure.

Motivational appeals are directed to the person's wishes and wants, either utilizing those in existence or creating ones to be utilized. Typically the persuader utilizes motivational forces already extant, although perhaps latent, rather than trying to create new sources. The latter normally takes an extended period of time and extensive resources in terms of contact, manipulation of stimuli, and money.

Although separated for analytical purposes, logical and motivational appeals are interlinked in achieving effects in persuasion. Seldom is one or the other operating alone sufficient.

This chapter has been concerned with the two major sources of proof—reasons for a person's feeling something to have been demonstrated—but other elements remain to be considered. Matters of organization, language and style, and delivery are integrally related to these appeals. Indeed, a logical or an emotional appeal must be placed in some order; it must be worded; it must be delivered into the channel. These appeals do not exist except in terms of these elements that remain to be discussed. Further, these reasons for proof are linked to the credibility of the source, the proof offered by the person making the communication. This form of proof will be treated in section IV.

DISCUSSION QUESTIONS AND PROJECTS

1. For more insight concerning the interrelationship of forms of proof you might run an experiment similar to Ruechelle's. Would judging the speech versus the manuscript make a difference? Would rating smaller units such as paragraphs increase agreement on classification of appeals?

2. Discuss the relationships between "reasonable," "logical," "probable," and "true."

3. In what senses is logic a science? In what senses is logic an art?

4. To what degree can the use of logic become a motivational appeal? To what extent can we acquire the desire to use logic as a tool in directing responses?

5. If a person knows he needs a good deal of praise and is

CONTENT

very concerned with having prestige and status, to what degree must he weigh this in testing the best career choice?

6. Using the approach of a set of factors that determine persuasion effect such as those in figure 10C, analyze one of your own speeches in terms of estimated impact.

7. Discuss the validity of the statement that people use reasoning powers and abilities in logical analysis only when motivated to do so.

8. Construct a speech or essay that stresses the use of rational appeals. Then, retaining the same goal, develop a communication that stresses motivational appeals. What are the differences in support forms? In appeals? In language? In organization? Utilizing your class as the assumed receivers, which version would be most effective? Why? Would a combination of the two versions be more effective?

9. Discuss how much source, topic, available materials, and receivers appear to determine the number and intensity of logical versus motivational appeals. Would it be valid to hold that poor communicators determine this in terms of source elements and good communicators more in response to the other factors?

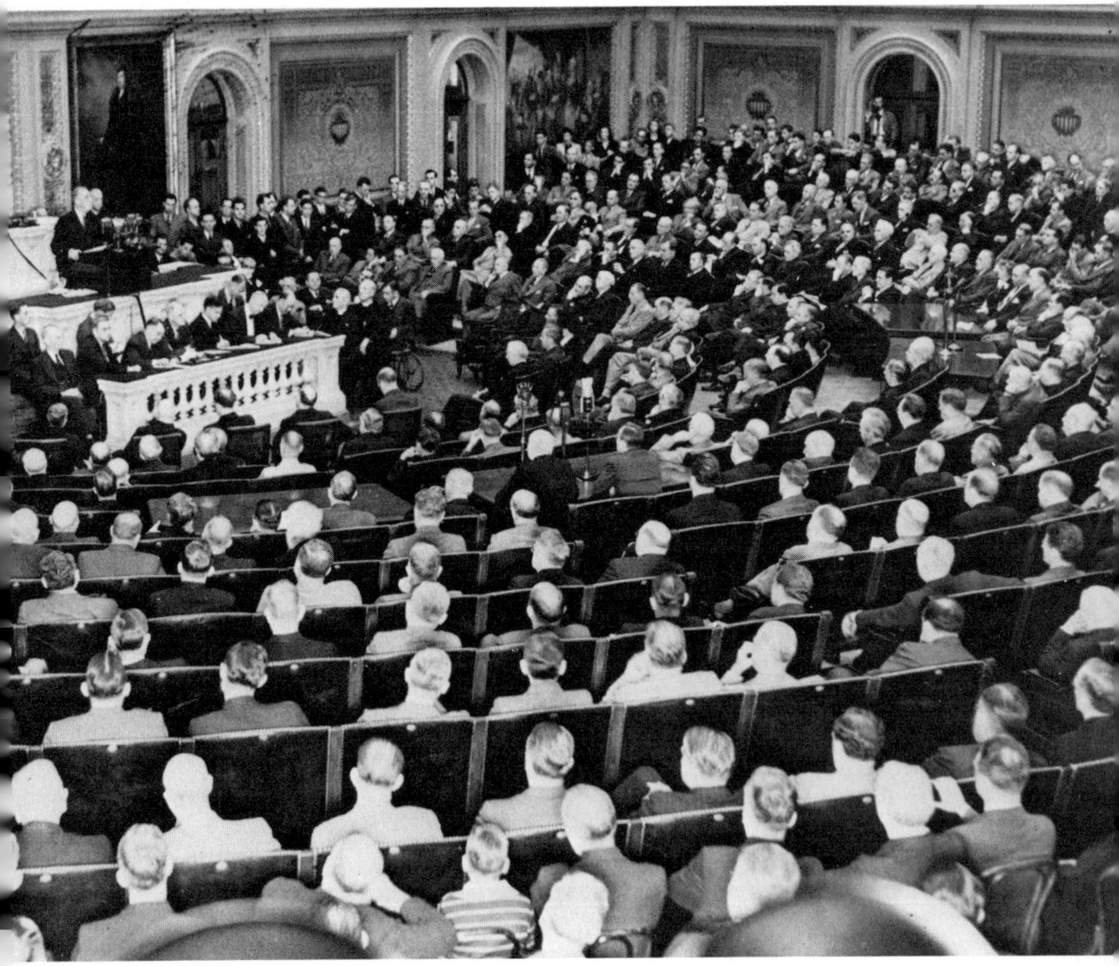

8 Organization

The value of good organization of message elements in a persuasive communication seems obvious. A proper flow of ideas at the sentence level and the right psychological and logical order of the material presented should help comprehension and acceptance. This attitude is reinforced by commentary on the importance of organization in speech outlines, criticisms on term papers, advice for writing essay examinations, planning agendas, and management.

But the results of experimental studies on organization have cast doubt on some of the simple assumptions about the value of organization. For example, learning has been found to be enhanced by at least moderate amounts of disorganization. A motivated learner becomes actively involved in trying to put a form on the material. Since active involvement is better than passive response, greater learning takes place.

Empirical studies provide a basis for examining the impact of certain organizational patterns and a start toward a clearer understanding of factors to consider in deciding how to organize material. The studies demonstrate there is no single formula for good organization. Again, consideration of the various factors related to the communication effort will suggest that one or another pattern is the best approach for a particular persuasion attempt.

This chapter briefly examines some study results seeking generalizations concerning the effects of organization and concludes by suggesting some elements basic to a theory of organization and its application.

A sentence has an organization, a form and order. A paragraph is a unit of organization. This chapter focuses on the larger units of a message: the relationship of idea to idea, of developmental pattern to developmental pattern. The next chapter deals with language and style.

PATTERNS OF ORGANIZATION

Empirical research in organization has concentrated on patterns or systems of organization. These studies have included questions of the importance of organization versus levels of disorganization, of primacy versus recency, and climax versus anteclimax order, and placement of types of material within the total message.

Organization versus Disorganization

Studies comparing organized versus disorganized communications have tended to employ retention, not attitude change, as the measure of effect. A mass of studies suggests that retention does not necessarily correlate with attitude change. Hence, differences in retention because of level of organization may not generalize to the question of impact in terms of attitude shift.

Written materials seem more adversely affected by attempts at disorganization than oral materials. In a review of literature on organization, Beighley found that with written communication, retention is greater for organized than disorganized forms.[1] In contrast, Petrie's examination of studies of disorganization of speeches yielded inconsistent results: some studies showed greater comprehension with organized speeches; some showed the degree of organization made no difference in retention.[2] Thompson found that although people who listened to a better-organized speech retained significantly more than did those who heard a less well-organized presentation, shifts in opinion were not significantly different.[3] Darnell found that organization manipulated at the sentence level did affect comprehension.[4]

The implications of these research findings are not clear. Disorganized written communications seem to produce greater loss in retention than do disorganized oral communications. Perhaps because of the linear

[1] K. C. Beighley, "A Summary of Experimental Studies Dealing with the Effect of Organization and of Skill of Speakers on Comprehension," *Journal of Communication* 2 (1952): 58–65.

[2] Charles Petrie, "Informative Speaking: A Summary and Bibliography of Related Research," *Speech Monographs* 30 (1963): 79–91.

[3] Ernest Thompson, "An Experimental Investigation of the Relative Effectiveness of Organizational Structure in Oral Communication," *Southern Speech Journal* 26 (1960): 59–69.

[4] Donald K. Darnell, "The Relation Between Sentence Order and Comprehension," *Speech Monographs* 30 (1963): 97–100.

nature of print and the expectations of the reader, disorganization creates negative response in terms of interest or some other factor that causes the loss in retention. Perhaps the organizational imperatives for speech differ: the receiver is more attuned to the necessity of integrating and putting structure into what she hears. Tests on listening suggest that a person's ability to structure material correlates with greater retention.[5] The receiver may be set for personal effort at structuring in the oral setting but less so with print.

Most experiments dealing with effects of disorganization have been conducted with student experimental groups in classroom settings. Students are typically motivated to gain information; perhaps with all but the extremely disorganized materials, they compensate for the disorganization by their efforts. Further, retention tests have usually been concerned with specific isolated facts, not involved concepts. Research in learning suggests that organization and structure become increasingly important as more and more complex ideas are presented, as one moves from facts to integrative structures. In most audience situations, listeners or readers do not have the set of the classroom student.

Primary versus Recency

The question of the impact of primacy versus recency in retention of material in communications has been studied both in terms of individual messages and in contradictory statements, either within one message or between messages.

Early studies of organization by Lund and Jersild favor primacy.[6] Material that occurred early in the communication was best retained. These studies laid the groundwork for the assumption of the law of primacy. However, later attempts to replicate the experiments yielded conflicting results. Ehrensberger tried to duplicate Jersild's study with tighter experimental controls and found recency to be favored.[7]

The Hovland group at Yale conducted an extensive series of studies on the primacy and recency issue and found that the generalization that primacy is favored in retention or attitude shift was not supported.[8] This was true when arguments on opposing sides of the question were used.

[5] Ralph G. Nichols, "Factors in Listening Comprehension," *Speech Monographs* 15 (1948): 154–63.

[6] F. H. Lund, "The Psychology of Belief IV: The Law of Primacy in Persuasion," *Journal of Abnormal and Social Psychology* 20 (1925): 183–91; Arthur Jersild, "Modes of Emphasis in Public Speaking," *Journal of Applied Psychology* 12 (1928): 611–20.

[7] Ray Ehrensberger, "An Experimental Study of the Relative Effectiveness of Certain Forms of Emphasis in Public Speaking," *Speech Monographs* 12 (1945): 94–111.

[8] See Carl I. Hovland et al., *The Order of Presentation in Persuasion* (New Haven: Yale University Press, 1957); Arthur R. Cohen, *Attitude Change and Social Influence* (New York: Basic Books, 1964), pp. 9–11.

Also, stronger arguments were found more powerful, whatever the position.

Gulley and Berlo found that material that occurred in initial or terminal positions could not be successfully contrasted, but material that appeared in the middle was least effective in terms of attitude shift.[9]

The overturning of the assumption of the law of primacy and conflicting results obtained have led researchers to speculations and to specific experiments that deal with the relationship of primacy and recency (as well as climax and anticlimax) to such factors as time of commitment, warnings against premature decisions, time of measurement, degree of audience interest. It appears that material placed in positions of primacy or recency is almost certainly going to have greater impact than material placed in the middle, other factors being constant. A number of factors must be considered before a final determination of the question of what produces primacy effects in one instance and recency effects in another can be answered.[10]

The question of climax and anticlimax order is related to primacy and recency. Operational definitions suggest that primacy and recency are matters of placement; climax and anticlimax deal with the psychological or perceived importance of the material. Climax suggests that the most important material occurs near the close of the communication; anticlimax suggests the reverse.

The research indicates that climax will be more significant in one instance, anticlimax in another. The interest the topic holds may be one factor in the question. Where the subject has interest value for the receiver, perhaps climax fulfills expectations, whereas anticlimax may be useful for a person who is uninterested in or more neutral toward the topic.

Placement of Material

Despite a greater paucity of research, or perhaps because of it, studies on the placement of certain types of material seem to yield clearer suggestions for persuasion than the areas investigated above.

Attention Factors

The basis for one generalization about the placement of attention factors was developed in chapter 5: attention factors need to

---

[9] Halbert E. Gulley and David K. Berlo, "Effects of Intercellular and Intracellular Speech Structure on Attitude Change and Listening," *Speech Monographs* 23 (1956): 288–97.

[10] For a brief summary of primacy-recency and some of the research studies that have treated specific factors, see Ralph L. Rosnow and Edward J. Robinson, *Experiments in Persuasion* (New York: Academic Press, 1967), pp. 99–104.

be distributed throughout a speech since attention tends to vary, being alternately lost and then regained. Furthermore, since any stimulus that remains unchanged tends to become tiring, change is necessary to retain interest.

Movement was shown to be an intrinsic factor in attention: organizational structure can provide the basis for movement, suggesting the progression of ideas and the development of thought.

Need Arousal

At what point in communication should motivation be stressed? Cohen found that opinion change is stronger if a need for the information is first created and then the information supplied.[11] This would fit with motivational theory that suggests that need precedes activity and motivation helps and speeds learning. Unfortunately, no experiments have studied the value of a compact versus distributed treatment of motivation. Should motivational elements be concentrated in one position, or should recurring efforts at motivation be made throughout the speech? Although the motivational forces need to be aroused during the early part of the communication, these forces should be strengthened throughout the speech.

Order of Positive and Negative Material

McGuire found that material that is more positive, more rewarding, more acceptable to the communicator should be presented first, less desirable material second, and least desirable material last.[12] Certainly this approach is consistent with the theories of selective attention and perception in that we tend to pay attention to ideas that appear to support our orientation and our attitudinal frame, and are thus rewarding to us.

Repetition

Jersild found that repetition of ideas and statements was effective in gaining retention and that spaced or distributed repetition was more effective than immediate repetition.[13] Other studies on emphasis, retention, and learning stress the value of repetition although points of diminishing return can be reached, with boredom and error setting in.

One value of statements of thesis, internal summaries and transitions, and concluding summaries may be this effect gained from repetition.

---

[11] Arthur R. Cohen, "Need for Cognition and Order of Communications as Determinants of Opinion Change," *Order of Presentation*, pp. 79–97.
[12] William J. McGuire, "Order of Presentation as a Factor in Conditioning Persuasiveness," ibid., pp. 98–114.
[13] Jersild, "Modes of Emphasis."

Presumably major ideas should tend to form the bulk of such restatements. Interestingly enough, studies show that specific factual information tends to be lost although the attitude shift and major claims may be retained.

PROCESS OF ORGANIZATION

Although the research on the impact of organizational elements on attitude change and action does not yield many strong generalizations concerning organization patterns, the rhetorical tradition and findings relative to learning theory, attention, and audience response generate a reasonably tenable theory of organization.

Developing an Organizational Strategy

Some of the factors that must be considered in developing an organizational strategy are the predispositions, set, and expectations of receivers; the nature of the subject matter and available material; and particular problems in setting, context, and medium limitations. Presumably the goal of the organizational pattern for the communicator is to obtain the maximum contribution toward his or her goal. The communicator will therefore consider problems in organization as they affect the motivation of attention and interest, comprehension, and acceptance of his or her purpose on the part of the receivers. Organization involves a logical pattern (the progression of ideas in meaningful relationships or patterns) and a psychological pattern (the impact upon the mind of the receiver in terms of the processes through which his or her mind is moving).

Clearly, then, it is as important to consider organizational patterns from a psychological viewpoint as from a logical viewpoint. This fact is often neglected by both novice and experienced communicators. A variety of standard patterns can be used to present material: chronological ones that move forward or backward in time; spatial or geographical ones; topical or arbitrary ones (for example, when we describe or present material in which no particular order of topics seems reasonable). For many persuasive purposes we need to use more complex patterns based on reasoning patterns: deductive, inductive, analogical, cause to effect, effect to cause, or effect to effect. The problem-solution sequence moves from awareness of a problem through analysis to suggested solution(s) and implementation.

Any of these patterns can be used; the situation must dictate which seems best. It is impractical to compare effectiveness of the various patterns since the impact will almost certainly depend upon appropriateness to subject matter, to audience, and so forth. Different patterns can also be used in one speech. While one basic pattern may be used to organize the major points of the speech, different patterns may be employed to develop the subpoints under the various major heads. Thus, one can look at the overall organizational pattern, the pattern for one main head and its development, or the developmental pattern for a subpoint.

Any reasoning pattern is a possible organizational scheme for the presentation of material to a receiver. Smaller units within a discourse may often be organized more efficiently and perhaps most effectively by putting them into structures following the demands of a reasoning pattern as to the movement of the ideas.

We may be less familiar with psychological patterns than we are with logical patterns. The motivated sequence is based upon the psychological response of the receiver. The first step is to gain attention. The second step is a need step, a motivational step. The third stage is satisfaction—the needs created are met through the presentation of material. The fourth step is visualization—the attempt to project the reality of what can or might be. The final step is one of actuation—a move to action if that is appropriate.

A final caution seems appropriate: quite significant differences in organization might produce no real difference in impact. But some form of organization is a minimum; people need some structure. Such an expectation needs to be met if negative effects are to be avoided. The exhaustiveness of the treatment of material is not the key factor in organization. The important question is in terms of adequacy to the needs of audience, topic, and special conditions.

A presentation can be divided into three sections: introduction, body, and conclusion. The basis for this division is not in the logical requirements of the subject matter but in the psychological requirements of the receivers. First, we will examine strategy in terms of these three divisions and then in terms of three audience classifications: neutral, friendly, and hostile.

Strategy for Introductions

The function of an introduction is to gain attention, draw attention to the topic, gain interest in it, and build goodwill toward the communicator.

Since attention is held only for limited periods of time and since forced attention becomes tiring, the introduction must lay the groundwork for maintenance of interest and thus gain nonvoluntary attention throughout the speech. The introduction must thus gain attention and direct this attention to the topic and materials of the communication so that the topic develops a degree of intrinsic interest. The reputation of the speaker may be such that she can hold initial attention on the basis of it. But eventually the material itself must develop interest value. Where the topic is salient to the audience, presumably a reference to the topic and its importance is a very effective introduction. Specific illustrations or other reality or proximate materials may also be good sources for developing interest.

When an audience is uninterested in the topic area, the introduction must begin one of the major tasks of the entire communication: creating interest in and concern for the topic area.

One major criticism of many introductions is that they seem irrelevant to a communication; indeed, they might fit literally hundreds of different topics and different communications. Some people seek set introductions that work in every situation. However, the validity of such formula approaches is challenged by the findings on primacy and recency. Since an audience is most likely to remember what comes very early and what comes very late, material in the introduction that is basically irrelevant to the purpose of the speech has a higher probability of being remembered. Few communicators would want to have irrelevancies remembered and the key points forgotten.

Material related to building goodwill toward the persuader and building credibility will be covered in chapter 11.

Strategy for the Body

The logical imperatives of the development of the topic are most relevant to the body of the communication. The introduction and conclusion are concerned more with psychological considerations outside the pattern of logical development. Thus, a communicator will look to the imperatives of subject matter as a factor in development of the organization of the body of the communication.

Because of the fluctuating nature of attention, the body of the speech should contain recurrent elements that have attention-gaining potential. Repetition of ideas is helpful; selecting material in terms of interest value for the receiver and using emphasis in the form of internal summary and transition statements pay dividends.

The organizational structure should suggest movement, evolution, process. Movement itself is a factor of attention. Organizational elements may gain from parallel structure as from familiarity, but the value of change and novelty must not be discounted.

Material included should maintain and enhance the motivational structure of the communication. Motivation will fluctuate. A basic physical drive such as hunger may persist until met, but more derived motivations, such as appeals to altruism, may not endure against competing stimuli with potential for motivational impact.

Motivation sources should be aroused and operative prior to the proposition because acceptance of the proposition depends upon the energy supplied by such motivational elements. Potential sources of motivation must be made fully operative as motivational forces if the persuasion is to be successful. A potential source of motivation may remain that unless clearly activated.

Reinforcement theory suggests that one should proceed from ideas that are supportive of and easily acceptable to the receivers and move toward less agreeable points last. Thus, for an audience agreed that there is a significant problem but not on the solution to that problem, a communicator would presumably profit from a problem-solution order. That is, she will build awareness of the problem, urge that something must be done, and then hope that this will lead her receivers to identify with her and to accept the point on which there is less agreement: the best solution.

Two-sided arguments are more effective for opposed receivers, for those who are well educated, and for those who are well informed about the topic area. The presentation of both sides of an issue also increases the inoculation effect. A speaker who wishes to refute an opposing argument is probably wise to develop the point in a positive fashion, then consider the negative argument and develop its weakness, and then restate the original position.

The complexity of the presentation should be adjusted to the capabilities of the audience. Too complex material will not be understood if it is presented too rapidly or with insufficient detail. Material that is too simple may become boring, and attention will be lost.

Strategy for Conclusions

The introduction has the advantage of primacy; the conclusion has the advantage of recency. Further, to the degree that motivation may peak and a climax pattern be employed, the conclusion presents a potential for strong psychological impact. The conclusion may include the repetition of key ideas, thus combining the value of repetition and restatement with the value of the position.

The conclusion may be the logical point at which the communicator attempts to gain commitment. This may be done by asking the receivers to declare themselves by a show of hands, orally, to each other, or to pledge on a card, sign a petition, or volunteer for an assignment. The persuader should facilitate commitment in any feasible way. The activity of the others in making the commitment will often reinforce a wavering individual, who will tend to do the same. Commitment increases the probability that an attitude change will be retained by setting in motion certain actions that will reinforce or increase the change in attitude.

In oral situations, the persuader may choose to conclude by calling for questions or comments from the receivers. This device gives an opportunity to discover areas of disagreement, to respond to those specifically, to restate and emphasize the main points, and to adjust to receiver concerns. The willingness to answer questions may also have a positive effect on the credibility of the source. Care in handling questions or comments is essential since the persuader should not antagonize and may be perceived as lacking crucial information or the ability to defend a position. Good advance preparation, as well as a tolerant and warm regard toward the audience, a communicated sense of respect, is needed.

Since the conclusion is so important, it warrants particular emphasis in preparation. It should be carefully planned, often outlined or written out in full and tested for probable impact. The conclusion is too important to be left to the inspiration of the moment, which often results in the communicator's lamely concluding, "Well, I hope you accept my idea. I guess that's about all I have to say." The conclusion has to give a sense of closure.

Strategy for Neutral Receivers

Many neutral audiences are not only without a strong opinion or any opinion at all on the subject being discussed but often have no interest in the subject either. Persuaders are usually grateful for any audience they can find. Thus, they may make presentations to groups that have little or no interest in the subject and whose reason for assembling is something quite remote from the persuader's interest. The students in a class may have little interest in the teacher's problems with baby-sitters. Commercial persuasion has the funds to buy access to the audience. The typical situation for most of us is that we have to find some other means.

A key goal for the introduction and for the entire presentation to the neutral audience is to gain attention and to transform this attention into interest about the topic area. This means heavy reliance upon factors of attention and motivational strategies. Ways in which the issue and the need for action are directly related to the receivers must be brought out. They must be made to feel involved.

With a neutral audience the persuader can often make a direct statement of the topic and purpose. However, the audience should not be placed too much on the defensive or on the alert that they will be asked for money or other possibilities that would reflect a commitment they are not thinking about. Such appeals may come later and sometimes follow an inquiry from the audience of how they may help.

Adjustment to the situation is highly important. If time limits are established, they should be observed. The conventions that govern the situation should be respected just as the other interests and activities of the receivers should be respected. But perhaps these interests and activities can be linked to the persuader's goal. The use of a question or forum period can be very useful. In asking questions, the receivers become involved. Further, those who have been interested and become concerned are most likely to participate. Many of these people may serve as opinion leaders for the others in the group who tend to remain silent or uninvolved. These receivers may lead the way for the group as a whole to become involved, and they may serve to keep the issue before the others in future interactions and activities.

The persuader should seek to channel response in ways that will be favorable to the goal. A small pamphlet or some material that can be passed out and taken home may reinforce the immediate effort and even produce a later response. References to newspaper, radio, or television materials relative to the topic may increase the salience of these materials and thus heighten the possibility of a delayed impact. A specific reference to something that will happen in the community or some recurring happening may be linked to the persuasion effort; thus, when that event occurs, the receivers will be reminded of the presentation and the persuader's concerns. Any indication of continuing interest in the topic is a significant achievement—perhaps the most difficult of the steps that may lead to a final change in attitude or action desired by the persuader.

Strategy for Friendly Receivers

A friendly audience is to some degree favorable toward the attitude, object or action to be urged by the persuader; however, there are many shades of opinion within an audience. Further, the proper action may be the subject of tremendous disagreement even if all feel they can agree upon the ultimate goal. Often the most bitter fights are between friends who are seeking the same goal but disagree about the means. In some instances, people initially favorable toward a point of view will become so dissatisfied by events that they will join the opposition with a great sense of self-righteousness. Thus, a friendly audience is not a guarantee of success for the persuader.

Since there are strong areas of agreement for those in the friendly audience, the persuader should identify the areas of agreement and reinforce the unity and cohesion of the group. She can announce a clear identification with the general goal and dedicate her effort to that goal.

Often an audience is friendly because they know the persuader, who may be functioning as a representative of the group. Even if not personally known, the receivers may still be relatively easy to analyze.

Knowing the subject matter and the various opinions relative to it, the persuader may be able to identify the various interests and subgroups that exist relative to the topic. Persuasion can be designed to accommodate these various groups. Indeed the persuader can often indicate that various actions are a realistic, practical compromise that is best for all concerned. The effort to find commonality among the views is an important one, for the persuader can represent the specific proposal as one that can unify the group. Past accomplishments can be used to move the group toward future actions, which are presented as similar potential gains.

Often the friendly audience needs to have a means of expressing their shared commitment. The persuader may simply function as an agent of the group in directing the activity. But even a friendly audience may need to be reminded of the importance of the issue. Often they need new information and new illustrations to reinforce and make vivid their commitment. They may need to obtain new evidence and new lines of argument to deal with counterpersuasion or to use in attempting to influence others to similar views. If the topic can be made highly salient for these people, they are likely to maintain an interest for a reasonable period of time. During that time, in interacting with others they may talk about the issue, try to influence others, and thus spread the influence of the work of the initial persuader. "Talk it up!" is particularly sound advice coming from the persuader to a friendly audience.

Strategy for Hostile Receivers

With a hostile audience the communicator will need to build a sense of some common identification, some community with the receivers. The ability of the receivers to accept and perhaps identify with the source may be a key to success for the position to be presented. They will think that if the communicator is a respected person, who is willing to treat their opinion with respect, and who is sincere and highly credible in his presentation, then they should give him or her a hearing.

Typically the persuader must orient the receivers to the topic and give them some sense of the purpose or goal. The tradition of concealing purpose is unwise in many instances. If the audience already knows the position of the persuader, a candid statement of some disagreement and willingness to examine both sides may be helpful. With some audiences an overt denial of effort to persuade can be useful, but this depends upon the knowledge and perceptiveness of the receivers, as well as the reputation of the source.

A sense of mutual respect and acceptance is essential with a hostile audience. Goodwill is necessary on the part of the persuader if it is to be achieved in return. The more controversial and emotional issues may well be downplayed somewhat. In dealing with a hostile audience, the persuader will need to exercise particular care in the selection of content. Explanations should be fair. Precise figures, careful quotation of sources who are highly regarded by the receivers is essential. A recognition that legitimate opposing views exist is essential. A two-sided presentation is almost essential. The refutation of opposing views should be handled carefully; sometimes a suggestion that the matter is close but that on balance the persuader's view might seem to have more merit is a useful tactic. The persuader should constantly seek to open up the receivers to future influences that may reinforce the persuader's approach. This may involve suggesting that people defer judgment until they read certain materials, think further about the issue, or wait until the results of some trial of a plan are reported and studied. In some cases the wisest effort is simply to delay the decision to act on their contrary purpose.

Dealing with a hostile audience is a challenging proposition. Mistakes in audience analysis or in adapting to the audience can be devastating. In some cases the better part of wisdom is not to make a presentation. The advice "Let sleeping dogs lie" is sound. The persuader needs to take particularly careful inventory of her or his personal characteristics. Some people are so committed on a topic that they cannot easily tolerate those who hold the opposite view. Others tend to become upset in handling questions that reflect disagreement. It is often easy to take the perspective of someone who is similar to us, but we find it difficult to take the perspective of people who are quite unlike us. It is hard to understand how they come to believe in and act on values or beliefs that we see so clearly to be wrong. If you cannot develop the ability to deal comfortably with these problems, it may be best in the short run to give the persuasion task to someone better equipped to discharge it.

APPLICATION IN OUTLINES

There are many ways of outlining and many uses of outlines. Some outlines are merely key words jotted on a card to remind one of the major points and to act as a psychological protection against the possibility of blocking in the middle of a speech. Other outlines are extremely detailed and so complete that the communication could be delivered almost verbatim from the outline.

An outline serves a valuable function where preparation time is adequate. It is the key tool for preparation of the persuasive communicator. It emphasizes ideas and the relationship of ideas and not the minutiae of the complete wording.

182   CREATION OF MESSAGES

Because the outline condenses and catches the essence of the idea, ideally in such a complete fashion that the idea is fully communicated in language that suggests the emotional as well as the logical toning, it enables the prospective communicator to examine several patterns: the psychological, the logical, the attention factors, the motivational sequence, the integral relationship of parts to wholes.

In many instances, communicators do not practice the material they plan to present; often it is not desirable or feasible to develop a complete manuscript. However, a communicator who has command of communication skills should be able to achieve the desired impact if preparation of the outline is adequate. Too many spend time practicing a speech that should be spent preparing it. Even if a manuscript is to be written, a careful outline should be constructed prior to the actual writing and rewriting. The manuscript should polish the style, not develop the structure of the larger elements of the discourse.

Here are some suggestions for preparing an outline, the best preparation you can make up to the actual moment of communication (each of you will develop your own variations with time):

1. Every relatively formal speech, essay, or article should be given a title. It may not be used, often it should not be, but when a title is needed, its absence is very distressing. Many communicators, particularly in the oral setting, are asked for a title and mumble something lamely, which the introducer repeats, equally lamely.

2. Every outline should contain a simple, clear statement of the communicator's specific goal. Often this statement will not be communicated to the receivers, but its very presence directs the preparation of the communicator on this specific goal. Everything in the communication should logically and psychologically be tested as the best means to achieve that goal.

3. Introductions should be carefully planned and perhaps even written out. Because introductions are so important, they cannot be left to chance. It is, of course, true that circumstances often force modification of introductions at the moment of actual communication, but wise preparation often saves the situation.

4. The body of a communication should be outlined in reasonable detail, probably varying from 25 to 75 percent of the total words to be used in the final message. When the material is unfamiliar to the communicator, great detail usually will be needed to ensure his ability to communicate fully and effectively. A communicator who knows a great deal about the subject may need an extensive outline to serve as a check on use of time so he doesn't become lost in minutiae irrelevant to his audience or expend his time without covering necessary ground.

5. Main heads and key ideas should be in complete sentences and catch both the style and emotional-motivational tone desired.

6. Subheads and certain specific supporting material may be presented in words or phrases if the material is sufficient to provide an adequate means of testing the idea for relationship, motivational elements, and attention value.

7. Outlines should summarize what will be said, not what will be done. "I will explain how the process works here" is not a useful statement in an outline because it totally begs the question. Rather the summary of the essence of the process should be provided so it can be checked for clarity and meaningfulness.

8. Conclusions often should be written out; in any event they should be planned very carefully.

9. Bibliographies should be included in outlines. Most people use similar topics and materials repeatedly in their communications. It is very embarrassing to return to an outline and find you have forgotten several main sources for the data.

10. Outlines should be preserved for future reference. Most speakers or writers have opportunities to develop future communications on similar topics. Thus, you can build on the old by improving and refining rather than merely repeating the initial steps of developing a communication several times.

The outline is not something done for the sake of doing. Its main function is to allow the testing for relationships, logically and psychologically, of the elements in the planned communication. The outline provides a means of highlighting the various processes involved and the various choices made to enable maximum development with least effort. An outline is usually reworked and revised several times and at several stages of the preparatory process. Of course this depends upon the significance of the communication. For the critic, the technique of outlining the message is a good means of examining the persuasive structure and highlighting the choices made. For the communicator the ultimate test of an outline is its efficiency as a tool to improve her effectiveness in achieving her goal.

SUMMARY

The significance of organization in producing communication effects needs further exploration through research.

Disorganization achieved by randomly ordering paragraphs need not limit retention of facts. Disorganization seems to weaken written communications more than it weakens oral communications. Further, randomization at the sentence level does inhibit retention. When dealing with complex generalizations or audiences less set for learning and persuasion, disorganization will probably be much more destructive.

No general pattern of preference for primacy versus recency or climax versus anticlimax order has been demonstrated. However, the initial and terminal positions are more effective in achieving retention than positions in the middle. Further, motivation needs to be aroused before the material that is to gain acceptance through the motivational forces is presented. When presenting mixtures of material, some of which will be liked, some of which will not, the more acceptable material (or at least a part of it) should come before the less acceptable material.

Repetition and restatement and the distribution of such material throughout the communication seem clear aids to retention and persuasion.

The strategy of the communicator in organization lies in accommodating the order of the material to the demands of audience, topic, materials, and particular influences. This demands consideration of both logical and psychological factors. The introductory and concluding sections of a speech pose particularly heavy psychological demands.

The outline is the major tool of message preparation. It maximizes the opportunity to test the various patterns of order and relation of ideas, attention devices, appeals, and relationship of the elements of the message to the purpose. The outline also becomes a useful device for careful analysis of the persuasive communication of others.

DISCUSSION QUESTIONS AND PROJECTS

1. In what, if any, situations can a very clear organizational pattern be harmful to the goal of a communication?

2. Experiment with casting the body of a message into different organizational patterns. Do some topics seem to fit in only one pattern? Does changing the pattern change the emphasis given to points?

3. What reasons can you offer for the findings of many studies that suggest comprehension of written communications is more impaired by disorganization than is that of oral communications?

4. Discuss how much a lack of knowledge of the goal of a communicator affects your response to an oral communication. To a written communication.

5. As an experiment the class may wish to compare the effects

ORGANIZATION

of a low, moderate, and high degree of disorganization on the audience. Both written and oral presentations could be used. What is the effect on retention of facts? Of a complex generalization? Does persuasion appear to be more influenced than retention?

6. Discuss the extent to which introductions and conclusions serve psychological purposes versus logical purposes.

7. Does the organization of an answer to an essay question on an exam make a difference in the grade received? What is your opinion? What do studies on grading practices show?

8. How much do you think the use of students in tests of effects of disorganization on retention of facts has affected the results? How might a typical nonstudent audience react?

9. Create a set of criteria to judge outlines for speeches.

10. To what degree is the process of thinking a process of organization?

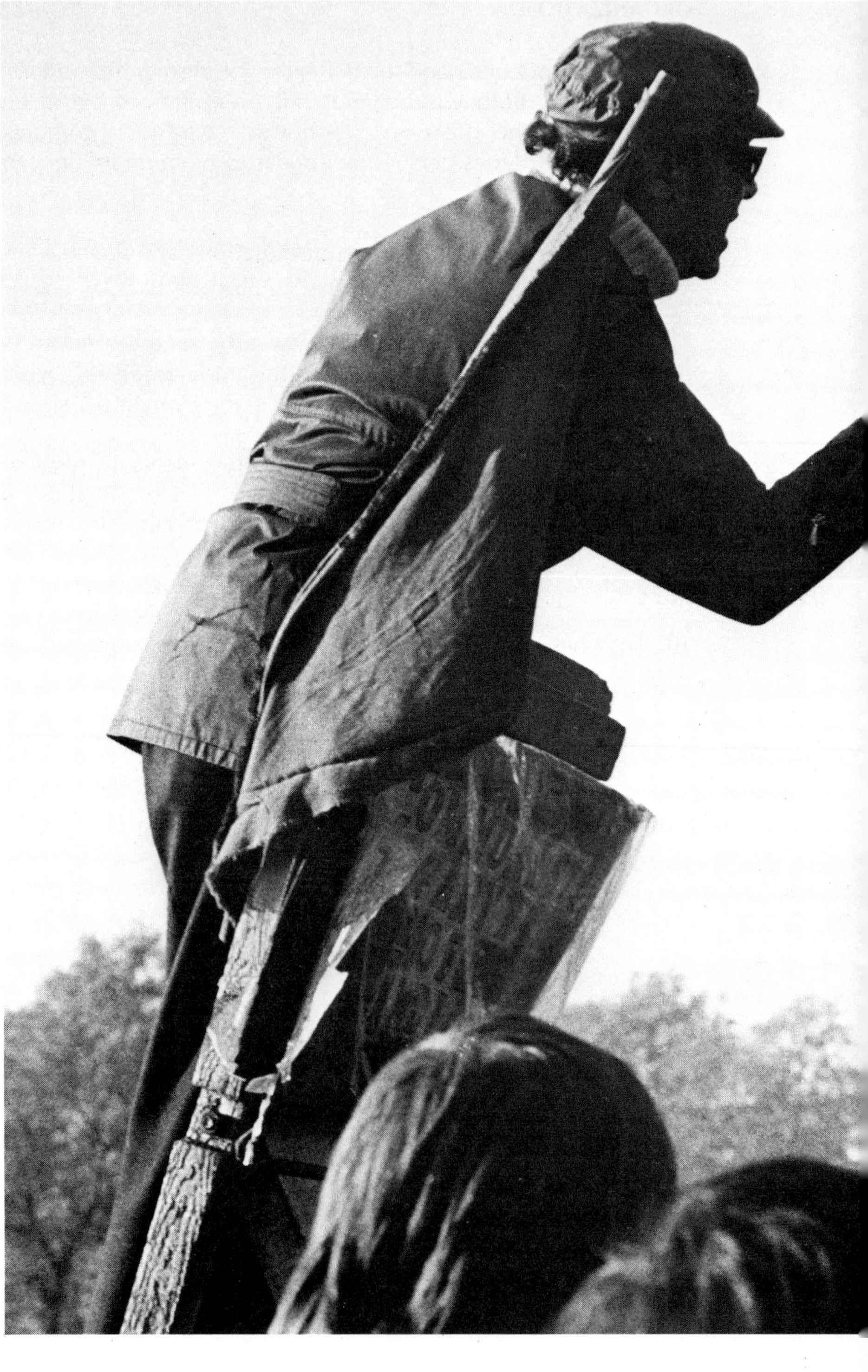

9 Language and Style

Thoughts and ideas are not messages. Thoughts must be encoded if they are to be communicated by stirring up meanings in the mind of the receiver. Hence, the creation of messages necessitates the use of language. This chapter is concerned with the nature and function of language and style in yielding persuasion effects. (Nonverbal communication is discussed in chapter 10.)

THE NATURE AND FUNCTION OF LANGUAGE

Our ability to use language has been termed the characteristic that distinguishes us from other animals. Other animals can learn to respond to symbols and utilize a language to a degree, but our ability to pass on knowledge and to transmit a culture through language is unique. Language is the instrumentality by which mind contacts mind. Like every other tool it has limitations that place restrictions on what can be done with it.

Language Defined

Language is an arbitrary system of abstract, relatively conventionalized symbols by means of which a social group interacts. A language can employ any sensory medium—visual, audible, tactile, olfactory—but generally we think of audible codes, visible codes, and the language code transmitted through audible and/or visible means.

Language is often defined in terms of vocal symbols. Linguists are increasingly focusing upon the oral symbol as the original medium of communication and also as the one most flexible and responsive to change. For purposes of this chapter I shall deal mostly with the language code, whether written or oral. I do not mean to minimize the differences between the printed and the spoken word in terms of the modality employed; the possibility of altering, enriching, or inflecting the language code with additional meanings in the various systems; or other important differences.

The terms in the definition develop several key points concerning the nature of language and its function.

Arbitrary denotes that language must be learned; it is not natural, inevitable, fixed. There is no necessary relationship between the word and the thing symbolized. In order to learn a language *"it is necessary for another organism to intervene and reward us each time we respond correctly. Since the intervening organism can reward a range of possible responses, the choice of the sound pattern 'chair' is quite arbitrary."* [1] This arbitrary aspect of language provides the basis for the point to be amplified later that words do not mean; people have meanings for words.

System means that language possesses pattern and order. Language has a syntax that can be studied in terms of the manner in which signs are used apart from what they signify.

Abstract is somewhat redundant because symbols are necessarily removed from the thing they symbolize. However, the word emphasizes that the symbol employed abstracts from the totality of the thing referenced and emphasizes some characteristics and not others. Alfred Korzybski made much of this point in his structural differential in which he pointed out that the reality of any thing involves an infinity of characteristics.[2] A ladder of increasing abstraction can be built as one moves from the label "Terry Smith" to a "junior," "male college student," "young man," "male." Each of these terms omits progressively greater numbers of specific differentiating characteristics. Many other similar systems can be built starting from "Terry Smith."

Relatively conventionalized indicates that a language is not uniform in terms of usages or responses (meanings) evoked in receivers. You and I in looking at these same symbols may have somewhat the same meanings

---

[1] George A. Miller, *Language and Communication* (New York: McGraw-Hill, 1951), p. 5.

[2] See Alfred Korzybski, *Science and Sanity* (Lancaster, Pa.: Science Press, 1933), and Irving J. Lee, *Language Habits in Human Affairs* (New York: Harper & Brothers, 1941), pp. 263–68. The Lee book presents many of the most compelling points of the tradition of general semantics, which is concerned with the many ways in which the meanings of symbols and words influence responses to one another and the world around us.

stirred up, but these can be only approximately identical. Our experiences are different, perhaps vastly so. Our frames of reference and the forces structuring our response are such that the symbols can be only relatively conventionalized. Each of us interprets the symbols in terms of our own perspectives. Some words evoke relatively similar responses across an entire society, whereas others evoke rather diverse responses even within a small subgroup. The hidden assumption of complete conventionalization of language produces many communication breakdowns.

Symbols are representations of things rather than the things themselves. Symbols stand in place of things or as signs of things rather than being the things. This does not suggest that symbols do not exist. They do. They can be counted and analyzed in ways totally apart from their representational function. Symbols can be studied without questioning their meaning. Some approaches to linguistic analysis focus upon the symbols and not the referents for which the symbols stand or the responses made to the symbols by receivers. In persuasion the primary concern with symbols falls under the heading of semantics—the science of word meanings in which we study the relationship between signs and meanings.

By means of which a social group interacts indicates the function that language serves. It permits mind to come in contact with mind; it permits the exchange of information. This does not mean that something is literally transmitted from sender to receiver but that a stimulus is used to stir up a meaning in a receiver.[3]

Meaning

A discussion of the function of language is obviously incomplete without reference to the concept of meaning. The function of language is "to express and elicit meanings. . . . *Meaning is inherent in the very definition of language."* [4] It seems common sense to talk about the meaning of messages. But this approach is fraught with difficulty. Messages are stimuli. Meanings are in humans responding to stimuli. Meaning, according to Osgood, Suci, and Tannenbaum, is a

---

[3] The use of this term *stirring up meaning in receivers* is due to the influence of the late Andrew T. Weaver. Professor Weaver stressed the limitations of words in communicating meaning and the idea that communication is never total: rather we should be amazed at the frequency of the "happy accident" of communication. Rather than bemoan the fact that communication is not total, he urged that we be surprised at the amount of communication that actually does occur given all the limitations involved in the process. Professor Weaver argued that no one ever tells a story to another. One induces another to tell the story to himself out of his experience.

[4] David K. Berlo, *The Process of Communication* (New York: Holt, Rinehart and Winston, 1960), p. 173. Chapters 7, 8, and 11 in his book are particularly relevant.

representational mediational process: "Words represent things because they produce in human organisms some replica of the actual behavior toward these things as a mediating process."[5] This mediating process may involve purely neural events; it does not necessitate actual behavioral response. Meanings are responses produced by these representational mediational processes.

George Kelly's construct theory reinforces the points made about the nature of language and meaning:

> Man looks at his world through transparent patterns or templates which he creates and then attempts to fit over the reality of which the world is composed. The fit is not always very good. . . . Let us give the name *constructs* to those patterns that are tentatively tried on for size. They are ways of construing the world. . . . In general man seeks to improve his constructs by increasing his repertory, by altering them to provide better fits, and by subsuming them with superordinate constructs or systems.[6]

Researchers have demonstrated that people differ in the number of constructs that they use in interpreting experience. On the average, women use more categories to interpret interpersonal relations than do men. In this sense women can deal more discriminatively and variously with people. Similarly one person may have a number of constructs to deal with one field of experience and few to deal with another field. Some people tend to be cognitively complex; they bring a number of constructs to any situation. Others tend to be less complex; they bring a small number of constructs. Thus, the symbol depends upon the person for interpretation, meaning, decision.

Kelly sees individuals as active—as "scientists" trying to understand and predict their world. Hence, meaning cannot be static. The categories used to interpret experience may change if they do not fit. A persuader often seeks to change the template through which an experience is seen.

We are accustomed to distinguishing between denotative and connotative meanings. Denotative meanings deal with the relationships between the sign (word) and the object or the thing referenced. Connotative meanings involve signs and objects, but the person making the relations becomes a key factor. Connotative meanings arise from the individual's particular additions in the representational mediational

---

[5] Charles E. Osgood, George J. Suci, and Percy H. Tannenbaum, *The Measurement of Meaning* (Urbana: University of Illinois Press, 1958), p. 7.

[6] George A. Kelly, *The Psychology of Personal Constructs* (New York: W. W. Norton & Co., 1955), 1:8–9.

process. Connotations have to do with the feeling or sense that a person has toward the object and sign (for example, a four-letter word for the sex act), sometimes to the object (such as a snake). Since denotation is to some extent specific to an individual and his or her experiential frame, the distinction between denotation and connotation must be one of degree, not of kind. Connotations generally shared become part of denotative meaning.

One of the most stimulating and seminal approaches to communication has been the investigation of Osgood and his associates into the dimensions of connotative meaning. This pursuit has resulted in the development of the semantic differential as an instrument to measure connotative dimensions of meaning. Arguing that qualifications are normally established through the use of adjectives, Osgood and his associates developed large numbers of bipolar adjectival pairs. Various subjects were asked to respond to a wide range of concepts in terms of these pairs. The judgments were then correlated, summing over concepts and subjects, and factor analyzed to determine the fewest numbers of independent factors that could explain the pattern of relationships that emerged.

Three major factors emerged, which have been confirmed in succeeding research. *Evaluation,* first in order of appearance and magnitude, is dominated by terms such as *good* and *bad.* This single dimension accounted for over half of the variance extracted (explained). It suggests the emphasis on judgment, value, worth, and goodness that characterizes us as human beings. The answer to the question "What does it mean?" as far as connotation is concerned seems to be one of value judgment. The importance of this factor has led many researchers to use the evaluative dimension of the semantic differential as a measure of attitude toward concepts.

The second factor to emerge was that of *potency,* with such terms as *strong* and *weak, hard* and *soft.* This might be termed a power factor. The third factor to emerge was *activity,* dominated by terms such as *fast* and *slow, active* and *passive.* Together these two factors approximately equal the magnitude of the evaluative factor. For concepts related to the sociopolitical sphere and to people, these latter two dimensions tend to coalesce into one labeled *dynamism.* Other factors also emerged but they tend to vary more in terms of the type of concepts analyzed or the nature of the respondents and to explain a smaller and smaller proportion of the variation in judgments.

It is difficult to estimate the importance of the connotative dimension of meaning in persuasion. But certainly the pervasiveness of the evaluative factor warrants the serious attention of the persuader. And the degree to which placement of concepts on each of these referential dimensions is determined by the receiver in terms of experience reinforces the importance of the receiver as the determiner of persuasion effect.

Language and Culture

How much a language is bound to a culture is of interest both theoretically and in actual persuasion. As suggested above, even within one general cultural framework, markedly different meanings exist for the same word. When communication becomes cross-cultural, even demanding translation of the language code, the complexities and potential barriers to communication are multiplied.

Edward Sapir and Benjamin Whorf are associated with the hypothesis that language characteristics have a determining influence on cognitive processes. Certainly evidence exists that languages differ with cultures or surrounding environments. Since the available cultural categories affect recognition and retention, different cultures categorize experience differently. For example, time and space may be coded differently, and in communication across cultures, one trips over these invisible cultural chains.

This suggests another limitation of language: it is not only an inexact tool for communication, but it also produces different initial perceptions and evaluations of the same objects or situations. What one sees is intimately linked to the categories one has available. Language is not the only factor influencing perception and cognition, by any means.[7] Further, this linguistic relativity can be counteracted to some degree. But to do so demands awareness of and sensitivity to the problems.

Culture is both an abstraction from behavior and a directive to behavior. We learn our culture so automatically and at such an early age that most of us are unaware of the degree to which we have absorbed it. A culture is a product, has a history, is selective in including certain ideas, patterns, and values, and is based upon a complex, interrelated set of symbols. Culture includes literature, art, and music; it also includes ways in which we prepare food and make tools, in our patterns of behavior and our ideas of goodness. We may think of culture as being the culture that is shared by the Western world or that of the United States or of one geographical section or even economic segment of the country. The latter are normally referred to as *subcultures*. We each may live in

---

[7] Harry C. Triandis, "Cultural Influences upon Cognitive Processes," in *Advances in Experimental Social Psychology*, ed. Leonard Berkowitz (New York: Academic Press, 1964), pp. 9–48.

LANGUAGE AND STYLE

more than one culture, and we can participate in several subcultures at the same time. The difference a culture makes can be seen in terms of a person's immigrating to another country and becoming acculturated. A person who moves from a small rural town to New York City faces a similar shift in cultures.

A culture shares certain beliefs; it holds in common a folklore, a set of myths, a series of rituals. The bicentennial celebration in the United States isolated some of the myth and folklore about the founding and growth of our country that we shared. In challenging the accuracy of many of those beliefs, scholars and the media alike were the target of anger and protest expressed by many who did not realize that their culture was not a truth.

Subcultures present a significant problem for the communicator. By definition the members of a subculture share certain rituals, myths, and beliefs, which are often reflected in a shared language unique to the group—unique in terms of words used or in the interpretation given to particular words, phrases, and nonverbal behavior (such as dress, movement, eye contact, a handshake). There is a tendency for elements from one subculture to move to the larger culture or to be shared with other subcultures—particularly those in close contact. Thus, many expressions and behaviors that were initially associated with black athletes have become shared by athletes generally. Similarly, the music, activities, and jargon of those at rock festivals have been somewhat transformed and partially absorbed by the larger culture.

The difficulty of cross-cultural communication has been illustrated repeatedly in the diplomatic and business worlds. Even the casual tourist encounters unexpected difficulty. For example, people in some cultures tend to stand much closer in conversation than people do in other cultures. Many Americans find it impossible to stand at a comfortable distance while talking to an Italian; the Italian in turn wonders why the American keeps moving away. An early dinner may be a 6:30 arrival in one culture, a 10:15 arrival in another.

Persuaders must be sensitive to the problems of communicating between two people from different subcultures. A well-intended comment may be seen as a slight. The attempt to use a nonverbal gesture to show identification may succeed in convincing the receiver that the persuader is out of touch: the effort to communicate a shared value may communicate exactly the opposite. Something as apparently simple as addressing a person as Ms. (or Miss or Mrs. as appropriate) may produce a frigid, angry response. When certain conventions are not widely shared in a culture or are in transition and rules for use of the convention not generally known, addressing a letter may pose a significant difficulty for the persuader.

THE NATURE AND FUNCTION OF STYLE

The term *style* is used in two characteristic ways: as referring to general, characteristic patterns of behavior, and as related to language choice and order. In the first sense we talk of the Ford style or the Carter style. Style in this sense includes typical patterns of organization, emphasis in support forms, voice, action and movement—anything that contributes to the image of the individual as a communicator. Those seeking to impersonate or mimic a communicator use a few of these characteristics, often with pronounced success.

The second, more limited usage restricts style to characteristics of language in terms of effects achieved through the choice and ordering of words. Although considering style in this more restricted sense, we need not lose sight of the interrelationship between language and other message elements. A "vivid, powerful phrase" delivered in a slack, slovenly manner hardly qualifies as a "vivid, powerful phrase" in terms of the listener's perceptions.

Style Defined

Although suggestions about the basis of a good style may differ widely, most writers agree that style is the way in which the thoughts of the speaker (or writer) are expressed. This includes word choice and order or syntax. This basic thought is expressed in a variety of ways and with different emphases.

Buffon, for example, saw style as the order and movement that one gives to one's thoughts.[8] Accordingly every communication has a style, and in Buffon's view style is the person. Each communicator has several different styles, varied in some systematic fashion in different situations, in different media, and in communicating to different receivers.

Carpenter approaches style from a different purview. Carpenter sees style as a departure from the norm. "Style is concerned with selection of words and their arrangement in sentences. Whether or not a specific selection of word or syntax *is* stylistic, however, depends on whether or not that choice favors an option which while grammatical departs from what would be customary and familiar in a particular situation."[9] Although this approach contains significant implications about how to achieve greater impact in one's style, it is not a necessary point of view

---

[8] De Buffon, "An Address Delivered before the French Academy upon the Day of His Reception," in Lane Cooper, *Theories of Style in Literature* (New York: Macmillan, 1922), pp. 170–79.

[9] Ronald H. Carpenter, "Style and Emphasis in Debate," *Journal of the American Forensic Association*, 6 (1969): 27.

concerning style. It seems best for our purposes to retain the notion that every communication has a style. Most writers on style have dealt with the impact and methods of obtaining a good style. At times *style* really meant good style.

Aristotle said good style was clear and appropriate, with any art concealed and the expression seeming natural and spontaneous. Herbert Spencer approached the same goal as Aristotle but with an emphasis upon receiver response: the best style provides the greatest economy of effort on the part of the auditor for perception, conception, and emotional response. Anything that demands increased effort for the same return is a less effective style. More intense response or deeper perception might demand greater effort rather than less intense perception, but this would fit Spencer's dictum about economy. Aristotle and Spencer provide the guidelines for a sound estimate of the function of style and the basis for developing a theory about achieving a good style. Too many people tend to view style as did DeQuincey: the art of treating any subject "ornamentally, gracefully, affectingly." From this emerges a tendency of emphasizing a style of excessive ornamentation, of "purple patches," of embellishment for the sake of embellishment. Style can be allowed to become more important than the content the style should be communicating. A means to an end may supplant the end itself.

Perhaps the emphasis of Longinus's "On the Sublime" is the best view: a mean marks sublimity, one of appropriateness of matter to language and the language to matter.[10] Great thoughts demand great expressions and great figures, but great figures and expressions without great thoughts are bombast. The term *mere rhetoric* has often been associated with such excessive efforts.

In persuasion analysis, style should be treated functionally in terms of effect upon the mediational processes of attention, comprehension, and acceptance. The best style maximizes effect. This may well demand beauty, but beauty is a means to an end and not the end itself.

ANALYSIS OF LANGUAGE AND STYLE

Style and language present significant problems for the researcher seeking to investigate their effects. The relationship between language and style and content is necessarily close. To substitute a word is to shade the meaning; to alter a phrase is to alter the meaning achieved. Thus an alteration in style is also an alteration in the meaning of the content. Carpenter argues that style can be altered without changing the content. Perhaps a change in word order or word choice changes

[10] Longinus, "On the Sublime," trans. H. L. Havell in Cooper, *Theories of Style*, pp. 97–159.

the style more than the content; yet the effects of both are confounded by being measured in terms of the same representational mediational process.

A number of measures have been used to study language and style: size of recognition and use vocabulary, variety in word choice, order, sentence forms, length of sentences, punctuation, ratio of verbs to adjectives, readability, interest, and communality of language. Readability scores measure word complexity and length of sentences; interest measures focus on personal pronouns and specific references. The measure of communality is typically the "cloze" procedure, in which words are deleted at arbitrary intervals, usually every seventh word, and respondents fill in with the missing word. These studies show that vocabulary size correlates with intelligence, age, and education. Oral speech has typically been found to make greater use of personal pronouns, verbs as compared to adjectives, and variation in sentence length and structure. Studies consistently show that people display significant variations in language and style depending on the situation and the medium employed.

Most of the studies in language and style are descriptive. They show that people differ, but these differences are not shown to determine effectiveness. The fact that people do vary style suggests that such variations are learned and indicates that variation in style is rewarded—that the variations are learned because they are effective. Further, common sense suggests that a single style is not appropriate for all situations and purposes. The persuader who can master a great range of style and adjust to various situations is likely to increase persuasive effectiveness.

Written and oral styles differ, although there is a great deal of overlap. Formal speech situations demand a more dignified, elevated style than an informal letter or memo does. Advertisers often use a highly informal, colloquial style in ads for one product and a much more dignified, formal style for a different product.

Interpretation of the research on language and style indicates that the persuader should develop a flexible, responsive style that adjusts to a range of situations, sources, receivers, subjects, and so forth. No one style is appropriate for all occasions. There is no perfect style.

Humor

Although closely linked to language and style, humor is more than a matter of use of language and a particular style. It is true that humor often depends upon language, style, and techniques of delivery to achieve the recognition "That's funny." Responses can range from the hearty belly laugh and giggles to a wry smile and a sense of warmth in recognition. Development of humor often depends on language characteristics such as punning, dialect, word choice, and on stylistic features such as suspense, antithesis, and other reversals closely linked to humor. Delivery in the sense of timing, use of the pause, inflections, and other nonverbal behavior that reinforces or links to the humor are important factors in achieving the effect of humor.

Because the role of humor in persuasion has been studied in only a few instances, no clear relationship of humor to persuasiveness has been identified. Most of these studies have been conducted in situations involving rather large audiences. But humor seems to play important functions in the one-to-one and small group situations where proximity and shared experiences might make its use even more effective than in certain large group settings.

Humor may do many things in the persuasion process. It can affect attention, and it often attracts interest. It can serve as a means of identification and polarization. We can laugh together, or we can laugh at things. Thus, humor can facilitate response and unify audiences. The technique can work effectively as a weapon of defense or rebuttal or even attack as in a "reduction to absurdity" strategy in which we try to extend a point or take a section of it and reduce it to an absurdity. Humor can serve many psychological functions: it can relieve tension or manifest aggression, superiority, or deference depending upon the target and the use of the humor.

Humor is a difficult weapon because it cannot always be controlled. Irony, satire, and subtle debunking often do not work because the audience fails to perceive the humor or reversal and so reacts in a fashion opposite to that intended by the persuader. Some humor can yield identification (as when parents share experiences in raising children) but it can also produce separation. Children if they overhear parents often feel they are being laughed at and not with. Kramer researched cartoons in magazines such as the New Yorker and found that they tended to portray women in service, sexual, or less desirable, less powerful roles as compared to men.[11] The humor in magazines such as Playboy has been an increasing target of many who consider it harmful, even for those who enjoy the humor.

It is wise to select humorous material or to develop the humor out of the subject matter and common experiences shared by persuader and the receivers. Humor that has no relationship to the subject may distract

---

[11] Cheris Kramer, "Folk-Linguistics: Wishy-Washy Mommy Talk," Psychology Today (June 1974): 82–85.

198   CREATION OF MESSAGES

the audience. Further, material that does not relate meaningfully to the subject may call attention to the effort at humor. If there is no response, the communicator may have to deal with an awkward situation in which a graceless move back to the subject may be the only alternative.

Most persuaders should avoid the role of comic and see humor as another potential to use in persuasion. Care should be taken that the humor is not going to be distracting. Humor that grows out of the material or the natural, easy relationship between participants seems very helpful. Often the warm and acceptive nature of the communicator permits the gentle humor to have its effect. In persuasion humor is a means to an end and not an end in itself.

LANGUAGE AND STYLE IN PERSUASION

The basis of evaluation of language and style in persuasion is the effect of these elements in determining persuasion outcomes. This approach yields a judgment of language and associated stylistic features in terms of their effect on the mediational processes of attention, comprehension, and acceptance. It is true that style has aesthetic dimensions. Communications evaluated from the view of the poetic are judged in terms of beauty. To some degree aesthetic response, particularly in certain situations, is an important key to persuasion effectiveness. Many communications are judged as having great beauty and as being a part of literature. Some communication efforts that are considered enduring works of art have been ineffective persuasive efforts judged from immediate response. The persuader's immediate concern is not with beauty and art, but with functional effect. As many Danish designs reveal, functionality and beauty are often closely related.

Attention

In the attention process, style should be used to select and direct attention toward desired elements. Hence, a style that draws attention to itself and away from the content generally mitigates against success. At times, empty but grand verbiage may achieve a desired end. These cases are probably fewer than communicators apparently assume them to be; probably the same objective could be accomplished in more desirable ways.

How can style affect the attention process favorably? Carpenter suggests that departures from the norm that are not incorrect are stylistic. To the degree that these departures must be novel, unusual, and have elements of change and variety, these methods serve to select attention.

Carpenter lists five general patterns of style: repetition, omission, suspension, schematic inversion, and schematic antithesis.[12]

Repetition involves redundancy, less variety of word choice, and parallelism in structure. The value of repetition in learning has already been observed. Furthermore, the economy of effort in perceiving redundant materials is clear. Redundant material communicates less information but increases the likelihood of transmission of information present. Of course unduly redundant material will become boring, and receivers will not pay attention. If no new material is being communicated, communication should cease.

Omission involves condensation—deleting words and phrases normally used. This omission involves a departure from the expected norms of redundancy. The response "Nuts" to the demand to surrender is more effective than one hundred words. *Suspension* yields a sense of delay and climax. *Inversion* involves a change in position from the normal, and *antithesis* places contrasting elements in contiguous or proximate positions. All of these patterns can draw greater attention to elements or materials than they might otherwise receive.

Use of various figures of speech provides rich opportunities to command attention. Word choice, possibilities in metaphors and similes, strategies in rhyme, rhythm, and sloganeering all draw attention. Rich (and appropriate) imagery possesses great attention value. The specific is often recommended over the general or the abstract because of its ability to attract attention. Appropriate use of figures of speech and similar devices can enhance attention.

The necessary fluctuation of attention suggests another tactical consideration. Not everything in a communication can receive maximum emphasis. Some things must be placed in the sun, some in the shade. Style provides the opportunity to highlight and shadow appropriately so that important and less consequential elements are appropriately stressed.

Effective style is often associated with proper use of support materials and motivational elements. Good support and strong motivational elements often evoke the patterns associated with a powerful style.

Style seems particularly noticeable when it negatively affects the attention process. Style that draws attention to itself through improper word choice, improprieties in usage, or inappropriate embellishment can be extremely harmful.

An examination of current communication habits suggests that both

---

[12] Ronald H. Carpenter, "The Essential Schemes of Syntax: An Analysis of Rhetorical Theory's Recommendations for Uncommon Word Orders," *Quarterly Journal of Speech*, 36 (1969): 161–68.

written and oral forms of communication are tending toward a more easily accessible style. A traditional dictum holds that oral materials must be relatively comprehensible immediately and written materials ultimately so. Increasingly in the United States, at least, that style seems to be preferred which renders material reasonably instantaneously accessible in any medium.

In many ways the mass media are tying groups into larger cultural communities. Certain pronounced localisms in phrasing, language choice, even pronunciation, therefore, become more distracting. The shopper who has bought a loaf of fresh bread only to be asked if she would like the clerk to "poke it for her" is less likely to think "How charming," and more likely to think "What a hick!" Unless one develops the style of a raconteur, such departures from the norm may draw attention, at least temporarily, away from the content.

Word choice offers many opportunities for negative attention. Excessive jargon—use of words unfamiliar to the receivers—will draw attention. The current slang of a teen group may not receive positive attention with an adult group. The speaker who always employs the term "fascist pigs" for policemen is likely to incur such negative attention values and to direct attention in such negative ways that the entire communication will result in negative persuasion. While the erudite speaker may achieve some degree of impact from using words that distinguish her from the audience, limits may soon be felt.

Unfortunately too few receivers ask for clarification, and in many communication settings, it is unlikely that a person would ask even if it were possible. The loss is partial in terms of comprehension of the content being communicated by the word, but an additional loss is in the attention directed away from other content elements in the search for comprehension of one or two words.

Efforts that betray work in the "reach for images" probably detract as well. Often communications seem stilted and lose attention value because they are too obviously studied efforts rather than direct communication of what one thinks or feels. The "smell of the lamp" can be a distracting stimulus.

Improper adaptation in level of usage and word choice can be very distracting. At one time, textbooks seemed intent on teaching students to communicate in patterns no human being had ever followed. Under the influence of Pooley, Fries, and others, descriptive studies have shown the falsity and the futility of such efforts. Current books on usage espouse the idea of adjusting the language to the level of usage appropriate to situation, receivers, and topics. Levels of usage are determined by the norms of the community in which the communication takes place. The norms of the law court are different from those of the public bar. Term papers are not written in the same fashion as letters to friends. We do not give a public speech in the same way we talk over the breakfast table. (If we do, one or the other is likely to be rather ineffective communication.)

Excessive departures from the norm may well be ungrammatical. In general, oral communications demand less formal usage than written communications operating within the comparable situation. An oral argument does not require the formality of the written brief; oral defense of a point does not require the conventions of the written defense. Excessively formal or proper usage can be as distracting and harmful as ungrammatical and improper usage. Only a boor, not a free soul, greets the queen of England with "Hiya, babe!"

Too vivid or too intense images can be as distracting as or even more distracting than images that are perhaps too dull and ordinary. In style the line between drama and melodrama is often crossed. With the current changing standards of style, the simpler and less vivid image is probably more effective in instances of uncertainty than opting for the more intense.

Unduly dull, repetitious, qualified, impersonal style will lose attention. Injunctions to use the blue pencil are legion. Thesis directors delight in telling doctoral candidates to employ "hairy-chested verbs," Anglo-Saxon nouns.[18] It seems pointless to repeat the injunctions, but perhaps valuable to attempt application again.

Comprehension

Proper word choice is the key to comprehension. The discussion of meaning stressed that meanings exist in people, not in words. Words stir up meanings that people have derived from their past experience, but words do not contain these meanings. Even denotative meanings vary widely; connotations may be diametrically opposed. A mother may shrink from the garter snake her young daughter offers so proudly.

Selecting the proper word depends upon an action of mind. We seek a word that to some degree impales the thought we have. But this is dependent upon our own clear perceptions initially, and we can draw only from the store of available words. Further, our linguistic habits tend to dictate the words we will choose. Every person develops patterns that

---

[18] Despite the antagonism I feel for almost all books on style and usage, I find one book enjoyable to read. Many of you might enjoy it as well: William Strunk, Jr., *The Elements of Style*, rev. E. B. White (New York: Macmillan, 1959).

render succeeding words highly predictable. Particular topics, themes, patterns, and slang come to characterize a person. We all have our own patterns of probabilities and predispositions in language choice.

Naturally the right word is dependent upon the potentialities and predispositions in language choice. The right word depends upon the potentialities of the receivers. The perfect word for the source may be meaningless to the receivers.

The search for the right word must be approached realistically. In a message that may contain a thousand words, one or two words rarely make the significant difference in comprehension, in the image of the speaker, in anything (although one word can be the determining factor of success or failure). Probably one right word could be found, but several words may serve effectively, and no known measuring instrument could detect any difference. Yet there is value in the search for the means to distill and disseminate the exact idea we wish to communicate.

Much of the effort we view as stylistic is an effort to clarify our own thoughts and conceptions. All of us have said, "I know what I mean but I can't put it into words." In my case I usually mean I cannot discriminate sharply and distinctly what I wish to communicate, but I have a vague feeling I am searching in the right area. Clear comprehension by a receiver seems heavily dependent upon clear comprehension by the communicator. The act of communication often results in even greater clarification for the communicator, who revises, perfects, and sharpens the ideas as he goes. Sometimes we do not know what we think until we find ourselves saying it. Sometimes the receiver through interaction is the key to the process. The receiver's questions or responses enable us to clarify our view.

Words existing in isolation may have almost an infinity of meanings. We work with a finite number of words to represent an infinite number of things. Furthermore, the university today is not the university yesterday or the university tomorrow. The term *love* means so many different things that the word alone means almost nothing. Fortunately, in communication our words occur in contexts. They are linked to other words. They are given by particular communicators in particular situations and to particular receivers. The statement, "I love persuasion," has a reasonable opportunity for adequate comprehension if made by a woman to a classmate while walking out of the class. The tone of voice can also make a big difference.

Certainly as tools of communication, meanings that words stir up are related to all the factors in the surrounding matrix; the word does not carry the whole burden.

Often special attention needs to be given to ensure comprehension of the meaning of a term or word as the communicator intends it. Definition becomes an important key. Definitions may be offered through restatement, through the context, by examples, by negation. Many of these techniques also heighten impact and serve to increase attention as well as comprehension.

Sensitivity to the receivers seems the key to ensuring comprehension. A communicator who can soundly estimate the experiences of her receivers and where they are in terms of the problem area and materials being used has a basis for developing a maximally effective style to aid comprehension.

The medium interacts with language choice and style to affect comprehension. Print permits a reader to reread, stop, use a dictionary, puzzle through the copy. Radio, television, film, and direct oral interchanges are transitory. Unless the material is on tape or some other reproductive medium and can be played and replayed at the convenience of the auditor, material must be caught relatively instantaneously. For close study most materials of this transitory nature are typescripted or replayed extensively.

Face-to-face oral communication permits questions and provides a variety of other feedback stimuli. Many oral communication settings involve almost constant interchange among people in a conversation, in small groups, or in one-to-one settings. Even without verbal feedback many visible cues to auditor response are provided, which can yield adjustments in order to maximize comprehension.

Acceptance

The persuasiveness of style is a complex problem. To change the style seems inevitably to change the content to some degree. Words are not identical; therefore, to change a word is to change the content (meaning) of the word. Hence we are faced with the question of the degree to which the change in content is persuasive and the degree to which the style is persuasive and how the two interact.

To the degree that attention and comprehension contribute to acceptance, style that maximizes these processes increases the potential for acceptance. Intuitively, it appears that style can do still more to yield acceptance. There may well be a persuasiveness of style per se; elements of style may directly mandate persuasion.

Some syntactical patterns have implications linked to persuasion. Redundancy seems to exert a compelling effect. Nazi Germany used the "big lie" technique and repetition of certain themes as keys to acceptance. In the 1964 Democratic National Convention Hubert Humphrey used parallelism in structure with the audience joining in shouting the repeated parallel response. Rhetorical questions use this same value of active audience involvement. Material must be styled to make such participation possible.

Images seem to compel assent in many instances. A well-framed image that seems correct and apt may be so appealing it is instantly accepted. Metaphors and similes may be so right that the person or thing never escapes the label.

The role of aesthetic appeal in yielding acceptance is a particularly difficult problem. Aesthetic responses can involve the person with the object to which he or she is responding. Participation may yield a sense of rightness that sweeps the person along. Assent may be derived from the flow of line, the impulse to associate oneself with the material. Poetic devices of every sort may serve the practical communicator talking of workaday matters.

Commercial persuaders often test various artistic elements, such as color, lettering, and positioning, in the layout of ads. They may evaluate product names at great length, and use different names in various test markets. Motivational research has led many advertisers to adopt words for associational rather than denotative values. Slogans can be extremely effective in gaining acceptance.

Kenneth Burke's rhetorical theory uses a principle of identification as the heart of rhetoric.[14] Persuasion occurs as the source and receiver become identified with each other through the linguistic strategies employed. Language is the most important tool employed to yield identification. The phrase "he talks my language" is a common indication of praise and identification. I may accept a person and her proposition and ideas if she uses words that link her with my ideas, my values, my reference groups. Certainly the Burkean principle of identification operates at levels other than stylistic, but stylistic identification is a major thrust.

As Burke notes, words as agencies or tools relate to the other factors in the persuasion matrix that motivate behavior: violent scenes demand violent acts and violent acts demand violent words.

In primitive societies one's name is often concealed because an enemy who knows your name has gained power over you. The confusion between the word and the thing is much emphasized in general semantics. People who might faint at the sight of blood may also faint at the mention of it. Vivid descriptions can make us feel the horror of a vicious crime. The tendency not to distinguish between the word and the reality the word presumably symbolizes suggests that style often has direct persuasive impact.

---

[14] Kenneth Burke, *A Grammar of Motives* (New York: Prentice-Hall, 1945), *A Rhetoric of Motives* (New York: Prentice-Hall, 1950).

Burke notes the power to name things is of great import. Joseph McCarthy's name became the label for an era in which a person's credibility was demolished in the eyes of many people because he could be claimed to be an "associate of known Communists." The confusion between words and reality will not be halted by injunctions to avoid such confusion. Certainly the problem affects the communicator who seeks to transmit as accurately as possible the reality he perceives as well as the intentional distortions of reality.

The limits of language and style as the direct cause of persuasion versus their role as mediators for other factors inducing persuasion cannot yet be assessed. The hand is often quicker than the eye; the word is often more powerful than the reality it symbolizes. The claim "Give me the right word and I will rule the world" is not a totally idle one.

Style can also affect acceptance negatively. Burke stresses the use of linguistic strategies that proclaim identity. But language can also proclaim isolation and separation. Words and style may mark one as of another camp, tribe, or persuasion. Other instances may be more subtle; the person who uses "allness" statements, either by implication or overtly, is displaying a different cognitive style from that of a person who carefully qualifies. Often this tendency to make sweeping statements is more a matter of the communicator's style and action of mind than of his or her actual perceptions. Yet differences in this respect could cause negative response.

Excessive and unfair labeling can cause a wave of sympathy or a reaction against the overstatement. A wolf may win sympathy for being excessively maligned.

An ill-chosen slogan or image can be disastrous. The slogan "Rum, Romanism and Rebellion" has been judged the reason Blaine lost a presidential election to Cleveland. A minister used the phrase in Blaine's presence and newspapers picked it up. The Democrats seized upon the ill-chosen phrase and retailed it widely. The negative reaction apparently swung enough votes that Cleveland pulled out a victory over Blaine.

Furthermore, the appropriateness of an image or of the style as a whole seems necessary to avoid negative response. An unduly embellished style may cause negative response. An audience roused to great expectations by the style may respond negatively to a "piddling" request. A speech to Iowa farmers that the speaker describes as "a discussion of the problems incident to and incumbent upon the tasks of an individual who is involved in the exacting requirements of removing wastes deposited by swine in areas where domiciled" is likely to bring rejection of the speaker as pompous and to create negative sets, which mitigate against acceptance of whatever he urges.

On the whole, if communicators follow the guidelines of seeking to accommodate to situation, message and purpose, medium, receivers, and to themselves and to stress economy in terms of the effort demanded of receivers to obtain an optimum response, style will probably develop in the desired direction.

Style has been said to be something to be "caught" because it cannot be taught. Certainly concern for the development of an effective style in persuasion is an important element in the success of any communicator. Often the polishing of style is the culmination of the sharpening process that began with the selection of subject, development of appeals, and structuring of messages. By concentrating on smaller units of material and seeking to maximize the effect of the linguistic medium in terms of attention, comprehension, and acceptance, the communicator should be improving his or her persuasive effort.

SUMMARY

Language is the means that a communicator uses to stir up meanings in receivers. As a tool language has built-in limitations. A limited number of words must symbolize an infinite number of things. Further, meanings are not contained in words; words only stimulate those representational mediational processes in receivers that we call meaning. Thus, words are stimuli for which people have meanings, but these meanings differ according to referential frameworks, which are at best only relatively similar and may be totally dissimilar.

Style is the form and order one gives to thoughts. Thus, since every communication has form and order, it has a style. The choices we make automatically and uncritically might be thought of as our natural style. But in fact a person's style shifts somewhat automatically with the medium employed and with the task. Thus, each individual has many styles. More effective communicators may be those who can adjust maximally to the demands of a given situation.

Different subject matter, different purposes, different occasions and media, different receivers and different sources all help to determine language choice and style. The effectiveness of such linguistic considerations as language choice and style may be evaluated in terms of their impact on the mediational process of attention, comprehension, and acceptance basic to persuasion.

Two major guidelines for judging style are the appropriateness of style and the economy of effort demanded of the receivers to achieve optimal attention, comprehension, and acceptance.

The problems of investigating the effect of style are many because of the confounding of changes in the meaning of content with changes in style. In working with stylistic matters a communicator is completing

LANGUAGE AND STYLE

and perfecting processes related to selecting materials, developing appeals, adjusting to receivers. In addition it seems plausible that style directly affects some degree of persuasion in its own right. Certainly the development of a good style in terms of maximizing impact on attention, comprehension, and acceptance is part of developing mastery of the persuasion process.

DISCUSSION QUESTIONS AND PROJECTS

1. What limitations does language have as a tool for communication? Could an improved language be developed that overcomes these limitations, or are they inherent in the nature of language?

2. Language is held to determine our view of the world in large part. For example, Eskimos have over twenty different words for snow. What problems would such a degree of specificity concerning snow give you if you were to talk with Eskimos?

3. Discuss some of the problems arising out of linguistic barriers that confront a nation such as the United States in trying to communicate to the people of a country through a means such as "The Voice of America."

4. Compare three or four samples of your own communication efforts in situations of varying formality and involving both oral and written modes. What differences do you see?

5. If a person has a style that seems identical in both oral and written modes and in formal and informal situations, does this denote a person who is truly himself? Is he likely to be an equally effective communicator in all situations?

6. Studies suggest that meanings of many terms differ systematically between blacks and whites. How would this difference compare to that between the affluent and the poor in general; urban versus rural dwellers?

7. Discuss the degree to which aesthetic dimensions of communication affect persuasiveness. What about films, plays, poems, and other creative materials that make a didactic or propagandistic point?

8. Language is always changing. What factors can you identify that force language to change? What factors are associated with change in language? You may wish to discuss vocabulary, syntax, grammar, and meaning.

9. To what degree is there a conflict between beauty of style and effectiveness of style in effecting persuasion? Many people feel that the age of the great orator is past, that beauty is gone, and that communication is becoming ugly.

10. Why should we continue to put up with variations in meaning? A group should establish meanings, publish the results, and thus solve the problem. What are the fallacies of this approach?

11. Do you believe that style in all media is tending toward adoption of the conventions of oral rather than written communication?

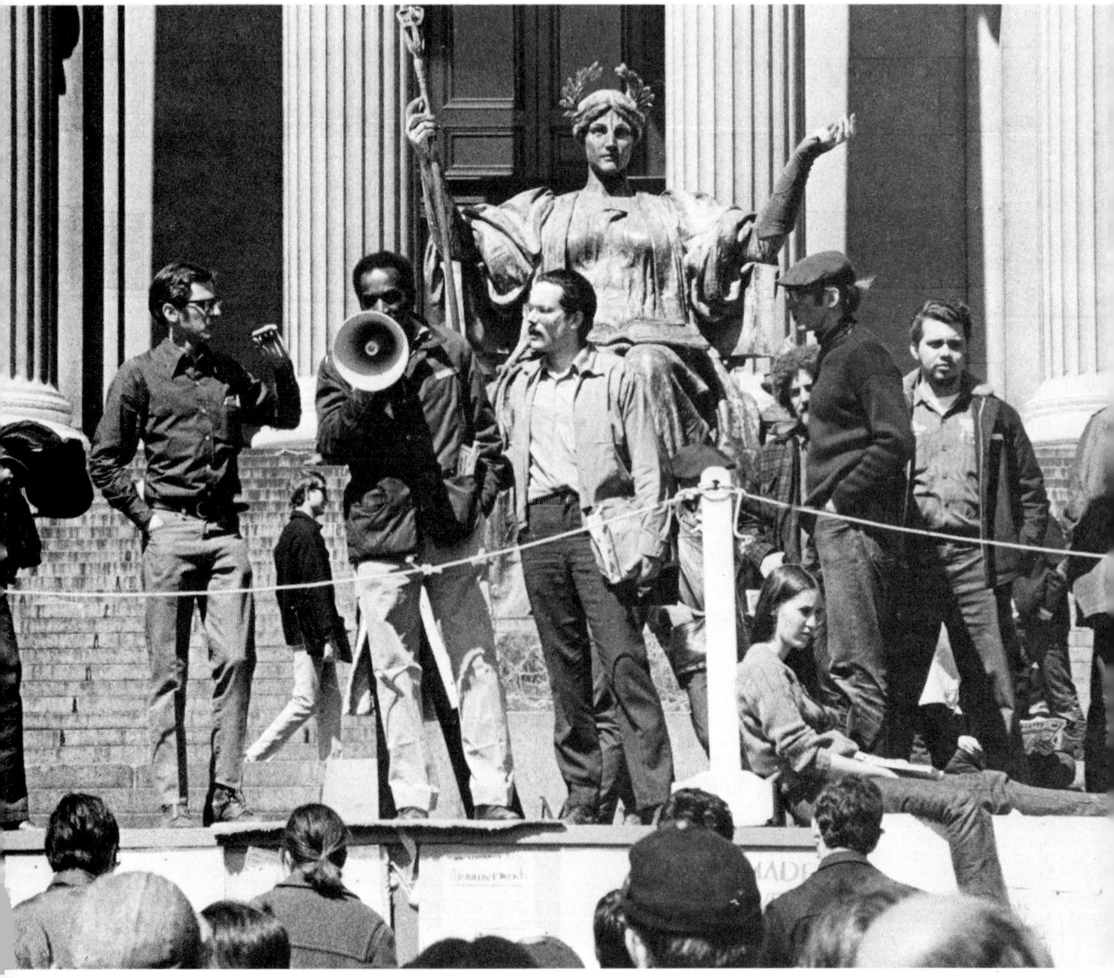

10 Delivery: Bringing the Message Into Being

A message comes into existence at the moment a signal is put into a channel. Delivery may be viewed as the process that starts with a desire to communicate an idea (a potential message) and ends with the creation of some message in one or more channels. The gap between the potential and the actual message may be almost nonexistent or so great that the two do not fit together. Although we tend to think of the delivery process as simple, it is quite complex. The ideas that exist in the brain are quite different from the characteristics of the sound waves in the air. The act of speaking may not seem complex until we remember that it took us several years to master the various sounds in the language. Delivery becomes so automatic that we don't have much conscious awareness of it as a process. But remember the slips of the tongue, the sentence begun, and the sudden block when we forgot the ending. Remember when you most wanted to sound calm and assured, and your voice shook or you talked too fast or the pitch was too high. Remember saying you liked something when your face and body shouted exactly the opposite.

Delivery is largely a matter of habit acquired through long experience. And we are unconscious of most of the actions we perform in giving our messages an existence. Perhaps popular books like *Body Talk,* workshops entitled "Reading People like a Book," newspaper columns about dressing for success, or the old saw "What you are shouts so loudly I cannot hear what you say" remind us of the power of delivery, of nonverbal behavior in persuasion. Most of the popularized materials place too much emphasis upon the body, voice, or attire without weighing all the factors that work together to produce an effect. One gesture, one posture can say many things; we make an error in assuming it says only one thing.

The delivery process is linked to the medium or channel being employed. A channel may transmit only a portion of the available stimuli. Radio does not transmit as many stimuli as television or color, sound motion pictures. Even listeners seated at comparatively great distances from a speaker do not receive the same cues as receivers seated in the front row.

Further, many people and processes may intervene between the placement of a signal in a channel and its reception. For example, in revising this paragraph, which was typed initially, I first talked it through, wrote it longhand, and then typed it. It will be typed again before going to the publisher, where it will be reviewed, edited, and set in type with space, arrangement, and typeface according to the style manual and machines being employed. Finally, the printed material will be picked up by your eye, and you will supply the meaning. This example is not atypical. Think of the intervening people, processes, and choices made between a word spoken at the press conference and its appearance in the evening paper.

This chapter examines the role of delivery in the persuasion process. It will not focus upon the slip between the idea and the expression or examine the effects of the mass media. Rather, it will focus on the effects of the voice and body as they bring the message into being in oral communication.

NONVERBAL COMMUNICATION

Delivery, bringing a message into being in a channel, raises the question of the relationship between verbal (the word or linguistic element) and nonverbal communication. Since people use the term *nonverbal* in various ways, it is difficult to keep the relationship between verbal and nonverbal clear. Harrison limits linguistic communication to "the vocal-auditory channel in speech and the visual channel in writing." [1] Anything else is presumably nonverbal. But the relationship is not simple. A spoken word is created with a certain force, at a pitch level or levels, rate of utterance, and quality. Movement, small and large, typically accompanies speech, and it often changes the meaning of the spoken word. Certain gestures have become so stylized they communicate more effec-

[1] Randall P. Harrison, "Nonverbal Communication," in *Handbook of Communication*, ed. Ithiel de Sola Pool et al. (Chicago: Rand McNally, 1973), p. 94.

tively than the spoken word. In some languages, such as Chinese, the same syllable spoken at different pitches is several different words.

We need to remember that the verbal and nonverbal go together as a unit. We may separate them for analysis, but they work typically as a unit, a gestalt, in which the whole is more than the parts, and the elements contributing to the whole are not easily analyzed. Nonverbal elements seem particularly important in providing cues that suggest the power relationships and the roles of the people involved, the interaction patterns, and appropriate behavior. In this sense they suggest appropriate means of feedback and proper turn-taking in interaction. Nonverbal signs communicate content—often reinforcing, sometimes modifying—sometimes more efficiently than any word might. In typical communication interchanges nonverbal signs contribute to redundancy; they reinforce by saying the same thing as other signs and thus help to improve the chance of communicating the desired meaning. When the nonverbal cues conflict with the linguistic codes, we have an interesting situation; as we shall see, often the nonverbal cues rather than the word control the interpretation given.

Harrison distinguishes four broad categories of nonverbal behavior. The first, *performance codes,* relates to movements and actions of the body (such as facial expressions, eye movement, and posture). A subcategory is used to include paralinguistic phenomena associated with speech (such as rate, pitch, tone quality, grunts, laughter, and malfluencies). The second category, *artifactual,* includes dress, furnishings, status symbols, and other objects relating to the communicator. The third, *mediational codes,* relates to the actions of the media on material (such as cropping photographs, rearranging the order of a taped sequence, adding music or sound effects). The fourth, *contextual codes,* has to do with the way we use space and time as signs in communication.

This breakdown points to significant factors in the persuasion process. The majority of this chapter will be devoted to a discussion of the performance codes, although the other three codes also relate to the performance code and to other aspects of persuasion and its effects.

Artifactual Codes

Personal appearance, including dress, hair style, and jewelry, is a significant factor in our impression of a communicator we can see. Judgments of sources are often closely tied to artifactual codes. The power of these elements is seen in the degree to which costumes identify characters in plays and movies. The story of Cinderella suggests the power of dress and appearance; even the sisters and stepmother did not recognize the beautiful lady who was the talk of the royal ball. Similarly, background settings, the decoration of the movie set or the placement of mementoes, the flag, desk, and fireplace in a presidential chat with the nation indicate the power of the objects with which we surround ourselves to prompt, influence, and direct the responses of receivers.

Every persuader must be aware of the specific setting in which a persuasive act is to take place. Distractions or inhibiting objects can be removed or changed. The setting should reinforce attention and give emphasis to the message. One questions the wisdom of expressing grave concern about the world's hunger problem after an expensive dinner of steak and all the trimmings, including a rich dessert. A contrast such as the persuader or those at the head table eating a dinner more typical of the world's population might have great impact. Another possibility would be to discuss the number of people that could have been fed a sensible diet by eating lower on the food chain and with reasonable portions. Whatever the adjustment, some accommodation to the artifactual codes seem called for in this instance.

Mediational Codes

These codes are concerned with additions or changes in a basic message by activities of media people. These codes thus are of most interest to commercial and campaign persuaders. Growing numbers of jobs in advertising and communications media are directly concerned with expertise in terms of the mediational codes. These activities in cropping a picture, using a slightly out-of-focus image, or adding sound or intercutting material parallel the work of the persuader in planning a message. The impact of the mediational codes is suggested by contrasting your response to an event or speech you observed directly and then seeing that event reported on television or in the newspaper.

Contextual Codes

These codes are often closely related to persuasive effects. In the previous chapter we noted the impact of different ways in which time and space as used in different cultures on cross-cultural communicacation. Hall has been particularly interested in analyzing the space relationships between and among communicators.[2] He has identified four different zones of interaction: intimate, personal, social, and public. Americans tend to maintain greater distances in the personal and social zones than do people in many other cultures. Two people directly facing one another may feel uncomfortable. But if they sit across a table or stand at an angle to each other, they are likely to feel more comfortable at a closer distance. People who are too close to each other may lean away, avert their gaze, or become apparently occupied by

---

[2] Edward T. Hall, *The Hidden Dimension* (Garden City: Doubleday, 1966.)

some neutral or common stimulus some distance away. A stranger may look at you in a room or while walking down the street, but eye contact is usually broken as you approach one another. If it is not, the failure to shift one's gaze may be interpreted as a threat, an insult, or an invitation, depending on various factors. The persuader needs to be sensitive to the way in which the receiver uses space and time in interactions. Persuaders may need to adjust to the other, or they may be able to modify the setting or adjust other factors so as to improve the possibility of success in persuasion.

SPEECH

This chapter emphasizes oral communication because of its comparative dominance both in terms of its sheer amount and its effectiveness, and the degree to which speech represents the maximal use of channels as compared to print, radio, or other more limited channels. Various electronic and multimedia channels combine many of the potentialities of the oral medium, but they do not provide a three-dimensional scene; they do not permit touch. Since the mass media demand a greater selectivity in what is presented and involve persons with expertise in a variety of aspects of communication, they often yield greater effectiveness than a simple speech or appeal that most of us might make.

The oral presentation of material involves the performance codes of nonverbal communication. We shall focus upon these in terms of the visible code and the audible code. In face-to-face communication and in television and film, these codes generally operate concomitantly with the language code, and the systems are fused for the most part in terms of their impact.

Obviously these systems can operate independently, and some media stress one element more than another. Generally, however, the three elements are perceived as fused. For example, symptoms of stage fright are manifested in voice, action, and language. Frequently judgments derived from all three systems must agree for the person to be labeled as having stage fright. Further, the audible and visible codes actually coalesce and are called "delivery."

Visual Stimuli

Visual stimuli impact upon receivers through their eyes. This category includes a host of stimuli ranging from the general appearance of a speaker (including height, weight, dress, posture, and other matters of personal appearance) to movement of all or part of the body, particularly the face, hands, and arms.

The significance of dress, manner, and personal appearance should not be overlooked. (These stimuli seem particularly relevant to judgments of the image or ethos of the communicator and hence will be discussed more completely in the next chapter.) The potential of such stimuli to act as selectors of attention, either positively or negatively, and to detract from comprehension and acceptance is clear. Perhaps the negative effects of visual elements are more obvious than the positive ones. Yet reports of famous speakers often note appearance, physical impressiveness, or other such elements as being significant aids to persuasiveness. This section, however, will discuss elements of movement and gesture and some questions specific to the visual realm, such as the role of eye contact in communication.

At one time, delivery was accorded possibly the central place in the study of oral communication. Visual elements received an emphasis equal to that given audible elements. The elocutionary movement brought to the United States and England a period in which training in complex systems with elaborate taxonomies of bodily action was a major facet of training speakers, public readers, actors, and dancers. The influence of Delsarte and and his approach to the teaching of movement and gesture was reflected in the training that many prominent speakers and teachers received and is still apparent in the teaching of disciples of Ruth St. Denis and Ted Shawn in dance. Modern training in oral communication is directly linked to many schools, initially private, that were established in the United States to offer training in physical culture and elocution.

A tendency exists on the part of many to denigrate the importance of delivery as contrasted to content in gaining persuasive effect, partially because of a tendency to separate what should be ultimately treated as unified. Certainly few professors would be happy to say they teach delivery. But comments that audiences make concerning speakers and experimental studies suggest that ignoring delivery is dangerous. For example, although the direct effect of specific elements of visible stimuli cannot be demonstrated, the total impact of the visible code is involved in the persuasive effect achieved.

Clark surveyed attitudes toward certain standards of public speaking. He asked over 250 adults of varying ages to rate a variety of elements from most essential to not essential. They rated gestures and certain elements of delivery as less essential than did textbooks. However, these raters saw certain matters relative to voice and such characteristics as "conversational quality" and "sincerity" as essential.[3] Clark's results

[3] W. K. Clark, "A Survey of Certain Audience Attitudes toward Commonly Taught Standards of Public Speaking," *Speech Monographs* 18 (1951): 62–69.

suggest that audiences do not regard any specific element of visual or audible appeal as necessary but that the various elements become essential as they contribute to general impressions such as "sincerity," "conversational quality," "poise," and "purposiveness."

The existing empirical evidence on the effect of visible action on audience retention or acceptance of content suggests that bad movement or weakness in action produces a negative effect. How much excellent movement or action has a positive effect is unclear. Presumably if visible elements can detract from the effectiveness of content, they can also reinforce content and make it more effective.

Gilkinson and Knower found that poor speakers were differentiated significantly from good speakers in terms of poor eye contact, limited facial response, and fidgeting, as well as by various vocal characteristics.[4] Whether these characteristics provided the basis for the judgment that they were poor speakers or the judgment that they were poor speakers was illustrated by these characteristics cannot be answered by descriptive studies. Henrikson found that student raters stressed negative aspects of voice and physical actions in identifying poor speakers. But content and material were most influential in picking the best speakers.[5] This suggests that delivery can limit success but delivery alone is not sufficient to produce success.

Judgments of sincerity, command of situation, poise, and liveliness are common reactions to many communications. What is the contribution of the visible code to such elements? The role of visible elements has not been demonstrated directly, but material relevant to stage fright would suggest that visible elements do contribute to these judgments.

There are many definitions of stage fright or communication apprehension. Some center on physiological measurements; some center upon the communicator's evaluation of nervousness or confidence level; others center upon judgments made by observers, either presumed "experts" or receivers in general. In a factor analysis of the visible symptoms of stage fright, Clevenger and King found three principal factors: "fidgetiness," which involves a variety of random movement; "inhibition," which relates to unnatural lack of movement and restriction of the normal range of responses; and "autonomia," which includes such elements as blushing, breathing heavily, moistening the lips, playing with a pencil.[6]

[4] Howard Gilkinson and Franklin H. Knower, "Individual Differences among Students of Speech as Revealed by Psychological Tests—I," *Quarterly Journal of Speech* 26 (1940): 243–55.

[5] Ernest Henrikson, "An Analysis of the Characteristics of Some 'Good' and 'Poor' Speakers," *Speech Monographs* 11 (1944): 120–24.

[6] Theodore Clevenger, Jr., and Thomas R. King, "A Factor Analysis of the Visible Symptoms of Stage Fright," *Speech Monographs* 28 (1961): 296–98.

To the degree that "excess tension" is a judgment made by receivers and suggests a speaker who is not in command of the situation and of self, these elements detract from the speech. To the degree that these elements draw attention to the problems of the communicator, they may detract from the communicator's emphasis. Receivers, particularly in face-to-face settings, often empathize with a communicator. If he is "in trouble," an audience may concentrate on the speaker, hoping he will succeed by at least finishing. Classes will give sighs of relief louder than those of the speaker when he finishes. Such concentration on the problems of the communicator must detract from the concentration upon the communication.

Situations differ in the demands that they place upon a speaker. A degree of tension is necessary for the communicator to work with maximum effectiveness in placing her message into the channel. But the appearance of unusual tension may take the ground out from under the speaker's efforts.

Movement and gesture can be overt or covert. An overt action is one that is perceived by a receiver; a covert action falls below the threshold of perception. But as learning theory shows, a stimulus that falls below the limen of perception may through summation of stimuli yield conscious effects. The totality of bodily response by the speaker may create effects that the receiver cannot link to any known stimulus. This operation of covert and overt elements of the visible code may explain a portion of the assumption that an audience can judge a speaker accurately.

The complexity of putting a message into channel is such that a communicator cannot possibly consciously control the elements. The multiplicity of muscles involved in framing sounds and the natural response of the total body to ideas mean that a communicator cannot control all of these factors. During normal nonstressful communication, we may respond with a good deal of bodily activity in posture, facial expression, and gestures, depending on the situation.

Cultures vary in the degree to which the visible code is emphasized. Certain nationalities are stereotyped as using hands, face, and body frenetically in normal communication. Other cultures hold all actions to a minimum. The expressiveness of stances, body line; movement of the body as a whole; or the face, limbs, trunk, and hands is demonstrated in dance. The variety of expressions in dance illustrates the expressive potential of the visible code and the degree to which it is influenced culturally both in terms of what is done and how it is interpreted.

The communication of meaning through the visible code has been investigated in a variety of contexts. Although nonverbal stimuli provide a basis for receiver response and judgment, the judgments vary. There is no systematic theory of nonverbal communication. Much of the emphasis in the study of the visible code has been upon the communication of emotions. For example, studies of facial expression show that people can identify emotional states portrayed with reasonable accuracy, but stereotyping also occurs. Actors' portrayals of emotional states are more accurately judged than portrayals by persons in real life.

The meaning of gestures is conditioned culturally. Two men would rarely kiss while meeting at O'Hare Airport or stroll arm-in-arm through the streets of Madison, Denver, or Salt Lake City. But such behavior would escape notice in many other cultures. Hall's *The Silent Language* treats the impact of culture in communication. He particularly stresses that manners and behavior, totally apart from the language code, communicate in ways we fail to realize because of our cultural orientations.[7]

I discovered that how men handle babies manifests whether they have had children of their own or are close to children. People can no longer tell me that they like children when they do not; the way in which they hold my son tells me what they themselves may not know.

Good visible action is action that as a minimum does not detract from the effectiveness of the communication; it does not detract from desirable attention, comprehension, or acceptance. At its best it maximizes desired attention, comprehension, and acceptance. Although the specifics of such action cannot be described, in general they must relate to the canon of appropriateness to source, situation, messages, receivers, and so forth. It is tempting to suggest that good action is exemplified by persons in normal communication situations in which they are not aware of being "communicators," but this is unwise. Much normal action, since it is learned and habituated, is probably as ineffective as many of the responses made in situations labeled as involving stage fright. We can accommodate to an astonishing variety of actions.

The subject of eye contact is prominently treated in discussions of delivery, although its exact value is unclear. In one test of its importance, students delivered memorized speeches to audiences with marked variation in the degree of eye contact. No difference in effectiveness was found. This study suggests the key consideration about the value of eye contact: in most situations it apparently makes no difference if the message elements are already fixed in every other respect. But this does not mean eye contact is without value. A major source of feedback in most situations involving face-to-face communication is through the eye. The speaker unconsciously and consciously receives a variety of cues to

---

[7] Edward T. Hall, *The Silent Language* (New York: Doubleday, 1959).

audience response. These cues enable her to adjust message factors. She may strive for greater attention; she may repeat for clarity; she may alter her treatment of a topic.

Although lack of eye contact is frequently reported as evidence of ineffective speakers, it is very doubtful if such speakers are ineffective because of the poor eye contact per se; this behavior is a manifestation of a larger syndrome. But poor eye contact is ultimately destructive because it limits the possibility of feedback that can be used to adjust the message to increase the effectiveness of the communication.

Audible Stimuli

Although certain visual elements have become so conventionalized that they function as symbols, we typically think of the audible sounds as carrying the burden of transmitting the language code. In rare instances (such as sign language) the linguistic code is transmitted through the visible code. Those aspects of the audible code relevant only to the transmission of the symbol were discussed under language and style. But this section will discuss the additions that the audible code provides, basically through variations in the four parameters of voice: volume, pitch, rate, and quality and the interaction of these four parameters.

Volume

In his survey of audience criteria for public speakers Clark found adequate volume to be rated as most essential. This is not surprising, for if a message cannot be heard, it can hardly exert the desired persuasive effect. Many situations occur in which the volume is loud enough that the message can be heard, but there is a sense of strain on the part of the receiver. This is tiring, and the attention focused on bringing the stimuli into greater clearness must detract from the energy available for comprehension and acceptance. Often the effort is so fatiguing that one simply stops trying to listen. An excess of volume has a similarly tiring effect: the sound can become oppressive, and one wants to "turn down" or "turn off" the speaker. Too, most of us resent being shouted at.

Pitch

Individual voices differ in normal pitch, range, and flexibility. Training can alter natural predispositions to a marked degree by either training a singing or stage voice or by corrective training to alter improper habits, such as unnatural pitches or monotones. The effect of such training is limited by natural factors; a soprano who persists in singing alto is likely to harm her voice if she continues the practice.

At one time it was widely assumed that certain voices were unsuited to particular tasks. Women were considered incapable of becoming powerful orators. They were also restricted in entering radio because some thought they "lacked a radio voice." Certainly the characteristics of older microphones did make sharp, thin voices, male or female, or persons with sibilant "s" problems very unattractive vocally. Inevitably people do differ in the degree to which their voices are judged as attractive, but this rarely eliminates one automatically from any role. Very effective communicators have had very "bad" voices.

Lack of variety in pitch has been investigated extensively. Variety within reasonable limits and appropriate to the elements involved is the key to effectiveness. Although variability in pitch will not necessarily increase effectiveness in a situation, it may. Within limits of appropriateness it should do no harm and probably can do some good. Unfortunately, no one has studied the effects of markedly improper pitch changes or variety in pitch that exceeds the limits of taste.

Rate

The most researched area of voice is the matter of rate. Perhaps because of radio's emphasis upon voice, a number of descriptive and experimental studies were conducted during the 1930s. The interest in rate has continued to the present day.

An extensive survey of work on rate in radio by Lumley disclosed some interesting anomalies. For example, while NBC recommended that its announcers speak at 170 words per minute, CBS recommended 113 words per minute. Lumley found that different speakers used different rates and that average rates for different kinds of material varied. The average for all radio talks surveyed was 162 wpm (words per minute).[8] Cotton analyzed a performance of Hamlet's soliloquy by John Barrymore. Through a complex procedure of estimating syllable duration, Cotton found that the rates varied from 15 percent above 300 wpm to 12 percent below 39 wpm.[9] Although these variabilities are extreme, even normal conversation displays flexibility in terms of rate.

Research suggests that fairly marked variations in rate, ranging from 100 or 125 to 200 or 225 wpm, do not alter comprehension. Harwood found that a sample of material judged to be "fairly difficult" in terms

---

[8] F. H. Lumley, "Rates of Speech in Radio Speaking," *Quarterly Journal of Speech* 19 (1933): 393–403.
[9] Jack C. Cotton, "Syllabic Rate: A New Concept in the Study of Speech Rate Variation," *Speech Monographs* 3 (1936): 112–17.

of the Flesch Readability Scale did display a significant dip in comprehension between the 175 and 200 wpm rate.[10] This suggests that difficult material may demand a slower rate. More complex material takes greater involvement and effort to comprehend; therefore, rate could reach a point where any further increase would result in a significant loss in comprehension.

In summary, rate can be varied sharply, both through the use of pause and through the length of time or duration given to individual sound units. Wide variations can be accommodated to the point where difficulty of comprehension exerts an upper limit. Descriptive studies suggest that speakers of the earlier part of the century probably spoke more slowly than those of today. But today averages of 150 or 175 wpm are not at all unusual, although certain situations indicate slower average rates. Too constant a rate, of course, may incur loss of attention because of the lack of variety.

Quality

The relationship of voice quality to effectiveness has received little investigation. Elements of quality probably account for many of the effects found in studies concerning voice as a whole. Quality is the result of the complex of factors involved in the production of voice, and variations in quality have been described by a variety of names—most of which are incapable of precise definition. Discussions of quality are often similar to judgments rendered by critics in reviews. Specific problems in tempo or pitch can be identified. But often the reviewer provides an extended dissertation on the strengths or weaknesses of quality by comparison to other singers of the past, or metaphors drawn from any possible bird, animal, or mechanical device. Inevitably the reader will be treated to descriptions of a legato phrasing that approached menthol green but was too restricted and pinched to be truly beautiful. (Thus in effect we all write our own reviews because we lack clear referents for these terms.)

Training can affect the quality of a voice. Unless there are special problems, a person who speaks with a fairly relaxed throat and who is not unduly tense and straining in voice production should achieve a reasonably effective degree of quality in voice. We cannot all sound like Marlene Dietrich, but why not relax and enjoy those who do?

Voice—The Interaction of the Elements

Although we may analyze the elements of voice to assess strengths and weaknesses, we typically respond to voice as something

---

[10] Kenneth A. Harwood, "Studies in Listenability, III. Listenability and Rate of Presentation," *Speech Monographs* 22 (1955): 57–59.

of a unity. Descriptions of desired vocal characteristics often suggest this unity. Speakers are advised to have good vocal variety or a flexible voice that is responsive to the content and the desired communication of feeling and tone.

Vocal effectiveness makes a difference. And the more complex or difficult the material or the greater the hazards of the situation, the more help good delivery can be. When everything is in the favor of the communicator, differences in delivery may not make a great deal of difference, and rather marked difficulties in voice production or delivery may not affect comprehension because receivers can accommodate themselves to a wide variety of characteristics. Yet good delivery does provide a positive factor. Under conditions of controlled distraction, for example, listeners retained more information from the speeches that were well delivered.[11] Beighley found skilled readers helped audiences achieve higher comprehension for complex and difficult material.[12] McCroskey noted that good delivery improved the effectiveness of a speech with good content, but good and poor delivery made no significant difference in the effect of a speech with bad content.[13]

In many situations voice has been shown to have a greater effect upon judgments of the source than upon persuasiveness of material. Bowers found that different delivery styles produced significant differences in the attitudes about the speaker but not in speech effectiveness.[14] Cantril and Allport presented a variety of voices to listeners who were asked to judge characteristics of the speaker ranging from age and height to personality. The receivers could often identify characteristics of the speakers accurately. There was, however, greater unanimity in agreement in judgment than in accuracy; persons tend to make stereotyped responses to stimuli.[15]

Importance of Delivery in Total Effect

Heinberg attempted to assess the comparative effectiveness of delivery versus content in judging general effectiveness. Through a regression analysis he discovered delivery to be almost twice as important

---

[11] John L. Vohs, "An Empirical Approach to the Concept of Attention," *Speech Monographs* 31 (1964): 355–60.

[12] K. C. Beighley, "An Experimental Study of the Effect of Four Speech Variables on Listener Comprehension," *Speech Monographs* 9 (1952): 249–58.

[13] James C. McCroskey, *An Introduction to Rhetorical Communication* (Englewood Cliffs: Prentice-Hall, 1968), pp. 207–08.

[14] John Waite Bowers, "The Influence of Delivery on Attitudes towards Concepts and Speakers," *Speech Monographs* 32 (1965): 154–58.

[15] Hadley Cantril and Gordon W. Allport, *The Psychology of Radio* (New York: Harper and Brothers, 1935), pp. 109–26.

as content in speeches of self-introduction. And he found delivery almost three times as important as content in determining ratings of persuasive speeches.[16] These results must be weighed in terms of the limited variety of topics used. Also, the speakers were students, and all were being rated by professional speech teachers. Speeches graded unfavorably may actually be as effective in gaining attitude and action change. And certainly the criteria that people employ in determining what to believe revolve around some factors not salient to teachers assigning grades to classroom speeches.

The importance of delivery in producing effects varies with the situation. If a speech is delivered at a volume too low to be heard, the delivery determines the absence of positive effect. If the delivery is so poor that it attracts attention almost solely to the delivery, it will inhibit persuasion. To the degree that delivery affects the image of a source negatively, it will harm the potential effectiveness; to the degree that it strengthens an image, it increases potential effectiveness. Ideally delivery should contribute to maximization of desired effects.

There is no formula for effectiveness in delivery. Every person must work within the possibilities of her or his own voice. But as a tool of communication the voice can be made more responsive and flexible. Specific disabilities may be corrected by professional speech therapists.

Delivery must be adjusted to the source, the message, the situation, and the receivers. Patterns and style in delivery change in terms of the whole culture over time as well as specific subgroups within the culture at any one time. The communicator who is sensitive to the qualities of the communication matrix should respond to these vocally and visually just as to other elements. The characteristic criteria of appropriateness and variety seem good precepts in moving toward good delivery.

Much has been made of the role of delivery in winning over people, and clearly delivery is important. We are often urged to develop an intimate, direct personal style, a conversational style. But *conversational style* is a difficult term to define. It may describe a sense or impression communicated but not the effort or skill needed to create this appearance. A person talking in her own living room does not have the range and fullness demanded in addressing a convocation of 500 people on "A Modern God-Myth."

A good delivery does not correlate with an image of a perfect delivery. A good delivery is unique and personal. An occasional malfluency, a slight mispronunciation, or a localism is inevitable. Tolerance limits are reached

---

[16] Paul Heinberg, "Relationships of Content and Delivery to General Effectiveness," *Speech Monographs* 30 (1963): 105–07.

where excesses affect credibility of the communicator and affect comprehension negatively. Differences between markedly different styles of delivery may be so minor that they produce no significant differences in effect.

COMPARATIVE EFFECTIVENESS

The rise of new media inevitably stimulates questions about comparative effectiveness of media. McLuhan has been an energetic advocate of the idea that the move he sees from the world of print to the world of electronic media has revolutionized the way in which people relate to the world through communication. This concern is not original with McLuhan; the rise of radio stimulated many studies during the 1920s and 1930s upon the comparative effectiveness of various media.

The comparative effectiveness of media depends upon questions such as: For whom? Under what circumstances? For what messages? For what purposes? No single generalization can summarize the comparative effectiveness of media because of the impact of the questions.

There are significant problems in researching the comparative effectiveness of media. How does one ensure that the same material is communicated in different forms? Should a TV presentation be only a picture of a lecturer, or should it permit exploitation of the possibilities of the medium? But such differences mean the message (as well as the delivery channel and process) is changed. How does one equate exposure time? It might take ten minutes to communicate some material through a lecture. In the same ten minutes most students could read that material through at least twice and have time to reread specific areas of difficulty a third time.

Delivery modalities can be compared in various senses depending upon the way *modalities* is defined. We might compare the four methods of presentation of speeches, typically called *impromptu, extemporaneous, manuscript,* and *memorized.* But these build in problems of preparation methods and time and are linked to presumed variations in visible and audible codes. We might compare a lecture with a dramatization or discussion. We might contrast a lecture with the use of a loudspeaker or tape to transmit the information, with a printed text of the material, and with a televised presentation of the lecture.

Only a few studies have been concerned with the method of speech presentation. Hildebrandt and Stevens compared manuscript and extemporaneous presentation and found that the styles did not differ in persuasiveness. But different communicators did differ significantly so the researchers concluded it was the quality of the communicator and his or her skills that determined effectiveness.[17] This suggests that a speaker with good communication skills may be expected to be good in a variety of presentation modes.

Impromptu speeches, those done on the spur of the moment without time for preparation, would presumably be more effective on the whole than those that permit careful advance preparation. But the other three modes that permit extended advance preparation may have no inherently distinctive characteristics. A well-delivered speech probably should sound much the same and involve similar patterns of delivery whether memorized, read, or delivered extemporaneously (with advance preparation but without word-for-word execution). Individual people may have distinctive problems with one approach, but these are probably unique to the people handling the material rather than the mode itself. True, some people reading a manuscripted speech sound like gifted four-year-olds reciting a Sunday school piece. But others proceeding extemporaneously may sound even less gifted. Receivers tend to accept the somewhat differing conventions of manuscript, memorized, or extemporaneous presentations. The very presence of the manuscript changes expectations to some extent.

Textbooks have given a great deal of stress to extemporaneous methods of presentation and delivery. It is true that many speakers sound more direct and develop more effective methods of delivery by utilizing the extemporaneous mode. This mode is very similar to much of the normal communication in which we engage. But other people are indirect and halting in utilizing the extemporaneous mode and need the text with them to be even reasonably effective. Presumably everyone could develop a good pattern of delivery in any of these modes, but if one does not have equal strength in all he would obviously employ the one best in terms of the total situation in which he finds himself.

Manuscript and memorized forms of presentation have some unique characteristics. Particularly in terms of language and style, the care possible in obtaining the right word or image may yield dividends. Further, a manuscript is probably essential in certain critical situations where the exact words being spoken are of great import. A person who reads from a manuscript should make fewer Freudian slips and probably has greater protection against the claim that she made a statement when she in fact did not. Putting things on paper can protect all parties in a dispute or negotiation. Often things need to be spelled out precisely. In that case the speaker may need to heed the call to put it in writing.

---

[17] Herbert W. Hildebrandt and Walter Stevens, "Manuscript and Extemporaneous Delivery in Communicating Information," *Speech Monographs* 30 (1963): 369–72.

A major strength of the extemporaneous mode is the opportunity to maximize the possibility of adjustment during the presentation of the communication. A speaker who has content well in hand but leaves the exact wording to the moment of delivery can adjust—and does so in part unconsciously—to the sources of information present in the communication situation. With manuscripted and memorized speeches, alteration is more difficult because the speaker's attention is directed to the precise wording. Also, the characteristics of the inserted material may be quite unlike the prepared material and thus call attention to itself.

When the extemporaneous method is used well, it can be uniquely effective. The speaker is communicating fully and directly to the audience. The idea is coming into reality for self and for audience at the same time in one sense. Often, I suspect, the extemporaneous speaker is seen as truly natural and sincere. Many very good extemporaneous speakers need to be taught the art of interpretation if they are to deliver their own speeches from manuscript or memory effectively. Certainly the extemporaneous mode of presentation is not the desideratum in all instances, but it has sufficient advantages that a persuader needs to develop a good command of the mode.

Discussion methods have been compared to lecture methods. Studies suggest both are often equally effective in transmitting information but that discussion offers some additional advantages in terms of attitude change and commitment to action. But the message elements and the relationships change so significantly that these variations represent changes in setting and not just in delivery. Hence this area will be examined in detail in section V.

Studies comparing face-to-face communication (typically speeches or lectures) with voice-only presentations and with printed versions of the message are numerous. The results show a great deal of agreement. Face-to-face presentations are more effective than radio-type presentations, which are still more effective than print. With complex material, print may be superior to oral presentation. When persuasion is involved, these tendencies for the dominance of the face-to-face mode and the audible code may be more marked than when information retention is the measure of effect.

The comparative advantage of the combination of the audible and visible codes over the audible code alone and over print seems reasonable, especially in terms of persuasive effect. Attention in face-to-face oral settings is usually more concentrated upon the communicator and communication, and there is some degree of insulation from outside distractions. Further, the potential for feedback and accommodation to the receiver is high in face-to-face interaction and almost nil in other situations.

The elimination of the visible code may be important. The visible code transmits cues relative to the nature of the source, thus affecting ethos. Further, the visible elements may reinforce material selectively and thus heighten effect as well as communicate emotional tension of the source, which may produce high empathic involvement.

The voice alone offers possibilities not available in print. The variety of inflections and shades of meaning possible with the human voice are truly amazing. Both connotative and denotative areas of meaning are markedly affected by elements of the voice. It is not exaggerating to say that the variety of communication resources potential in the oral face-to-face situation exceeds those of any other medium. Our own skills are the richest resources for communication, and we should not overlook their immediate availability.

SUMMARY

Messages come into being as a potential message is put into a channel. Typically oral communication in the one-to-one setting permits fullest use of the visible and audible codes. A unique advantage of television and film compared to print or radio is that these media come very close to reproducing the full variety of stimuli found in direct personal communication through speech while offering other advantages as well.

The audible and visible codes seem important for the tone, feeling, and emotional meanings they contribute to the message beyond their contribution to denotative meaning. When the audible, visible, and language codes are maximally integrated, the impact may be so good that the contribution of the audible and visible elements is not perceived. But when they are not so well integrated, specific awareness of the negative effects of monotone, bad gestures, distracting mannerisms, and lack of vocal variety develop rapidly.

A good delivery is not any certain delivery; it must be defined within the context of the communication situation. Minimally delivery does not detract from the processes of attention, comprehension, and acceptance. Ideally it contributes to maximization of persuasion effect, either directly in its own right, through its role as the transmitter of other material, or through its indirect effect on such characteristics as the ethos of the communicator. A good delivery, then, must be responsive to the situation and presumably flexible in permitting such response.

The oral modality is powerful. Laboratory studies suggest that the audible and visible code can significantly reinforce or contradict the language code, particularly in persuasion. The unique power and availability of the oral medium make it an excellent means to employ. But certainly

DELIVERY: BRINGING THE MESSAGE INTO BEING 229

other media have particular strengths and occasions that call them into being. The power of speech should not be understated but neither should it be overemphasized as the only real communication mode.

DISCUSSION QUESTIONS AND PROJECTS

1. How much does the visible code communicate denotative meanings during normal conversation? During speeches?

2. If a person raves about a marvelous speaker, such fine gestures, such a beautiful voice, but has almost no reaction to or memory of the content, what is your judgment of the effectiveness of the speaker? In what ways is he or she a success? A failure?

3. Do you agree with the implication of some experimental studies (such as those by McCroskey cited in the chapter) that delivery only makes a difference with good content or with more difficult content?

4. Chapter 10 argued that there is no absolute standard for a good delivery. What minimums should characterize any acceptable delivery? What criteria may be created to test for good delivery?

5. What differences in delivery do you think characterize manuscript versus memorized versus extemporaneous speeches? What positive and what negative effects would these differences create? You or your class might attempt to check the validity of your assumptions by monitoring a few speeches in each mode and tabulating frequencies of the predicted items.

6. What are some evidences you have seen in cross-cultural communication in terms of the visible code? What is your response if strangers touch you while talking to you or if they never meet your eyes?

7. Does labeling a situation a "speech" situation inhibit natural delivery characteristics? If so, why? Probably you have a sense of what being "natural" means. Why do you feel some things are natural?

8. What stereotypes about delivery do you associate with

various groups (for example, Greeks, Italians, the English, blacks, foreign-born, preachers, politicians, suburbanites, farmers)?

9. What is the effect of pronunciation in speeches? What about mispronunciations? How does this compare to spelling problems in written material? Why do you think there are more variable effects associated with pronunciation than with spelling? Or are there?

10. Discuss the adjustments in delivery made by a speaker presenting an idea to a large audience at a formal convocation versus the speaker presenting the same ideas in an informal conversation in someone's living room.

11. What advantages does print have over the oral medium of communication? What limitations? Are these advantages and limitations inherent in the nature of print?

IV PARTICIPATIO

11 Ethos: Creation and Effects
The Nature of Ethos
Definition
Dimensions of Ethos
The Creation of Ethos
Extrinsic Ethos
Intrinsic Ethos
Consequent Ethos
Ethos as Ethical Proof
Effect of Extrinsic Ethos
Effect of Intrinsic Ethos

S SOURCES

12 Persuasion and Effects upon the Source
Significance
Persuasion of the Self
Reinforcement
Commitment
Cognitive Balance
Effects on Action
Before the Communication Act
During the Communication Act
After the Communication Act

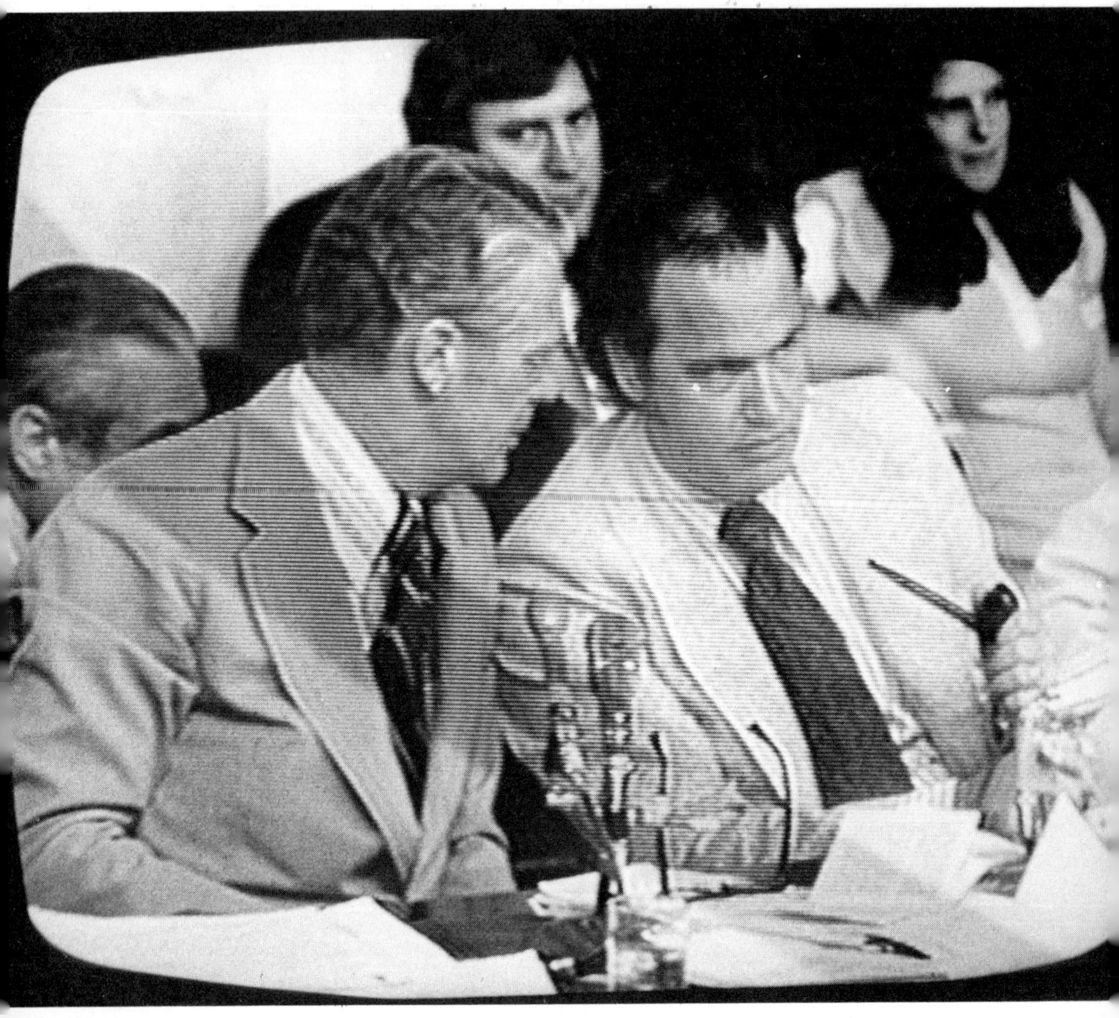

11 Ethos: Creation and Effects

Ethos, the image of the source, is a powerful element in persuasion. Under a variety of rubrics the concept of ethos has received the attention of many rhetorical theorists and experimentalists from classical to contemporary times. Ethos has become the subject of concentrated experimental investigation. Indeed, more research on this topic has been reported in recent communication journals than on any other single concept specifically related to communication.[1]

THE NATURE OF ETHOS

Aristotle perceived ethos as a powerful proof supplied by the source himself and through judgments made of his character, sagacity, and goodwill. But later the stress upon judgments of the source made by auditors became intertwined with questions concerning the intrinsic goodness and morality of the individual and his persuasion efforts. Further, when rhetorical theory was under the dominance of a faculty psychology, logical and emotional proofs could be easily identified with mental faculties but judgments concerning a source seemed less clearly linked to a faculty of the mind. Ethos tended to lose its sharp focus as a major source of proof. This confusion was later compounded by a tendency to adopt terms researchers employed in social psychology: *prestige,*

---

[1] A summary of research findings to 1963 is in Kenneth Andersen and Theodore Clevenger, Jr., "A Summary of Experimental Research in Ethos," *Speech Monographs* 30 (1963): 59–78.

source credibility, expertise. In looking for explanations of persuasion effectiveness, various analysts turned to the "magical personality that persuades," "the mesmerizing personality," when other explanations fell short.

The confusion of approaches and the tendency to name when one did not explain has produced a lack of consensus concerning the nature of ethos. The variety of approaches necessitates careful analysis of the nature and role of ethos in persuasion. This chapter is at once a definition and a theory of ethos.

Definition

Ethos is the image of the source held in the mind(s) of the receiver(s). Fully operationalized, ethos is the total of the receiver's(s') responses to all possible questions about the source. Typically in measurement only a limited number of questions is employed to estimate the image. Thus, the image of the source corresponds to the psychological concept of attitude toward the source and measurement involves the collection of opinions.

Three distinctions implicit in the definition of ethos provide a basis for more extended discussion: ethos is determined by receivers; ethos may change over time; ethos is measured at different times as related to a communication act.

Perhaps the most important distinction is that the image or ethos of a source is determined by the receivers, not by elements in the message or other stimuli in communication and not by characteristics of the source. Stimuli in the message may be deliberately designed to effect a specific impression of the source, or any one of the many stimuli in the message may have an effect upon that impression. But the stimuli must be clearly distinguished from the resultant ethos. The stimuli gain meaning only in terms of the receiver. A communicator may reveal that she is a registered, lifelong Republican. This may improve her image for some, harm it for others, and have no effect on the image held by many others. A source may be quiet and reserved. But a stranger who happens to observe him cutting loose at a party may not perceive the true nature of the individual.

This should not suggest that what a person is and what a person does is irrelevant to her or his image; far from it. But the meaning of these things is dependent upon the person who perceives these stimuli. And the image may be either negative or positive.

The ethos of a source can be thought of in many different ways. An image may be an average of the images of any defined set of receivers. We may be concerned with the national image of the President, or we may focus upon his image in terms of a specific subgroup such as youth, the business community, the press corps of foreign countries. The image could be defined in terms of any one receiver.

It is also possible to talk about the variability of the image. In some instances a source may have a relatively congruent image; a wide variety of people see him in approximately the same way. In my persuasion classes, fairly general agreement exists in almost every class, and has existed among the classes over the last sixteen years, as to Queen Elizabeth's image. Richard Nixon, however, has displayed wide fluctuations in image; the variability within one class is often dramatic.

Although it may be profitable to use the average image of a source in dealing with a given audience, the variability of that image among the receivers may be extremely important. Certainly an image can change in time. John F. Kennedy was not as well known or favorably evaluated as Richard Nixon during the early months of the 1960 campaign. In November Kennedy was elected President. His image was highly favorable for a time after his assassination. As the years have passed President Kennedy's image has become less favorable in terms of the perception of his achievements and his personal style. A popular person who espouses an unpopular cause often becomes somewhat less popular. We may evaluate someone we liked greatly six months ago quite negatively today. Winston Churchill was out of the mainstream of British life in the 1930s for an extended period of time. The same elements that caused him to be outside the mainstream were largely responsible for his becoming prime minister during the war years.

Certainly many things affect the ethos of an individual at a moment in time. But the communication act provides the maximum opportunity for a person to affect the image that exists in the minds of his or her receivers. Therefore it is particularly useful to talk of ethos at certain key points in the communication act and to attempt measurement prior to the communication, during the communication, and after the communication.

Extrinsic or prior ethos is the image that exists up to the moment of the presentation of the message by the source. It includes the prior reputation of the source, the endorsements and introduction received, behavior, and appearance up to the time of the inception of the message. The extrinsic image may fluctuate over time. If the image were measured at a series of points prior to the actual message presentation, one might trace the fluctuation and identify the factors producing it. Often the persuader or researcher is interested only in obtaining an estimate immediately prior to the actual message.

Intrinsic ethos is the image created in receivers during the transmission of the message. Message elements are assumed to be of significant importance, but reaction of other receivers, the channel employed, and extraneous elements will contribute to this image created during the communication act itself. In normal situations, the image created during the communication act must be affected by the prior extrinsic image and interact with it. The intrinsic ethos may be measured at different points in time during the message presentation. Intrinsic ethos is of obvious importance. The changes that occur in an image during communication graphically illustrate the dynamic nature of communication. While the intrinsic image is being changed or reinforced, it is simultaneously changing and reinforcing other factors. It is determining effects at the same time it is being affected.

The consequent image—the image that exists after a communication act has been completed in the sense that the transmission of message has ceased and closely associated activity has been completed—is the result of the interaction of the extrinsic and intrinsic factors related to the ethos, as well as the images themselves and any subsequent influences. The consequent image may also be measured at various intervals. Usually the image is measured almost immediately after the persuasion attempt, but it may be measured on a delayed basis. To a significant degree, the extrinsic image for the next communication act is the consequent ethos as it has evolved since the last communication act.

Since the image of a source changes with different receivers, at different times, and at different stages of a communication act, it needs to be stipulated in terms of the particular receivers in question and the particular point in time. Awareness of these parameters is basic to an understanding of ethos.

Dimensions of Ethos

Aristotle stressed that the ethos of a source was determined by judgments of his character, sagacity, and goodwill made on the basis of choices manifested during the communication act. Aristotle's approach has provided the basis for many later discussions of the dimensions of ethos. The philosopher typifies the approach in which a person analyzes communication and then sets forth his estimation of the key factors without empirical verification.

Most early efforts to measure the ethos of sources essentially used this approach. Sources were judged by a critic or experimenter or by a number of persons who ranked them comparatively in terms of the level of their ethos or prestige. In many instances, various linear rating devices were employed to obtain ratings on a variety of categories felt to be related to ethos. Typically these ratings were utilized with the assumption that ethos remained fixed throughout the communication act and was the same for any topic and possibly any audience. Later researchers associated various sources with various statements on a rotation basis. Change in acceptability of the statement was held to provide a measure of prestige.

All these early measures tended to have one or both of the following weaknesses. First, many confounded the measure of ethos with the measure of persuasiveness. Frequently one could not determine if ethos made no differences in persuasive outcomes or if there was no difference in ethos. Second, measures of ethos that tried to be independent of persuasion effect were dependent upon intuitive assessment of what was or was not a relevant dimension of ethos.

Contemporary research has moved the analysis of the dimensions of ethos from speculation to empirical derivation. A number of researchers initially used the evaluative dimension of the standard semantic differential as a measure of attitude toward the source. Recent researchers have utilized the procedure of factor analysis to determine empirically the dimensions of the image of sources.

Andersen created a semantic differential specifically designed to measure ethos by drawing upon a variety of terms utilized in discussions of ethos and upon terms drawn from the three dimensions typically found in previous investigations utilizing the semantic differential. Undergraduate students responded to a variety of well-known personalities but received no messages attributed to these persons. Analysis of the results indicated that two major referential dimensions were employed in making judgments about these potential sources. These dimensions were identified with the evaluative and dynamism dimensions found in previous analyses. However, whereas the three major factors account for approximately 50 percent of the variance in standard analysis, Andersen found that his two factors accounted for over 60 percent of the variance. The evaluative dimension accounted for 45.6 percent of the total variance, and the dynamism factor accounted for 15.9 percent of the variance. Scales that loaded on the evaluative dimension were honest–dishonest, moral–immoral, fair–unfair, sympathetic–unsympathetic, good–bad, reasonable–unreasonable. Sincere–insincere, open-minded–biased and likable–unlikable also were strongly but not as purely related to the evaluative dimension and were not used in the final instrument designed to measure ethos. Scales that loaded on the dynamism dimension were interesting–uninteresting, strong–weak, fast–slow, aggressive–nonaggressive, and active–passive.[2]

Since 1960 several researchers have employed similar techniques of

---

[2] Kenneth E. Andersen, "An Experimental Study of the Interaction of Artistic and Non-artistic Ethos in Persuasion" (Ph.D. diss., University of Wisconsin, 1961).

factor analysis applied to different settings or different classes of people. Berlo, Lemert, and Mertz used four types of sources: public sources and personally known sources with no relationship to topic and public sources with relevant and irrelevant topics as related to areas of competency. In one analysis four factors—labeled safety, qualification, dynamism, and sociability—were found. A second study, which employed adults drawn from the local community rather than the students used in the first study, found three factors explaining 60 percent of the total variance: safety, qualification, and dynamism.[3] McCroskey in a series of studies found two major categories, which he labeled authoritativeness and character. In later studies with highly specific people such as spouses, friends, and so forth, he found a greater number of dimensions that explained a great amount of the variation. A study of television newscasters produced three major factors labeled reliable–logical, showmanship or dynamism, and trustworthiness.[4]

Although they differ in many respects, these and other studies are congruent to a large degree, considering the different situations and audiences studied. Evaluation of the source is the most important aspect of images that we hold. Andersen found only one general evaluative dimension when sources were not personally known and not linked to messages. Later studies that linked sources to messages tended to find at least two separate factors of an evaluative nature: trustworthiness or safety and expertness or authoritativeness. Dynamism is a usual but less important dimension of source images.

Most studies of ethos have focused upon the "average image" of the various images toward a source held by a group of receivers. In so doing the studies have concentrated on isolating dimensions of meaning that are common to large numbers of people evaluating large numbers of sources in many different situations. This means that dimensions of judgment that might be specific to one type of source, one particular setting, one persuasive topic, or to one or another particular subgroup of receivers or even of each receiver individually have not been studied. It is interesting to note that when sources are linked to specific messages in specific settings, we have a greater number of dimensions isolated than when we talk about the communication sources generally. A specific source (such as spouse) produced more precise and a greater number of dimensions than sources generally.

[3] David K. Berlo, James B. Lemert, and Robert J. Mertz, "Dimensions for Evaluating the Acceptability of Message Sources," Research Monograph, Department of Communication, Michigan State University, 1966.
[4] David Markham, "The Dimensions of Source Credibility of Television Newscasters," *Journal of Communication* 28 (1968): 57–64.

Researchers who have been following the techniques of George Kelly in trying to identify the individual dimensions or categories of judgment that individuals bring to particular sources, topics, or objects have demonstrated that people have a great number of categories that they use to interpret some stimulus object, say a speaker. But many of these categories are unique to one person or shared by some people and not by others. The very specificity of the analysis means that we cannot generalize widely across people except to say that they average a certain number of constructs or some people tend to have more than other people.

Such approaches are most useful when we deal with one source and one receiver or with a limited number of receivers dealing with a limited number or class of sources. Research into a theory of ethos will be able to make use of these techniques in many respects. Unfortunately the technique becomes less useful when we deal with large numbers of people or when we want to be able to sum over many situations, sources, and people in a quick, economical way. Then the approach of a fewer number of standard dimensions will be employed as the means of measurement.

The research findings support a view about the complexity of images. First, we probably have a rather generalized impression of a source not linked to any particular setting, message, or purpose. Sources known by reputation or who are not of much importance to us probably have less clear-cut, less well-focused images. Indeed we are not aware of having an image of these people at all in most instances. But when asked questions about people we know only vaguely, we nevertheless do make predictions about them; thus we have an image of those sources. Even when we do not know the people, a small amount of information about them provides a basis on which we infer certain characteristics.

When we know prospective sources well, or once we begin to respond to messages and to the other elements of the communication-binding context, we have much more complex and specific images. If we restrict our interest to specific types of sources or specific settings, we can find three, four, five, or more dimensions shared in common by large numbers of people. Obviously if we examined the individual categories or interpretation of each individual receiver, we could find many more categories. Yet some individuals may work with only six or seven, and a few others may range as high as twenty or more.

As a source becomes more remote in time, less associated with a particular communication act, the image may become more general and involve fewer dimensions. Both the number and the variety of dimensions that will be employed in making judgments about the source will vary with situations. In this sense there is no one image of a source;

the source does not have an ethos. We have one image for one person and one image for another. We have one image at one time, a different image at another for the same receiver. We may be judged in terms of one set of dimensions when we act in one role or for one persuasion goal and with a different set when we act for a different purpose or in a different role. (Are you reminded again of the dynamic, changing nature of the communication process? Are you reminded of the importance of the communication-binding context that holds the various factors together as they interrelate?)

THE CREATION OF ETHOS

People are normally concerned with creating and maintaining a favorable impression or image in the minds of those with whom they interact. For all of us, creation of a good image is normally an ongoing goal. But this problem is often particularly relevant to the communicator who will inevitably create an image in the process of communication if he does not already have one. This image may be a key factor in determining success or failure.

Because the materials that shape an image differ at different times with relationship to a communication, let us analyze the factors that contribute to extrinsic ethos and then those that contribute to intrinsic ethos.

Extrinsic Ethos

The image that exists in advance of a communication is based upon judgments about the source derived from experiences associated with the source. Receivers may have no direct experience with a source and yet possess an image of that source. Experiences with other sources and with persons of similar referential memberships, along with reports and endorsements of others, provide a basis for judgment. Even the medium and the occasion may contribute to the image.

Presumably an extrinsic ethos may be potential (the image is entirely unformed). When the receiver is stimulated by an event or question, however, this potential image may come to be more consciously perceived. Since this image is potential in many instances, highly inconsistent elements may exist. Indeed, even consciously held images may contain a degree of contradiction just as do other attitudinal structures.

The image that is formed and its degree of positive or negative orientation depends upon the meaning the receiver gives to the information about the source. Four categories of information about the source contribute significantly to the image: experiences with the source, either direct or vicarious; facts known about the source, particularly those that indicate referential class memberships; endorsements of the source offered by others; and immediate stimuli leading to the actual communication.

An important factor in determining the image of the source is prior experience with that source. In most communications we are not being exposed to the communicator for the first time. We have interacted with him or her before—read, seen, or heard him or her in some context. We have daily contact with other students, weekly contact with club members, a multitude of daily interactions with family and neighbors. The experiences provide both the basis and the reinforcement for an image once it is formed. We have vicarious experiences with many sources. Through the mass media we are given information about newsworthy people. We sense the pressures during a cabinet meeting. Other people pass information on to us about experiences with others in such a way that we may experience these events vicariously.

Facts about the source may be true or only assumed to be true. We may know of specific matters on education, positions on questions of public policy, age, work. These facts take on meaning largely to the degree they serve as an index of "referential class membership." On the basis of these facts we place the individual within contexts or classes and can then apply our stereotypes concerning these classes to the person as an individual.

The operation of these referential class memberships and their power is unclear. Although we would all like to believe we judge on merit, it is only possible to the degree that we know the merits. In the absence of specific contact we may be forced to judge on the basis of expectations associated with roles, status, referential class memberships. The knowledge that a speaker is liberal, an Elk, a labor union leader, black, and happily married with three children certainly creates a different expectation from conservative, a Rotarian, president of a small, privately owned company, white, thrice married with no children.

The belief that people tend to judge others through stereotyped patterns should not be carried to extremes. Yet it operates even when people protest that it does not. During a disturbance in Ann Arbor an undergraduate accosted a policeman with the assertion he was "a fascist pig." The policeman pointed out that he held a master's degree, spoke three languages, and was a veteran of Vietnam. The college student who was calling upon the policeman to "free himself" from his prejudices seemed at least mildly annoyed by these claims.

People do classify occupations, clubs, and interests as differing in prestige and status. These relative judgments depend upon the person making them, but society as a whole has certain generalized assessments in all of these areas. Many studies show the effect of labeling a source as college professor versus a student or the surgeon general versus secretary of the Communist party of the United States.

Endorsements of a source may affect image. Empirical support for this theory is offered by a number of studies that have demonstrated that ethos can be manipulated through endorsements offered in the introduction. Harvey demonstrated that the ethos of the introducer affects the ethos of the person being introduced.[5] Thus, a person who receives a positive endorsement from a well-regarded individual may develop a more favorable ethos than a person who receives a positive endorsement from a negatively evaluated source. Politicians speak of the kiss of death being administered when an unpopular person or group endorses a candidate. Henry Wallace was hurt by his refusal to denounce the support of the Communist party in the 1948 election.

The role of endorsements and the relatively unconscious level at which they operate is illustrated by McCroskey and Dunham, who found a sponsorship effect in many situations. The presence of a teacher during an experiment was found to confer an ethos upon the source and material being presented even when the teacher in no way endorsed the material.[6] Persons who agree to appear at the head table of a political candidate or at a charity dinner confer an endorsement upon the proceedings, whatever the intent. Indeed, the analysis of who is and is not present for a candidate's speech provides important insights concerning his or her support. And such sponsorship can be overcome only with difficulty in many circumstances.

Stimuli relative to the immediate presentation of the communication may also affect the image. A person given exposure by one of the mass media gains some status. A person who has written for *Harper's* gains a degree of prestige she might not have received for writing in the Sunday supplement. One important function of the mass media is conferring legitimacy—warranting a person as a newsmaker, worthy of coverage. Television is severely criticized as offering a platform for any radical who threatens to burn down the country or commit mayhem on its citizens. By offering exposure, the media are charged with legitimating these people as leaders, as anointing them with power no one had given or could give them. The media have tried to downplay such presentations

---

[5] Ivan G. Harvey, "An Experimental Study of the Influence of the Ethos of the Introducer as It Affects the Ethos and the Persuasiveness of the Speaker" (Ph.D. diss., University of Michigan, 1968).

[6] James C. McCroskey and Robert E. Dunham, "Ethos: A Confounding Element in Communication Research," *Speech Monographs* 32 (1966): 456–63.

and to limit access to those who have established a position in some way. But events in which one person or a terrorist group takes captives or makes bomb threats present special problems. Publicity is one demand of such groups. But the publicity can have a contagious effect: one mad bomber quickly produces four others. Extensive publicity given to one terrorist band frequently produces similar actions on the part of other, hitherto unknown, bands.

Any actions that a communicator makes immediately prior to a communication may provide a basis for judgment if the receivers are in a position to see these things. His selection as a speaker for the occasion may confer status. His dress, his manner in relating to others, his responses to things happening around him may all contribute strongly to his image. Indeed, first opportunities to see the communicator often involve conscious attempts to size him up, to feel him out.

The effect of these various stimuli will certainly depend upon three factors: the consistency of the various stimuli, the power of the stimuli, and the number and temporal duration of the stimuli. Further, the effect is likely to depend upon the importance of the source in the life of the receiver. One remembers many things about one's boss and proportionally fewer things about a person who has no clear relationship to one's goals.

The importance of the source, his saliency for the receiver, likely determines the degree to which the image is consciously formulated and used as a basis for response by the receivers. A person who is of key importance probably has a clear image, one that is sharply discriminated in terms of specific factors. Predictions of his behavior can probably be made precisely in terms of specific knowledge and past experience. A person who is less important or only vaguely known would not have such a finely discriminated image. For such a source the more general referential dimensions probably account for the judgments made.

Intuitively it would seem that prior experience of a personal nature would be the most important determinant of the image. Extensive prior experience not only provides the material for formulation of an image and the motivational forces that impel such a formulation but also provides the reinforcement and the opportunity for selective perception and exposure that should fix the image. In the absence of such a fixed image, the general reputation, the referential class memberships, and the endorsements of others are likely to weigh more importantly.

Extrinsic ethos, then, is a mental construct derived from the association of various stimuli with a source. Of particular importance in the creation of this mental image are previous experiences with the source, facts including those that provide a basis for establishing referential class memberships, endorsements, and stimuli relative to the immediate setting of the communication.

Intrinsic Ethos

Intrinsic ethos is the image of the source created during the message transmission. The stimuli arise from the source, the message, the occasion, the audience, and the channel. Since ethos is concerned with judgments of the nature of the source, the communicator is presumably the key factor affecting the judgments. But the nature of the communicator must be inferred from what is done within the total matrix of the communication act.

Many writers advise the persuader to be a good person, to be sincere, to work for the best interests of the receiver. But a person may be doing this while the audience forms a quite different impression. To create a favorable ethos one must not only be an honest person but also be able to communicate this through behavior that leads the audience to draw that inference.

The message is probably the most significant key to the image created during the communication act. Dress, manner, personal appearance, and utilization of the visible code come into play in visual communication settings. The voice comes into play in audible message situations. The message is the instrumentality by which the source can maximally affect the stimuli impinging upon receivers. The choices made explicitly and implicitly in the message and in presentation provide the basis for estimates of the nature of the communicator drawn by receivers.

The communicator has a prior image that will affect perceptions of the communicator during the message itself. Because of selective perception, the tendency will be to perceive the source in accordance with the prior image, particularly if that image is well established. Relatively marked departures from that image might be necessary for the audience to begin to alter the image. Certainly the prior image interacts with stimuli presented in the actual communication setting in determining ethos.

The communicator can continue to utilize some of the same classes of stimuli that helped to determine the extrinsic image. She may provide, overtly or covertly, facts about herself and reveal certain referential class memberships. She may refer to past experiences and contacts, particularly those with any or all of the receivers. She may consciously work to achieve identification with people, attitudes, values, and beliefs that are valued by the receivers. She can offer endorsements of position by techniques ranging from casual mention of a statement to citation of evidence.

The topic and purpose selected, the materials in terms of lines of attack, appeals, forms of support, and reasoning, language and style, and delivery (if the audible and visible codes are used) provide the basis for many judgments about the source.

In most experimental studies several factors within the message have been varied in the attempt to modify ethos, partially because of the belief that one factor may not be sufficient to alter the image and that a composite of items may be demanded. In many instances the assumption was made that the changes created different levels of ethos in the receivers. When no differences in persuasiveness or comprehension occurred, it was impossible to know if differences in ethos did not develop or if differences in ethos were not related to these effects.

The relationship between speaker image and the topic or concept has been investigated through the congruity model, which predicts that two concepts linked by an assertion or an association will tend to exert reciprocal pulls on one another and take on the same connotative meaning. Thus, a receiver who hears a communicator support an attitudinal position will tend to place the two at the same point in semantic space.

Tannenbaum predicted attitude change toward communication sources when associated with written messages presented to college students. The correlation between predicted and obtained results was a positive 0.91, confirming the hypothesis.[7] But the same hypothesis applied to public speakers produced results only somewhat better than chance. Bettinghaus hypothesized that more factors were involved in oral than in written presentations. When the congruity model was expanded to four elements—speaker, central proposition, speech composition, and delivery—the results were much closer to the predictions.[8]

The implications of these findings for ethos are clear. In associating himself with topics and ideas, the speaker takes on the values associated with these ideas. If he associates himself with materials viewed positively by receivers, his image will tend to improve. If he associates himself with negatively valued concepts and ideas, his image will move in a negatively valenced direction. The causes one associates himself with and the quality of the efforts made on their behalf affect speaker image.

Some of the ways in which message elements may affect or effect an image have been examined experimentally. One important area that has not been assessed is the relationship of logical and motivational elements

---

[7] Percy Tannenbaum, "Initial Attitude Toward Source and Concept as Factors in Attitude Change through Communication," *Public Opinion Quarterly* 20 (1956): 413–25.

[8] Erwin Bettinghaus, "The Operation of Congruity in an Oral Communication Situation" (Ph.D. diss., University of Illinois, 1959).

to the image derived. Researchers have usually contrasted the effect of materials of "high credibility" with material that emphasizes logical appeals. Alternatively, they have compared high and low credibility speeches but with the variations in the level of credibility not induced by variations in logical and motivational elements.

Procedures designed to improve one's ethos do not necessarily enhance persuasiveness. But interpretation of the findings is not easy. One researcher compared speeches designed to induce high credibility with speeches that had a clear, logical structure. The speeches dealt with political issues in a political year. Another compared speeches designed to induce high credibility with logical speeches. To ensure equal length, the logical structure in the speeches of high credibility was practically eliminated. In the absence of specific measures of perceived ethos, it is impossible to determine which of the two types of speeches engendered higher credibility. Considering the training of many college students it is quite possible that the presence or absence of logical proof affects the image of the communicator. The "logical" speeches may have induced higher credibility than the "credibility" speeches.

The nature of the motivational appeals utilized also provides a basis for estimations of the source. Janis notes, for instance, "If the communication is perceived as having an obvious intent to manipulate the emotions of the audience, disbelief would be the expected reaction."[9] Selfish appeals offered as a basis for our action may cause negative response. Motivational appeals at levels far in excess of the valid level of appeal may rebound sharply.

Thus, logical and motivational materials should be viewed not only in terms of direct effect as proof but also in terms of the contribution they make to the ethos (positive or negative) of the communicator. Such matters as citation of evidence, good organization, inclusion of both sides, demonstration of the authoritativeness of sources cited as evidence, and variations in the support used may all contribute to the ethos created. But the effects of these elements have not yet been sufficiently established. In some instances they appear to make a difference; in some they do not.

The language and style employed may affect the image created. People judge status from cues contained in language used. Language does create different images although not always in predicted directions. Delivery also influences images. A number of studies suggest that excessive vocalized pauses, malfluencies, or other problems in delivery may inhibit the formation of a positive image. The effect is not unvarying, however,

---

[9] Carl I. Hovland, Irving L. Janis, and Harold H. Kelley, eds., *Communication and Persuasion* (New Haven: Yale University Press, 1953), p. 86.

for dress, manner, and personal appearance also affect judgments of sources.

Judgments related to the competency of the speaker seem related to judgments of speaker image. Hildreth filmed a series of speakers who first supported the side with which they agreed and then supported the side with which they disagreed. In judging the films audiences did not evaluate sincerity reliably; the more competent speakers were considered more sincere, no matter which side of the question they were supporting.[10]

The fact of communicating on a given occasion may affect prestige. But the environment, the formality of the occasion, the display of flags, and the prestige of those sitting on the platform may all contribute to the image created. To a degree the persuader can manipulate these factors to maximize impact. Hitler used many techniques in manipulating elements of setting and occasions, which contributed to image values.

The audience may collectively affect the image created. Tremendous emphatic response and wild applause should enhance the image as contrasted to muted rumblings and boos. An extremely negative audience reaction such as markedly hostile questions will put the communicator on the spot and may lower the image created.

The media seem to confer certain positive image elements upon the communicator because he is being allowed to use the medium. ("It must be so; I read it in a book.") Also, the medium may reinforce or detract from the image by the way it communicates the person. Nixon's personal appearance as contrasted to Kennedy's on the first television debate in 1960 was considered a key factor in the resultant comparative improvement in Kennedy's image.

Although innumerable studies demonstrate that images can be created or altered in laboratory settings, it appears to be easier to do in introductions that create extrinsic ethos than during presentation of messages that create intrinsic ethos. Repeatedly studies that qualify persons by occupation or expertise (college professors versus college sophomores seem favorite choices) create the effects desired. But manipulation of message elements seems much less effective in achieving desired differences.

Two important questions arise: Why is intrinsic ethos more difficult to create and alter as desired? Do these laboratory findings generalize to real-life communication?

---

[10] Richard Hildreth, "An Experimental Study of Audience's Ability to Distinguish between Sincere and Insincere Speakers" (Ph.D. diss., University of Southern California, 1953).

Three major factors may explain much of the problem in creating desired differences in intrinsic ethos in the laboratory: sponsorship effects, lack of topic saliency, and general trust in communicators. The sponsorship effect has already been described. The presence of the teacher or any other authority figure supplies a sponsorship, which results in higher levels of credibility or trustworthiness. ("If this wasn't good they wouldn't be taking our time to present it.") Such sponsorship may balance the effect of elements that may create a less favorable image.

Topic saliency is even more critical. Experimentalists select topics for research that are not highly salient to minimize the possibility of contamination from outside influences and to make effects easier to see since less salient attitudes are typically easier to shift. But since topics are less salient, the receivers are not as motivated to put forth the effort necessary to make careful discriminations and to detect what may be relatively subtle differences in content. And since the attitude objects are relatively unimportant to the receivers—not involved with their own values and attitudes—any of a variety of approaches may easily shift them. But if the topic were more important to the receivers and if the action or decision made did significantly affect their lives, judgments of the acceptability of the person urging the ideas and of the ideas themselves would be more important.

Finally, the very fact that the communication is presented gives it some merit. Generally communicators are accepted and trusted in the absence of any reason not to do so. A normative standard may operate in which sources not personally known to receivers are evaluated in a positive manner.

Does this same pattern hold for nonlaboratory settings? Quite unlikely. Normally communication sources and receivers are to some degree linked in utilizing communication to accomplish their personal goals. Unless the material holds interest and has some level of saliency, it is doubtful if the receivers will even expose themselves to the communication. To the degree the materials discussed make a difference, the decisions to accept or reject based upon what is being communicated will be quite different from those in the laboratory.

When does an intrinsic ethos emerge? At what point in the presentation of message do source images begin to shift? Traditionally communicators are urged to create goodwill and build a favorable ethos in the introduction. Receivers seem to concentrate on forming an impression and making judgments about a communicator during the first part of a communication; they then tend to become more involved in the ideas and the content. Of course, elements affecting the receivers' image of the speaker continue to occur throughout the message.

Brooks and Scheidel studied the shifts in image that occurred during a speech by Malcolm X. There was an extremely sharp rise in the favorability of the image very early in the speech, then a slight decline, a small rise, and finally a gradual but rather consistent decline in favorability of image.[11] This study reinforced the idea that shifts in image occur often as a result of introductory material but also demonstrated that changes in image continue to occur throughout a communication.

Consequent Ethos

What is the relative contribution of extrinsic and intrinsic images to the consequent image? Presumably the dominance of prior versus immediate stimuli in determining the image depends upon factors similar to those affecting any attitude. The prior image is largely dominant when it is well established, in part because of selective perception and in part because the source probably does not modify behavior so significantly that a new image is brought into being. When certain conditions exist, it is possible an image could undergo a major upheaval. When meeting friends we have not seen for many years, we tend to respond to them and they to us as we did years ago. With the changes the years have brought, we may be surprised about the changes in each other. But where previous interaction has been frequent and extensive, it is unlikely (although possible) that a sharp shift in the image will occur.

An image measured immediately after a communication interchange should be capable of relatively fine differentiation. Further, the image will probably be particularly associated with the topic. Over time the association between source and topic will diminish as the specificity of the particulars of the communication-binding context diminish. The image will rather naturally lose specificity in terms of the number of independent dimensions of judgment and tend toward fewer, basic referential dimensions. This loss over time may surprise someone who expects "to take up where we left off a few days ago."

Other factors also affect the consequent image. Succeeding events or ideas associated with the communicator can affect ethos. For example, if a persuader predicts certain unexpected results and these results do occur, the image of the source is likely to become more positive. This technique is often used by people seeking to deceive the "pigeon" in a con game. Small bets or other minimum commitments meet with significant successes. Finally a major sum of money is committed—and disaster follows.

---

[11] Robert D. Brooks and Thomas M. Scheidel, "Speech as Process: A Case Study," *Speech Monographs* 35 (1968): 1–7.

Consequent ethos may change rapidly in the period immediately after a communication act. But as longer periods of time elapse, the change typically becomes less and less, and the image becomes relatively stable. The importance of the communicator to the individual receiver and the probability of future interaction are likely to determine the degree to which succeeding events are associated with the persuader and thus likely to affect the image. People often seek out information about a persuader—particularly if in doubt about the person or the persuasive goal. In this case significant changes in image are possible long after the act of communication is completed.

ETHOS AS ETHICAL PROOF

Actions or matter related to sources by receivers create or alter images of those sources in the minds of receivers. But it is not enough to know that images exist and can be altered. We must ask how images operate to produce effects in the persuasion process. The term *ethical proof* is normally used in a narrow sense as the role of ethos in offering the direct warrant for acceptance of the proposition urged by the source. Viewed more broadly, ethical proof may be defined to include all the ways in which the image of the source produces effects in the persuasion process, both directly and indirectly, positively and negatively.

In considering the role of the image as a causal factor in persuasion, we must remain cognizant of the audience-centered nature of ethos. A stimulus may affect one receiver positively, another negatively. Similarly the same image held by two different receivers may produce different effects.

Since the same stimulus may create a positive image for one receiver and a negative image for another, no formula for creation of a desired ethos is possible. In essence, as the source becomes identified with behavior, beliefs, actions, appearances, and material that are positively evaluated by receivers, her image moves to the positive. As she identifies with or is identified by the receiver with negative elements, the image becomes less favorable.

Similarly it is impossible to say how an image will function in every communication situation. Sometimes a person is selected for his incompetency. The right person for one job is thoroughly wrong for another. One type of leader is needed at one time, another at a different time.

The effect of ethos on persuasiveness has been investigated to an extensive degree. The way in which the image interacts with other elements in producing effects has not been well investigated, but analysis suggests certain ways in which the interactions presumably operate.

Effect of Extrinsic Ethos

Innumerable studies show that the prior ethos of a communicator is linked to the success of communication efforts. The same material may achieve different effects when linked to sources with different prior reputations or prestige. It has been shown that extrinsic ethos is related to impact on political, social, religious, and economic issues as well as on matters of aesthetic judgment and personal taste. Thus, a favorable prior image increases persuasiveness in many instances. This is, of course, not universally true. A sound prior image may not be sufficient to cause significant differences in persuasion although it often is. Certainly one cannot depend on prior ethos to be sufficiently powerful to accomplish the persuasive goal.

In many instances the image of a potential source is a factor that brings the receivers into the communication setting. We may buy a book by our favorite author, see a movie by our favorite director, make the effort to hear a speech by a famous radical. We expose ourselves selectively to communications, and the image of the source may be a powerful factor conditioning that decision.

One's extrinsic ethos may enable a source to command the use of a given media. A known writer will be accepted for print, whether in a popular or a scholarly magazine, whereas an unknown author with the same message might be rejected.

Finally, the prior image of a source gives him a point of departure in his own planning and preparation. In a communication the source may analyze (correctly or incorrectly) the potential receivers and estimate the image they hold of him. He may then condition his preparation by deciding to include or exclude certain types of material and by deciding how to proceed and at what pace in terms of the image the audience presumably holds of him.

Extrinsic ethos has usually been investigated in terms of its persuasive outcome. But how does the prior image exert this effect? In some instances the image may produce the effect quite directly. An authority highly regarded by a receiver presents a claim or is quoted in a speech as making a claim. In the absence of contradictory information the receiver accepts the claim. The power of this prior image is such that in some instances in research an incredulity effect is introduced. Subjects respond with the statements, "He could not have said that." "That must be out of context." "I don't believe it." The basis for this incredulity must lie in expectations about the source that are strongly violated in the material with which the source is associated.

Most communication situations demand more concern with the interaction between prior image and the material than suggested by the direct effect above. Prior image not only brings people to a communication situation but also gives them a set toward the communicator. Selective perception may also occur. Different sets will produce different degrees of attention and predispositions to accept or reject a variety of claims and varied potentials of emotional response.

Since these points relate to interactions with message and intrinsic ethos, they will be discussed in the context of the next section, which deals with intrinsic ethos. But these sets and predispositions toward communicator and hence her communication are the most powerful effects of prior ethos.

Effect of Intrinsic Ethos

Intrinsic ethos in normal communication is the result of the interaction of the extrinsic ethos with the stimuli operative in the communication situation. In the persuasion process, the image will affect both the source and the receiver. The source will make adjustments to the image that she perceives the audience holds and will attempt to modify that image. Similarly the audience will respond to the image they held and to any modifications of it during the communication. Actually, four images operate at any communication situation.

Let us begin with a hypothetical source, John Doe. First there is the real image, the true John Doe. This is John Doe as we shall never know him because it is the person in totality: what he is and is not; his potentials and his limitations; his attitudes, his beliefs, his values.

The second John Doe is the source's image of himself. He believes he is a certain type of person. True, he builds his picture in large part from other people's reactions to him, but, still, this is his personal picture. When he seeks to project his true self, he is trying to project the second John Doe. The true John Doe serves as a limit on the second image. The second John Doe may feel he is free as a person, but the reality of his true image may limit his ability to communicate this freedom.

The third John Doe is the audience's image of the man. They believe John is a certain type of person. (This is the image we index by the term *ethos*.) The image may or may not be close to the true John Doe and it may or may not be close to the second John Doe.

The fourth John Doe is John's perception of the nature of his image held by the audience. In interacting with others, John needs to have a picture of what these people think of him. Because this is normally a concern to all of us, John works to derive an accurate picture of his ethos with the audience.

In a communication all four images of John Doe come into play. John is ultimately limited by the reality of what he is and what he is capable of doing. He may convince himself and others that he can solve math problems in thirty seconds. If John cannot solve the problems he cannot. Sooner or later reality serves as a limit the other images cannot transcend.

How John sees himself determines some aspects of his strategy. The variance between how John sees himself and how he thinks the audience sees him may lead John to extensive efforts to correct the audience image. If John misanalyzes the image that the audience holds of him, he may implement a brilliant strategy that totally backfires because it is the perfect strategy for a problem he does not have. Of course, the audience's image of John helps to determine effect.

In many instances the four Johns (or the four images of the same John) may be very similar. Then, in some senses, John may be fairly well off. He sees himself realistically; he can do about what he thinks he can. The audience holds a reasonably realistic assessment of him and does not place demands upon him he cannot fulfill. Within limits John is probably a basically well-adjusted person.

When the four images are widely at variance, various difficulties are at least potential, if not actual. The audience may set expectations John cannot meet and thus punish him in some way for the failure. The Bay of Pigs incident caused particular consternation and negative reaction among those who had seen Kennedy as approximating the "White Knight without error," perhaps without realizing the extent of their commitment to this image. The response many expressed, "How could he do this to us?" or, as one student put it more directly, "How could he do this to me!" indicates the conflict between expectation and reality. Often teachers attempt to grade students by the degree to which they live up to their potential. If the student's potential is overestimated by the teacher, she is punished for a failure that was really not of her doing but a result of the faulty image which the teacher held.

Persuasive Effect on Proposition

Differences in reputation, prestige, or ethos as a totality and differences in specific dimensions of ethos such as evaluation, trustworthiness, expertise, or dynamism can produce significant differences in the acceptance of a proposition. But many studies have also found that significant differences in images do not produce differences in acceptance. Perhaps the differences in image are not great enough to make any practical difference. Perhaps other sources of proof serve as equally effective bases in mandating acceptance. Perhaps ethos makes the difference only when other forms do not. Perhaps the image of the source in some cases is simply not a relevant matter in determining acceptance.

Just as ethos can induce belief, it may not be a sufficient basis for acceptance. Some elements related to topic saliency affect ethos. When topics are nonsalient, mere assertion may be almost tantamount to acceptance of an idea for a short period of time, particularly if the image of the communicator is somewhat positive. More salient topics may show less shift even with high levels of ethos.

Another factor affecting ethos may be the nature of the topic area. Research suggests that majority opinion may be as powerful as or in some instances more powerful than expert opinion in shifting attitudes. Thus, a person who perceives the majority of society or a reference group as upholding one view may be resistant to contrary expert opinion. Since the reliance on expert or majority opinion varies with topic, source characteristics may be more of a factor with some topics than with others.

Ethos may interact with characteristics of the message and thus affect persuasion. For example, high prestige sources are able to use higher levels of fear appeal; sources with higher initial trustworthiness were more effective when they used stronger fear appeal communications than when they did not. Differences for communications with low initial trustworthiness were not significant but tended to favor low fear appeals as more effective.

McCroskey has completed an extensive series of studies on the factors affecting ethos and also on the relationship of ethos and elements in the speech message as they interact in affecting outcomes. In summarizing his research McCroskey indicates that good evidence increases the effectiveness of sources with moderate-to-low credibility initially, raising both the ethos and the persuasiveness, but has relatively little effect with high credibility sources or if the audience is already familiar with the evidence.[12]

The power of ethos is also related to the question of the degree of proof necessary to induce a change in attitude. To what degree are units of proof additive? To what degree are they mutually supportive? Are we to follow a model in which three units of ethical proof, three units of motivational proof, and three units of logical proof equal nine units of proof and thus should move a person nine units on a change scale rather than six or three? Or is it possible that three units of motivational proof, three units of ethical proof, or three units of each kind present move the receiver approximately three units on the acceptance scale? There are undoubtedly interactions among the proofs, and there are

---

[12] James C. McCroskey, "A Summary of Experimental Research on the Effects of Evidence in Persuasive Communication," *Quarterly Journal of Speech* 55 (1969): 169–76.

limits on the degree to which people may reasonably change. Some of these limits are the results of the instrument used in measurement, others the results of the nature of human beings. A small degree of proof may shift an attitude; much larger efforts at proof may yield little additional gain.

The effect of ethos must be considered in terms of its contribution among the totality of forces that affect persuasion. These interactions are subtle and complex. In many instances where differences in ethos have not correlated with persuasion, other factors may have caused the shift, and ethos was not a factor.

The nature of the auditors may also affect the operation of ethos as a proof. Rokeach notes that "closed-minded" people are relatively dependent upon authority as a basis for their decisions. Others who are oriented toward information, reasoning, and evidence are less swayed by authority. Although closed-mindedness has not correlated with the effect of ethos in many studies, the possibility of this relationship does exist. Certainly research in suggestivity shows that people vary in their susceptibility to prestige suggestion.

Persuasive Effect on Ethos

One effect of any communication is to create an image. In fact, the persuasive goal of many communications is either to create a particular image or to alter in desired ways the image that exists. Such change may be necessary as a basis for future persuasive efforts or instrumental in accomplishing one's goals. In large part a leader may be picked on the basis of image. We cannot know what issues the President will face in the next four years; hence we must vote for the candidate we feel will face those choices in the way in which we would prefer. Stands on current issues may be important, for they tell us about predispositions to respond in given ways in future instances.

The concrete implications of ethos for future persuasion efforts may be illustrated through figure 11. If you were being asked to pick a leader, whom would you be likely to select from the class? Your choice, of course, depends upon the needs of the position, but there are certain people you would not consider and others you would. In many cases the most important outcome of a communication would be the image established.

There is always the possibility of a boomerang effect. A person who is highly respected may markedly lower ethos through association with negatively evaluated materials, ideas, or other elements of content. This possibility is illustrated in a study of the effects of a satire directed at Joseph McCarthy. Judgments of McCarthy were not lowered by the

258 PARTICIPATION AS SOURCES

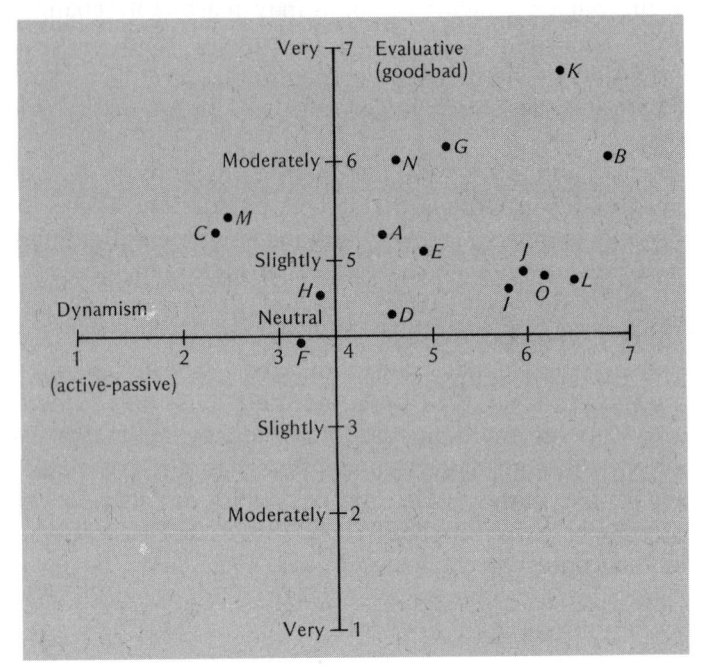

Figure 11. Consequent Ethos. Fifteen Persuasion Class Members in the Eyes of Their Classmates at Conclusion of Final Speech.

satire, but the image of the sponsoring agency was.[13] Sereno found that high ethos sources who support ideas opposed to the beliefs of the receivers for whom the topic was salient were evaluated significantly less favorably after the presentation of the communication.[14]

A communication may be weighed not only by its effect on the proposition urged but also by its effects upon the image of the communicator. A communicator may move her image in a sharply negative direction through only one communication. This is a factor many communicators will need to weigh.

Ethos as Mediator for Other Elements

The role of ethos is conventionally viewed as a direct warrant for persuasion. But what of the contribution that ethos makes in other respects? For example, we are unlikely to accept many of the claims of

---

[13] David Berlo and Hideya Kumata, "The Investigator: The Impact of a Satirical Radio Drama," *Journalism Quarterly* 33 (1956): 287–98.

[14] Kenneth K. Sereno, "Ego-Involvement, High Source Credibility, and Response to a Belief-Discrepant Communication," *Speech Monographs* 35 (1968): 476–81.

those we distrust; we may examine their reasoning more carefully; we may actually check the evidence they cite for accuracy. Such actions will affect the efficacy of their logical proof and their ability to mount motivational appeals.

Presumably a minimal level of ethos is necessary for logical and emotional proofs to achieve effectiveness. For example, low credibility sources cannot use high levels of fear appeal effectively. Lacking a certain minimal ethos, logical and emotional proofs simply may not function.

The interpretation of meaning may also be a function of ethos. The statement "The country must do for the individual what he cannot do for himself" inevitably takes on a different meaning if attributed to Franklin Roosevelt or to Herbert Hoover in the 1932 election campaign. The statement "It was a tough evening!" takes on one meaning if an older person says it, quite another if a college coed uses it to mean something very positive and favorable.

Attention is related to ethos as well. Consider those identified in figure 11. Certain communicators in that class were seen as slightly dull, uninteresting, and undynamic and evaluated as neutral, neither good nor bad, neither honest nor dishonest. The set of the audience may well be one of lack of interest or apathy when those people speak upon the next occasion. One can mentally picture the persuasion class slouching lower in their seats, doodling, steeling themselves for a dull five minutes but trying not to show this to the classmate giving the speech.

Figure 11 indicated the average image created by individuals in the minds of their classmates during the course of a term and as it existed immediately after the final speech. Figure 12 has a somewhat different focus. Here we see the variety with which the same source is viewed by a number of individuals. Each of the people represented in terms of average image in figure 12 could also have been presented in terms of the individual reaction that contributed to that average.

The effects noted above about the average response can now be projected variously in terms of given individuals. Some of the employees who work with this warden will have one set, be prepared to respond in certain ways toward what he says; others will have markedly different sets and responses.

Another way in which images work is suggested by figure 13, which represents the image of an average inmate held by a number of workers who deal with inmates. Certainly this set would be presumed to differ with different inmates as these workers came to know them. But this composite is suggestive in the way in which the individuals would approach tasks in which they relate to the individuals. For example, because

260 PARTICIPATION AS SOURCES

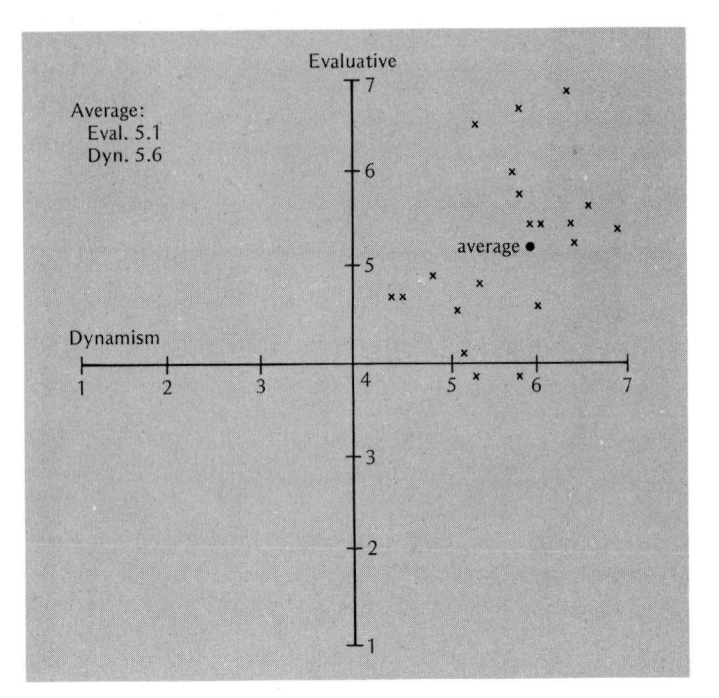

Figure 12. Image of a Warden Held by His Employees.

guard C generally sees prisoners as being more powerful and active, he may be more alert to dangers of escape and more cautious about the possibility of being trapped in some way by the prisoners. Guard D, who has the lowest evaluation of the prisoners, sees them as quite passive and nonpowerful; prisoners are losers in all respects. This image would also condition response. Guard D might be less alert to problems of prisoner revolt and also less prone to accept anything prisoners say as true. Further, his attitude may affect the inmates' images of themselves.

A number of additional, interesting hypotheses can be generated from examining these figures.[15] But even the brief treatment accorded them here suggests the multiplicity of ways in which ethos may interact with

---

[15] The materials used in figures 11, 12, and 13 come from specific classes that I have taught. The data are extremely limited in terms of sample size, and there is no claim that these are typical or representative findings. However, they suggest ways in which such research can add insight concerning potential or actual communication effects. In my own classes we often use these as the basis for creating solutions to a hypothetical problem in how to change an image or to predict what would happen in certain situations and how this impact could be altered.

ETHOS: CREATION AND EFFECTS

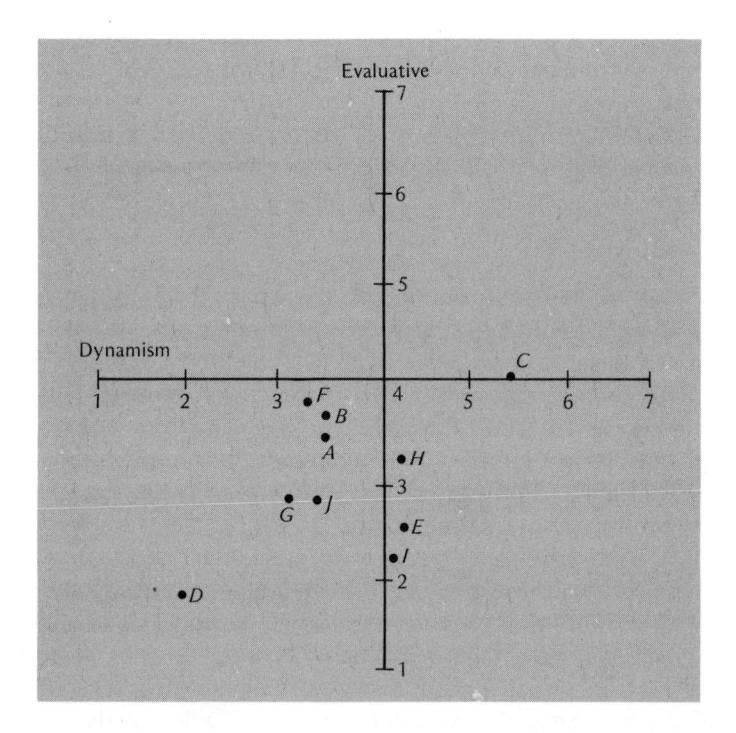

Figure 13. Image of an Average Prisoner Held by Prison Guards.

other elements in contributing to ultimate effects. Certainly these relationships contribute support to the idea of the extreme complexity of interaction that results in a comparatively singular "effect" of the persuasion process. At least, it is "singular" as compared to the multiplicity of things contributing to it.

Effects of Ethos in Time

The effects of ethos on the persuasiveness of messages are limited temporally. A sleeper effect occurs, at least in some instances, when source and proposition or message elements become disassociated over time. Thus the differential effect in persuasiveness from an attribution of message elements to a source may be lost. A negative source coupled with a message may engender negative shift in acceptance; a positive source may engender quite positive shifts. Over time, however, the message and source become disassociated. Acceptance of the proposition should then increase for the group who heard the material attributed to the negative source and decrease for those who heard it attributed to the positive source. The findings of Weiss and Kelman and

Hovland bear this out.[16] As specific confirmation, Kelman and Hovland found that the reinstatement of the original linkage of source to message by specifically recalling the source produced a significant trend toward reproducing the original pattern as contrasted to the results for those receivers who did not have the original source-message linkage recalled.

SUMMARY

Ethos has been defined as the image of a source held in the mind of a receiver. Image is a property of receivers and is determined by their response to the source and to the stimuli associated with the source. This image may be studied in terms of individual auditors, although often we are more interested in the average or composite image for large groups of people. We may focus upon the communicator's image at particular times; extrinsic ethos, the image prior to a given communication; intrinsic image, the image created by a given communication; and consequent ethos, the image that exists after the completion of a communication. These measurements are arbitrary in terms of time, and measurements conducted at various times within these larger divisions show changes in image as well.

Receivers, actual and potential, have images of sources. The dimensions of these images as investigated through factor analytic techniques indicate that judgments particularly center around evaluation of the worth of an individual. One researcher focusing upon prior images found a general evaluative dimension. Others focusing upon messages linked to sources have found two independent evaluative dimensions: one centering around trustworthiness or credibility, the other around knowledge or expertise. Another dimension of less weight is related to the dynamism, which includes power and activity, of the source. Different situations, different sources, and different receivers produce variations in the dimensions of source image, but these general dimensions seem reasonably common to a variety of situations, sources, and receivers.

Extrinsic ethos is related to information and experiences associated with sources. Experience, real and vicarious, seems particularly important in establishing extrinsic ethos, particularly if the experience has been relatively strong in terms of frequency or saliency to the individual.

---

[16] Carl Hovland and Walter Weiss, "The Influence of Source Credibility on Communication Effectiveness," *Public Opinion Quarterly* 16 (1961): 635–50. Herbert Kelman and Carl Hovland, " 'Reinstatement' of the Communicator in Delayed Measurement of Opinion Change," *Journal of Abnormal and Social Psychology* 48 (1953): 327–35.

Other facts, including referential group memberships, endorsements offered by others, and appearance, contribute and may be of strong weight in certain situations.

The communication act represents the maximum opportunity for the communicator to affect her or his image both for immediate and delayed purposes. Therefore the source's response as manifested in behavior, particularly message behavior, is important to the image she or he creates. The choices a person makes, conscious or unconscious, offer a basis for the receivers to draw inferences about the nature of the individual. These choices are important both for items that are elected and things that are not done. An appeal not made may tell us more about an individual than one that is made.

The images that result from the interaction of prior elements and those of the immediate message contribute to the consequent ethos of the communicator. Presumably this image is more finely differentiated and also more linked to the specific proposition immediately after the communication than it will be later.

The image that is created or that exists may work positively or negatively for an individual. But whether it works or not is specific to the receiver and to the situation. Just as the image is determined by the response of the individual receiver judging the nature of the source through the materials available, the use of this image as a warrant and its interacting with other elements in the persuasion process are also dependent upon the individual receiver.

In general, extrinsic ethos will be a key factor affecting the image as it develops through the communication. Further, it may afford the communicator a chance to be heard by drawing an audience and providing an available medium. The ethos of the source may be a sufficient cause for acceptance, although this presumably varies with the nature of the receiver, the topic under discussion, its salience, and other elements within the communication setting.

One important goal of a speech may be to create or alter an image. In this instance particularly, the communicator must be sensitive to the effect on his ethos of what he does, as well as the persuasiveness of his message. Indeed, concern with one's image is an element presumably present to some degree in almost all interaction.

The interaction of ethos with other elements in the persuasive process both in terms of creation of ethos and in the operation of ethos has been extensively investigated, but the high volume of research in the area of ethos should yield further insights in the near future. The insights already gained illustrate the complex interrelationships involved in the persuasion process.

DISCUSSION QUESTIONS AND PROJECTS

1. Discuss how the creation and change of an ethos is similar to the creation or change of an attitude.

2. What problems are encountered in understanding persuasion if ethos is considered a property residual within a source? If defined as stimuli in a message?

3. What do you estimate is the power of a prior image to persist unchanged versus the power of stimuli in a communication to change the image? Discuss your answer in terms of a specific instance.

4. What instances have occurred in your experience where a communicator created an image sharply at variance with a prior image? Are these cases mostly ones in which you had limited contact with the source? Are some of these cases instances where you had known a person for a long period of time but had limited recent contact?

5. Utilizing figure 11, contrast your strategy in approaching a hostile audience to the action recommended in your speech if you are speaker K or B versus C or M.

6. This chapter suggests that a person for whom the four images (the reality, his image, receiver's image and his image of the receiver's image) correspond may be relatively well adjusted. Is this valid? To what degree?

7. Talking with a friend with whom you were very close in the past but have had little interaction for two or three years often produces very real stresses in communication. To what degree is this a problem in the area of ethos?

8. What can a person do to avoid approaching others in terms of images based on the past rather than the present?

9. Discuss the ways in which ethos is related to other forms of proof. How do these proof forms contribute to ethos? How does ethos contribute to the operation of these other forms of proof?

ETHOS: CREATION AND EFFECTS

10. Discuss the technique used to create a favorable ethos with a hostile audience. With a friendly audience. Contrast the two techniques.

11. Design a speech or written communication whose basic goal is to create a favorable ethos.

12. As an experiment measure the ethos of class members before and after a round of speeches. Discuss the reasons for major shifts.

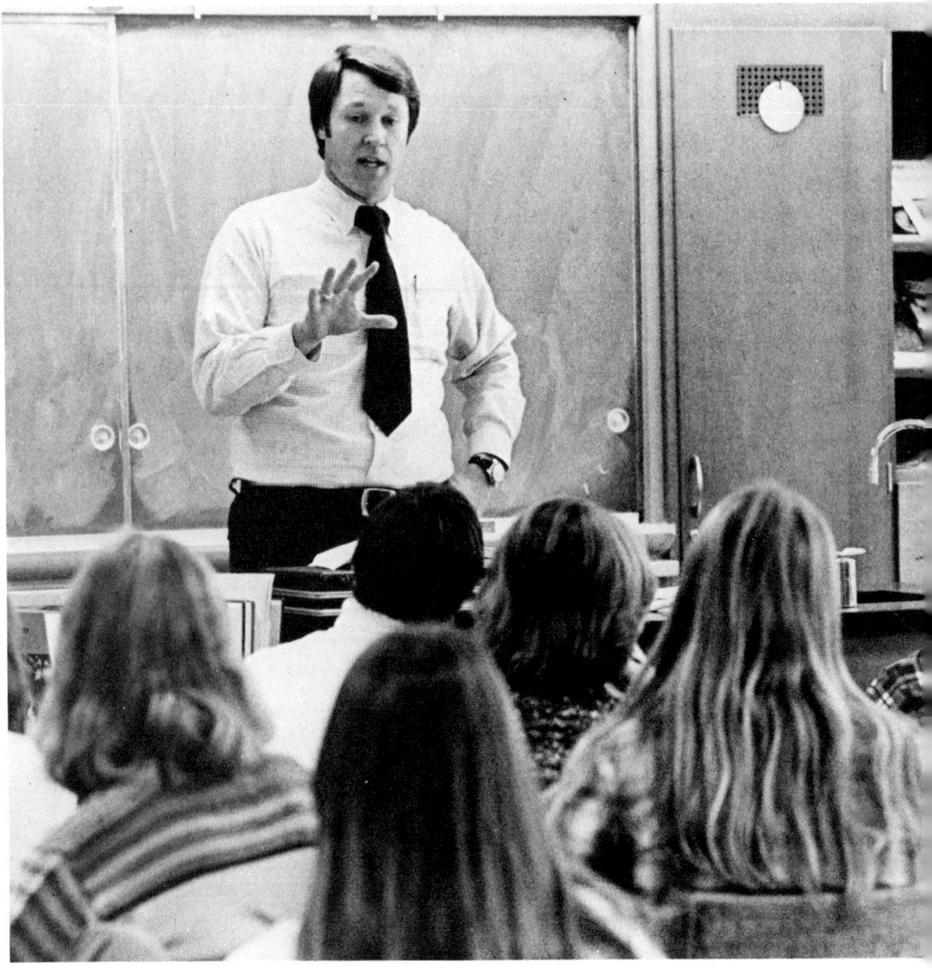

12 Persuasion and Effects upon the Source

In approaching the persuasion process we inevitably think of the body of effects realized in the receivers. But what are the effects of the persuasion process on the source? To the degree that persuasion serves as an instrumentality that the source employs as a means of accomplishing goals, the effects engendered in receivers are relevant to the future actions of the source. A successful persuasion effort may place the source in a position to accomplish his or her goals. An unsuccessful persuasion effort may result in a redoubling of efforts, radically revising strategy, shifting to new goals, or abandoning the effort.

But there are other effects upon the source. The behavior of the source immediately before, during, and after a communication effort is affected directly by the persuasion process. More far-reaching effects may also occur. The source may perform a good deal of self-persuasion: she may become more or less committed to her point of view, or she may shift to another point of view because of adjustments made to her own behavior, as well as the response of others. Her persuasion efforts may place limitations on her future behavior, shift her self-image, alter available choices. The effects on the source are an important aspect of the persuasion process.

SIGNIFICANCE

Of what significance are the effects the persuasion process produces on the source? The answer to this question lies in an examination of some of the important effects and an evaluation of their import on the source in terms of his attitudes and behavior.

Some effects of the process on the source are long-term and relatively difficult to isolate since they are the result of an ongoing process rather than any one element in the process. Other effects are short term and can be related to one element in the total process. Thus a sudden surge of negative feedback may increase the tendency to vocalized pauses; anticipation of an important speech may produce heightened tension.

The significance of effects related to conditions that exist immediately before and after a particular communication event and during the presentation of the message will be discussed in the final section of this chapter. The matter of self-persuasion will be discussed in the next section of this chapter. There are, however, a number of comparatively long-range effects whose significance should be identified now.

The most obvious effect upon the source is whether he achieves his immediate goal in the persuasion attempt. If he does, he can proceed accordingly. To the degree that he does not, he can make adjustments either by continuing his persuasion efforts, changed or unchanged, or by altering his goals in some respect.

Participation in the communication act may also serve other functions for the source. He may gain some enjoyment from this activity. He may have a good deal of catharsis. He may have reassured himself about his status, his ability, his capacity to make a difference in some way. Perhaps he has had the reward of being noticed or hearing himself talk.

These immediate effects need to be related to more long-range effects, the most important of which is that his participation in communication continually conditions his patterns of behavior, his personality, and his self-image. Communication is the primary instrumentality by which we mediate with the world. Therefore, the effects we achieve in utilizing this process are important to our perceptions of the nature of the world. Our successes and failures are indexes of our ability to cope with the world and the accuracy of our world view. This effect is related to all of our communication efforts but particularly to our persuasion efforts. When a source is consciously motivated to seek a certain effect, the results of that effort will clearly have importance to the source in proportion to the strength of the motivational forces that impelled him or her initially.

To the degree that we seek to win a response to our communication efforts, all communication contains persuasive elements. Presumably some favorable response is the general goal of our efforts but even a negative response may be better than no response at all. A person who does not receive any notice of her efforts often engages in activity that will receive negative reward in one sense but that does provide the positive reward of being noticed.

To illustrate how our persuasive efforts affect us, let us assume that a communicator is relatively successful. Her communication efforts are rewarded in that she moves toward the accomplishment of her goals. She is given feedback indicating a positive response to her and her efforts. Her perceptions of the world are accurate because other people accept them and operate in terms of them. Since this person is being rewarded, she tends to persevere. She will continue to use the persuasion process as a means of accomplishing her goals. Further, in receiving such reinforcements she should develop enough security to profit from error. Differential reinforcement will provide a basis for adapting her efforts in more effective ways. Negative feedback can become positive in that she learns from it.

In contrast, someone who is relatively unsuccessful may attempt to use communication to achieve her goals and fail. Her world view and perceptions are not accepted by others; they do not act on them or come to the same conclusions that she does. She may alter her goals and may develop new tactics. But the motivational forces acting upon her press her to make adjustments in some way. Without a basis of past successes, it is possible that reactions to a pattern of failure may create negative results over the long term.

No one incident would produce a general pattern of response, but the effects of the communication process over a period of time could produce marked effects. Once the patterns of failure or success are established, they may intensify the previous pattern. For instance, a person who has had a fair amount of failure in communication may become more worried and come under greater stress. This stress in turn can cause the failure of efforts that might otherwise succeed, and so the cycle becomes one of recurrent intensification.

As a response to failure, a person might adopt new strategies to seek the old goal. He might abandon the goal. He might redirect his energy in any number of constructive and nonconstructive ways. He might find newer, more effective ways of proceeding. But he might also withdraw and cease to compete in the area of ideas. Such withdrawal can be destructive both personally and in terms of the contribution lost to the society.

Such a pattern could also typify an entire group. Many groups have withdrawn from the persuasive arena, perhaps because they have not been successful and often because they have not even been permitted a reasonable degree of access to the process or given any prospect of success. These people are forced to turn to alternative means, less desirable ones, if they are to be felt as a force in the total society. Many minorities such as blacks and Spanish Americans have been forced into this situation at times.

This analysis seems simplistic because it leaves out a number of other interacting factors and because it generalizes a pattern that may take years of an individual's life or a generation or two in a society. But the effects of the persuasion process on the source are clearly relevant to decisions concerning the use of the process itself. Although it is conventional to record the successes of those who use the process effectively, one should also note the failures and the effect of those failures.

An individual's world view is conditioned by the persuasion process. A world view may be confirmed and established or contradicted and shattered. Certainly the response of others is a key element in determining reality when that reality is not fixed. Justice, morality, love, truth, and virtue can be defined in terms of one's fellow man. The person who finds himself out of step with others may become a Richard Cory.

The personality of the individual is clearly related to the persuasion process. Personality, defined as the integrated and dynamic organization of the physical, mental, moral, and social qualities of the individual as manifested in social interaction with others, is inextricably linked to communication. Communication, particularly persuasive communication, becomes the operationalization of our personality. Thus, the persuasion process is the behavioral manifestation of the source's personality. Not only does an individual judge his personality through the response to his communication, but, since the response affects the individual, it shapes his personality. In essence, then, the persuasion process as one of the most significant aspects of our communication behavior is not only a manifestation of the person and her or his personality but it also simultaneously serves to shape and form each person in a direct, significant way.

A further, somewhat more specific, effect of a source's communication behavior is that it imposes limitations and restrictions. By committing ourselves to a position, we set other people's perceptions in part, and we also provide an anchor for our own actions. Having given our word, we are held to it even when others do not hold us to it. Having said we will never do x we are left with a ticklish problem as events push us closer and closer to x.

Our communications also refine and shape our thinking process. It was suggested earlier that responses to communication efforts condition our world view as they offer confirmation or varying degrees of contradiction to it. But the same thing occurs within the individual. The stimulus to communicate causes us to draw upon our mental resources. Acting in part as a result of external stimuli but also on internal resources

PERSUASION AND EFFECTS UPON THE SOURCE

in terms of material supplied by past experiences and various patterns of response, we group ideas in alternative ways. We think about things. We turn over alternative possibilities. But often the clearest testing, indeed the stimulation to engage in such action, occurs in response to a specific persuasive situation. This activity occurs overtly in many persuasion settings, particularly when the persuasion has not been preplanned. We can watch the communicator struggling with the idea, phrasing it, rewording it, restating it, and over a period of time bringing it into clear focus and meaning for self and perhaps at the same time for us. At times all of us are surprised at what we have said. And after reflection, we may be even more amazed that "Yes! I do believe that!"

Surely other evidences of the general, persuasive long- and short-term impact on the source of participation in the persuasive process could be cited. But these few points suggest the vital way in which the process of persuasion has many elements of feedback that influence the source.

PERSUASION OF THE SELF

Self-persuasion is one of the effects on the source that result from participation in the persuasion process. Through involvement with and presentation of messages, the source's own attitudes, beliefs, and actions are affected. The potential for such effects is always present although it may not occur in every instance. Some of the these effects are mediated by the audience, and others relate to the effects of the process directly upon the source without reference to receiver response. It would not be valid to insist that the most important impact of the persuasion process is upon the source. But often the impact upon the source's beliefs, attitudes, and actions is an important effect of the process, and in many instances such effects may be the only ones or the ones of most consequence.

Self-persuasion results from at least three patterns: reinforcement, commitment, and cognitive balance. It is helpful to consider two contrasting situations. In the first situation, the source is advocating an action or attitude in accord with her or his own views and actions. This is the situation we think of as normal in most persuasion activities. In the second situation the source is advocating a belief or action in conflict with, perhaps even directly contrasting with, her or his own attitude or actions. This latter situation is called *counterattitudinal advocacy* and has been given much attention in laboratory studies in communication and social psychology. It is easy to understand situations in which a persuader is advocating her or his own beliefs, but it is less clear how someone comes to advocate something that is counterattitudinal.

Most of the research in counterattitudinal persuasion has used undergraduate students as subjects. Much of the controversy over interpretations of findings has involved the issue of the effects of the experimental situation in producing distorted, biased results. The validity of this criticism seems reasonable, since researchers typically find results supporting their hypothesis even when running a study similar to one in which the opposing viewpoint was supported. The minutiae that could be presented regarding this controversy include several books and hundreds of journal articles.

The possibility of advocating views that partially or perhaps fully conflict with one's own attitudes and actions (at least prior attitudes and actions) is quite real. We are often in the situation in which a white lie is accepted. We are often polite and courteous and overtly helpful to people. These actions may result in our expressing opinions or doing things that conflict with some aspect of our attitudes or previous behavior. Those who work in the advertising and selling professions frequently find they are working on a product or presenting ideas that are not in total agreement with their own opinions. We may work as a representative of a group or act as an agent for others even though we opposed the particular view or choice that was adopted. On a personal level, spouses defend the choices of their mates even if they personally disagreed with the choices and argued against them. Circumstances often place us in a situation in which we present ideas or advocate solutions that depart from our own preferred ideal or solution.

Reinforcement

The response of individuals or the group collectively may be a positive or negative reinforcement for the persuader. In talking about commitment and cognitive balance patterns of self-persuasion, we shall discover that the effects largely result from the relationship between the source's attitudes and actions, while the response of the receivers is largely immaterial to the effects. In the reinforcement pattern the response of the receivers is typically essential in the process.

The reinforcement pattern of self-persuasion utilizes a learning model as its explanation. Since attitudes, beliefs, and values are learned and since receivers can selectively reinforce actions and statements of the source, receivers may provide a learning experience for the source. Learning that occurs during the persuasive interaction may produce a change in the source's beliefs, attitudes, values, and actions.

Reinforcement may affect the salience or importance of the attitude, it may affect the tenacity with which a position is held, or it may shift an attitude. For example, a source communicates an idea. She receives applause, acceptance, and a variety of forms of highly positive feedback.

She may then tend to hold this position more firmly, may become even more positive toward the concept expressed, and may be motivated to persuade more people on the same topic by this reinforcement. Negative reinforcement would tend to produce opposite effects.

The potential for self-persuasion through differential reinforcement arising from a receiver is perhaps best seen in a one-to-one conversation. The speaker transmits an idea and the receiver responds. If the response is perceived as positive by the first speaker, she is likely to continue to talk about the idea. Often in the relative freedom of a seminar or in talking with a colleague, I will float an idea as a possibility. If it is received favorably, I tend to like it and may continue to examine it further. I may later talk about the idea with others and think about its ramifications. If it continues to look promising and positive reinforcement continues, I may insert it into one of my lectures. Indeed, several of the ideas in this book followed much that pattern. Early negative response to the ideas might have caused them to be dropped even though they were valid and useful.

All communicators are in a vulnerable position. In making statements we place ourselves in a public position. We may receive a good deal of pressure to conform to accepted opinion, particularly if the topic is controversial. We are likely to be quite conscious of feedback. As communicators we are seeking a change in our receivers, and we are not on our guard against being influenced by the receivers. Thus, certain processes may influence us. We have noted previously the operation of suggestion. Several studies have focused upon distraction hypotheses—a person learns or is persuaded to a particular view while focusing on something else, thus being distracted from a particular issue.

Persuasion is thus a two-way process. The source setting out to influence others may be strongly influenced; indeed, that can be the key effect. In some instances the strategy of persuasion is based on selective reinforcement of a source's communication. The source is only an apparent source and the real persuader is basically quiet.

The potential for self-persuasion based on the reinforcement of the receiver seems particularly powerful when the source's own attitudes are somewhat in flux. Suppose a source was considering the possibility of some change in pattern of behavior. If he received positive reward in "suggesting the remote possibility that," he would typically become more predisposed to that change. Indeed the promotion of change in a system often involves leading others to suggest changes voluntarily which are then adopted. Having participated in proposing the change and being rewarded when it is adopted, the individual is motivated toward acceptance of such change and also toward the possibility of other change. If the individual can be induced to begin making statements that can then be reinforced, he is well on the way to "talking himself into a new ball game."

It is impossible to tell how much self-persuasion results from differential reinforcement by the receivers. But inevitably a great deal of influence is possible in this situation. Since our communication behavior is a major way in which we mediate with our world, our attitudes and beliefs will be prominently featured in our persuasion efforts. Thus, any feedback has the potential to influence and shape these attitudes and beliefs and our future actions. Some adjustments presumably do not shift attitudes at all. We may simply not try to talk about that issue with that audience. Or a negative response from an audience may make us even more certain we are right. The status of the receivers, the degree to which they serve as an important reference group by which we judge our attitudes and values, will certainly affect the potential they exert for changing our attitudes. To offer a person a chance to try his or her ideas on others may be the best method to put the ideas to rest.

In some cases communicators have been prisoners of their receivers. The court jester who failed to make the king laugh could be in trouble. Politicians develop the floating of trial balloons to a fine art. Leaks from a high administration source may be followed by official confirmation if the response is favorable. Or complete denial may follow if the reaction is markedly negative. When in doubt, members of the House of Representatives are often advised to vote the district to ensure reelection.

Surely the source has possibilities other than conforming entirely to receivers or refusing to attempt to persuade. But just as the source can influence receivers, so the receivers can influence the source. The options and the possibilities operating through selective reinforcement seem about equal in both directions. The response of receivers is not the only factor involved in any change of attitude by the source. But the type of reinforcement is one part of the test that an idea receives.

Commitment

A second avenue to self-persuasion is commitment, which increases retention of effects and makes the translation of attitude into overt action more probable. If this effect operates on receivers, it should also operate on sources. Indeed the act of commitment required in many experiments is that the receiver become a source by making a public affirmation of acceptance or belief.

If such a limited public statement or holding up of one's hand induces greater likelihood of action, the act of commitment implied in voluntarily setting forth one's support of an attitude or action in a communication should mean that this holds for the source. Certainly the attitude is likely to increase in saliency, and this in turn will produce important consequences. When a person is asked to take an oath on the Bible, the effect of the commitment involved in making a public statement is heightened through a symbolic ritual. But even under ordinary circumstances the public statement of a belief is of some importance.

The reasons why commitment binds a person more firmly to certain attitudes and beliefs may result in part from reinforcement and in part from the relationships of cognitive balance involved between an attitude and an action. A person who spends extensive amounts of time working for a political cause can hardly admit that the cause was without value and just incidental.

Whatever the underlying factors involved, commitment functions in a self-persuasive way. The very act of communication often indicates a strong degree of commitment on the part of the source, and this commitment seems strengthened by the act of giving it public utterance. Even though others may urge the source to abandon her efforts, she cannot: "I gave my word." To the degree that she presents arguments, offers reasons, and seeks to involve others in acceptance of her view, she takes on a moral commitment of responsibility for what she urges.

Becoming involved sharply alters the saliency of the issue. Once a person is involved she tends to discover more information, to become involved with other people who provide additional evidence, to seek out information to support her cause. Her selective perception and exposure become strong factors. Her associates reinforce her commitment. Her initial commitment therefore leads to actions that strengthen that commitment.

Cesar Chavez, leader of the strike against the grape growers in California, began with a general interest in bettering the lot of the Mexican-Americans. He thus joined organizations seeking to better the role of the Mexican-American. As time passed he devoted more and more of his energies to the cause. He endangered his health and sacrificed far beyond the conceptions of most of us in a struggle that could well prove fruitless. But in a sense each act of the past demands certain additional acts in the future. Thus commitment leads to a committed person, and a committed person often is not totally free to choose.

Cognitive Balance

The pressures for agreement between actions and the source's cognitive structures that underlie these actions constitute the basis of the final pattern of self-persuasion to be examined. The messages a source frames are actions that presumably operationalize a source's attitudes, beliefs, and values. When these actions are at variance with the attitudinal positions, pressures to bring these attitudes into agreement with action may exist. A number of balance models may be utilized to discuss the ways in which decisions that determine the elements in the message are reached. But the cognitive dissonance model focuses upon postdecision behavior. Since the message represents a decision, changes in attitude that follow have often been investigated through the cognitive dissonance model.

The cognitive dissonance model is a means of explaining shifts in attitudes of a source when behavior and attitudes are discrepant. When action and attitude are not in balance, cognitive dissonance may be created. Festinger and his associates identify cognitive dissonance as a mental tension possessing drive properties. Let us assume that a source says certain things in a message that are not consonant with his attitudes. If he perceives the discrepancy, he will be under pressure to resolve the cognitive dissonance created. He may disavow the message, reinterpret it, or in some way rationalize it to make it consistent with his attitudes. He may dismiss the incident as insignificant, or he may tolerate the discrepancy. But one way he may eliminate the tension is to change his attitude. In effect he presents a message and then persuades himself to a new attitude to justify the message.

A typical experimental study might be this: several students are asked to make statements that conflict with their attitudes. For doing this they are promised varying levels of reward. Some may refuse to complete the task, but others will agree. The task being completed, the researchers are interested in what changes in attitude, if any, the sources have undergone. Interestingly enough, those most likely to change attitude received the smallest amount of reward—an amount just sufficient to induce them to make the contra-attitudinal statement.

Other researchers agree that attitudes change but disagree about the basis for the change. Bem argues for a self-perception theory.[1] When situations are ambiguous or the person doesn't have a clear internal guide or justification for behavior, he tends to act like an observer of his own behavior. The students in the previously mentioned experiment are in an ambiguous situation. They performed a task and were asked their attitude about it. They were then rewarded for misleading others about the interest value of the task. Those who were offered a sufficiently large reward could easily interpret their behavior as reasonable, as that which most people would do in the situation given the large reward. But those given a minimal reward are faced with a possible inconsistency: how could they have misled a fellow student for such a minimum reward? They try to interpret this situation by looking at it as if through the eyes of an observer. Their behavior suggests that the task really must not have been so boring after all or they would not have done what they did. So

---

[1] Daryl J. Bem, "Self-Perception Theory," in *Advances in Experimental Social Psychology*, ed. Leonard Berkowitz (New York: Academic Press, 1972), 6: 2–62.

they change to (report) a different attitude, which seems to be sensible in light of their interpretation of the situation.

A number of other interpretations for contra-attitudinal shifts have been offered. Recent analyses have focused around the various justifications that can be offered. The importance of the behavior and the attitude is one factor. If the matter is unimportant or has no effect upon other people or the source's perception of self, little or no change in attitude should be expected. If the behavior is relevant to other people and may mislead them or may cause them to misperceive the source, then greater potential for attitude change exists. Most people can tolerate small discrepancies. Some can tolerate a significant degree of discrepancy between a perceived attitude and another attitude or action without changing any of the elements involved.

The interpretation or justification that the person can offer is important.[2] If the action is easy to explain or justify, then little change is expected. People weigh both their internal motivations for and against the action and also any external costs or benefits that may arise out of the situation. Thus, if there is a slight balance in favor of an action and a strong external incentive to perform the action, the action would be performed, and there would be little need to change attitudes. When there are not strong incentives for the behavior, when the behavior contradicts a previous attitude or action and the behavior is seen to have some importance, there will be some degree of change in the attitude linked to the behavior.

The theoretical rationale for many of these changes observed in laboratory experiments is as yet unclear. Several different theories may explain the same effect. But the research does say that the source's persuasive activity is important. When the justification of that activity is not readily apparent to the source in terms of her or his understanding of the reasons for the actions, changes in the perception of the importance of the issue or of the attitudes held may occur.

The behavior of the source in the persuasion process is an important activity that has the potential for a variety of significant effects upon the source's own attitudes and future action.

EFFECTS ON ACTION

Participation in a communication effort exposes the source to many direct influences. The source's own attitudes and future actions may change. And the behavior of the source in the immediate situation

---

[2] Harold B. Gerard, Edward S. Conolley, and Roland A. Wilhelmy, "Compliance, Justification, and Cognitive Change," *Advances in Experimental Social Psychology* 7 (1974): 217–47.

also may be determined to a large degree by the efforts to influence the behavior of others.

Before the Communication Act

Much of the behavior of the source before the communication act is related to preparation. According to the importance of the occasion and the audience, the source may devote extensive time and effort to this process, including extended research on audience and topic, and painstaking care in tracing the steps of preparation suggested in chapter 6.

The anticipation of persuasion may also affect relationships with potential receivers. A good deal of the attention of the source may be devoted to developing and maintaining a favorable ethos. A source may develop a strategy that involves manipulation of setting or receivers in preparation for the particular persuasion effort. Thus, in many instances the persuasion strategy is being implemented in tactics that occur well in advance of the communication. Therefore the source's behavior is being determined in large part by the demands of strategy and the tactical considerations involved in its implementation. The source voluntarily assumes many of these constraints since his strategy calls for them, and he may assiduously proceed to manipulate as many of the variables in the situation as he can to make them conducive to the message presentation.

Many people condition behavior over a long period of time to contribute toward persuasive efforts. Membership in a number of clubs is helpful to the person desiring awards as the "big man on campus" or as the outstanding young man of the United States by the Junior Chamber of Commerce. Involvement and participation, becoming known by others in many groups, may be instrumental to future goals. The behavior of the source in advance of a communication effort may reflect elements of long-term planning as well as items specific to the immediate communication situation.

Inevitably there are some elements that the source cannot control. Other factors may necessitate the source's adjustment to them rather than vice versa. The source can only respond as best she can to certain choices that she is given; she cannot determine all choices.

A marked degree of tension may occur immediately prior to the communication or continue during and after it. When this tension becomes sufficient for the source to notice it, it may be labeled stage fright. The concept of stage fright is usually related to the oral communication situation; *mike fright* is often used for problems relating to media transmission; such terms as *test-taking behavior* or *writing block* may be used for situations involving writing. Certainly such tension is found in many diverse situations.

Under normal conditions the tension aroused is largely proportionate to the demands for energy and action placed upon the source. Much of this tension represents both physiological and psychological preparatory stages. Under normal circumstances this tension contributes to heighten effort for one can literally do more, think more rapidly, react more quickly. Of course the tension can become excessive and thus prove detrimental. Certain students "block" on written tests or only on speeches labeled "final." Most people learn to accommodate themselves to the tension. Released in activity both mental and physical, the tension is helpful. When it is excessive, the effects may be seen in a variety of patterns. Although these patterns can be detrimental, the problems created must be extreme before they are sufficient to account for any significant negative effects.

During the Communication Act

Putting a message into a channel is extremely complex. Multiple internal systems are at work to produce the symbols and to invest them with meaning: the entire critical apparatus is at once supplying, testing, rejecting, and offering alternatives. Further, the communicator is monitoring the sources of feedback—some from the process of message presentation and some from any receivers present.

Feedback a speaker receives from the message and audience and by a writer from the message may lead to adjustment in behavior. To some degree the communicator may become the prisoner of the feedback. Typically the feedback provides an opportunity to adjust the strategy and tactics being employed. The source may consciously choose to ignore such feedback but unconsciously be affected. Often a persuader consciously elects to modify behavior. Even under the best conditions the source may not interpret feedback correctly, and different people vary in the degree to which they can elicit and utilize feedback.

Although feedback can be helpful in enabling the source to improve persuasive efforts, it can also be detrimental. Sometimes to know what the receivers are thinking or to think you know what they are thinking can be detrimental. For example, feedback can be detrimental to some elements in delivery. Increases in tension, a judgment that the presentation is not going well or that the audience is reacting negatively often produce an increase in malfluencies and a poorer vocal quality, as well as less effective nonverbal communication. In some instances when the persuader perceives the feedback as too negative, he or she may abandon the task either because he or she loses a sense of control and cannot proceed or because of the fear that more harm than good is resulting.

Unanticipated feedback can be quite a shock to the persuader. Lecturers who are interrupted by hecklers or a question often find it difficult to resume the presentation. Or if they do resume, it may be with less effectiveness. Of course, this situation can work in both ways: sometimes the interruptions or questions help the communicator be more effective. One example of a negative effect occurred in a contest debate a few years ago. In one debate I was unable to understand a point, and I apparently looked at the speaker and showed my confusion. In great distress the debater stopped and asked me not to respond in any way. It was disturbing to see me react, and it would be better if I didn't look at the debater at all. I had violated the expectations of the debater in the situation and clearly was inhibiting communication.

Extensive research shows the ability of feedback to help people to improve skills and to acquire greater competency in particular tasks. Feedback in the form of echoed sounds and repronounced words helps the child to acquire acceptable pronunciation of sounds and words. Feedback in the persuasion interaction may have similar effects for the growth of communication and persuasive skills. Feedback can have both positive and negative effects, and much of the effect depends upon the source's sensitivity to feedback and the reasonable interpretation of that feedback.

The source must be sensitive to the degree to which the feedback of the receivers can draw the source from a planned presentation into areas not covered in the planning or for which the source is not as well prepared. This is most obvious in the case of questions posed to the persuader by one or more receiver. Aspects of the issue may be raised that the source has not previously considered. This can be particularly detrimental if the receivers believe the matter raised is important and one that the persuader should be prepared to answer. A series of questions can lead a persuader far from the original planned approach and into situations in which he or she is largely at the mercy of those who were to be persuaded.

After the Communication Act

Completion of an act of communication almost inevitably involves some release of tension as well as some assessment of the impact of the communication. In responding to the persuader, the receivers may well be influencing the persuader's immediate behavior and the behavior that is likely in the near future. If the presentation is judged successful by the persuader, the persuader is likely to be reinforced in her or his beliefs, likely to persuade on this same topic again, likely to have good feelings toward the receivers and to want to interact with them again. Most of us persuade relatively similar audiences on the same or similar topics in somewhat similar situations. Thus we tend to become habituated to certain appeals, certain techniques, if they appear successful.

The response to the persuasive effort affects the nature and quality of future interactions. If, for example, a couple fails to agree about where to spend a vacation, the failure tends to color the relationship and may affect many other aspects of it.

It is important to weigh the emotional effects of the persuasion activity on the source. In addition to the sense of release, there can be positive feelings of self-worth and self-satisfaction associated with a reasonably successful attempt. The more important the occasion to the source, the greater the sense of release may be. Sometimes people who are very calm and very much in control throughout a presentation discover they are quite tired, feel weak or even a bit shaky after the presentation effort. The act of persuasion can be a high, psychologically and physiologically, and there is a sense of coming down off the high. Many politicians report a great sense of energy and the ability to work intensively for long hours during a campaign, much as an athlete has for an important game.

Even when persuasion is not successful, there are often positive emotional responses. A great sense of catharsis may occur. "I had to do it, I had to make the try, I am glad I did." Often people feel the need to make an affirmative statement even if they perceive it will fail to move the receivers. People simply enjoy the process. Some appear to treat persuasion much as a game, a challenge; they like to test themselves. Others get the satisfaction out of the cause or the quality of the effort they put forth. One of the factors that motivate people to attempt persuasion is the effort at self-definition. Another factor is one's sense of self-worth or self-esteem. To the degree participation in the activity serves these needs, the response to the effort will be positive and self-reinforcing.

A final effect of participation may be that the source comes to accept what cannot be changed. If the source has made a valiant effort but lost, he or she can be congratulated by others and taken into the unified group moving on to the next problem. We do not give enough importance to this effect, which is an extremely significant outcome of the persuasion process for sources. The active involvement permits acceptance of a reality that otherwise might have been more painful. Perhaps in the short term the sense of loss is momentarily greater, but in the long term the activity provides a basis for rationalization and for acceptance of what was opposed.

SUMMARY

Persuaders are not free agents in the persuasion process. They are limited by the resources available to them and by the realities of the situation in which they function. They cannot easily avoid certain effects that result from their participation in the process. Persuasion is one way of trying to influence the environment, either people directly or through people some of the forces at work in the environment. But in this process the source is being influenced and sometimes greatly changed by the people or other factors in the situation.

The act of persuasion places the persuader in a somewhat vulnerable position. The decisions to persuade and those made in the course of the persuasion effort are closely tied to a person's world view, goals, and personality. Response to her or his efforts will shape the world view, goals, and personality—or at least have the potential to do so.

The efforts of the communicator may produce self-persuasion; the persuader's own actions and attitudes are affected. Through reinforcement, the effects of commitment, and attempts to balance cognitions and actions, the source may well alter his or her opinions, attitudes, beliefs, and future actions. The receivers may act upon the source either to anchor a position or increase the propensity to shift an attitudinal position toward or away from one pole. These effects may be deliberate on the part of the audience. Some effects in certain situations may be the accidental results of pressure to conform; others may result wholly from the source's interpretation of feedback, and the interpretation may be inaccurate. Commitment may increase the saliency of an attitude and modify it in terms of strength or position on a continuum. A number of conditions exist that may lead to some discrepancy between prior attitudes and action in terms of message elements. One way of adjusting to this discrepancy is to shift attitude to match the action. Although this is obviously not a universal response, it does occur in many communication contexts.

The source seems particularly susceptible to influence through cues received during the communication situation. The source may condition his behavior by strategy and tactics adapted to meet his perceptions of the best procedure. This adaptation may be comparatively constant over long periods of time. And, of course, situations occur that the source cannot control—then he or she must react as well as possible. During and immediately after the communication, the source may be strongly affected by the feedback, both from his own assessment of the message and other elements and the response of his audience. These may serve as his basis for sharp modifications during the message presentation and also for future plans.

While persuasion effects upon the source are not the most important elements of the persuasion process, they are significant and relevant. If we ignore the effect of participation upon the source, we have an incomplete view of the process of persuasion and its effects.

DISCUSSION QUESTIONS AND PROJECTS

1. To what degree do you feel free to fail in a speech, even one presented in a classroom? What effects does your attitude regarding failure have on your behavior as a communicator?

2. What potential for a persuasion strategy lies in the power of reinforcement to affect the "communicator's" behavior? Can the apparent persuader be made the persuadee? Could this be a highly effective persuasion strategy?

3. Can you provide instances where you clearly recognize self-persuasion as operating in communication situations in which you have participated?

4. Discuss how much one's communications reflect personality, how much they are personality, and how much they form personality. Can these interactions be successfully distinguished?

5. The class may wish to conduct experiments with feedback. The feedback conditions may be determined in advance or simply left to class response. For example, positive response can be shown by having the audience hold up a green paddle, negative by reversing to a red side, and neutral by not showing the paddle. What negative effects would you predict from such direct and immediate feedback? After adjusting to the system, would communicators improve persuasiveness from such methods of feedback?

6. Assess the degree to which a source may be the prisoner of receiver response. You may wish to compare situations, personality types, or roles.

7. Does the potential for effects upon the source increase or decrease the contribution that the persuasion process makes to achieving the goals of the source? Of the receivers? Of society as a whole? Does this process limit dissent, for example?

8. Often college debaters are required to debate both sides of an issue. What would you predict about their final position? Would you expect them to believe in both the affirmative and negative cases they present?

V USE OF CHANNELS

13 Relationship of Channel and Setting
Nature of Communication Channels
    Personal Channels
    Mass Media–Channels That Amplify
    Comparison of Personal and Mass Media Channels
Nature of Communication Settings
The Interaction of Channel and Setting

AND SETTINGS

14 The Persuasive Campaign: Multiple Channels and Settings
The Nature and Function of the Campaign
Planning the Campaign
Executing the Campaign
Effectiveness of the Campaign
    Voting Behavior
    The Problem of the Unreachables
Confrontations and Campaigns

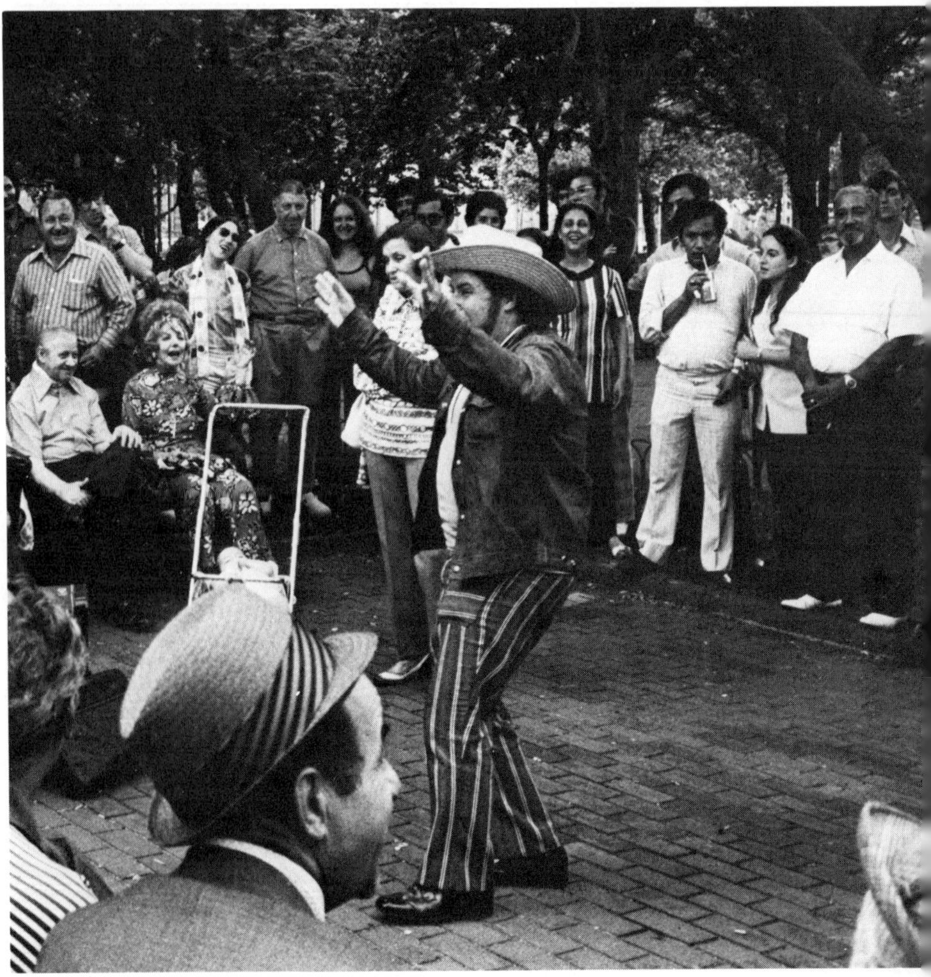

13 Relationship of Channel and Setting

Channel and setting affect the results of the persuasion process directly, interact with other elements, and also have a particularly close relationship to one another. Certain settings seem to mandate certain channels, and certain channels almost inevitably involve certain settings.

Chapter 10 discussed the use of channels and the comparative effectiveness of different channels. Chapter 4 analyzed situation as a factor related to audience analysis. This chapter will examine the nature of certain communication channels and settings and the relationships of the two. The next chapter focuses upon the integrated use of communication media and settings in persuasive campaigns that are extensive in terms of time and numbers of people involved as persuasive agents and receivers.

NATURE OF COMMUNICATION CHANNELS

Any sensory modality can be employed as a communication channel. Thus stimuli may be transmitted using the senses of sight, touch, hearing, smell, and taste.

The processes involved in using any of the available mediums to express oneself and in picking up and interpreting what someone puts into or onto a medium (since communication involves imposing form upon matter) are complex. In mass media the steps and the numbers of people involved between an initial expression of an idea and the ultimate reception of that idea are many; the possible relationships and interactions are beyond easy description. A television announcer reading a few lines on camera is only a small part of the total process by which the lines came to be communicated. Further, the sounds the announcer makes and the movements of her body are subjected to many transformations before the television receiver translates the signals back into audible and visible stimuli, which approximate those picked up by microphones and cameras in the studio.

Although an interest in persuasion does not necessitate an understanding of all the complexities of the various mass media, certain factors are important.[1] Gaining access to the mass media and making effective use of them are extremely difficult problems in persuasion, particularly noncommercial persuasion.

Communication channels may be categorized in many ways, in terms of degree as well as kind. Initially we will distinguish two very general classes of communication channels: personal channels and mass media channels.

Personal Channels

Personal channels permit comparatively private point-to-point, person-to-person(s) contact. Personal channels provide opportunity for a comparatively high degree of interaction of source and receiver(s) and alternation of the roles of source and receiver. Personal channels operate in settings that permit relatively direct adaptation to one another, accommodation of particular interests and influences in an immediate way, and, often, control and manipulation of the setting. In personal channels we can identify the individuals who place messages in the channel.

Accessibility to the material in the channel is limited. Wiretapping, spying, electronic surveillance, even the steaming open of letters are efforts to violate the private nature of personal channels. In many instances even the attempt to violate this privacy is against the law.

The same basic sensory modalities are used in personal channels as in the mass media although we use different labels. Writing or typing suggests a personal channel; print suggests a mass medium. A conversation in the living room is more private than a panel discussion in the classroom, and both are more personal than a televised panel.

We may differentiate three personal channels employed for rhetorical

---

[1] Marshall McLuhan has become the popular spokesman for the idea that the channel or the medium employed is more important than the content in the channel. McLuhan does not give attention to the role of the people and businesses that control the media. Without disparaging the importance of the medium, we should note the importance of the people and the processes by which the media operate, since the persuader gains access to the media only through these people.

purposes: speech, writing, and personal agents. Variations exist within these three channels, including the use of instruments such as the telephone, typewriter, telegraph, loudspeaker, and visual aids.

Speech

Speech, the form of communication that is produced without recourse to instrumentalities outside one's own body, includes dance, song, sign language, pantomime, as well as "talk." Speech is a mosaic—a mosaic that includes the linguistic code, the various inflections of vocal variety (rate, pitch, force, and quality variation), posture, gestures, and gross movement. These factors interact with others in the persuasive process to form meanings that are stirred up. The speaker employs more than one channel, and these channels are capable of transmitting a great variety and hence a complex matrix of symbols.

Speech is often identified as the communicative form with the most potential for effect. This belief, supported in part by empirical evidence, arises from many sources. In part it is attributable to this greater variety and the mosaic characteristics of the medium. Greater empathy may develop. The receiver may "feel into" and identify more closely with the experiences of the communicator. Further, the potential for arousing emotional response and achieving identification seems higher. But many of these effects may be less the result of the channel and more the result of the settings in which the channel is used. In the directness of face-to-face communication, the situational forces may account for more of the effect than the channel. Of course the setting and channel work together, and the interactions are such that the single causes and the strengths of the various causal factors are impossible to separate meaningfully in the practice of persuasion.

Speech remains the preeminent means of communication utilized in our daily lives. The electronic media of radio and television and also film are making speech (at least in some senses) an even more dominant mode of communication.

Writing

The written word is often seen as a recorded form of the spoken word. But speech and writing are different. The words in the manuscript are not the same as the alternate rarefactions and condensations in the air. Movements of the lips, tongue, and body are not the same in speaking as they are in writing. Nor are the activities of the eye and ear the same in reading a manuscript as in listening to a speech. But writing can be distinguished from the mass medium of print. For example, print does not reproduce the uniqueness and almost total illegibility of my handwriting.

McLuhan asserts that the rise of mechanical type and print is responsible for the tendency of Western literate culture to have lost much of the power of memory and certain uses of speech. McLuhan argues that we have stopped remembering things because we can write them down and retrieve them.[2] And we often use writing as a means of testing ideas and trying alternative structures.

Although writing has come to have certain strategic uses for preparation as contrasted to speech, it does have functions other than as an aid to memory or a replacement of memory and as an aid in testing structures and relationships. Writing has a degree of permanency. Exceedingly complex material may be reviewed, reread, reused. Even if not instantly intelligible, the material may become ultimately intelligible. Writing lasts until it is lost or destroyed. The letter tends to be kept until answered; the telephone message may vanish in the face of competing pressures the moment the phone is cradled. Often the only reminder of the telephone call is the monthly bill from the telephone company. In contrast a letter must be torn up, thrown out, burned, fed to the goat, or destroyed in some other way.

Obviously, too, writing may be used as a personal channel when speech is impossible. The letter home, the note on the roommate's desk, the paper or final examination written so the professor may study it at her leisure all indicate this use. And writing may be used for emphasis. An oral commitment is one thing: it gains power if put in writing. The spoken promise is hard to offer as evidence, even to the person who made it.

Personal Agents

A third means of personal communication is to employ an intermediary—a personal agent. Often in difficult situations, which may range from international crisis to a broken romance, some person is chosen as the go-between. This procedure is formalized in many ways: we appoint ambassadors, we need numbers of people to link institutions with those served. In our personal interactions friends often assume the role of personal agent on our behalf—often without our being conscious of that fact. A friend may find a way to resolve a dispute when the people directly involved cannot.

There are ritual elements in the use of intermediaries or personal agents. We tell things to the agent that we would not dream of telling the person directly. Yet we know that the agent will share the information with the other person. We cannot sit down at the same table together, but we can negotiate through a friend. This technique applies to nations

---

[2] Marshall McLuhan, *The Gutenberg Galaxy* (Toronto: University of Toronto Press, 1962).

who will not establish diplomatic relations with one another and to people who have just had a fight. Often the problem would be resolved eventually, but the use of one or more intermediaries permits the dispute to be resolved more quickly and with less strain than if the two tried to talk it out directly, each attempting to persuade the other.

Personal agents need to be chosen carefully. They are not passive links between people. They are independent channels of communication. Their skills are called upon, and they make decisions and influence what happens in their own right, as well as acting as a transmission device. Also, we may select a particular agent because the agent has access, prestige, connections, or other factors that are essential to the success of the persuasive attempt.

The use of personal agents can become a center of controversy, raising sensitive ethical, moral, or legal issues. Agents act not only for us but in terms of their own goals and their own perceptions. They act in what they perceive our best interests when we might disagree with their judgment. Some may be offended by use of a personal agent. And the intermediary can "botch the job" for any number of reasons. Business firms have come under severe attack for using intermediaries. Payments for the work of the intermediaries have been seen as bribes rather than payment for services. In some countries the intermediary is a normal means of doing business, and a certain amount of money (sometimes a bribe) is expected as a condition of doing business. But we must remember that many legitimate professions and people work as intermediaries. We respect the good real estate agent, the sensitive marriage counselor, the consultation firm that finds the right person for the corporate presidency. Many people work as agents for others and are respected for the contribution they make to both the initial persuader and the ultimate receiver.

It is surprising that we do not focus more directly upon the role of the personal agent or intermediary as a medium or tool in the persuasion process. We see many of these individuals as persuaders and do not think about them as agents for another. And in our personal life we see such intermediaries as normal parts of life. Children ask one parent to persuade the other that the children should have a trip to the park, a vacation, or a new car. Friends tell us that our spouse has a problem and needs our help right now. We expect friends to be working in our best interest even when we may not know of it.

The possibility of the use of a personal agent as a channel or means of persuasion is a major strategic decision. We need to become sensitive to the opportunities available and the limitations of such possibilities. More and more people are serving the role of intermediaries in our service society. Issues as to responsibility for their actions are becoming an increasing focus in our society. Responsibilities of businesses for the action of their agents are clearly established. The responsibilities in our private activities are typically not matters of law and are much more complex.

Mass Media—Channels That Amplify

Although the mass media may communicate some sense of a personal, direct approach, they are not point-to-point private communications channels. Access to material in the channel is not restricted in the mass media; on the contrary the material is available to anyone who wishes to obtain it. The message is published. The mass media involve a number of people who do not function as sources but are essential for placing the message into the channel. Mass communication demands a system and an organization. The audience, or at least the potential audience, is "relatively large, heterogeneous and anonymous."[3] Finally, in many instances in the mass media the actual source of the message is extremely difficult to identify. Often the source becomes an institution in which actual responsibility and control of the message is almost impossible to discover.

The mass media involve institutionalization. The mass media and their specific agencies exist because of the potential to return a profit. (Here I speak more directly of the United States than of many other countries, in which portions of the mass media exist for reasons other than the profit motive.) In the United States the mass media are operated by commercial institutions whose goal is to deliver an audience to potential advertisers or communicators who will pay to reach this audience. From this viewpoint the informational, entertainment, and educational functions performed by the mass media are incidental. Presumably, if profit could not be made from delivering audiences to potential communicators, the media owners and operators would switch to a more profitable business.

The mass media, particularly television, are often treated as channels that reach the total audience or at least an audience that is undifferentiated from other audiences. Such a view impedes the understanding of certain factors that are central to the functioning of the mass media used as persuasive channels.

Audiences reached by various mass media or by any part of a medium can be differentiated. The audience for television is not the same as the audience for a best-selling nonfiction work. A magazine entitled the *Million Dollar Farmer* clearly reaches a different audience than does

---

[3] Charles R. Wright, *Mass Communication* (New York: Random House, 1959), p. 13.

Woman's Day. The advertisements for diesel tractors, five-bottom plows, and self-propelled combines from the *Million Dollar Farmer* would surprise the reader of the New York City edition of *Time.* Many radio stations have found success in programming only the top fifty tunes or programming to Spanish Americans, blacks, or farmers.

Access to the mass media depends upon the communicator's either being able to buy space or time or being accorded coverage by those controlling the media. Freedom of press, of expression, of access to the public airwaves is guaranteed. But access does not mean that we will be allowed to use the medium. Of course, in some countries access to the mass media is regulated by government fiat. But in any country access often depends upon more subtle issues. If we can help to deliver an audience to those who will pay for the chance to reach that audience, we will be given access. Indeed, we will probably be paid for a freelance article, for a performance, for our work as a singer, dancer, announcer.

If we cannot help to deliver an audience to others, we must obtain that audience for ourselves. To pay is one solution. The mass media involve the activities of many people. And these people must be compensated for their time and for their skills. If a reasonably guaranteed audience comes with the presentation, we must compete at the going market rate. We may submit a book to a vanity press if the traditional publishers reject our volume of poetry. But even here the typesetting, the pressman, the bindery, and the various materials must be paid for, and the operator of the press must reap a profit. And, of course, we are promised no market. The extensive advertising campaign may include only a listing in *Books in Print* or advertising in the columns of three magazines in three lines of print in the classified ads section.

We may be news. If we are, the media may provide us with access. But someone must make the decision that we are news. And, of course, being news is a comparative matter. Other items can push us off the broadcast or cut the presentation from a ninety-second newsclip to a thirty-second one. And no one needs to be malicious in this action for it to occur.

The list of channels included in the mass media is almost as varied as the number of people writing on the mass media. Let us consider three categories: print, film, and the electronic media of radio and television.

Print

Print has the advantage of relative permanence and ease of access. Almost everyone in our culture reads, and thus the message is available in a readily consumed form. Print is also portable. It can be carried to the beach, the bathroom, the plane, the train, or the breakfast table.

Because of this flexibility print can be used in a great variety of ways. It can reach the consumer via the billboard or bumper sticker. It can come as a direct mail advertisement, a free shoppers' guide, a handbill, a newspaper or a magazine to which we subscribe, or a book, particularly a paperback, that we may discard after reading. Print can become a collection of handsome books bound in fine leather and shelved impressively.

The computer promises a great expansion of the potential of print. Newspapers may become cheaper or at least costs may be kept low. Perhaps the newspaper will be printed in homes much as the wire services transmit copy. The computer can be programmed to type letters that appear personal: they are typed, your own name and address appear upon them, and the names of two other people in your community who are also receiving these special invitations are included.

The value of print for potential permanency, for ease of handling and storage, and for personal accessibility is unlimited. Of course, much of what is printed can be thrown away without much concern.

Film

Film has been discovered: everyone is making film, above, below, and on the ground. The film as an artistic, entertainment, and informational medium has long been important. But increasingly, film is available to make a personal statement, to use as a vehicle by which we may communicate rather than passively receive a message.

Film provides a relatively permanent record and can combine picture, sound, color, and a variety of special effects through various photographic tools and such techniques as editing, montages, cutting, juxtaposition, and time-lapse photography. Film has typically been seen as a more artistic medium than much of the print or electronic media. But it is increasingly utilized as an informational tool.

Films can be used as powerful persuasive media. They serve propagandistic functions; witness films made by the Nazis for use in World War II. Films can stimulate discussion, promote group interaction, provide a point of departure. And they can be used to make powerful persuasive points. The Hollywood film has often been criticized for the picture of American culture and values it has communicated to Americans and to the world. Much of the new force in cinema involves highly personal statements of directors expressing viewpoints about the horror of war, about peace, about life or death, or about reality or fantasy.

Film is used extensively in television. Commercials on television are almost always filmed. The possibilities of film are being extensively exploited by commercial persuaders. As a means of noncommercial persuasion efforts, film will probably grow exponentially in the next few years. It seems an excellent means of developing a persuasive message that can be communicated without the problems involved in getting time and visibility on television.

Electronic Media

In contrast to radio, television, the newest mass medium, receives a disproportionate amount of attention in some ways. The television set and the television industry as a whole have emerged only since World War II. Just as the automobile revolutionized life, so did the television industry; its growth and development revolutionized the mass media in many senses.

Television does certain things very well. The immediacy with which television can bring events to the public is unquestioned. I cannot forget watching that Sunday morning as Oswald was shot in Dallas, and I heard a friend from undergraduate days, Tom Pettit, say, "He's been shot!" The thrill of the first trip to the moon was greater for seeing it happen. (Yet letters arrived at the networks complaining about the cancellations of regular programming.)

Television delivers a vast audience to advertisers. And a person given coverage on network television may achieve more national attention in one night than from a cross-country tour.

Radio remains a very powerful tool nevertheless. Although the television audience is often larger, radio may deliver an audience that can be targeted much more specifically. The cost is sharply lower and the ease of access much greater in many instances. Further, radio is available in almost any configuration from a rather specific segment of the local audience to a much broader general audience.

Television has been accorded particular attention as changing the nature of political campaigning, as introducing new problems in terms of evading public responsibility, as threatening our children through violence, as a key factor shaping the amount of public reaction to the Vietnamese war. Unfortunately little of this impact has been documented and demonstrated although many have asserted it.

Comparison of Personal and Mass Media Channels

Personal and mass channels share certain elements in common but differ quite significantly in others. It may be useful to note some differences in terms of the strategy and tactics that can be employed in persuasion.

1. Channels differ in the permanency with which the message is made available. At times the fact that speech and television are

transitory may be a great asset. Extensive repetition can be used to overcome some of this transitory effect. Also, written or printed materials may be used in conjunction or as supplements, often with cumulative gain in effectiveness.

2. Channels clearly differ in terms of privateness. Although the mass media are limited and can be differentiated in terms of the audience they reach, the material in the mass media is public, published, and accessible. This is not true of private channels. Often material in private channels is given more weight because of that privateness.

3. An important consideration in the use of channels is cost. Initially it would seem that private channels are cheap and mass media expensive. But, in terms of people reached many of the mass media, which are expensive in terms of total cost, are cheapest in terms of cost per thousand receivers. Letters seem cheap. But a business may find that a letter costs two or three dollars to produce without counting the postage stamp.

4. Personal and mass media channels are often best used in combination with one another. The salesman from the national company may gain entrance to an office because of recognition of the company, which results from extensive advertising in the mass media. In turn, the salesman may get the order that would never be obtained in any other way.

5. Cost must be evaluated in terms of ultimate as well as immediate effectiveness. Many advertisers advertised during World War II even though they had no products available for the general public. But the image was important when they resumed production after the war.

6. Personal agents are often overlooked as persuasive channels. Agents can act and communicate information that source and receiver could not exchange directly. Yet each recognizes that the other is aware of the sharing of that information. The agents may also bring special skills, talents, prestige, or other additional influences to bear.

7. The privateness of personal channels can be used for "disguised" tactics. Thus, a communication may be undertaken totally for the benefit of an apparently unintended receiver. The overheard stock tip may be given more credence than the urgent recommendation of one's own broker.

8. Written materials may capture spoken items. A manuscript that a speaker overtly reads may later be offered as evidence of what the speaker said. Notes taken on a public lecture or jotted down after a telephone conversation may be given greater credibility than one's recollection of what was said and done. Furthermore, a tape recorder or other mechanical devices can be employed to capture the message.

9. Certain products are more conveniently sold via one medium than another. Probably toilet bowl cleaners and toilet tissue are sold much more effectively and economically through the film techniques

RELATIONSHIP OF CHANNEL AND SETTING

and the devices utilized in the television commercial than through any other procedure, including direct, personal selling.

10. Channels differ in the degree to which a selected target can be reached. A personal channel offers the maximum opportunity to reach a known person. Even the habitual watcher of the NBC evening news may miss a night. The mass media offer many choices and strategic alternatives to reach a variety of definable, specific target audiences.

11. Presumed effectiveness of personal channels in many cases may be more the result of situational factors than of inherent differences in the effectiveness of the channel.

12. Many people do not expose themselves to significant amounts of the mass media or may focus upon the entertainment functions of the mass media.

13. People who are interested in an area tend to utilize sources within the mass media that provide maximum information concerning that topic. This usually means they turn to printed sources.

14. Some people tend to be extremely heavy consumers of mass media, exposing themselves not only to more of one medium but also to a wide variety of media.

15. The mass media function more as reinforcing agents than as change agents. Demonstrations that the mass media are direct sources of effects in receivers are largely lacking.

NATURE OF COMMUNICATION SETTINGS

Communication takes place within the context of a particular occasion-setting-environment. Situations could be classified by degree of formality, structure, purposiveness, privateness, numbers of receivers, similarity of receivers, responsiveness, and so forth. Any of these continua would yield some insight about communication settings and their effects. But an approach that combines a consideration of size with situational-environmental factors seems particularly useful in identifying important variations. Four settings will be differentiated: face-to-face settings in one-to-one, small-group, and target audience situations and non-face-to-face mass media settings.[4]

One-to-One

The one-to-one setting is typically a face-to-face situation but includes letters, memos, telephone calls, or other means by which two people interact. This setting involves the personal channels of communi-

---

[4] This division parallels—and was suggested by—Howard H. Martin, "Communication Settings" in *Speech Communication*, ed. Howard H. Martin and Kenneth E. Andersen (Boston: Allyn and Bacon, 1968), pp. 58–84.

cation at their most personal and private level. The intrusion of another person almost inevitably changes the things said, the topic of conversation, the pattern of interaction. Letters that I write knowing that my wife will read them before I send them differ from those I write that she will not read. (This is not to imply that these differences are necessarily significant any more than they are always consciously intended.)

The one-to-one setting provides maximum opportunity for interaction and freedom from a variety of external restraints. Yet constraints inevitably still exist. The one-to-one settings are often not seen as persuasive. Husband and wife interact so casually that they do not perceive these interactions as involving persuasion. The couple who are dating frequently, the family talking with one another, the friends talking over coffee or pausing momentarily in the hall to chat typically do not perceive these as persuasive settings. Thus, the barriers against allowing oneself to be persuaded may be set aside. The sense of mind free to meet mind is often felt strongly. Yet these are probably the most important of the persuasive exchanges in which we engage, at least as far as our own personal, private lives are concerned.

The privacy and directness of this situation can be used to good advantage. Heads of state at times dismiss the interpreters and talk one-to-one. Often the setting can be deliberately selected and manipulated. The favorite dinner, good records of mood music, the relaxing drink can all be predetermined. Opportunity for maximum exchange of roles, of searching out needed information, of revealing the real self are provided in this setting.

Small Group

A small group can be defined as three or more people interacting together with each having full opportunity and access to the role of communicator as well as the role of receiver. Thus, practically, a limit exists on the size of the group and the conventions and expectations of the people involved. The group might range up to fifteen or even to fifty people in certain instances. In other cases four or five people might be "performing" for a larger audience and thus not properly characterized as a small group.

Small groups exist to exchange information, to solve problems, or to have a social occasion. Indeed many small-group settings are social in nature; others are associated with work groups; some few are voluntary associations such as clubs or planning committees.

The small-group setting is rarely identified as being a persuasive setting. Yet it is one of the most important. Indeed, our public lives are largely determined by our activities in the small-group setting just as the one-to-one setting is probably most important in our personal, private lives.

Persuasion is as much a reality in the small-group setting as it is in any communication setting. In business, community action, developing national legislation, determining the political nominee of a party, the small group is the key to the outcome. Decisions are typically made by the few people in the group. Often these decisions are reached in bitter confrontations. Sometimes compromises can be achieved and differences accommodated; sometimes someone wins and someone loses. These decisions may in turn be translated to other groups for action or implementation. The decision of a few people in General Motors may affect the lives of literally thousands of workers, affect the national economy, and result in marked shifts in contemporary life.

The small-group setting has been widely researched under such rubrics as group dynamics, group discussion, negotiations, game theory in small groups, group therapy, sensitivity training, T-groups, and so on. Unfortunately the behavior in these settings has not often been evaluated in terms of persuasion. Yet one who seeks to solve the puzzle, to win the game, to get the best deal, to win the support or recognition of others overtly creates a persuasive setting.

The small-group setting has many implications for persuasion. It provides much of the opportunity for interaction and exchange that characterizes the one-to-one setting. Yet by the introduction of greater numbers of people, one induces the additional constraints of the individual's relationships to each of these people and his personal goals in terms of these people. One may "toady" to the teacher, another may seek to cut down his classmates' performances. Certain conventions and roles may create patterns in terms of interaction. The history of the group is a strong factor conditioning its present behavior. The setting may be manipulated to some degree. If problems of pressing urgency are discussed at 12:05 during the lunch hour in a room without chairs, decisions will soon be forthcoming.

In a small group one loses the ability to control so completely the stimuli that impinge upon the receivers. The other people are free to introduce contrary and competing ideas. Attention cannot be focused so completely upon a given set of stimuli. Setting in terms of environment cannot be manipulated as freely. The patterns and conventions that structure the group may be difficult to alter. In contrast, the one-to-one setting and the speaker-to-target audience both provide greater opportunity for control in these respects.

The literature on small groups is so extensive and the task in reinterpreting the terminology and the approach in terms of a more general and universal persuasion theory so great that it cannot be undertaken here. But the insights concerning the general persuasion process do apply with adaptations to the specifics of the small-group setting, and the material on small groups can contribute significantly to the development of insights about persuasion in general as well as persuasion in the particular setting of the small group.

Source to Target Audience

This setting may still be a face-to-face situation or it may involve less direct interaction. Many of the source-to-target audience situations approximate those of the mass media in some ways. The key to distinguishing this setting is that interaction between source and receivers and alternation of roles are still possible on a relatively immediate basis. In mass media, although such interaction is ultimately possible, it is on a delayed basis.

This setting normally involves a relatively large audience in a situation perceived by those involved as essentially one of communication flowing from a source to the receivers. Each individual if asked could clearly name his or her role. Certain conventions constrict the actual as contrasted to the possible actions of sources and receivers.

First, since the people perceive themselves as having certain roles, they will behave in terms of the conventions of those roles. Audiences will rarely interrupt a speaker in a formal lecture or banquet presentation. If they do, it will generally be by applause or other brief interjection. Rarely will a question be posed or a dialogue ensue. (Conventions differ in different settings within one country and certainly in different countries. In Canada and England political speeches involve a good deal more heckling by the audience, and the speaker is evaluated by his or her ability to handle the interruptions.)

Second, the audience is largely self-selective. Thus, the audience that attends a public lecture on Greek oratory is motivated to attend and to expend the time needed. Those who watch a football game differ in many respects from the audience at a ladies' wrestling match or a chamber music recital. Even a speaker on the soapbox in a public square is dependent upon the audience members to decide whether they will become auditors. Generally, then, the target audience chooses to become the target audience and expends some effort to do so.

Third, this communication setting is typically seen as an influence one. Often the audience is homogeneous and friendly to the source's intent. At times the situation is perceived as being one of information transmission. Yet there is almost inevitably an awareness on the part of all that influence is truly one potential in the situation. Some people may be on guard to resist the influence; others come prepared to yield to it and to participate fully. It is surprising how many people come to a "spontaneous" riot with the ammunition that will be needed during the riot. And, of course, in attending the theater or a football game, we set ourselves psychologically for participation in the experience. If we do not, the event often seems to fall flat.

Fourth, the very definiteness of the situation contributes a series of expectations that must be mediated in some way. The communicator anticipates the communication opportunity well in advance and is expected to be prepared for the occasion. Communication is judged in terms of standards and expectations held by the audience.

Finally, the source-to-target audience situation blends into a situation that is closely comparable in some ways to the mass media. The easiest distinction is that in the former situation the interaction of the receivers with speaker, writer, musician, actor, or athlete does affect the behavior of the source in an immediate sense. The receivers are active agents in affecting the progression of the message. They may indeed modify the stream. The response of the audience may contribute to the presentation and alter it and thus the effect. In the mass media this possibility does not exist in any immediate sense. Lack of readers may cause a work to go out of print, or a program may be canceled for lack of viewers or because it offends the sponsor, but these operate on delayed rather than immediate bases.

Mass Communication

The mass communication label conjures a setting in which vast numbers of people are assembled and focused upon a common stimulus. This description is, of course, untrue. This setting of mass communication is really not a setting in some senses, for the audience is dispersed, scattered, and fragmented. The receiver may be an individual, perhaps two or three people are focusing upon the television set, although five, fifty, or five hundred may be in the motion picture theater. The total audience reached may be in the millions, but these millions are reached in many cases as discrete individuals. Perhaps the ultimate example of this separateness and dispersion is the audience for a book; almost inevitably a book is read alone or in practical isolation.

One of the clichés about television is that it comes into the living room, the recreation room, and the bedroom. Despite the canned laughter tracks, it does not operate with the audience facilitation of the motion picture film, which eschews any thought of canned-laughter tracks.

Not only is the audience fragmented and discrete in most instances of the mass communication situation, but also any feedback cannot affect the creation of the message that has already been presented and published. It is complete; it is frozen in channel. Of course, the receiver may destroy the book or the police may confiscate a film, but essentially these actions do not affect the availability of the message for others.

The audience for any item of the mass media is also self-selective. We decide to read or not to read a book or even, by habit, whether to read books at all. We decide to watch Carol Burnett or the news, or we never tune those programs in at all. The sheer amount of stimuli available in the mass media means that no receiver can consume even a small portion of it. Of necessity we must choose among that which is available. We must apportion attention given to the mass media in terms of attention given to work, recreation, family, and all the other things that command our attention.

Comparison of Communication Settings

Certain strategic implications arise from the considerations relative to the differences in settings.

1. Settings differ in the degree of interaction and the immediacy of interaction that are possible and in the conventions that exist and govern the interaction. Thus the one-to-one and small-group settings permit extensive interaction and very immediate interaction, and the conventions of the settings tend to encourage relatively free interaction. In target audience settings and the mass media, immediate interaction is limited by accepted conventions that may vary from situation to situation and nation to nation and by the lack of immediate feedback in the mass communication situation.

2. Audiences are always self-selective. But in the smaller, more personal settings, there is less perception of being a source and receiver and of being in an influence setting. Further, exposure in these settings becomes part of one's normal ongoing activity, part of one's life. Exposure in target audience situations or to the mass media involves more of a sense of choice, and, particularly in the former case, demands action on the part of the potential receivers to place themselves in the setting.

3. With the exception of film, most of the mass media communicators can do little to control the setting, the size of the audience, or the number of interacting receivers when the communication is received. This is determined by the receiver.

4. Settings that involve relatively few people permit direct adaptation to the receivers on the part of the source and to the source on the part of the receivers. Situations in which relatively large numbers of receivers are being reached limit the specificity of adaptation

and move the communicator to deal with more generalized averages that can be estimated for receivers.

5. In many instances, participants in one-to-one and small-group settings do not perceive these settings as persuasive situations. In many of the larger target audience and mass communication settings, people are more sensitive to the possibility that these settings are influence settings, and they may selectively expose themselves on this basis.

THE INTERACTION OF CHANNEL AND SETTING

Channel and setting have particularly close relationships as factors in the persuasion process. Since certain settings seem to mandate certain channels and certain channels lead to certain settings, the two interact closely in determining the effects of the persuasion process.

Mutual Determination of Use

To select a one-to-one setting is necessarily to select a personal channel of communication. To hand a person a brochure, sit back while the person reads it, and then depart could not possibly justify the cost involved. This setting and the effort involved in getting into this setting mandate the additional advantages that can be exploited in speech. Of course, the message in the one-to-one setting may be carefully pre-planned. Yet questions may interrupt the flow: the phone, baby, or husband may interrupt. Other unexpected elements may arise to modify the anticipated message.

To select any of the mass media also involves a complex network of decisions not only about the final message being put into the channel but also about the procedures in creating that message. We must prepare or have the message prepared according to the imperatives of the medium. We must select the medium, the time, and the message in terms of the audience sought. We must call upon the resources and talents of those skilled in the use of the medium. We must link into a very complex system in such a way that we use the system rather than having the system render us meaningless or ineffective.

Mutual Determination of Effect

If certain channels mandate certain settings or certain settings mandate certain channels, it will be difficult to find the causal relationships between these elements that operate independently and the interactive effects. In some instances the one-to-one setting has unique power. But is this because of the use of speech or the adaptation of the message consciously or unconsciously to the specific receiver? Or does this effect arise from the conventions of attention, and feedback and interaction that the setting calls forth? One is free to turn off the television; it is more difficult to turn off a boring host at a party.

Often in research identical messages are contrasted to measure the power of a medium. Thus print, a radio broadcast, and a live speaker may be contrasted. But print, the spoken word, and the face-to-face speech are not the same message. Nor is the same message necessarily equally adapted to the three media. The settings also change—in real life certainly, and almost inevitably the laboratory conditions are modified. There is relatively little audience interaction in reading the print. The focusing and moving together in response to a stimulus may create effects in the radio situation that simply cannot occur in the reading situation.

The conventions of the setting may affect and predispose audience response in ways totally unrelated to the channel. But the channel may also create some expectations unrelated to the setting. Thus, the novelty of television seemed to be a factor that led early experimenters to seize upon the televised teacher as more effective than the same teacher in the classroom. But when the novelty wore off, the difference in effectiveness vanished.

SUMMARY

This chapter has explored the close relationship of channel and setting as interacting elements in the persuasion process.

Communication channels may be differentiated as either personal or mass media. Personal channels are private and point-to-point, and material in the channels is restricted. Speech, writing, and personal agents function as personal channels. Print, film, radio, and television serve as mass media channels, the material is public and "published." Access to the material in the channel is dependent upon the receiver's selecting the material, although the material is available to all who seek it.

Channels differ in terms of the numbers of receivers easily reached, cost, the degree of institutionalization, the ease of access to the medium, and the degree to which the message may be conceived and transmitted by identifiable individuals. All of these elements affect the choice of the channel to be employed.

Settings may be differentiated in terms of many continua. Separation into one-to-one, small-group, source-to-target audience, and mass communication settings may be accomplished in consideration of size of the group involved, the environment, and the immediacy of interaction. These factors contribute to decisions of key importance in determining the ultimate effect of the persuasion process.

Finally, the interaction of channel and setting is such that the use of channels and settings is linked. The nature of the channels and the stimuli transmitted, the settings employed and the conventions relative to these settings interact to make the determination of cause and effect relationships between these factors and ultimate persuasion effect extremely difficult.

DISCUSSION QUESTIONS AND PROJECTS

1. Plan a persuasive message on a topic that presumably has appeal to a wide range of audiences. Then note the changes you might make in extemporaneously presenting the message to a variety of audiences. (Perhaps a tape recording or reports from a team of classmates as observers would be valuable.) What changes did you make? Why? Which changes were conscious on your part? Did the changes enhance effectiveness?

2. Begin with a speech by a student or one by some noted speaker. Read a manuscript of the speech; then listen to a tape of it. Watch a film or a television tape of the speech if one is available. Do the same things impress themselves upon you? How does the medium interact with the message in yielding these results? What changes occurred in the environment or setting as you focused upon the message in these different settings?

3. Contrast the use of filmed versus live television as a persuasion medium. Do you perceive differences in immediacy? What are the strengths and weaknesses of each approach?

4. In every age the death of the spoken word is pronounced. The theater of the absurd, contemporary music, light shows, and "doing your own thing" have all been cited as contemporary evidences of the death of the word. Is the word dying? In what senses? Or is the word being reborn?

5. What forces shape the content of the mass media in such a way that it is favorable to the commercial interests who buy space and an audience in the media? What counteracts these forces? You might talk specifically in terms of dangers of smoking, the poor safety record of the automobile, or some other current instance.

USE OF CHANNELS AND SETTINGS

6. To what degree is a news anchorperson like Cronkite or Chancellor a reporter? To what degree can he or she be identified as a source for the messages he transmits? To what degree a persuader?

7. What are the implications of an aesthetic medium such as a play, novel, film, or any other work of art being used as a persuasive instrumentality? Can aesthetic decisions be made except from a frame of reference, a persuasive point of view? Why should we pay money to attend a play or a movie only to be subjected to the persuasive efforts of a writer or director?

8. Is a book truly a means of communicating to a mass audience? In what sense do any of the mass media reach the mass audience?

9. What strategy would you employ in using various media and settings in trying to influence a policy decision reached by your university? (Don't forget the possible use of personal agents.)

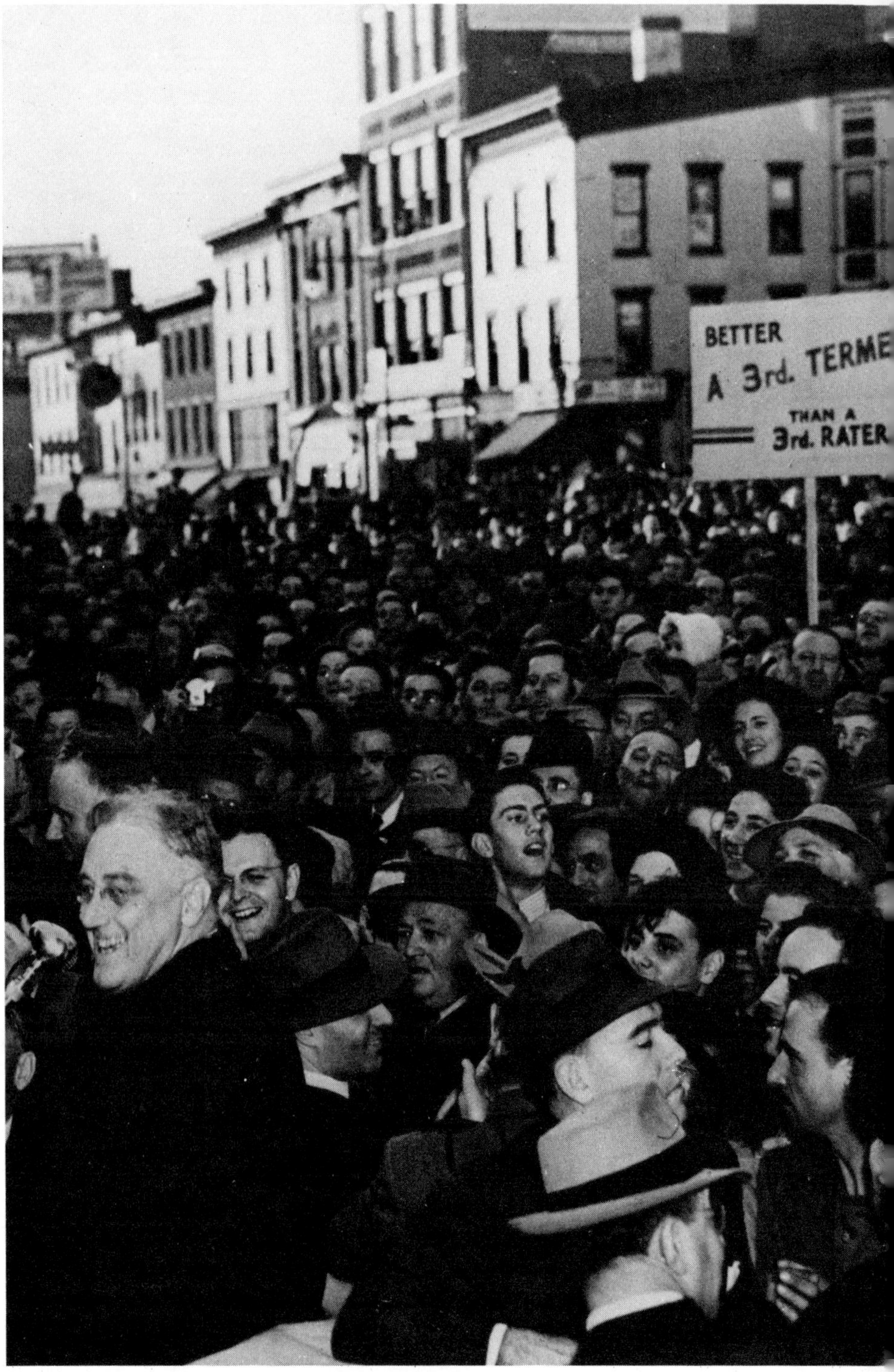
BETTER
A 3rd. TERME
THAN A
3rd. RATER

14 The Persuasive Campaign: Multiple Channels and Settings

A few persuasion efforts may be described as one-time attempts, but, in general, any persuasion effort is only part of a continuous series of persuasion efforts. This is true whether we view persuasion as a persuader, a persuadee, or societal observer.

What creates this impression? In part it may be that people in every era face the same questions. *Faust, Madame Bovary,* the *Ethics* of Aristotle, and *Paradise Lost* speak to us all. Then, too, certain issues in each generation so capture public attention that many become involved in persuasive efforts relative to those issues. Thus, the guarantee of medical care by the federal government was an important issue in the United States in 1930 and will continue to be one in the 1980s. However, more specific reasons for this apparent continuity of persuasion efforts exist.

Our persuasion efforts grow out of our commitments to beliefs, attitudes and values, and actions. Our actions are likely to relate to attitudes and values that are salient in a particular situation. In discussing religion or politics we draw upon the attitudes and values that characterize our views in these areas. If strongly committed to a certain policy as desirable for our company or our department, we evaluate favorably those proposals and actions that implement the policy. In casual conversations, in making day-to-day decisions, or in recommendations for hiring, firing, or promoting we act within that frame of reference.

The relevant bases of action change from situation to situation. Further, actions rarely result from only one commitment or belief. Indeed a person whose life revolves around a single commitment that dominates action in diverse situations is obsessed and neurotic.

Most individuals recognize that significant persuasion goals cannot be achieved in a day. The sales representative may work two years to make the first of a continuing series of sales. A manager may work many years to establish the procedural reforms within her department that she sees as needed. Further, a temporary victory may not be sufficient to ensure winning the war. The teenager may agree to keep her room picked up and do so for a month. But persuasion often has to be continued or renewed if the change in behavior is to endure.

If someone is animated by certain enduring values and commitments and if repeated persuasion efforts are necessary to gain or to continue success, a pattern of ongoing persuasion may characterize the individual. In a sense we have but one speech and we spend our entire lives making it. Obviously the speech adjusts to the specifics of situation and audience. But certain patterns and dominant themes may characterize each of us.

As receivers we function as the target of myriad persuasion efforts. If those around us are engaged in a series of extended persuasion efforts, we become the target of such efforts. We are the target of persuasion efforts originating from political parties, the pulpit, and charitable crusades, as well as efforts to maintain or enlarge the market for products and services—from beautification to plumbing.

As she stands talking to us through the screen door the canvasser for the United Fund may feel she is engaged in a simple, isolated persuasive appeal. Yet her appeal is linked to a pattern of previous campaigns and our giving in those campaigns. It is related to the reports in the newspapers, on radio and TV; to the billboards and to the red line on the thermometer prominently placed downtown that reflects the progress of the campaign. Any one appeal, any one speech is only one fraction of the total mosaic of the United Fund campaign.

Society incorporates the persuasion efforts of many individuals and groups. An individual may see himself as acting independently in supporting a point of view. Yet that particular act is only one part of a larger pattern of many groups and individuals who are supporting, opposing, or ignoring that particular viewpoint. The derivation of a public policy is the result of many individuals and groups interacting about that issue or policy.

The observer may identify the various campaigns—the competing systems of persuasion—that coalesced to pass a local bond issue or to alter the shape of a prospective constitutional amendment. Those opposed to a particular campaign may identify it as a massive propaganda effort or as a conspiracy directed against societal values. Those supporting the campaign may see it as a valiant effort to arouse and inform an indifferent public to problems regarding the survival of the entire nation.

Understanding the interaction of forces in persuasion campaigns is of great interest to many disciplines. The political scientist and the historian study campaigns ranging from election campaigns to legislative campaigns conducted by lobbyists. Social scientists are interested in persuasion campaigns for many theoretical as well as practical considerations. Sales representatives, advertising agencies, political parties, and candidates are interested for many purely practical reasons.

The identification of persuasion campaigns and the description of the many varieties present significant problems. To develop and test even a comparatively limited theory concerning campaign persuasion provides enough problems to last the behavioral scientist many years. Currently the efforts seem to be divided between researchers who want to describe and identify the main features of various persuasion campaigns and attempt some preliminary identification of the relevant factors and those who offer advice on how to do it—typically on the basis that they did it.

The complexities of dealing with a persuasion campaign can be briefly illustrated by recalling the movement to "stop the war in Vietnam." Opposition to involvement in Vietnam presumably existed on many levels before there was any U.S. involvement in that area. This opposition was salient only to those who could in some way see this as a potential action by the government and thus a source of concern. Once the involvement began, the commitment was slow and gradual. The country was not faced with the call for a declaration of war in this instance.

Opposition to the conflict in Vietnam was undoubtedly being voiced before most of the American public even saw it as a war. When the opposition began to be heard it appeared to be a single congressman, a negative reference by an acquaintance, an expression of concern by a commentator. Over time a number of voices began to question the extent, the manner, and the validity of U.S. involvement. People who opposed the war began to draw together into groups to communicate with one another and to identify and articulate certain common arguments. As the movement grew, some groups that had formed in opposition dissolved. But other groups were born. They began to attract more public attention. They began to draw support in the form of money and volunteer workers and were accorded the status of newsmakers to be covered and reported by the various mass media.

New groups continued to form. Some were local chapters of a national group that had formerly operated a small printing press by the voluntary efforts of three people. Various preexisting groups began to expand their concerns to include the war or even to make it their central concern. Thus, in time, the anti-Vietnam movement grew so that the Vietnam war became a central issue in the nation and affected the political lives and the personal choices of many Americans.

To analyze the "stop the war" movement is an exceedingly complex task. The actions of many individuals and of many groups are involved. No one individual, no one group provided the key to the movement. The interests of many groups and individuals were quite diverse, even conflicting; yet each contributed toward the growth of the movement as a whole. The ways in which the movement affected individuals within the society, the ways in which the movement interacted with other movements and other issues and shaped and altered these movements and issues and was in turn shaped and altered by them are so extensive as to prohibit description.

In one sense the movement against the Vietnamese war had a limited life. In another sense the allegiances formed, the commitments made, and the interrelationship of this issue to other elements in the life of the nation and in the lives of individuals is such that the movement will affect Americans and America for at least a generation, maybe much longer. The current women's movement has followed the same general pattern. Its effects will similarly continue for generations.

Much of the persuasion that individuals initiate or receive and much of the persuasion in society cannot be identified as part of a persuasive campaign. Paradoxically much of the persuasive interaction that occurs within a society is not part of a planned persuasion campaign; yet that persuasive interaction occurs only because of a campaign. Further, the success or failure of the campaign often depends upon persuasive interaction that occurs outside the planned campaign structure. To see the relationship between a campaign and the totality of persuasion efforts that relate to the goal of any campaign, it is necessary to define and then to explore the nature and function of the persuasion campaign.

THE NATURE AND FUNCTION OF THE CAMPAIGN

A persuasion campaign is relatively extensive both in time and intensity and involves large numbers of people who perceive themselves as working together to achieve a specified goal that can be accomplished only by affecting the attitudes and/or behavior of large numbers of receivers. Such a campaign will usually involve the use of all available media, but in some situations, both historical and contemporary, only one medium might have been or might be used.

The persuasion campaign may be differentiated from an extended effort by an individual or from the many individual campaigns that characterize a movement. Individuals engage in relatively extended campaigns to achieve some goal. People have devoted their entire lives to pursuing success. And every medium from letters and telegrams to impassioned love poems, billboards, and skywriting has been used in pursuit of a woman. While there are many analogues between a persuasive campaign as defined and the efforts of a single individual, I shall restrict the use of the term *campaign* to situations that meet the definition set forth.

Persuasive campaigns should be distinguished from movements. A persuasive campaign has a structure. Campaign workers feel linked together in a structured, cooperative effort to achieve a specific goal. Even within this limitation, a wide range of campaigns exists. The Republican candidate for county coroner mounts a campaign. So does the Republican candidate for county clerk. The candidate for the United States House of Representatives, the party candidate for senator, the presidential and vice-presidential candidates all mount campaigns for office. These campaigns are independent in some respects, yet linked in many others. Both the individual and the party campaigns depend upon many of the same factors as determinants of success or failure. Money and support may flow both from the local candidate to the state or national candidate and to the party and vice versa.

Unfortunately there is no convenient label to distinguish the campaign of an individual, such as the presidential candidate or the candidate for sheriff, from the larger campaign, which might be identified as the Republican party campaign. Perhaps we might term the individual's campaign a *microcampaign* and the large entity, which is the total of the similarities and distinctive features of all the party efforts, a *macrocampaign*. Success or failure of either the micro- or the macrocampaign must involve a consideration of the other.

Even macrocampaigns, however, can be distinguished from a movement. A movement involves a number of identifiable, separate, and distinct campaigns. Movements tend to be more extensive in time than do campaigns. Further, the goals of a movement are rarely unitary; they are often only vaguely defined and typically involve a number of relatively independent goals as steps toward achieving the goals of the movement—the antiwar movement, the free-silver movement, the populist movement, the black-power movement. Movements center around ideas; campaigns tend to focus around specific products, people, or actions. Of course, movements are reflected in campaigns to elect specific people, to gain legislative enactments, to achieve certain actions. But in many cases the success or failure of the movement in accomplishing a specific goal is not of great consequence to the movement. A movement is usually not dependent upon any single leader, although a single leader frequently is present at a particular time.

A persuasive campaign that exists with relation to a product is a sales or marketing campaign; related to an individual it is typically an election campaign; to legislation, a legislative campaign. Campaigns mounted by those opposed to our view are typically "propaganda campaigns."

The term *propaganda* has come to have such a negative connotation that the word is rarely employed in common usage except in a pejorative sense. Dictionaries define propaganda neutrally as the spreading of information, ideas, or material designed to further one's own cause or to damage an opposing cause.

In general, a persuader identifies campaigns with which he or she is associated as informational, educational, public-spirited, or sales campaigns. A persuader allows opponents to organize and execute propaganda campaigns as they wish, but he or she is aware that much of the research on propaganda and propaganda techniques can be of great value to a persuasion campaign.

Although the complete persuasion campaign involves many and diverse characteristics, three important processes are common to all of them: organizing and sustaining the persuasion effort, using multiple media, and using the multistep flow of communication.

Organizing and Sustaining the Persuasion Effort

To have any hope of success, a persuasion campaign must be organized. In order for the people involved to function as a unit, some provision must be made for a division of responsibility and effort. An organization must be developed that permits decision making and that monitors the campaign, directing and redirecting efforts and workers as needed. Organization is essential not only to plan and initiate the effort but also to sustain the campaign a sufficient length of time to achieve its goal or until the campaign is lost.

Since the next section deals with the organization of campaigns in terms of the planning stage and the following section deals with implementation, let us focus briefly on the reasons for sustaining the persuasion effort over a relatively extended period of time.

First, a persuasion effect tends to disappear in a relatively brief period of time unless it is reinforced. A change in a belief or attitude may persist for a brief period of time unless a means can be found to reinforce this change and perhaps to continue the evolution toward a still greater change.

Second, many persuasion efforts are directed toward goals that are not particularly salient to an individual. Although we may be predisposed to contribute to the United Fund, there are certainly other matters in our lives that are of more immediate importance. Further, the success of the campaign depends not so much upon getting a contribution as upon getting a relatively significant contribution from those who do contribute.

Third, some campaigns are forced to continue over an extended period of time. A candidate must often run in the primary to secure the party nomination. Then she must continue to campaign until she sees the polls close on election day. (Then she may begin her next campaign.) To allow her campaign group to disintegrate, to disappear from public view, or to appear to exhaust herself or her ideas can be disastrous.

Fourth, a campaign often takes a good deal of time. Workers must be recruited. In part these workers will be obtained during the actual campaign. Volunteers may be obtained by other workers. Interest in the campaign may be slow to build. It may take time to reach the various media and to utilize these media in effective ways. We cannot ring all the doorbells in a community in one night. It takes time for the personal contacts and interactions by which influence is spread from person to person and from group to group.

Fifth, changes and progress may occur gradually. In some instances the public must first be made aware of a problem; attention can then be focused upon the proposed solution. The issue may be put on the ballot, and finally the campaign will culminate in winning or losing the vote. This issue might not even be placed on the ballot without an aroused public opinion, and apathy might condemn the proposal to failure even if placed on the ballot.

Finally, sustaining and building the momentum of a campaign may be essential to the very survival of the campaign effort itself. A billboard may do little to change the voting decisions of the public, but the billboard may reassure the workers in the campaign that the campaign is on the track and moving forward. If the campaign is not sustained, if it loses momentum, the workers may lose a good deal of morale, and their effectiveness may sharply diminish. The danger of this happening and its adverse effects both on those participating in the campaign and the public at large is represented in the popular concern of candidates in elections that they may peak too early.

Using Multiple Media

Campaigns use the available channels of communication, drawing upon both mass media and personal channels. Every campaign will not use all the media. For example, a local bonding election will rarely involve television or magazine coverage unless in a large metropolitan community that possesses one or more local television stations or if the issue possesses larger implications.

Some campaign communication is directed at those within the campaign. The workers' efforts must be channeled and coordinated. Material and information that the workers can use in their own persuasive efforts must be supplied. Further, the communication within the campaign organization as well as that directed to those outside it is important in maintaining the morale of the campaign workers. The personal communication from the leaders and officials within the campaign structure is of great importance to morale. But the evidences of the campaign that appear in the mass media are particularly likely to be noted by the worker; research findings clearly indicate that material in the mass media first reaches those who are most interested and most favorable. The active campaign worker is in this category.

Some degree of saturation of the target with stimuli relevant to the campaign is essential. The major themes need to be repeated, and the receivers need to be immersed in relevant stimuli. Eventually the material first noted by those sympathetic to the campaign will be noticed by the neutrals and those less interested. As the stimulation continues, interest will grow, and the object of the campaign will become more important to those who were formerly uninvolved.

Different media reach different people. The more educated tend to rely more heavily upon print than do the less educated. Different types of material attract different receivers. A newsworthy statement by a politician may be covered on the evening news, but a paid thirty- or sixty-second spot may reach those who watch sports or situation comedies but do not watch the news.

The use of many media and the concentrated and extensive use of the several media may have a summation effect. A single stimulus may go unnoticed, but a whole series of stimuli may break through to the consciousness of the receiver. Further, the very amount of coverage may make the issue become important in the eyes of the receiver; it may cause him to take a position or to seek to legitimate the position he has by reference to groups or individuals with whom he interacts.

The sense of personal contact with the campaign or the campaigners is exceedingly important. In local elections where the candidate must become known, personal contact is of urgent importance. The neighborhood coffee hours, appearances at the plant gates at the change of shift, the walk through the shopping center, appearances on news programs or local "meet the candidates" nights become important means of reaching the voters. For example, only two local candidates for office have interacted with me on a direct personal basis in the last seven years. Both have received my vote. One who stopped me in a shopping center to introduce himself as a candidate for judge had been campaigning for several weeks although I did not recognize his name. I suddenly began to notice advertising, statements, and material related to his candidacy.

On the basis of what I read, I voted for him. Yet without the personal contact I probably would have read none of the material. In the second instance I was invited to a neighbor's home to meet the opposition party's candidate for mayor. In the course of a question and answer session I posed several questions to him. He responded specifically, and I thought appropriately, to these questions. I never had the opportunity to pose these questions to my party's candidate nor did they come up as significant issues in the campaign. I voted for the opposition party's candidate for mayor. (He lost.) The personal contact is not the sufficient explanation of my voting in these instances, but my vote would probably not have gone as it did without these contacts.

The mass media serve important functions in campaigns because of their ability to determine who or what constitutes news. A magazine may decide to run a feature article on an individual. The local radio station may interview the mayor concerning support for a local tax drive. In the Detroit area television stations run films of new cars during newscasts. New features are mentioned, the film clips provided by manufacturers are attractively done, and the date for the introduction of the new cars in the local showrooms is announced. In many areas of the nation such material does not qualify as news.

Much of the impetus given local charity drives, local politicians, local bonding and community tax issues, and school board problems is provided by the local media that treat the material, and the claims and counterclaims as news. The local media provide the major means for waging competing campaigns.

Commercial advertising campaigns or national political or legislative campaigns draw upon the expertise of professional ad agencies and public relations firms. Such campaigns involve access to skilled professionals who sell their expertise in campaign persuasion and in creating and distributing messages through media. These professionals are particularly sensitive to selecting the media in terms of desired target audiences and matching messages to media potentialities and limitations. A grocery store may stress one feature or try to establish a particular image in a television commercial. But the store will utilize an extensive series of prices for particular products in the newspaper ad. In addition special coupons for stamps or cents-off may be featured. A national firm may spend millions in a wide array of television, radio, magazine, and point of purchase promotions. Advertising campaigns or new products may be carefully tested in selected markets to determine the best way to market the product. Often the marketing techniques are the key to success; the product itself and its merit may be almost inconsequential. This is particularly true if the product is competing in an area where differences are extrinsic rather than intrinsic to the competing products.

In contrast, the local plumber may simply rely upon past customers, word of mouth, and a quarter-page ad in the Yellow Pages that advertises emergency night and weekend service. (This usually means she has a telephone answering service.)

Every campaign will involve strategic decisions concerning the media. These decisions revolve around availability, cost effectiveness, access to the media as news, relationship of messages to available media, and the target audience that can be reached.

Use of the Multistep Flow of Communication

The multistep flow of communication theory has produced a good deal of insight about the spread of influence in society. The hypothesis originated as the two-step flow of communication in a 1940 study of voting behavior in Erie County, Ohio, residents.[1] A number of succeeding studies have clarified the theory as it relates to campaigns and the spread of influence. In brief, the theory holds that certain people serve as opinion leaders. They expose themselves to greater amounts of media and are more influenced by information in the media. In turn, they influence others through direct personal contact, passing on the media material and acting to legitimate and certify it. Even though the information may reach some individuals directly, the opinion leaders still may function to legitimate the material.

Research has shown that opinion leaders may vary in terms of the issue. Further, opinion leaders exist at all levels of society. Rather than two levels that consist of opinion leaders and those who are influenced by the leaders, a hierarchy of opinion leaders exists. Thus, some key influential people reach certain other influential people who in turn pass on the influence to still other individuals.

What makes a person an opinion leader? In part it relates to his or her knowledge. In this sense anyone may aspire to become an influential source. In part it relates to the values and attitudes that one personifies and with which others can identify. It also relates to one's status or prestige—whom one knows. To a degree the opinion leader functions much as a reference group does. The reference group gains power to the degree that the individual identifies with it, regards it favorably, and perceives himself or herself as gaining power or something of value by belonging to it.

The power of opinion leaders is demonstrated by the fact that communication directed to opinion leaders rather than to the rank and file

---

[1] Paul F. Lazarsfeld, Bernard Berelson, and Hazel Gaudet, *The People's Choice* (New York: Columbia University Press, 1948).

is more effective in achieving acceptance by the rank and file. The use of opinion leaders is basic to the success of a campaign. Since opinion leaders exist at all levels of society, they cannot all be identified or involved in the campaign in a controlled fashion. The influence that these people exert in mediating between various sources of communication and those people with whom they interact is an important factor in determining success or failure.

PLANNING THE CAMPAIGN

Whether the object of a campaign is a new bond issue, an increase in the university's appropriation, in student power, or in sales of Vicks, a campaign involves both extensive preplanning and a process of controlled execution. The time consumed in planning may well exceed that involved in executing the campaign. The planning and execution stages may also overlap, particularly if a series of sequential stages is involved. No one sequence will be followed, but certain patterns or stages in the planning and execution phases can be described.

The Initial Planning Group

Before a campaign can come into existence some individual or individuals must see the need for one. This need may be perceived by a company manager, the board of directors, members of a club, or by various individuals in whom this awareness develops either singly or through social interaction. For the campaign to begin, an individual—more typically a group—must prepare and plan it. This planning committee—group or individual—marks the start of the campaign.

The initial planning group typically comes into existence without significant public attention. This is not always true, for an official may announce the appointment of a blue-ribbon committee to study a problem, often as a way of countering heavy public pressure for action. In the deliberation and planning stages, however, the committee work normally is private rather than public. The committee or the recommendations that the committee makes may later move into more public, visible activity.

Initially the planning committee must face two questions: What is the nature of the matrix in which the problem must be tackled? What is the nature of the problem itself? Obviously these two questions are interrelated, although they direct attention to somewhat different aspects of the total problem faced in planning the campaign.

The success of the campaign depends in some way upon decisions by people outside the campaign structure. Sales of a product, high viewer ratings for the television program, or a successful effort to raise property taxes are all dependent upon the actions of the receivers. Thus the planners must know the economic, social, and political elements that affect these receivers. They must analyze the prospective receivers of the campaign persuasion efforts as rigorously as any persuader working with a single audience. Audience analysis is a key to planning the campaign.

The committee that fails to consider the present attitudes and beliefs—the situation in terms of the totality of factors relevant to the specific community—dooms its efforts to failure. The school board that loses three bonding issues and simply announces a fourth with no provision for changes in the campaign, no alteration of the proposal, and no effort to reach or mobilize new workers is not realistic. Of course, it may take comfort in that it is giving the community one last chance. This attitude should do much to help defeat the proposal and guarantee the board members a feeling of self-righteousness.

The problem itself must be studied. What are the factors that contribute to the problem? What are the effects of the problem on the community and on the various individuals and groups within the community? What are the alternative solutions? What is the best or most acceptable solution? What should be the goal of the campaign in relationship to the imperatives of the problem?

The committee must establish a campaign goal out of this consideration of the problem area and the matrix of relevant social variables. Once this goal is established, the committee must consider the acceptability of the goal to the community. They must identify anticipated responses of various individuals and groups. Further, they must carefully consider the possibility of significant counterpersuasion efforts. Indeed, mounting a weak campaign must result in formation of a massive countereffort that may not only defeat the specific campaign but alter the potentialities of the future for some extended period of time.

Developing the Campaign Strategy

Presumably the initial planning group identifies the goal of the campaign and assesses the important factors related to the probabilities of success or failure. Once the goal of the campaign has been established and the key variables that will affect the success of the campaign determined, the forming of campaign strategy can begin.

Often this step involves expanding the initial planning group in any of several ways. In some instances those with special expertise may be hired, consulted, or involved on a voluntary basis as active members. Often a church building committee finds that its fund-raising drive is successful only when a company that specializes in such campaigns is hired to advise or to execute as well as plan the campaign. The politician may hire an agency or firm to do an extensive survey of the electorate's stand on many issues and perception of the candidate. This information is a portion of that needed during the campaign planning. In other instances the committee may consult with important figures who for one reason or another cannot overtly serve on the campaign committee.

The planning group may be broadened by bringing in influential figures who carry weight in the community—whether a local town, state, or national community. Or groups that will be affected by the proposal and that have a potential stake in the results of the campaign may be consulted; perhaps a representative or officer in the various groups will be placed on the planning committee. The value of this technique is suggested by the response to a series of televised programs on sex education produced and aired by WITF-TV, Hershey, Pennsylvania. Representatives from the state department of education, various religious leaders, doctors, nurses, community leaders, and the station itself were involved at every stage in preparing the scripts for the series. Extensive efforts were made through these representatives to supply information to their respective constituencies. Finally, a massive effort was made to create public awareness of the series. Many church, school, and medical groups cooperated in creating viewing and discussion groups for each of the five programs in the series. The series won awards, and the community responded with praise. Almost no protests, crank calls, or negative letters were received. Much of the credit for this lack of militant negative response may be given to the artistic and informational quality of the programs. A large part is also the result of the involvement of all the groups who might have been responsible for structuring any negative response. Further, the endorsement of these respected groups and community leaders undoubtedly did much to establish the credibility of the series.

As planning continues, the general strategy of the campaign must be determined. Once the general strategy has been outlined it may be possible to delegate responsibilities of various sorts to subcommittees or to specific persons. Some issues regarding strategy for the campaign have already been indicated, but suggestions about the main questions that must be faced and key functions that must be discharged are valuable at this point.

> 1. The theme of the campaign must be established. This may involve determination of the major types of appeals and the individuals who will play important public roles in the execution of the campaign.
> 2. The use of the various media and the means of gaining access to them must be determined.

3. The procedures by which the content and materials used in the campaign will be developed, executed, and transmitted to the public must be determined.

4. The method of finding, hiring, or recruiting the persons needed in the execution of the campaign must be determined. It takes many workers to ring the doorbells of even 50 percent of the homes in a city of 65,000.

5. The internal communication and decision-making structure of the campaign organization itself during the execution of the campaign must be determined. Every person in the campaign must have some means by which he or she is linked to the central figures directing the campaign. In some campaigns many workers do not know who gets the money they have collected. They do not know whom to call about a problem they encounter.

6. Procedures for feedback and for evaluating the success of the campaign at various stages and procedures for making necessary adjustments must be established. In some instances procedures can be pilot tested on a small segment of the community or with a comparable community. Often the campaign will move through several stages, and various elements can be emphasized or deemphasized as needed.

7. The key figures in the community whose actions on campaign positions will largely determine success must be identified. The term *legitimizers* designates those individuals in a community who, while they may not become actively involved in a campaign, could prove devastating if they opposed it.

8. Plans for initiating the campaign and executing it in such a way as to build momentum and a climax, if that is appropriate, must be developed. If the start of the campaign is news, if the public can be made aware of the campaign, the campaign is obviously off to a good start. To a degree campaigns such as the United Fund make use of the news media to reinforce campaign efforts. Further, the news media and the reports on the campaign stress the competitive aspect: certain companies go over the top; others fall short. Finally an attempt is made to create some suspense as the campaign draws to a close. Will we make the goal? Will the workers have a victory dinner? Will the urgent needs of the community be met?

9. The economic problems associated with the campaign must be assessed and dealt with. Commercial campaigns are carefully monitored in terms of various costs and the probability of return. Several popular ad campaigns have been discontinued because they were not increasing sales sufficiently despite the fact that the public enjoyed the ads. Voluntary campaigns must find people to donate time and to advance the campaign. But certain costs are inevitable. Arrangements must be made to meet these. Many political campaigns have been hurt by money arriving too late or not enough money being

available. No campaign can ignore the problem of deriving sufficient funds or gifts of time and service to compensate for lack of cash.

Certainly planning is not enough to ensure the success of a campaign. Some campaigns hardly risk any significant possibilities of failure; some are essentially doomed from inception even with the best efforts. But a number of campaigns stand a reasonable probability of success, with the outcome determined by skill in planning and executing the campaign. Indeed, in many instances if the preparation has been carefully done, the legitimizers won, the opinion leaders and key influentials carefully identified, the media and messages carefully planned, the campaign may essentially be won before any of the members in the community at large are made aware of the campaign itself. This is not to say that the public as a whole could not reject the campaign goal; it is to suggest that the patterns of human behavior being what they are, it is highly unlikely.

EXECUTING THE CAMPAIGN

The strategy for execution of the campaign is laid during the planning stages. If the planners are sufficiently astute, the campaign may follow exactly as planned. Certainly opportunities exist to improve the campaign as it progresses. Unanticipated problems may develop. All the problems of the campaign cannot be anticipated; all the variables cannot be controlled as the campaign progresses. Some important elements of the implementation stage are:

1. Keeping the communication channels open within the campaign organization. Communication must continue to go from the planners to the workers, and the workers must be able to pass useful information back to the planners or to seek aid from them.

2. Adjusting to changes. Factors that are totally beyond the control of the campaign planners and indeed perceived as normally unrelated may become very important. A sudden scandal concerning one of the agencies under the control of a state official may affect chances for reelection. Other stories and happenings may dominate the news and focus attention on other matters. In attempting to implement a planned campaign in favor of the Panama Canal Treaty, President Carter did not expect the focus on Bert Lance.

3. Responding to counterpersuasion. In many instances a campaign creates or stimulates counterstreams of persuasion. A group that favors a tax increase may stimulate formation of three or four groups to oppose that increase. An increase in the advertising budget by one company may be countered with an increase or a change in the pattern of advertising by a competing company.

4. Moving with the flow of events and the campaign. There is a pattern to the development of issues. The evolving public opinion moves from a growing awareness of a problem area to a search for solutions. The campaign that reiterates the need for concern may lose to another group that suggests and seeks immediate implementation of its solution. In contrast, there is little value in extensive discussion of the costs of two comparative solutions until the public accepts the view that a problem exists that calls for something to be done. Further, a campaign must have a sense of movement. To repeat the same material endlessly may sell cigarettes or ring the chimes at McDonald's golden arches, but it rarely will sell Cadillacs or pass endless referendums that increase property taxes.

5. Putting recruits to work. During the course of a campaign on a community issue or a charity or political drive, many people may volunteer services. It is very helpful if these people can be put to work. An important figure may feel slighted if her offer of help is refused. A citizen who rings doorbells, stuffs envelopes, or answers the telephone becomes even more committed by this activity. And a committed person is more likely to influence those with whom she interacts on a personal basis. Furthermore, by membership in the campaign the individual may become an opinion leader for a time because of whom and what she knows. Any campaign worker spreads the influence of the campaign through a network of friends and associates.

6. Evaluating the campaign. Either to modify and improve the campaign as it progresses or as a basis for future campaigns, it is important that a campaign be evaluated and analyzed as it progresses and in a postmortem whether the campaign succeeds or fails. Campaigns with similar goals may be attempted next year, next week, or in the next town. The insights from one campaign may be of great value in contributing to the next one.

EFFECTIVENESS OF THE CAMPAIGN

The persuasion campaigns that have been most carefully evaluated are those that have been operated by or for commercial persuaders. Much of this information is the property of the companies or agencies associated with the campaign. But the campaigns in which most of us will engage probably do not parallel those of the commercial campaign in many respects. Despite the growing popular view that a candidate or a bonding issue is sold like soap, such analogues have serious limitations. An extensive and growing body of literature exists about the voting behavior of the American public. Thus, we may examine the effectiveness of campaigns as related to voting behavior and suggest applications to other campaigns.

Voting Behavior

On the basis of the many studies on voting behavior, certain generalizations have emerged that are valid for many elections.

1. Media exposure increases interest and commitment and solidifies existing preferences. The media act to crystallize and reinforce rather than to generate conversions.[2] This general finding characterizes the function of the mass media in study after study and not only those relevant to voting behavior. The mass media, just as other communication channels, transmit a wide variety of messages whose net effect is to reinforce present positions. Only rarely does the content transmitted effect conversions.

As Lang and Lang note, the value of this finding is limited.[3] The studies are normally conducted during a relatively short period of time, essentially that of the campaign itself. In a period of competing streams of persuasion, the pattern of past voting, the reference groups in which one finds himself, and the patterns of past exposure to information all suggest that this may not be the ideal time to study the effects of communication messages or channels in order to discern their potential effect in changing human behavior. Studies over a longer period of time might be of more value.

2. "Persons subjected to cross-pressures have been found to be particularly susceptible to conversion, to be unstable in opinion and thus susceptible to reconversion, and to tend on occasion to lose interest in the issue altogether."[4] These cross-pressures may arise from competing stresses of reference groups, opinion leaders, various attitudes and beliefs, and past commitments and patterns.

3. Many voters remain unaware of the major issues in an election.[5] Their vote is the result of party loyalty, reference group patterns, particular cross-pressures that may arise. Many of these voters make up their minds relatively late in the campaign and are least informed on the issues. For example, many voters know little more about candidates for the United States Congress than their party affiliation.

4. Particular issues rather than the general stance and pattern of behavior or commitments of the elected official may determine success in obtaining reelection. The elected representative may be

---

[2] Bernard R. Berelson, Paul F. Lazarsfeld, and William N. McPhee, *Voting* (Chicago: University of Chicago Press, 1954).

[3] Kurt Lang and Gladys Engel Lang, *American Voting Behavior* (Glencoe: The Free Press, 1959), pp. 217–35.

[4] Joseph Klapper, *The Effects of Mass Communication* (Glencoe: The Free Press, 1960), p. 96.

[5] Angus Campbell, Philip E. Converse, Warren E. Miller, and Donald E. Stokes, *The American Voter* (New York: John Wiley & Sons, 1960).

bound by constituents to vote in given patterns on one or two particularly salient issues: race may be a dominant factor in one instance and unwavering support for labor unions in another. An elected official appears free to act in many areas of policy but is sharply constricted in a few limited problem areas.

5. Often changes in patterns of voting are the result of a negative reaction against the person or party in office rather than a positive affirmation of the program or policy of the newly elected person or party. Further, the changes in voting patterns are often the result of the voting of people who are less interested and less informed about the issues at stake.

These findings suggest that the major function of an election campaign lies in retaining one's supporters and arousing sufficient interest to bring the supporters to the polls. A significant number of votes must be conceded to one's opponent, and the balance of power may lie within an extremely small percentage of the electorate who can be induced to vote and influenced to vote in the desired way.

Certain of these findings suggest generalizations concerning campaigns in general. Decisions are often made on the basis of appeals other than facts and in the absence of a clear understanding of the relevant issues. The findings about the effect of the mass media, the importance of the multistep communication flow, and the importance of personal contact to mediate between source and the vast bulk of receivers appear significant for all campaigns.

In many campaigns the actual differences among candidates, products, or solutions are minor, if not absent altogether. In these instances the campaign must create a difference in image or in certain beliefs relative to the assumed differences. Many such campaigns are highly successful. Perhaps the receiver is sufficiently rewarded simply because he or she believes he did buy the best product or find the best solution.

The Problem of the Unreachables

Every campaign fails to reach a large number of people who are potential targets for the persuasion efforts. These people are unreachable for a variety of reasons, and their importance varies with the nature and goal of the campaign.

Certain individuals appear to be beyond the reach of any medium of communication except one-to-one communication. In some regions of the country and in some segments of most communities, access to much of the mass media is extremely limited or nonexistent. Even today many people are functionally illiterate, and many who could read do not.

People select from among the available stimuli those that they wish to consume. Some simply do not listen to news, or they exclude whole classes of stimuli from their attention. The experiences of many people have been such that they do not respond to appeals or material that they receive. They have heard the pledges, the promises, all the words before. Nothing happened then; nothing is happening now; why should anything happen in the future?

It would be easy to assume that the unreachables are quite unlike the people reading the pages of this book. Nonsense. You are as unreachable in many senses as any of those we might instantly identify as unreachable. The reasons for being unreachable may differ. Because of our attitudes, our habits, or orientations, we may not be interested in a whole class of appeals. The minister may labor to attract you to her services. Having decided the church is not relevant, you are insulated from many of the situations in which the minister might have the opportunity to give you her message. Further, having reached your decision you are free to go on to other important issues—searching out the relevant things. From the minister's point of view, you are an unreachable.

The sheer amount and intensity of the persuasion efforts directed at us by commercial persuaders may well insulate us from most of that persuasion. We become unreachable.

Certainly no one can be reached by every campaign. This is not possible in any civilization that begins to have a degree of complexity. However, being an unreachable or having a large number of unreachables may have some serious implications and ramifications.

In every election those who take the greatest interest and who are the best informed about issues and candidates are those who are most committed to a party or candidate. As a nation we are often concerned about a voter turnout of 40, 50, or 65 percent. But if the additional votes come from people who are basically among the unreachables, who are uninformed and unconcerned with the issues and the facts bearing upon the election, what is the value of reaching them and turning them out to vote? Is policy better? Are better people elected to office?

In many instances fractional changes in votes, in patterns of behavior, or in buying habits can have powerful effects. A change of 1 to 1½ percent of the voters may indicate a 2 or 3 percent shift from Republicans to Democrats and thus elect a different candidate. A shift of even 1 percent of the buyers from one toothpaste to another would affect profits markedly, could result in a shift in advertising campaigns and agencies, and might lead to the introduction of a new competing toothpaste. Toothpaste seems largely irrelevant to most of us; the passage of a bond issue or the election of the President is not irrelevant.

In essence, any campaign reaches only a few people. Many of the people who are reached are the opinion leaders. Through their actions and their mediational influence, the campaign affects many others. Opinion leaders have significant power that they may not realize and that they may not use properly.

Finally, the unreachables may not be totally a negative factor. As issues and problems become more urgent, these people provide a reserve whose weight may be felt. The unreachables also provide a dampening effect against too sudden shifts from one pole to another. Rather than a society marked by a series of abrupt changes, the pattern is one of gradual change and evolution. In time realignments occur, and new patterns emerge. A single campaign may be too limited a time space to offer as a basis of judgment. Over the long term, patterns change, institutional loyalties are altered, life-styles are modified.

When a campaign is concluded the losers tend to wax philosophical: "We have fought the good fight; we stood for truth. History and the future will judge, the time for this idea and this program will come." Often the future verifies this view. More often it does not. In the short run a campaign is seen as a success or a failure. But was the effort to gain a federally sponsored health insurance program during the 1930s a failure? The glow of victory may become ashes tomorrow. And a phoenix may arise from the dead fire. In the short run it is difficult to know if the campaign has brought victory or defeat. In particular instances the result is clear and certain, but perhaps in those cases where the results are most important in terms of our future and that of our society, the results are least clear.

CONFRONTATIONS AND CAMPAIGNS

Confrontation can play a role in any persuasive setting. In general persuaders avoid being perceived in a hostile stance against the receivers. But confrontation can be a strategy or a tactic used in persuasion. Confrontations most typically occur in association with campaigns or social movements. We institutionalize confrontation in certain situations in which two or more persuaders appeal to the same group of receivers. Confrontations between two positions are often presented in the form of debates in which the two sides appeal to a third party to choose between the points of view presented. The debaters respond to each others' presentations, to refute opposing arguments, and provide additional support for their own position. Such persuasive situations exist in the courtroom, legislative-parliamentary debates, and in many public forums.

Confrontations are not always intellectual exchanges of ideas with decisions left to the judgment of interested or disinterested third parties. They often occur between two parties trying to persuade the other to accept a different point of view or to negotiate a compromise between the two. This situation typifies bargaining and negotiation sessions. Each attempts to gain the best deal, and both understand that some compromise may be involved. These are meaningful persuasive situations: each respects the right of the other to come to a voluntary agreement and recognizes the right of the other party to present their best persuasive case. Such persuasive situations are represented in labor-management contract negotiations, plea bargaining in legal cases, trying to sell a used car, establishing a new treaty between nations, or working out new provisions in a contractual marriage. In many senses the negotiations are a specific persuasion setting, and general patterns of persuasion apply.

Negotiations of this type often have touches of confrontation that go beyond the presentation and defense of ideas. Workers may threaten or go on strike; management may lock out or fire the workers. Wars are threatened over fishing rights or boundary claims. Threats of violence may be employed and actual violence may be involved. The right to assembly, to petition, to free speech are protected by the Constitution. But fifteen thousand people marching thirty abreast may limit the rights of uninvolved people. A crowd blocking the doors to a classroom building saying, "You better not go in there to teach your class," may produce a confrontation between people in that one or more individuals are having customary activities or rights violated by other people.

The 1960s and 1970s reminded us of the use of confrontation, of body rhetoric, of symbolic protest of various sorts as means of persuasion, tactics that are as ancient as our existence. That they are old does not mean they are right or wrong either morally or legally or that they are effective or ineffective. In fact, there is some presumption that the historical movement has been from a confrontation in which physical force decided the issue to a confrontation in which mutual choice without the necessity of physical force has decided the issue. We shall look at the ethical implications in section VI; let us now look at the function of confrontation in persuasion.

Confrontation typically occurs during a campaign or societal movement, although obviously individuals have confrontations. A person may create a scene in a store, refuse to pay a check or a bill, refuse to let someone by in the crowded aisle. Much of the analysis that follows will be relevant to such confrontations, but the focus will be on confrontations as part of a campaign.

Techniques of Confrontation

Confrontations can result from a variety of symbolic acts—from marches, protests, and vigils to threats of violence and actual violence, which risks death or results in death. Confrontations typically cannot be limited to parties directly involved; they inevitably have the potential of affecting people who do not see themselves as involved in the situation. Those seeking the confrontation may believe that all people are actually involved and that the confrontation is necessary to stir up everyone.

Terrorists have attracted an increasing amount of attention. They normally affect a number of people who are not directly involved in the persuasive issue—if, indeed, the persuasive issue can be clearly identified. Terrorism presents a difficult problem because police, governments, business, or families of hostages do not wish to deal with the terrorists, but the threats to human life cannot be ignored. Terrorists seek to deny choice to the hostages who are involved as well as to the parties negotiating. The demands are to be met. Since terrorists seek to deny any choice to the receivers, terrorism does not fall within persuasion as I have defined the term. Rather it falls within the category of totalitarian persuasion (which will be discussed in chapter 16). Excluding terrorism, there are still many other instances of confrontation as a tool of persuasion.

Many techniques used to produce confrontations are within the law and are protected by the law. In such instances those using the techniques are entitled to the protection of the right. Most of the civil-rights marchers of the 1950s and 1960s were entirely within the law. In some instances police and other authorities cooperated by assisting the marchers in some of the same ways that police manage traffic for a parade. In other instances police and private citizens violated laws in preventing people from marching, from attending movies or church services, from being served at lunch counters, from voting or registering to vote. Sometimes this activity occurred when people sought service or sought to attend. In many instances the activities occurred at night and included beatings, burning homes, or threats. One characteristic of confrontations is that they produce retaliatory responses; the stakes become higher.

Most legal confrontations involve demonstrations, marches, rallies, petitions, sit-ins, stand-ins, continuous requests for service, and so forth. Some confrontations are claims or statements that are sufficiently powerful and dramatic that they produce the effect of confrontation even if the physical implementation that we usually associate with confrontation is lacking.

Civil disobedience often parallels legal confrontation but goes beyond by breaking a law—either the law that is the target of the persuasive campaign or other laws as a means of dramatizing the goal of the campaign. Violations can be of a wide variety: some people have refused to pay a portion or all of their federal income tax; some protested the Vietnamese war by burning draft cards, refusing to report for induction, or destroying Selective Service files; people protesting a new highway have chained themselves to trees, lain down in front of bulldozers, picketed the site, and gone to court for an injunction as well.

Some people practice civil disobedience and desire to be arrested, jailed, or otherwise treated in accordance with the law or normal procedures. Others seek to avoid capture and refuse to cooperate in any way. Those who violate the law that is the target of the persuasive effort often seek a court test of it. Many laws have been ruled unconstitutional only because they were tested through active civil disobedience. Other protests evolve into a confrontation, and laws are tested as a result. For example, the student who wore a black armband to school probably did not expect to be punished by school officials nor anticipate the court tests that ultimately ruled that the right to wear the armband was symbolic protest protected by the First Amendment.

Thus, confrontation can ensue from the action of various parties. Receivers or members of the general public who are not targets of the persuasive effort may become involved, threaten violence, and produce the confrontation. Many protesters, in fact, hope that their techniques will produce an overreaction or an illegal act on the part of those responding to the protest. Often the scrupulous adherence to legal actions and a nonviolent response to violence is an important aspect of the success for the protester-persuader. Many people involved in nonviolent protests in the civil-rights movement were carefully prepared—even put through training procedures—to respond nonviolently when hit or spat upon.

Functions

The most obvious function of confrontation is to gain visibility for the campaign. In many instances visibility is the only goal. But in many instances the desire is to present the protesters in a favorable light. Thus, the effort may be made to provoke others to unwarranted action, or individuals may be selected to participate who will arouse sympathy or create an identification with many others in the society. The confrontation is news. News coverage may be only the start of the attention drawn by the confrontation. Editorials, letters to the editor, discussion of the matter between and among family members and friends throughout the community may follow. Comments may be offered from the pulpit; speakers may comment upon the incident in a variety of public settings; expressions of support or condemnation may come from a variety of sources. In all cases, attention is drawn to the confrontation. Indeed, at times dealing with the confrontation becomes the issue for the public, not the goal of the persuaders in provoking the confrontation.

The second most important function of the confrontation is the effect upon the persuaders involved in planning and executing the confrontation. A variety of effects will be observed. Those involved typically become more committed to their goal and also find positive reinforcement in participation. Acting on or promising to act to implement some belief or attitude has the effect of strengthening the attitude by making the attitude more resistant to negative influence, by increasing its ego involvement, and often by increasing the degree of positive commitment to the position. There is frequently a sense of transformation in that the commitment becomes a deeper, more basic value position. This effect is noted in many cliché phrases: "I stood up and was counted"; "I marched for freedom."

Certain secondary reinforcements are closely associated with participation. Being involved in such group activity in a cause that is more than a personal, self-serving one is exciting. Torchlight parades and rallies give a lot of vigor and pleasure to a political campaign. There is a thrill of marching as one of hundreds of soldiers marching along during a review of troops. The planning, working to make the occasion a success, joining with hundreds of friends and strangers in some effort is exciting. It certainly is different from the day-to-day humdrum that we usually do.

The third function is to attract others to the campaign. Often the public attention causes others to perceive this as a matter on which they need to take a position. Some may join because they are "cause groupies," but the majority will give some degree of considered support to one side or the other. This may take the form of talking positively about the campaign, but it can involve giving money and time and actively participating in some way. Obviously this is a major gain as the campaign draws new members and new support—the campaign is on the march to victory.

Effects

The effects of confrontations as part of the persuasion process are as many and varied as the effects that can be linked to persuasion generally. Some specific effects can also be associated with confrontations, at least in the short run, and some of the consequences could persist for quite a period of time.

One danger is that confrontation may become conflict. People who are toe-to-toe, fists clenched, and eyes narrowed may find they cannot control the situation. An unexpected move on the part of one may trigger an unwarranted and harmful response on the part of the other. Police and army troops are presumably trained in handling weapons and in being responsive to orders. Yet the training is not always complete. And personalities differ and results vary from situation to situation. A sudden movement is supposed to produce an instinctive response of turning and being ready to fire. The tension of the confrontation can be beyond the ability of the people involved to handle when emotions run unexpectedly high. More than one person has been punched out for calling me a name and vice versa. It is easy to misanalyze an audience, particularly under stress conditions when audiences are less predictable. So one possibility with confrontation is an escalation to conflict and violence that is beyond that deemed acceptable by any of the parties involved.

The confrontation may have a negative impact on the general public and those who were formerly uninvolved. In this instance the confrontation may well prove counterproductive and hamper achievement of the goal. Indeed, the campaign itself may be slowed or the participants isolated and eventually disband in their frustration. When to use the confrontation, how far the confrontation may be allowed to go, and who shall participate in the confrontation become very basic decisions.

Inevitably a confrontation will inconvenience one or a few people in many situations. Since those planning the confrontation will be limiting the freedom of others in the exercise of their rights, the ethical and moral questions of such action must be weighed. In general, the response of the public is tempered by their judgment as to the proper weighing of such issues. If those involved have not weighed such matters the practical impact can be very bad. But in another sense, this failure undermines the legitimacy of the persuasion effort itself, and this may have consequences for those giving their time and energy in the campaign. They may become disillusioned and abandon the campaign. Many campaigns have failed because the majority within the campaign could not support the excesses of a few of the fellow campaigners. This possibility can be particularly likely if the actions are associated with the leaders of the campaign rather than some of the followers.

The impact of confrontations must be weighed in terms of the general society. Confrontation has a disquieting effect upon the public. Indeed, this response is a desired one in many confrontations. But society can tolerate only a limited amount of stress. Too many confrontations can have an unsettling effect upon the society. This may cause inattention to needed reforms. It may produce fear that results in a repressive atmosphere or a neglect of basic rights of legitimate protesters-persuaders. This danger to society and to the rights of others protesting in their own right is a relevant concern. It is probably asking too much of those caught up in the necessity of their movement to weigh this issue, but people within the society must, and they will respond to the campaign partly in terms of this judgment.

SUMMARY

Many persuasion efforts, whether by individuals, groups, or in terms of issues, can be viewed as campaigns. To provide a more limited area for analysis, a campaign was defined as a persuasion effort extensive in time and in the numbers of people involved as sources and potential receivers. Campaign workers have a sense of unity about the organizational structure and the goal sought. Some campaigns (microcampaigns) are specific and limited (an effort to be elected city clerk). Other campaigns (macrocampaigns) involve a number of separate and distinct microcampaigns that are linked to a somewhat larger structure. A political party's campaign every four years will involve every level from President of the United States to an infinity of local township, city, and county elections. A movement spans a larger number of campaigns and focuses around an idea or an issue that may continue over several years, perhaps decades.

A campaign is often essential—whether to elect an official, gain or increase a product's market penetration, or meet the goal of the Community Fund—many goals demand a sustained, organized persuasion effort. The campaign provides a means of strengthening adherents, stabilizing any changes gained from former neutrals or opponents, and meeting counterpersuasion campaigns.

To exploit the potential of a campaign fully, campaigners use multiple media to stimulate interest, to reach the most people, and to stimulate the flow of communication from opinion leaders to others who are largely reached through the opinion leaders.

A campaign may be visualized in terms of the organization and planning stage, the execution stage, and the evaluation stage. Actually the three stages overlap, although such sequentiality as exists tends to follow this pattern.

Planning necessitates a number of strategic decisions regarding the people involved in the planning stages, the appeals and devices to be used, the messages to be created, the media to be employed, and the method of organizing and executing the campaign. Often the success or failure of the planning and organizational stages determines the success of the campaign even before any execution is attempted. The execution stage of the campaign demands a system for altering and modifying the strategy, as well as implementing it.

The campaign does not always result in success. The existence of one campaign often creates several countercampaigns. Some must fail (at least to a degree) if others are to succeed. Campaigns face the same parameters that determine receiver response that an individual persuader faces. Even without any counterpersuasion the campaign may fail. The campaign goal may be totally nonsalient for the receiver, and the effort to reach the receiver with any communication may prove unsuccessful. Studies of voting behavior and other campaigns suggest that individuals are likely to proceed in accordance with previous behavior and beliefs. Attitudes and actions are normally reinforced rather than dramatically altered.

A vast body of the society is only potentially reachable in any campaign. This group of unreachables provides a reservoir that may be tapped by more intense or more effective persuasion efforts. And this reservoir can dampen the possibility of sharp swings from one point of view to another. We are probably lucky that people's buying habits do not change overnight. Any organization, whether a family, a club, a nation, or the world, must have some stability over time. Constant change means that change is no change. Change is only relevant in a structure in which consistency provides a basis for change.

Campaigns often involve confrontations of one sort or another. Many confrontations are ritualized in the form of debates, court procedures, or legislative-parliamentary debates. But others involve a decision to use a demonstration, rally, protest march, or some other activity to draw attention to the cause. At times some demonstrations become full-fledged confrontations either by design of the demonstrators or by the response of the targets of the demonstration or the general public as a whole. Some confrontations violate laws or patterns that are the target of the persuasive effort. At other times violations occur in the process of protesting or as a means to produce the confrontation. Decisions to use confrontation as a strategy in persuasion must be weighed carefully. While confrontations often attract public attention and concern, reinforce the demonstrators in their efforts, and attract new support, they can also be counterproductive. The public can react negatively by viewing the confrontation as excessive or unwarranted. The public or the intended targets may act so as to hamper or even destroy the campaign. The chances of escalation of the confrontation into a conflict that produces violence and unacceptable results for all concerned are strong. And confrontations place a strain upon society and its institutions that may outweigh the justice of the cause of the protesters-persuaders.

DISCUSSION QUESTIONS AND PROJECTS

1. Identify the similarities and differences among a commercial product campaign, a political campaign, and a public-spirited campaign such as a millage increase for the schools or a charity drive. What can the politician or the public-spirited campaigner learn from the commercial campaign?

2. What are the implications of creating product differentiation where no substantive differences exist? Is this necessary in a complex, consumer-oriented society? Is this essential in every society? If the consumer believes in the difference, is he

getting his money's worth? What are the ethical implications involved in this issue?

3. The many books and articles on recent presidential elections provide fascinating insights concerning campaign persuasion. Interestingly enough, different observers come to quite different, completely antithetical conclusions in some instances concerning the things that work in campaigns. Many interesting questions can be posed on the impact of the media on campaigning and the role of media in local election campaigns. Perhaps it would be useful to ask if political candidates can be merchandized like soap, cigarettes, or any television personality.

4. Identify one or more hypotheses about campaigns that might be examined in a field study of a campaign conducted in your school or community.

5. Your class may actively cooperate in or undertake a campaign. You could volunteer to publicize and increase participation in a school or class election. Some persuasion classes have campaigned in local charity drives. In one instance students identified several important issues on campus. These issues were researched and persuasive speeches given to the class as to the methods needed to achieve solutions. Where the class reached reasonable consensus, efforts were made to implement the solutions by directing persuasion campaigns at appropriate students, teachers, or administrators. The motto of one effort was "We can't leave activism to the activists."

6. Examine the use of media in a current campaign. How was access to the media obtained? What are the similarities and differences in message content and the way the media are used? Whom do the different media seem to be reaching? How could the media have been used more effectively?

7. Identify the opinion leaders on your campus. Include administrators, students, faculty, and alumni. Then identify the legitimizers. Are these the same people? What explains the differences in the two lists?

8. If you want to create a controversy, seek to identify the opinion leaders in your class, perhaps by sociograms or some

other technique. Why did these people become opinion leaders?

9. Research one of the campaigns in the civil-rights struggle, protests against war, the women's movement, or various protests against one or another governmental actions or laws. The project could pay particular attention to the use of confrontation as a technique within the campaign and look at both the internal planning and effects of the confrontation as well as the impact upon outsiders.

10. Discuss the problems involved in keeping confrontations manageable both from the viewpoint of one planning the confrontation and the proper responses of police or other community agencies to protect the rights of the uninvolved, as well as those who are participants in some sense.

VI PERSPECTIVES

15 Ethics and Persuasion
Ethical Dilemmas of Persuasion
Approaches to Persuasion Ethics
Toward a Pragmatic Solution
A Guide to Action

16 Totalitarian Persuasion
Presuppositions of a Totalitarian Rhetoric
The Totalitarian Leader
Strategic Considerations
Effectiveness
Blending of Democratic and Totalitarian Rhetoric

PERSUASION:

17 Evaluating Persuasion Effects
Complexities of Measurement
Estimation of Individual and Societal Effects
Persuasion Criticism

18 Creating a Response System to Persuasion
The Goal: Putting Persuasion to Work for the Receiver
Planning the Response System
Accepting Responsibility

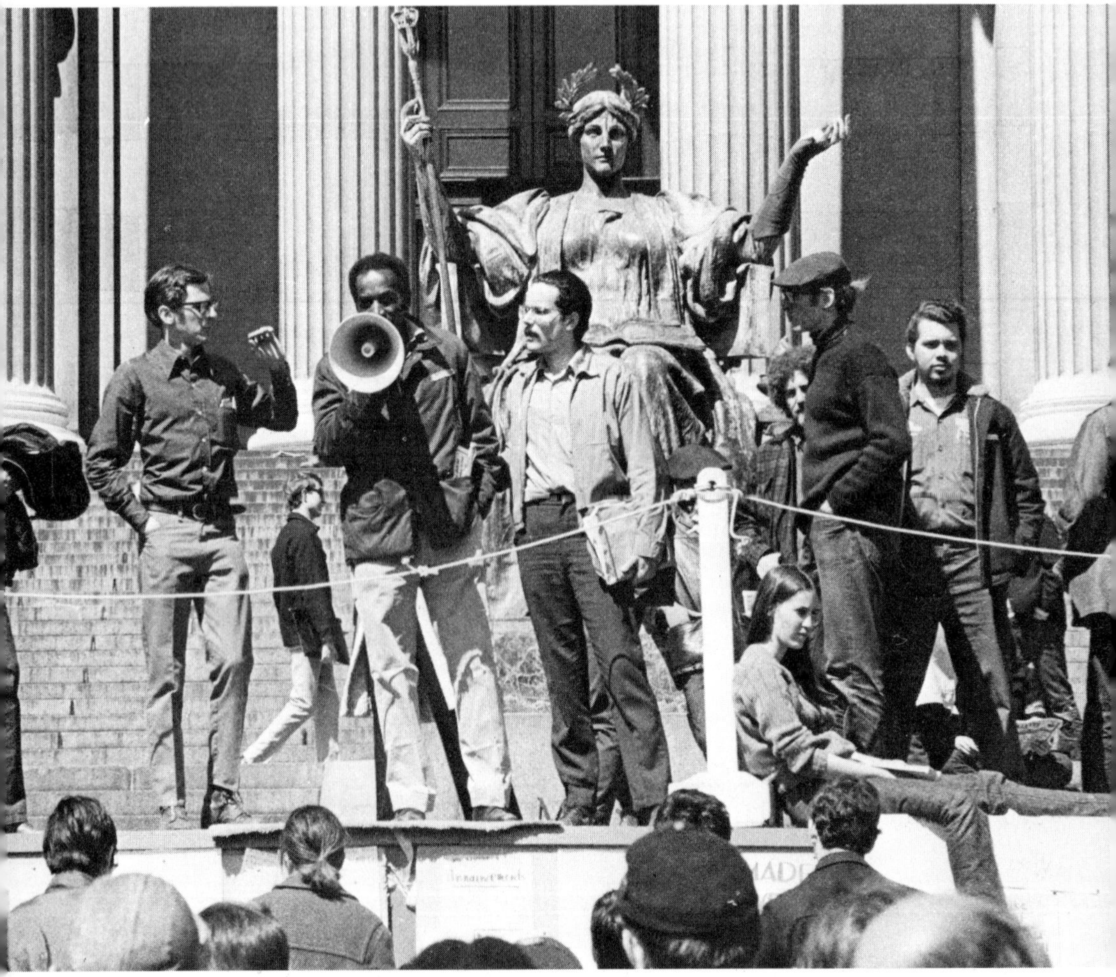

15 Ethics and Persuasion (WITH MARY ANDERSEN)*

The existence of a relationship between persuasion theory and practice and ethics is incontestable. The existence of that relationship and its nature have, however, been the subject of much dispute among writers on persuasion. Although most agree that applied persuasion involves ethical questions, many do not feel that persuasion theory and ethical theory have any relationship except in applied persuasion. Further, the way in which ethics is related to concrete application is disputed. Some settle for listing a set of prescriptive dos and don'ts. Others attempt to relate their ethical standards in persuasion to a variety of philosophical positions. Still others feel that this is an area in which individuals decide in terms of their own ethical standards; hence, it is not a subject that can be usefully treated in a textbook or a classroom since everyone has his or her own standards.

We believe that ethics is intertwined with the theory of persuasion. As the persuasion process has been examined and a theory formed in

---

*Mary Klaaren Andersen, M.A., the University of Michigan, is currently completing a doctoral dissertation at the University of Michigan in which she is examining the relationships between persuasion theory and ethics in a number of leading textbooks in the field of speech communication. The classification systems utilized and the research in the various sources cited are almost entirely the product of her work. The actual writing and the viewpoints expressed are a combination of both authors'. Although there is general agreement on many points, there are still some individual variations. The view of one author and then the other has prevailed at these junctures, but both support to a reasonable degree the conclusions reached.

the previous chapters, a number of ethical presuppositions have been involved. Each individual must form her or his own theory of persuasion ethics and maintain a continuing awareness of it. To this end, this chapter examines some of the ethical dilemmas implicit in persuasion and attempts to answer those dilemmas. The chapter discusses efforts to apply ethical systems to persuasion theory and practice and suggests some steps in moving toward a pragmatic solution to the problem of persuasion ethics. It concludes by stating one view of an ethical basis for participation in the activity of persuasion.

Although we proceed in an essentially descriptive, inductive manner, we do suggest some of the implications—weaknesses as well as strengths—of the various approaches. The reader may adopt any one, a combination, or a variation of the positions described. In no way do we, or should we, assume your responsibility of choosing the best position.

ETHICAL DILEMMAS OF PERSUASION

A dilemma is a question that admits of two answers, neither of which is desirable or, at the least, both of which lead in turn to further dilemmas. The questions that confront us in the relationship of persuasion and ethics may not be dilemmas in the sense of admitting of only two alternatives. Rather, the questions may be more in the nature of trilemmas, quadri-, quinque-, or even octalemmas. Perhaps these questions are best seen as *n*-lemmas in that we cannot always define the potential dimensions of the one question.

As a basis for this chapter we need to examine briefly the nature of ethics and the relationship between the concepts of ethics and values. As an area of philosophical inquiry, ethics is the systematic study of value concepts: good, bad, ought, should, right, wrong, and the basis on which we apply such terms. Ethics asks questions about the principles of morality, the science of the good, the nature of what is right. Ethics can also refer to an individual's moral principles (for example, "His ethics are very bad"). When the term is used in this sense, the context will make this clear.

A person's values mediate between ethical questions and the person's actions. If, for example, we believe that every person should and does act in terms of self-interest, this value position represents an answer to an ethical question, and the value will affect our behavior in a wide variety of situations.

In examining the relationship of ethics to persuasion, we are investigating the nature of what is good or bad, or proper or improper in terms of persuasion theory and in terms of persuasion in concrete situations.

Are Persuasion and Ethics Related?

In one sense all succeeding questions are included in the question of whether persuasion and ethics are related. If they are not, no further questions about the relationship of the two need be posed. (With the problems of some of the succeeding questions, the easy road might be to insist they are not related and move on to the next chapter.)

The study of persuasion at the level of forming a theory of persuasion may have no ethical component. Thus, Aristotle's *Rhetoric* has been seen as simply describing what does and does not work. Persuasion theory that only describes a system that is complete within itself may be treated as removed from ethical considerations. By analogy, a knife is neither ethical nor unethical; ethical considerations arise only in its use.

Yet Aristotle spoke of rhetoric as the "offshoot of ethics." Persuasion functions within the larger, total philosophical system of Aristotle in which the ethical implications were clearly recognized. Persuasion involves decisions about the means employed to reach ends. The persuasion process also involves decisions about the ends to be sought both on an immediate and a delayed basis. Hence ethical decisions about the important and unimportant, the valuable and the valueless, are inevitably involved. Furthermore, ethical decisions related to persuasion have impact not only as ultimate judgments of good or evil but also as pragmatic implications of effectiveness. As Aristotle noted in his doctrine of choices, any choice provides a basis on which another may make a judgment about the ethics of the person doing the choosing. An unconscious choice may be even more revealing than a conscious choice.

To treat persuasion as concerned only with describing and as a system complete within itself ignores the interrelations of the persuasion process and the individual and the society. The "big lie" is sometimes effective, but one factor relative to that effectiveness will be the judgment that some receivers make about how ethical the appeal is. Although it may be effective in some respects in the short run, one must ask questions about its effectiveness in terms of other aspects and in the long term. If one effect is to cause receivers to distrust other persuaders, this has some relevance to the persuader. It is not easy to divorce ethical elements from short-term effects; it is impossible to divorce ethical questions from long-term effects. If the two are divorced, we must exclude many of the effects of the persuasion process that are the most important to us.

Should Ethics Be Discussed Abstractly or Concretely?

In part the answer to this question is linked to the type of generic ethical theory to which an individual subscribes. A *deontological* approach uses a formal, predetermined moral criterion. Individuals have a duty to perform or not to perform certain actions whether they can perceive the good or the rightness of these actions or not. Actions are obligatory regardless of consequences. "One cannot tell a lie even to save another life" is a possible tenet of a deontological ethic. The formal criterion of rightness is based in God, conscience, or Immanuel Kant's "categorical imperative." In following this approach we would merely list the formal moral criteria and possibly indicate applications of them.

In contrast, a *teleological* approach focuses upon the consequences of an action in producing greater good than the alternatives. No behavior is intrinsically right or wrong. A judgment is made based upon the result or the tendency to produce good results. Good results may be interpreted through a variety of standards such as tending to personal benefit, pleasure, or happiness; fulfilling the potentialities of the self; social utility; or minimizing suffering (a negative formulation). Long-term effects must be given full weight, not just the short-term effects. As Hume noted, it is all too easy for us to be attracted by the short term and neglect the long term. In following this approach we would provide a basis for or an estimation of the good effects and show how this good can be determined in some concrete situations as a basis for generalizing to other situations.

A discussion of ethics that is not geared to one specific situation must include some of the general issues regarding the application of ethics and can, at most, provide suggestive instances of applications in concrete instances. Indeed, moral rules come into conflict at times, and we have to choose the best solution.

Is There a Value in Saying Anything about Ethics?

You have formed a set of ethical standards long before reading this book. Therefore, some argue that there is no point in saying anything about these questions, for you have already set the answers. This position overlooks two points, however: (1) You have also been persuading and being persuaded or not persuaded for years. Yet you have been drawn to reflect upon, examine, and improve your understanding and mastery of the persuasion process. (2) There may be value in a person's more conscious examination of the basis for her or his beliefs than in a possibly uncritical acceptance of values that have been handed down by parents, culture, and society as influenced by one's own past experiences. Untested values are likely to shift radically when challenged. Also, a person often has inconsistent ethical standards. Once this discrepancy comes to light, motivational forces exert some pressure for resolution of the conflict.

The impact of such an examination of our own present ethical standards and possible alternatives is impossible to predict. This does not mean that such an examination will be wasted effort or that there is only one answer. A set of ethical standards should be no less subject to self-evaluation and change than any other belief of similar importance.

Should One Persuade Lacking Certainty?

Anyone who considers using persuasion must confront certain ethical dilemmas. One of the most critical is the necessity to persuade, to act, to accept without being certain of the belief in question. We may lack certainty about a variety of factors. Each of the following problems is related to the larger issue of persuading when lacking certainty.

Lacking Certainty of the Validity or Truth of the Goal

Usually one persuades without being absolutely sure that what one is urging is ultimately best for oneself, the receiver, society in general. Some people assume the posture of certainty (even misleading themselves), perhaps because they are ultimately more insecure; some may be too stupid to realize the possibility of error; others may be so uncertain that they take no action at all. Inevitably the decision to persuade or not to persuade is equally a decision, and both alternatives carry ethical implications. If we wait until we can ascertain who is unquestionably the best candidate, the election may be long since over, and both candidates have died. To delay until one is sure the stock will rise means the stock has already risen. Taxes are by no means certain, and death is only ultimately certain (and some are beginning to wonder about that certainty).

Lacking Certainty about Effects

Even if we assure ourselves that we have a valid truth to communicate, we still do not have full knowledge of the effects. We cannot predict the effects of a message, even a truthful one. We may succeed in arousing action so intense that we find it irresponsible. Or an approach may be so mild that it produces no effect. Or even being mild may produce wildly intemperate reactions. We cannot know all that is to be known about our actual, let alone potential, receivers.

Lacking Certainty about Ethical Values

Despite the long search for ultimate ethical values, we have yet to agree upon what they are. Many have agreed on one or more, but others have disagreed just as vehemently either about the value itself or about its application. We may become convinced of the validity of our ethical code. Here, as in other instances, we have varying degrees of certainty of what is the right application according to the situation. Others will not share this same code. Values and codes apparently endorsed by groups or the society may differ sharply from that of an individual. The receiver may have a different code from that of the persuader. How does one go about persuading when faced with contradictory or nonparallel codes? Toleration of diverse ethical codes is essential to those involved in persuasion. Lacking such toleration we would prefer people who are less sure of their code. Often the most committed people are the most intolerant.

Can Ethical Elements Be Separated from Pragmatic Questions of Effectiveness?

This final dilemma returns to the initial question of the relationship of ethics to persuasion but in a different sense. Earlier we noted that judgments of receivers in regard to ethical elements affected the effectiveness of a persuasion effort. The chapter on ethos showed that the credibility and trustworthiness of the source affect the persuasiveness of messages.

The apparent answer to this question is a compromise because separation is only partial at best. Within our own ethical system, we are limited in the choices we can make; this limitation and the choices we make can limit identification with the receivers and be a barrier to our effectiveness. On the other hand, if we discard our code and act only in terms of the code of the receivers, we are untrue to ourselves; if the receivers perceive our action, our effectiveness will almost certainly be limited. Pragmatically we are not free to take on any appearance to suit the moment. Our values operate unconsciously as well as consciously. We cannot free ourselves from their operation totally even if we wanted to. Often, fortunately, there is no conflict between what we perceive as fully ethical and what may be most effective.

Certainly ethical elements affect our effectiveness just as effectiveness has some impact upon the ethical system. To be ineffective may sometimes be unethical, as well as the reverse. To recognize the intertwined nature of the abstract and the practical considerations of ethics seems an essential basis from which to begin consideration of various approaches to problems of ethics in persuasion.

APPROACHES TO PERSUASION ETHICS

A variety of approaches to applied persuasion ethics can be identified. One typical distinction is the identification of an approach as

ETHICS AND PERSUASION

relative or absolute. But relative approaches face the question of "relative to what?" Absolute approaches face the problem of application in the many varying situations. Standards may be absolute, but they are often relatively applied. We shall distinguish four general approaches: a situational or relativistic approach; emphasis upon nation state or cultural ideas (for example, an approach in terms of a democratic ethic); an approach based upon assumptions relative to human nature; and an approach based upon a series of generally accepted prescriptions offered apart from grounding in any particular philosophical-psychological approach. These categories overlap and need not be minutely differentiated in order to provide useful insights.

Relativism: A Situational Ethics Approach

The situational ethics approach is one in which ethical standards are derived on the basis of particular instances and the prevailing standards relative to those instances. An ethical relativist would be comfortable saying that a lie may be justified in a situation where telling the truth would hurt others and the truth serves no useful function. In other situations, the failure to tell the truth could be more destructive than telling an unpleasant truth. Some people ought to be told the truth if they ask whether they are going to die. Others should not be told. What is ethical and unethical is determined by the speaker, the receiver, or the critic in terms of the factors operative. Obviously any relativistic approach must ask, "Relative to what?"

Relative to Receiver's Standards

One approach suggests that the persuader is concerned with adapting to her audience; therefore, she should attempt to determine the ethical standards that her audience holds. In this view the task of the persuader in ethics as in other areas of persuasion is an adjustive, adaptive one. She seeks to adjust and accommodate to the values and ethical standards of her receivers. Ethics here is not a problem of forming standards but of discovering them through audience analysis. If an audience expects hyperbole and character assassination in a political speech, then these are not unethical. These same techniques employed in a scientific discussion of a theory of physics would be. The techniques of suggestion and emotional appeal in the Kate Smith war bond drive are justified by the acceptability of these techniques for this purpose on this occasion. They were acceptable to her World War II audience. Similar appeals for U.S. Savings Bonds today would be silly and unacceptable in the eyes of most people.

Relative to Factors in the Entirety of the Communication-binding Context

This view holds that the concern with the audience's ethics is too narrow. Rather, all the elements in the communication must be considered: the situation, the audience, the speaker, the relationship of source to audience. This totality is then weighed as a basis for determining what is ethical. Although this view suggests the larger context must be considered, it does not indicate how items are to be weighted or related to yield an ethical standard. Each individual could do this on the basis of experience and values. This view stands as a bridge between a focus upon the receivers' ethics and the focus upon some other basis for answering "Relative to what?"

Relative to Certain Generalized Goods or Goals

A variety of different goals or goods can be identified. Presumably once this is accomplished, actions (persuasive efforts) can be judged by an individual by how much they produce or tend to produce these goods. Different people may yield different judgments.

One goal that has frequently been suggested is social utility. What constitutes social utility? It may be perceived in terms of the utilitarianism of John Stuart Mill: the greatest good for the greatest number of people. But what constitutes this greatest good? Maintenance and survival of the group is perhaps a minimum view. Usefulness in terms of meeting the group's or individuals' needs as a minimum and as providing a basis for further growth and development in desirable directions could also be included. Usefulness is sometimes answered in terms of the immediate audience. This suggests that apart from the assumption that what is good for General Motors is good for the nation, General Motors should still do what is good for it and never mind the larger audience. Such narrowness of interpretation must be tempered by the question of short-term versus long-term judgment. What is good for today may be harmful tomorrow; one must bear in mind the point in time relative to a judgment.

Relative to Means and Ends

Relativistic approaches tend to focus somewhat upon the ends as justifying the means. If the end is seen as sufficiently worthy, the end may justify the means. If the ends do not justify the means, what does? This is not to suggest that any means is justified by any end or that every means possible could be justified by any end.

All relativistic systems face the problem of answering "Relative to what?" Each individual through experience and cultural and family conditioning comes to accept certain standards and to hold certain values.

The relativistic approach suggests that one weigh the factors in the situation in order to estimate the best ethical decision in that situation.

Many quasirelative approaches suggest one or more rather absolute standards, which guide one in relating the various factors in the situation so as to determine what is ethical. Even the most absolute standards seem to raise questions that can be answered only by weighing the situation. The more complex the issue, the truer this appears to be. And even the most relativistic approaches postulate some basis to answer the question "Relative to what?"

Democracy Applied to Persuasion Ethics

Some writers on ethics have attempted to define ethical standards more clearly and absolutely than they feel has been done by the relativistic approaches. One effort has been to define ethics in terms of the imperatives found in the character of the nation state or culture. Since the reader of this book will presumably exist within something viewed as a democratic society, probably the United States, I shall examine this approach in terms of ethics as derived from democracy or from the values of this country.

Democracy places great emphasis upon the dignity and worth of the individual in the ability to reason and make choices. Thus, strong emphasis is given to the role of reason by many who approach the ethics of persuasion in terms of the democratic nation. Haiman, for example, argues that items that short-circuit the thinking process of receivers are inherently unethical because they violate the democratic method of freedom of informed choice.[1] Suggestion, deliberate omission of materials contrary to the view expressed, and deliberate use of nonrational appeals are unethical. Haiman realizes the problem of drawing the line between what is reasoned discourse and what is not. One can admit that people are motivated by various needs and drives and still argue that they can best mediate these and solve their problems by using their faculties of critical judgment. One can accept many techniques of identification, appeals, and attention devices that are a means of reaching people to enable them to respond critically to the material presented. The ultimate question is not whether people are affected but whether they ought to be.

Exceptions to this demand for reasoned, informed choice may exist in

---

[1] Franklyn S. Haiman, "A Re-Examination of the Ethics of Persuasion," *Central States Speech Journal* 3 (1952): 4–9, and "Democratic Ethics and the Hidden Persuaders," *Quarterly Journal of Speech* 44: (1958): 385–92.

emergencies such as war or great personal danger. But Haiman would want clear evidence of overriding urgency before he would violate the commitment to reason. The development of man's capacity to reason is a good to which our democratic society is committed.

Wallace also develops an ethic related to four beliefs he identifies in a democratic society: dignity and worth of the individual, equality of opportunity, acceptance of freedom within the restraints of law, and a belief that everyone can comprehend the nature of a democracy.[2] Wallace believes that persuasive efforts must intrinsically meet these goals. The means employed must serve to offer "good reasons" and to meet the standards implied by acceptance of the four beliefs.

A variation upon the emphasis of the values peculiar to the democratic state is taken by Eubanks and Baker, who stress the role of identification of general societal values.[3] They draw upon the work of social psychologists who have identified certain common values (such as goals of well-being, wealth, skill, enlightenment, power). They argue that since these values characterize the culture, they may be validly used as tools of persuasion within the society. And by implication, appeals to these values would be highly effective methods of persuasion if the values characterize large numbers of people within the culture.

While accepting the approach of drawing ethical standards from the nation state or prevailing culture, Day differs from the writers noted above. At best, identifications of specific values that characterize a society should be seen as descriptive statements, not as identifications of positive values that should be accepted or taught. We need not confuse what is with what should be.[4] Day sees the value of democracy as lying in a commitment to democratic debate, to the clash of ideas. He argues that our commitment must be to full and complete debate and not to the idea that any one advocate has to present all sides or to use or not use a certain technique. We must commit ourselves to the positive value of full and complete debate and not to reasoned discourse per se. Presumably, with full debate, ideas will ultimately be accepted for intrinsic merit, not extrinsic factors such as how they are presented.

Haiman, Wallace, Day, and many others argue for an ethic relative to means more than to ends. The means employed must serve certain functions apart from the immediate goals that are sought. Haiman and Wal-

---

[2] Karl R. Wallace, "An Ethical Basis of Communication," *Speech Teacher* 4 (1955): 1–9. See also "The Substance of Rhetoric: Good Reasons," *Quarterly Journal of Speech* 49 (1963): 239–49.

[3] Ralph T. Eubanks and Virgil L. Baker, "Toward an Axiology of Rhetoric," *Quarterly Journal of Speech* 48 (1962): 157–68.

[4] Dennis G. Day, "The Ethics of Democratic Debate," *Central States Speech Journal* 17 (1966): 12.

lace argue that to short-circuit the imperative of reasoned discourse is to be unethical even if the immediate goal is highly desirable. Day, in contrast, emphasizes the existence of a larger total process rather than the actions of one individual within it. Even those who identify the prevailing social values as acceptable keys to persuasion stress a means approach more than an ends approach.

Nature of Man Applied to Ethics

The final approach grounded in a philosophical-psychological view emphasizes human nature. Although we categorize Thomas Nilsen's treatment of ethics as arising from an emphasis upon the nature of man, he comes to many of the same conclusions as do Haiman and Wallace. Nilsen focuses upon the rational capacity of people and the importance of the self-determining personality as a basis from which he derives a moral obligation to contribute to such growth when possible. *"The ethical touchstone is the degree of free, informed, rational and critical choice on matters of significance in their lives that is fostered by our speaking."* [5] This approach is used to judge both the means employed and the ends sought in a persuasive effect.

Full development of physical, intellectual, emotional, and spiritual potential can take place only within a communicative process, within a community. Although we cannot be totally certain of the effects of our actions or always be able to judge whether something is good or bad, we are still responsible for our actions in terms of the dictum of contributing to significant choice.

Wieman and Walter focus upon the unique nature of the human being in terms of having the ability for symbolization and the need for appreciative understanding.[6] Symbolization makes it possible to have mathematics, history, and philosophy, as well as love. Through appreciative understanding people come to accept others to a degree, to understand how they think and feel and thus make it possible to fulfill our need for communication. An ethical act, then, is one that enables people to meet these needs for symbolism and appreciative understanding; an unethical act limits or destroys these possibilities. From this point of view ethical rhetoric promises to create the kinds of communication that will eventually transform the individual into the best that he or she can become.

This approach may be exemplified by audience analysis. One has a

---

[5] Thomas R. Nilsen, *Ethics of Speech Communication*, 2d ed. (Indianapolis: Bobbs-Merrill, 1972), p. 46.

[6] Henry Wieman and Otis Walter, Jr., "Toward an Analysis of Ethics for Rhetoric," *Quarterly Journal of Speech* 43 (1957): 266–70.

positive responsibility to analyze the audience, to come to understand and share in their stance toward communication goals and methods. This is not only a pragmatic need but also an ethical one.

These theories that stress the unique features of humans return to an emphasis upon effects rather than means. They also become more relativistic in judging what does or does not constitute an ethical act.

Agreed-upon Prescriptions

Many writers have not identified a philosophical-psychological basis for ethics. They have settled for listing prescriptions, often of a negative sense. This approach is akin to describing some generally accepted values, but it does not grapple with the larger questions relative to ethics nor does it always provide a guide for judging when we have committed a sin.

Usually the prime injunction is to be good. Sometimes this is simplified to the injunction that one must be completely sincere. But sincerity may not be enough; one can make mistakes most sincerely. So one must first be good, presumably acting from a purity of motives and from a position of moral rectitude; then sincerity is not only automatic but also valid.

There are a number of specific prohibitions: it is unacceptable to falsify evidence, distort facts, deliberately use specious reasoning, deceive about intent or be insincere in supporting a proposition one actually does not. Irrelevant emotional appeals, totally extraneous attention devices, or other factors that have no legitimate association with the subject matter are also prohibited.

Finally, dealing with human values is more important than selling chewing gum. But one begins to wonder whether selling cigarettes is not linked more to values than to chewing gum. It is not clear just where selling a product leaves off and selling something like the Vietnamese war begins.

TOWARD A PRAGMATIC SOLUTION

In offering some indication of the variety of approaches to the problems of ethics in persuasion we have begun to take some steps toward a pragmatic solution to the problems of relating ethics and persuasion. In this section we wish to consider two further points: the question of acceptance of responsibility and the possibility of adopting a 200 percent theory of mutual responsibility in which each participant seeks to accept complete, personal responsibility for the persuasive outcome.

Acceptance of Responsibility

In talking about an existentialist view relative to rhetoric, Robert Scott offers an important point relative to responsibility. An existentialist views truth not as an outside objective reality but as something each person identifies in terms of experience. One should speak from a strong sense of personal commitment, Scott argues. Not being an exact science, persuasion deals in probabilities, and one must bear the consequences of uncertainties. Scott believes that we must face decision without "the comfortable certainty that God is on our side. . . . If we can overcome our disposition to inaction and take responsibility for the consequences resulting from our action in ambiguous situations, then we may act ethically." [7]

The minimum step in solving the problem of ethics in persuasion is to be willing to accept some degree of responsibility for one's self and one's actions. This is true both in terms of actions as a persuader and actions as a potential or actual persuadee.

The first step toward acceptance of responsibility would appear to be an effort to form one's ethical standards and values and remain sensitive to their relationship to many elements in the persuasion process. This suggests the need for some sense of integration and consistency in one's values and actions.

Ethical decisions are not made apart from other decisions in persuasion. Decisions about the most effective logical structure and the balance of logical and emotional appeals have both immediate and long-term ethical implications. And these ethical implications are as relevant to decisions as factors of time, attention needs, acceptability, and audience position. An unethical appeal may well jeopardize success. A particular technique may cause the communicator to be evaluated as unethical even though his or her immediate goal is achieved. This image of being unethical may be a problem for the communicator in future persuasive efforts. As a minimum, the communicator and the receiver who accept responsibility for deciding what to do are forced to consider the pragmatic implications of ethical matters.

A related aspect of accepting responsibility is a sensitivity to the power of words. "Sticks and stones may break my bones but words will never hurt me." "It was only words—I didn't hurt him." What is "mere" about words? Words are actions; they are a response of a source; they are a stimulus to the receivers every bit as much as a clenched fist or a smile. Can anyone really believe that greater hurt comes from sticks than from

---

[7] Robert L. Scott, "Some Implications of Existentialism for Rhetoric," *Central States Speech Journal* 15 (1964): 275.

words? Does shooting a gun involve greater responsibility than issuing the order to fire the gun? Words are actions; they are our primary mode for acting upon our environment and upon others. If we assume responsibility for our actions, we assume responsibility for our words.

The 200 Percent Responsibility Theory

Despite the fact that we may not have solved the problem of reaching ethical decisions for ourselves, we are continually seeking to structure the decisions that others make. Similarly, we are constantly the target of persuasion efforts of sources who may or may not have an ethical framework that we might accept. Although aware that we do not have certainty about the ultimate answers, we must nevertheless act and react. The 200 percent theory of responsibility may provide a mechanism for dealing with ethical responsibility that has practical value. Explicit in this theory is the belief that responsibility for ethical decisions devolves upon us equally whether serving as source or receiver, as intended or accidental receiver.

As Source

When we function as sources we presumably accept some responsibility for ensuring that the ideas we are communicating are justifiable. We submit them to a multitude of tests in terms of our experience, our prejudices and biases, our habits, our feelings, our logic, our ethical standards. Presumably any idea, any communication, is tested at some level consciously and unconsciously before we communicate it.

In testing ideas, in planning communications, we are operating within our own frame of reference. But the ideas and communications may not meet the tests of other people using other frames of reference. The source should assume responsibility for the effects of his action. This assumption of responsibility both in terms of emphasis and degree will be determined by the values of the source. If self-interest is the only relevant parameter, then he assumes responsibility in that he will test the results by how conducive they are to his self-interest in both the short and long term. Reasonably, then, the source should be willing to assume 100 percent responsibility within his frame of reference for what he achieves.

This acceptance of responsibility may be easier to see when one is working for a totally selfish interest. It becomes less clear if one accepts an ethic based on social utility or development of the personality of the receiver to the optimal condition. How can a person accept 100 percent of the responsibility for what happens here since clearly the receiver is not being manipulated in the same sense that is attempted with a totally selfish goal? Yet to the degree that the source has the power to affect the receiver, he can assume responsibility for that power. Even though a source knows that his understanding of the process of persuasion is limited and that his insight into the receiver is necessarily limited, he can still act from the assumption that he has responsibility.

In persuasion a source is not only forced to decide the goal of persuasion, he must decide how to persuade the intended receivers. He tests the ideas not only for himself but by the ways receivers can be led to accept them through the use of the logical, motivational, and ethical appeals employed. If a source can find no logical, motivational, or ethical reason why his receivers should accept his proposition in terms of their frame of reference, he has an indication of a question relative to his responsibility.

As Receiver

As an active agent in the persuasion process the receiver also bears responsibility. Just as the source will test materials in terms of his perceptions, so the receiver similarly tests materials in terms of his or her perceptions. Clearly the systems may differ. From a pragmatic viewpoint the receiver will profit from testing for himself. Totally apart from his own self-image, his desire to be seen as critical and rational and as making his own decisions, the receiver has practical reasons for drawing his own conclusions. The source may have a quite different ethical, logical, and motivational system. The source may be deliberately exploiting the receiver to benefit the source but harm the receiver. Or the source may be well intentioned but lack the specific knowledge available only to the receiver that causes the persuasive goal to be undesirable. Indeed, if the source knew this information, perhaps he would have changed his goal.

A later chapter details some ideas about building a response system to persuasion when functioning as receiver. If one can judge and evaluate which is present and if one can have some choice, one has responsibility. Again, even though a receiver may not be fully able to exercise control, it seems useful to assume as much control and responsibility as we can. Since we will bear the consequences of our actions whether or not we are fully responsible for them, we can just as well assume the responsibility even if we fail to fulfill it totally.

Values of the System

It seems logically contradictory to regard the source as having 100 percent responsibility for persuasion efforts and the effects of those efforts and simultaneously view the receiver as having 100 percent responsibility for the effect of the persuasion effort. However, this seems a desirable condition.

Source and receiver are two different people. They have different perceptions, with minutely or markedly different value systems. Just as a conclusion that is supported by more than one piece of evidence and more than one independent line of reasoning has greater probability of being valid, so a persuasion effect that results from two relatively separate, independent assessments would likely turn out to be a more beneficial one to the receiver and to the society at large and in many senses to the source.

Further, if either source or receiver defaults on responsibility, the other active participant presumably continues to shoulder sufficient responsibility to provide some protection for both. If we cannot trust others, we can at least trust ourselves, whether as persuader or persuadee. And in trusting ourselves we can put others to work to assist us in our efforts.

To assume that one can carry 100 percent responsibility for anything is a nonsensical view. We cannot choose our society, our language, our experiences and culture. We cannot have sufficient knowledge to know all that needs to be known either about the problem or about our receivers to have the burden of complete responsibility. Yet we may well be better off assuming responsibility we do not have than refusing responsibility that we do have. The burden of responsibility can become so heavy that it can crush an individual. But surely we do not act alone. Support surrounds us in the persuasion millieu, in the testing of ideas, values, beliefs, and data that are ongoing in our lives and in the lives of others.

To assume responsibility may be to commit a sin of undue pride. There are limits to what we can do, to what we can bear. Pride in having responsibility can become treacherous. We must accept the limitations that reality imposes.

A GUIDE TO ACTION [8]

From the point of view of our roles as persuader, receiver, and observer, the function of ethics should be to provide specific, practical help in our day-to-day lives. Our ethical principles should be dynamic guides to our actions in the persuasion process.

We do not start from zero in our search for an ethical system. Rather, we have acquired a rather complex set of interrelated principles through living in our culture, the influence of families, groups, and societal institutions, and our individual experiences. One way to form a moral

---

[8] This section has been greatly influenced by Professor B. J. Diggs, Department of Philosophy at the University of Illinois at Urbana-Champaign, in his treatment of Aristotle, Hume, Kant, and John Rawls.

code is to take our actions, opinions, and feelings and try to state our principles as explicitly as we can. Then we can test these principles to see if they meet the standards that we believe they should meet if they are to direct our behavior. We can test whether they seem generalizable as useful guides for others as well as ourselves. And we can move beyond such statements as "I feel," "I was taught," "I guess," to provide arguments and factual bases for the claims.

The Basis of the Code

We begin with the assumption that there is no preexisting set of rules that governs our persuasive activities. Rather, those rules that exist and those that we may create grow out of the factors that are linked to persuasion. We need to pay particular attention, therefore, to the nature of the people involved and to the nature of the activity of persuasion itself.

We need one another. At birth we need others to survive. We need others to help us grow. We need others to maintain a normal human existence. One part of the fear of being old and slowly dying is the thought of losing contact with people—their ideas, their thoughts, their feelings. Our complex society affords me the chance to share thoughts with others I have never met. The society permits me to pursue interests in teaching, in listening to opera, in travel, in hiking, in playing with my son, that would not be possible in a less complex setting. I can find a surgeon who can operate on a ruptured disc so I can again walk and sit without pain. The society gives me vastly increased opportunities to pursue a variety of interests and goals. Other people create possibilities for me that I could not have without them.

To be human is to be active in seeking to understand and control one's existence. To exist as a human being is to make choices. The choices we make affect our lives and those of others leading variously to happiness, pain, joy, opportunities, obligations. When we make choices we are inevitably tied to questions of what choice we ought to make, to ethical questions.

Communication as a whole but persuasion particularly is a means of interaction with other people. Persuasion acts to increase the complexity of our society and it is a result of that complexity. Persuasion brings us the stimulus to make choices and material that is helpful in making the choices. Information in the data sense is not enough; we need to know alternative interpretations, implications, possible outcomes of acting on those data in various ways.

Each of us has a right to make our own determination about what is good for us. There are many different life-styles pursued with remarkable success although with failure as well. There is no one way and no one goal. We test for the good life by rejecting approaches that do not work. People should not be forced to live a life they do not wish to live. But their life must not limit the possibility of others living their lives with the same right of choice. You might like to be the queen of the universe; that does not mean I will be your subject.

The fact that we are interdependent social beings means that we must create means of interacting, making common decisions, testing alternatives for society as well as individuals. We need to establish institutions that will protect our right and the right of others to develop their own life plans. Hume posits a "general will" as a necessary characteristic of a society. It provides rights and privileges, duties and obligations which regularize much of our activity. Persuasion is the means by which we develop this general will and it is our means of participating in the formation and change of that general will. Other alternatives such as force are not as good.

In a society there are many functions to be performed. We can take on or refuse a job tied to one of these functions. All of us contribute in more than one way by assuming roles: we take a job, run for an office, become a parent, are a friend, advise a scout troop. There are rights and duties associated with these roles, most of them widely known. So if we accept a role, we in effect accept the rights and responsibilities that go with it. Those around us feel they have the right to demand that we fulfill the obligations as well as enjoy the rights. If we do not, they will blame us and punish us. We may be fired from the job; be ousted from office or not reelected; lose our children by their decision or that of the courts; our friends may cease being friends; the members may stop attending scout meetings or those responsible for the program may replace us. We do not have to take on these roles, but if we do, we cannot be surprised that there are rules to go with them. We do not have to play a game, but if the game is to work and people play it with us, we must agree upon and abide by some rules and change those that do not work.

The Code Evolves

If we accept these bases, the code must take them into account; it must fit to them. These bases lead me to form the following as guides for our action in persuasion.

Persuasion is the best means to resolve differences between and among people. It is preferable to force and coercion; to anarchy; to random, uncontrolled change. Persuasion is valuable because it opens the possibility of new ideas and opportunities for the self. It permits the previ-

ETHICS AND PERSUASION

ously unthought thought, the unseen vision. It enables us to test our ideas in terms of responses of others without actually having to commit them to a dangerous reality to test them. It permits us to create shared institutions, which increase our possibilities individually and collectively.

Because persuasion is valuable we must preserve it and use it. It must in some sense be regularized to function within some shared rules or constraints. The exact rules and constraints are of less importance in many instances than the fact that they are mutually shared. The game won't work very well if your set and my set of rules do not match up. But we can play one set of rules one time and another set the next. We are very good at doing this, and there is not a necessary inconsistency. I play a game with one set of rules with my son and a different one with my wife and a third set with my friend. And the game is more enjoyable and rewarding for all involved with these different rules. But note: the rules are openly shared, they are publicly announced, and they are agreed upon.

Generally persuasion functions best when it increases the self-esteem and the mutual esteem of all those involved: persuader, receivers, and those not immediately involved but who may be affected by some aspect of the activity. Our moral sense leads us to affirm this view; it seems sensible and desirable as an idea. But the tenet is affirmed by practical consequences as well. Violation of this tenet may cause people to cease using the process, thus limiting its value for both those immediately involved and also for the larger group as well.

People who violate this essential premise of the persuasive code should be restrained. We must hold ourselves and others to the obligations imposed by the code. Such restraint must be appropriate to the situation. The person must know the rules or be responsible for knowing them. Either the game is played by the rules that exist or new ones must be created. A person who consistently lies to us must pay the penalty of our not believing future statements, cutting ourselves off from that person, and our telling others what a liar that individual is. If we lie, we must expect the same consequences even if we argue we have a right to lie.

Some people do not want to live by the rules because they can do a lot better for themselves if we live by the rules and they do not. But notice: they want us to tell them the truth, they want us to believe them; otherwise they lose more by lying than by telling the truth. A very few liars can so disrupt the system of mutual trust that the system very quickly breaks down. Therefore our responses to infrequent lies by a friend tend to be relatively severe if the issue is at all significant to us. After all, a friend should be the last one to want or need to lie to us.

We must be willing to provide others a sense of our ethical code, the rules we live by. Further, we need to be able to offer a rationale for those rules if we wish our mutual relationship to be bound by them. We have the right to ask the same of others. They do not have to do it; we do not have to continue the relationship. In cases of interaction that are essential to the welfare of the group or society, certain rules are so important that the group establishes regulations and laws that all must follow and enforce.

Generating Decisions

The task of applying these general guides in specific situations is a task much like many others in persuasion. We start with general principles and decide upon the best way to apply them in a particular setting. One important step is analysis to estimate the various ethical standards being used by the people involved. One function of the interaction may be to identify more fully the standards that are being employed. Typically we must infer such standards. A persuader rarely says, "Yes, I lied to you." But judgments can be made on the basis of what we know and what we can find out. If all involved hold to the same code, the people will not be as susceptible to being hurt, at least in the short run.

A device suggested by Immanuel Kant can be very helpful in helping us decide which ethical action to use in a specific situation. Taking into account all the factors, generate an ethical statement or premise, a guide to specific behavior that you can universalize. You decide to use a particular motivation appeal, which may not be relevant to the topic. Should all people in this situation act in this manner? If not, if special pleas or exceptions must be made, the ethical value of the act is probably negative. In persuasion we are accustomed to functioning as source, as receiver, as observer, or not immediately involved. We can take the perspective of each of these people. Would I as receiver, as persuader, as observer, as not immediately involved agree that the action is right? If not, further thought and different action are called for. It might seem that the observer is the best test. The observer still brings biases, habitual ways of dealing with things to the judgment. We need another perspective, that of the impartial judge, concerned to make the best determination.

Finally we must always be sure to weight the long-term consequences heavily. As Hume warns, we are easily drawn to desirable short-term results. We fail to weigh the possible long-term effects or we undervalue them. It is easy to want to win the election, the sale, smooth over the rough spot without realizing that in time this success will destroy our chances of success and those of many others as well. All politicians suffer from the credibility gaps created by some.

A general statement of this code may be helpful: *Persuasion is a process of value to people generally and individually.* We need to preserve it, and thus we must regularize its conduct in some ways if it is to continue to be effective in serving us. We need to work within certain standards of ethical practice. The most basic of these is to conduct our activity so that respect and esteem of self and others is enhanced in all the parties involved—at least to the extent that is possible. This concept both favors the continuation of the process and makes this specific use of it maximally helpful. When we accept certain roles, we must understand that obligations go with them and that we will be rightly blamed by others if we violate them. We generate reasonable ethical guidelines in a situation by taking into account the interrelationships of the factors involved and then forming a guide to action that takes into consideration our general principles and that we would be willing to universalize as valid for all people. We may test this universalization by considering the viewpoints of receiver, persuader, observer, and impartial judge concerned to obtain the best judgment. And we need to be aware of the long-term as well as short-term consequences and fairly weigh the long-term ones.

John Rawls employs an interesting rhetorical device in constructing *A Theory of Justice*.[9] He suggests we envison ourselves as people in a position in which we do not know our roles in society. We do not know if we are wise or stupid, rich or poor. He asks us, "What principles would you mutually accept as binding in the society?" I suggest we could adopt the standards set forth above in that original contractual-negotiating position and that the test of them in the actual society would confirm the value of the principles.

This code means that all of us need to work at understanding the persuasion process as fully as we can. Many of the guides to ethical behavior can be implemented only if we can weigh the impact of the means and ends being employed. We need to predict long-term societal effects as well as short-term individual effects. The reverberations of even one persuasion act may echo through a society or our own and other people's lives for a long time. Perhaps now you can see areas for choice about the persuasion process that you could not perceive when you began chapters 1 and 2. Ethical decisions are not made just in advance of persuasion or after persuasion but most critically function in our doing of persuasion.

SUMMARY

In this chapter we have discussed the relationship between ethics and persuasion at a theoretical and applied level. Our thesis is that individuals must assume the responsibility for forming their own

---

[9] John Rawls, *A Theory of Justice* (Cambridge: Harvard University Press, 1971).

ethical code relative to persuasion. This code needs to be consciously formed, and it must be capable of being put into operation. The code should bear a relationship to what is done in persuasion just as other elements of persuasion theory bear a relationship to what is done.

The discussion of ethical problems is a discussion of the meaning of value terms such as "good" and "bad" and systems for their application.

A variety of approaches to ethics in the persuasion context may be taken. Some are more relativistic in focusing upon the determination of what is ethical in terms of one or all the factors of a situation. Even here, many relativistic theories suggest one or more ultimate standards by which one answers the question, "Relative to what?" Some absolute approaches postulate a good or goal based either on a perception of the nation or culture in which we live or upon human nature. But even here the judgments in the situation are necessarily somewhat relative to the operative factors. Some ethical systems focus more specifically upon means; others are more concerned with judgments based upon end effects.

In every ethical system one faces the issue of putting into operation a system of values in a complex situation in which one cannot have certainty about what the short-term effects are and can have only very limited insight about long-term effects. Perhaps as persuasion theory comes to include better and more powerful descriptions of the relationship between types of stimuli and types of effects we will have more insight about how to make ethical judgments of something as good or bad.

Each person has a responsibility to form a system of values or ethical code. It is desirable both for immediate practical reasons of self-interest and for more altruistic reasons that a person accept responsibility for what she or he does in persuasion as receiver and as source. There is nothing "mere" about using words—using words is the most powerful form of action we know.

Individuals can profitably employ a 200 percent theory of responsibility in which, whether as source or receiver, they seek to assume total responsibility for their actions in persuasion. For maximum effectiveness of the persuasion process in its contribution to individuals and society, it is valuable if both the source and receiver in any persuasion process simultaneously act as if they have full responsibility. It is better to assume responsibility that one cannot fulfill than to deny a responsibility that one does have. The burden of responsibility cannot be allowed to become too crushing—one can accept responsibility for an error and learn from that error rather than being defeated by it. This burden of responsibility is shared with others around us. We have the insights and understandings transmitted to us from our culture and derived from our experience to aid us.

Since persuasion as a process is valuable, we need to regularize the conduct of the process to maintain its effectiveness. The most essential ethical principle is that we conduct our activity so that respect and esteem, both of self and others, is enhanced in all the parties involved to the extent possible. When we accept certain roles, we accept obligations that go with them and understand we will be blamed or punished when we violate the expectations. We generate reasonable ethical guidelines in specific situations by taking into account the interrelationships of the factors involved and forming a statement of ethical principle to guide the action that we would be willing to universalize for all to follow. We need to understand that such a universalization must take into account the interests of all people, not just our own. And we must weigh both the long-term and short-term effects in judging the desirability of our acts.

Ethical decisions are not made just in advance of persuasion or after persuasion, but most critically function in the doing of persuasion. Any choice we make has ethical dimensions; those of persuasion are no exception.

DISCUSSION QUESTIONS AND PROJECTS

1. John Foster Dulles has often been quoted as suggesting that the Arabs and the Israelis solve their problems in a Christian fashion. What problems do we encounter in communication across cultures because of divergent values and ethical codes? What steps can be taken to overcome these difficulties and maintain respect among all concerned?

2. What ethical standards, if any, does a receiver have a right to demand in a communication? Of a communicator? Do these differ with different relationships, situations, cultures? If so, how?

3. This chapter alluded to the problem of determining when an individual can assume responsibility—for example, a child for her actions, a mentally disturbed person for his behavior. How can a communicator resolve this question of the amount of responsibility receivers can bear?

4. To what degree can an absolute ethical standard be free of relativity in its application? To what degree can a relativistic position be free from an absolute standard?

5. Ethical considerations are involved at both the theoretical and applied levels of persuasion. To what degree is this view valid and useful?

6. For purposes of class discussion an analysis of the ethics manifest in a series of class persuasion efforts or famous persuasion efforts could be made. The relationship between what one believes her or his ethics and values are and what the class perceives them to be in terms of an actual communication can be a revealing subject of study.

7. Discuss the ways in which the ethical system employed and the values appealed to by the source in the message affect the ethos of the source. Can questions about ethics be divorced from questions about ethos? Even if one argued that he had no ethical responsibility in persuasion, would he be forced to some consideration of ethics because of problems of audience acceptance related to ethos and motivation?

8. To what degree do all arguments ultimately involve ethical presuppositions? Can we remove ethical questions from the majority of arguments that could be employed in dealing with problems which are highly involving to us?

9. In a paper set forth the ethical code that you have formulated and offer a rationale for it as useful for persuaders in general. Or you may wish to offer a critique of the code that we have set forth in this chapter.

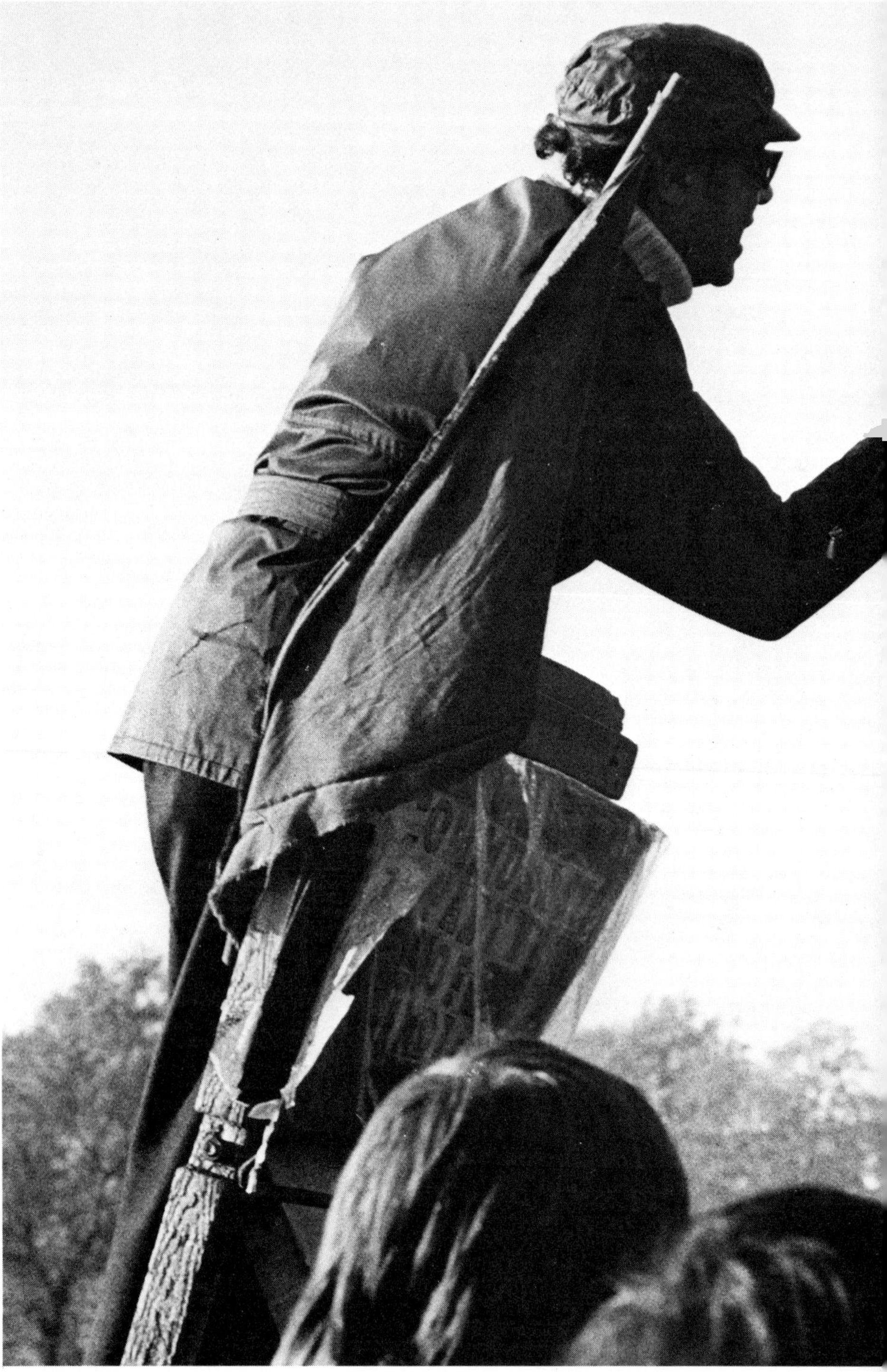

16 Totalitarian Persuasion

In setting forth a theory of persuasion, certain assumptions must be made. The theory presented thus far has generally assumed conditions in which a democratic-individualistic persuasion is possible. In addition, certain assumptions (not always identified) about human nature and the values to be sought in our actions have been made. Everyone has been presumed to have access to persuasion as a tool to be employed. Receivers have been viewed as free to decide whether to participate in the persuasion process and free to make decisions in terms of their own values, needs, and desires. Persuaders have been free to choose to persuade and the means to employ. Persuasion through the competition of ideas has been seen as a means by which people individually and collectively test alternatives and make choices. Persuasion is an instrumentality by which we accommodate ourselves to one another and to our society and environment while seeking change in one another, our society, and our environment.

The theory assumed a value in each individual's making her or his own choices, whether those decisions were right or wrong. Each person has been viewed as having the right and the responsibility to form and test her or his own conception of the good both for the self and for others. Mutual respect and self-respect are basic to persuasion, and the process should further enhance these characteristics. Although not a necessary presupposition, the assumption has been that given sufficient information and adequate access to competing streams of persuasion, individuals, often operating from quite different bases and for quite different reasons, will make sensible decisions. Finally, accepting responsibility for one's decisions is an important value: If one is to err, one should accept more responsibility than is feasible rather than the reverse.

We can postulate different assumptions, however, and form a quite different theory of persuasion. The different theories could agree on many of the same procedures and instrumentalities as being effective.

This chapter outlines a theory of totalitarian rhetoric. The framework is necessarily incomplete. In many instances the generalizations and the corollaries that have been offered in other sections of the book would be fully acceptable to a person developing or utilizing a totalitarian rhetoric. Thus, Hitler could declare repeatedly that public speaking was the most important means of achieving the goal of the Nazi party.

The label *totalitarian* may be ill chosen because it arouses a signal response of an immediate pejorative nature. But it can also be used denotatively. Many feel that a totalitarian theory is the only tenable type of persuasion theory in certain situations. To alter persuasion efforts by moving from a totalitarian to a democratic rhetoric would not only change the form of government of some nations, groups, or families but also might result in the complete destruction of the nation, group, or family. A totalitarian rhetoric is not only feasible; it can and does work and work exceedingly well, at least in some senses.

PRESUPPOSITIONS OF A TOTALITARIAN RHETORIC

The most basic assumption that underlies a totalitarian rhetoric must be that some have the right to decide for others. The basis of this assumption may vary. A meritocracy may be envisioned in which the best minds decide for the inferior minds. Hitler's *Mein Kampf* unabashedly argues that the best minds must rise to the top as advisers to the one man who must make the decision. Plato's view of meritocracy was more gentle. Plato envisioned men as naturally being led to accept that which was best for them. Indeed, the function of rhetoric was to lead people to do that which was best for them. A family assumes that the parents have the right to make decisions for the children, at least for a time, although the parents presumably accept a responsibility to provide the tools by which the children are ultimately freed from this constraint.

The basis for the ability of some to decide for others—and typically for the few to decide for the many—demands some justification. Usually this "right" is given a philosophical justification. Generally the control involved is easy if it is justifiable. Thus, a king may rule by divine right; once this view is accepted, the king's persuasion is largely accomplished. Or it may be argued that "might makes right." Or God may have ordained the situation. It may be necessary to torture the heathen to get him to accept God as his Savior—then to kill him before he has the opportunity to backslide and thus lose his immortal soul.

Inevitably, it seems, with the assumption of ultimate "right" for some to rule others goes the assumption that ends are sufficient to justify means. The consideration of the use of means therefore becomes largely a pragmatic one. It is not desirable to slaughter humans if this action breeds more ills than it cures. But if it cures more ills than it brings, then obviously it has merit as a solution and justifies careful, logical consideration. The values having been clearly fixed, logic becomes the ultimate tool to ensure the achievement of these values. One thing that is surprising about many people who are viewed as mentally ill is how fully, completely, and rationally they proceed within the system they have formed.

THE TOTALITARIAN LEADER

The totalitarian leader is usually charismatic—at least to those he leads. Charisma in theology refers to a divinely conferred power or gift. Christ and the Apostles had charisma. From this it is a short step to the conception of a charismatic leader as one who holds power or authority over large numbers of people through some special powers or personal qualities. The source of this charisma may vary since it depends upon the perceptions of many people. Tremendous physical strength, ability to endure pain, unusual patience, fame, great wisdom might all contribute to a charismatic leader. A person who has tremendous power and creates great fear has charisma as a result of this fear and awe. A person who is tremendously loved can also have this image.

If a totalitarian leader does not have charisma, it is usually essential for him to develop it if he is to survive. Perhaps in a democratic society this is less true; living with greatness becomes tiring. The British voted out Churchill, the French, De Gaulle, in favor of far less magnetic and awe-inspiring people and got along more comfortably and easily, at least for a time. But a person in a totalitarian setting who lacks charisma seems in danger of being deposed forcibly and instantaneously.

Three different archetypes of totalitarian leaders may be sketched: the mother–father–benevolent dictator, the tyrant, and the demagogue.

Mother–Father–Benevolent Dictator

Undoubtedly the most likable of the totalitarian leaders is the person perceived as a "mother" or "father" who functions as a benevolent dictator. We might also identify this type of leader as an accepted authority. As Rokeach notes in *Open and Closed Mind*, the closed-minded person places trust in authority figures. Many of us place trust in the doctor—a person of special competency. We may find it a relief to surrender ourselves to the father. Tyrants may be regarded by their subjects as a father figure. Despite the tyranny—or what may be perceived by outsiders as tyranny—the people feel they can give their burdens to him. Beneficence to some may mean malice to others.

It seems logical that the tyrant seeks to assume the role of beneficent parent who in punishing unruly children suffers far more than they. Indeed, this illusion is assiduously cultivated in many ways. Lenin is still the father image for succeeding communist rulers. Each in turn seeks to take up the mantle of Lenin and his name; his image is constantly maintained and reinforced in the persuasion campaigns that the Soviet government directs at its people.

Although the mother–father figure may appear the most attractive, she or he may not be any the less the totalitarian leader. If kind, firm rules cannot be violated because of power to compel or to punish, they are authoritarian. However, to be a mother or father figure is not necessarily to be a totalitarian leader.

Tyrant

The least attractive of the leadership images in totalitarian structures is the tyrant. The implication of the label goes beyond the use of fear and the ungloved fist. There is often the suggestion of capricious variation—the procrustean bed created in a mood of whimsy. Thus the tyrant may utter "Off with their heads" for any reason or no reason at all. And those who in turn act as his agents derive a sense of power from the act.

This image is more a Hollywood version than reality. The pragmatic tyrant would seek the maximal power and control by his actions. He and his agents must use tyranny in a strategic way. The tyrant is willing to resort to force and sheer power to compel by whatever means necessary. A man may be held captive, not by threats to his own life, but by threats—and the high probability of their execution—against his wife and children.

While the mother–father figure holds her or his position largely through the acceptance of her or his role by those concerned, the tyrant more obviously holds his position by his power to compel. His power rests upon the certain ability to enforce his decisions, however capricious. The Inquisition may have acted in the name of the church and of God, but the power that imposed sanctions, including death, was a more earthly force. Every society has some means of implementing the decisions and laws established through the governmental structure. But in the totalitarian situation, the decisions reached are those of a few people, and enforcement may proceed without any appeal.

The tyrant uses a blend of force, fear, and persuasion. Once the commitment to force is made and that commitment is obvious to the members of his family, the group, or the society, fear becomes a significant factor in anything potentially linked to the interests of the tyrant. That fear acts to control the actions of many and some actions of everyone. Potential conflicts may never arise. Counterpersuasion may be "voluntarily" limited, and response to active persuasion may be nil. Actual use of force may be quite limited: force may remain largely potential, particularly if the tyrant has relatively complete control and responds reasonably to the situations he confronts. In time the tyrant may assume the role of the mother–father or utilize the techniques of the demagogue to gain popular assent to her or his leadership and policies.

The Demagogue

The demagogue in many ways is the most fascinating authoritarian leader. Demagogues exist in every society whatever the blend of totalitarian and democratic decision making. The United States has had numbers of demagogues although the specific names listed differ with those doing the listing.

The roles of agitators and demagogues are easily confused. Many agitators are demagogues but by no means all are. Those opposed to the agitator may use the label *demagogue* either because they genuinely perceive him as one or they know the value of such a label.

An agitator seeks to create a public opinion that favors a change in a situation. Agitation uses all available communication means and is essentially "a persistent and uncompromising statement and restatement of grievances."[1] The demagogue agitates without regard to truth and in terms of his or her own goals and personal commitments, which may or may not be antithetical to the interests of society. Demagogues are one class of agitators.

In much of the literature, the demagogue is treated as seeking to gain power, and his authoritarian nature is shown largely in terms of the relationship to his followers. Demagogues exert authority over their followers in exceedingly tyrannical ways. Discipline must be maintained; the slacker must be shaken off, and one must be prepared to sacrifice oneself or a member of one's family to the cause.

---

[1] Charles W. Lomas, *The Agitator in American Society* (Englewood Cliffs, N.J.: Prentice-Hall, 1968), p. 2.

But demagoguery also can be a strategy for governing once a person has gained power. The demagogue may rouse great popular support and command sacrifices in the name of the party, the cause, the leader. Much of the posture of the mainland Chinese government as seen by Western eyes represents the use of demagoguery. China is surrounded by imperialist enemies who seek to crush it but who will always fail. The people must watch constantly for those counterrevolutionists within their ranks. Children must denounce fathers, wives their husbands; an individual must denounce himself because the revolution demands it.

Generally the demagogue arises from among the people that he leads. He is one of them; yet somehow he is more, for he is divinely called or ordained by Providence to lead. He is surrounded by efforts to destroy him; yet he is unvulnerable. He is a martyr who is bullet-proof.

The demagogue is the authoritarian leader who will most consistently employ persuasive devices labeled negatively as propaganda techniques—techniques that short-circuit reasoning. The demagogue will use scapegoats, bandwagon appeals, namecalling; he will attack real or imagined enemies and use every opportunity to exploit societal malaise when that may be used to his advantage.

The three faces of father, tyrant, and demagogue do not appear as distinctly in any real situation as they have been sketched. Each face contains elements of the others, and these features may be seen at various moments. Many elements are shared with more "democratic" persuaders. The presence of these images is a matter of degree rather than absolute separation.

STRATEGIC CONSIDERATIONS

Totalitarian persuasion uses strategy. One does not rule in any absolute sense in the face of unceasing civil or guerrilla warfare. Gaining the fullest control means gaining acceptance from those who must follow. Persuasive techniques as well as force and coercion will be employed wherever feasible.

If the followers can be led to internalize certain values, then duty, conscience, and superego will lead to the desired actions. And this is preferable to imposed actions through force. Loss of creative talents and the professional and educated classes who tend to resist most obviously the totalitarian structure (unless they are part of it) constitutes a grave threat. Hitler lost many who were urgently needed, and many of those people were instrumental in bringing about the ultimate defeat of Nazi Germany. The Berlin wall has contributed to the growth in prosperity and betterment of life in East Berlin and East Germany since the leak of so much of the best of the population has largely been stopped.

A totalitarian persuader has certain strategic decisions to reach concerning methods that are not as available to persuaders in free-choice settings. Some of these key factors follow.

Control of Access to Communication and Content

One key decision concerns the regulation of access to communication channels and control of the content in them. One mark of the totalitarian society is that access to the channels of communication—particularly mass communication—can be controlled. What is presented on television, in the newspapers, and on the radio may be carefully controlled by agents of the power structure. The government may actually control the media, both access and content, through its agents who operate it.

The media may be allowed to operate with concurrent or delayed censorship. A newspaper may appear with a blank space because the censor deleted a story. Newspapers or magazines may be confiscated and the responsible persons punished severely. The possibility of punishment for any action cannot be overlooked even if the state does not censor directly during publication. The publisher may be jailed and her business either closed down or taken over by the state. A publisher subjected to such pressures may be unduly cautious. Since she cannot be certain what will bring the wrath of the totalitarian leader upon her, she probably acts most circumspectly. The uncertainty of her position may cause her to be far more cautious than if she were directly monitored during the process of publication.

Control of messages is certainly important. The totalitarian leader may cause certain messages to appear that otherwise would not. He can, as examples in many nations demonstrate, cause history to be rewritten at will. He may act to prevent other messages from being heard. Thus competing information may be blocked by obstructing the channels in which content cannot be controlled. Nations expend great energy in blocking newscasts of other nations or prohibiting certain newspapers, books, movies, or even music and fashions of dress. Monopolistic conditions are difficult to maintain even at the level of the mass media, and one-to-one interactions cannot be regulated directly.

The importance of this control of messages is suggested by the efforts given to careful study of the messages that do appear. The number of paragraphs devoted to a person in a state publication or the order of persons on the reviewing stand becomes a significant key to shifts in governmental policy and relative power of people within that structure. The content of communication media is of greater importance in understanding a closed, totalitarian society than it is a freer one.

Content Manipulation

Content is manipulated in part by blocking out various sources of and kinds of content through control of access and censorship of the media. But the potential for control of the content that is available is even more important. History can be rewritten as the current regime wishes it to be. A parent can lie about past happenings just as much as a totalitarian regime can cause encyclopedia articles to be changed. Problems in division can be presented in terms of gains for the state and the ratio of imperialists versus defenders killed. Operas may record the struggles of a young man against the peasant mentality that rejects the state or contain a soaring aria protesting against the bureaucratic chains of the dictatorship that deny a visa.

Since the totalitarian society seeks right action and belief and does not stress the value of free choice, there is no reason not to make the fullest use of the educational system, the communication system, the instruments of the state to produce right actions and beliefs. Propaganda techniques of all sorts may be employed. Constant repetition of the party line can be coupled with appeals to prejudice, patriotism, the "big lie," and any other helpful propaganda device. Many themes can be employed for motivational purposes: we exist in a hostile world and must defend ourselves; we have been cheated or robbed by force of our birthright, wealth, rights; there is a conspiracy against us on almost every side; the army of the invaders is at the border; the world is divided between the enemy and us; the enemy is ruthless and stops at nothing; our enemies are the cause of all our problems; they are powerful but they shall not defeat us; they surround us, they are great evils—we are unconquerable; the enemy is Jew, Negro, Protestant, Catholic, heathen, capitalist, imperialist, communist, youth, the old ways, the state, the revisionists, the Americans, and on and on.

It is difficult not to laugh at those who seem so easily misled by such appeals and such techniques. Yet we can see instances in which people within the United States have seen an enemy in the form of the government, or some opposing group or some idea as being devoted to our destruction, and thus any technique of resistance is justified. Shortly after I wrote this section, events in one country in Africa indicated the validity of the analysis. The irrational dictator used so many of the themes in the course of a few weeks that I was astonished.

Not everyone can be brought to change opinions in a desired direction under monopolistic conditions, but many can be. It is impossible to control content completely even if the graffiti that appear at dawn are removed by sunrise. Such a process of "reeducation" demands an extended period of time, perhaps even generations. But some totalitarian regimes may have the time. While evidence exists that most brainwashing is of limited success with most people, it does affect some. And brainwashing is used with people who have different experiences and values built up over a period of time.[2] This is not analogous to attempts that range from cradle to grave.

Control of Reward and Punishment

Persons in power in a totalitarian structure can reward or punish on an immediate basis. Followers know that rewards and punishments can be direct and swift. Rewards need not depend upon the evolution of economic, social, or natural functions: a person may be lifted to or moved from a position near the pinnacle of power by a simple gesture of the key authority figure.

Learning theory emphasizes the importance of positive and negative reinforcement and the factors of immediacy and strength. Authoritarian structures provide greater opportunity to teach by using the control of these factors than is given in freer choice interactions.

Blend of Force, Fear, Reward

Elements of force, fear, and reward can be manipulated easily in a totalitarian structure. A person can be punished or rewarded without right of appeal. Both possibilities become equally potential without action on the part of the person so destined because no element of choice is available. The tyrant is most likely to use force and hence fear in a direct sense, but the use of fear, force, and reward can exist in almost any combination.

Fear may be less important for what it causes people to do in a positive sense than for what it causes them not to do. One may not risk talking to friends or using the channels and the messages that cannot be reached by the authority in direct control. When your friend denounces you and

---

[2] Much more material relative to total manipulation of the environment and the people could be drawn from the research done on brainwashing during the Korean War. Schein suggests that even though relatively complete control was maintained, brainwashing was only limitedly effective. The analogy is limited in that the prisoners had an extensive prior history in a different setting and were not reared within a controlled environment. And, they perceived themselves as prisoners. The latter factors would be reversed in the case of a totalitarian state. See Edgar Schein, Inge Schneier, and Curtis Barker, *Coercive Persuasion* (New York: W. W. Norton, 1961).

is hailed as a hero because he overcame the falsity of the ties of friendship, fear can be pervasive. Television melodramas feature the policeman experiencing great anguish because he is forced to make the agonizing decision to shoot down his boyhood pal. We understand the necessity of this. So others can see the necessity of selling one's father into slavery. The question becomes one of the values that are at the apex of the hierarchy.

The totalitarian society makes great use of pressures to conform. Certainly the massive apparent endorsement of certain values by reference groups is a factor in defining reality. Further, one needs to exist in some kind of relationship with others; one needs acceptance, liking, reward. Is it not better to receive a warm bed, a meal, and money than to be beaten into submission and forced to perform the same action anyway? Fear of the unknown and the awareness of the potential retribution are certainly available as reinforcement.

A totalitarian persuader may function as a terrorist in dealing with the people that fall under the persuader's control. And interestingly totalitarian persuasion is strongly directed inward—toward those who are controlled. The face placed upon persuasion presented to those who can still make choices is different. The role of torture, of physical and mental pain and compulsion, of imprisonment as an instrument of totalitarian persuasion is hard for us to understand if we have not lived with these possibilities. And the risk is not just to the individual but to family, friends, and even casual acquaintances.

What is the reality of torture? It hurts to be hit. An electric shock hurts. We have battered children in our society. But the use of torture by one adult against another? Torture by one adult who has no personal grudge or claim against the other? Torture by those who act as leaders, presumably responsible for our protection? But that assumes we have rights to be respected, choices to be weighed and honored. Torture is a reality as an instrument of government in many nations. It also exists in families in our own community. Nor surprisingly those who are tortured tend to torture in return. A battered child tends to become a parent to a new battered child as this legacy is passed from generation to generation.

All of us can envision being sent to jail or to prison, but we cannot appreciate the full reality of what jail and prison may be like unless we have experienced it. We sense the meaning of loss of control over our lives, the inability to maintain relationships with those who matter to us. We do not comprehend fully the idea of concentration camps and forced labor, however. But dissidents in totalitarian regimes suggest that imprisonment is preferable to being treated as a mentally disturbed person. In the latter case, drugs and treatments are used both to punish and to alter perception and understanding. The risk is that one survives as a vegetable or in such a state that one would not will survival if a choice was permitted. To be destroyed as the person one was and yet to live on seems an anomaly; one is not physically dead but the self does not exist.

Creation of Desired Values

Perhaps the most important strategic consideration is the creation and/or utilization of desired values. As Erich Fromm pointed out, the most effective means to control people is to lead them to internalize authority. Once internalized, the desired values and patterns accomplish the control desired.

Some values may relate to personality characteristics. Many writers on totalitarianism have focused upon characteristics of individual members as a way to understanding the totalitarian system. Fromm sees the ideal follower of an authoritarian mode as enjoying commitment to something larger than himself. His role is submission, and his power as an individual comes in that submission. The individual gains through his participation in the community. Anyone who has swung along as one marcher in step with hundreds of others in a battalion parade has some estimate of this power of community even when he knows the community is meaningless in a personal sense.

Other personalities such as the closed-minded person described by Rokeach suggest relationships to the authoritarian structures. An interesting question concerns the comparative frequency of these various types in authoritarian versus nonauthoritarian groups or societies. What are the similarities between participants in a John Birch Society in the United States and those in a tight communist cell in Russia? How much are appropriate personalities or a range of personalities natural? How much are they shaped by the state or other groups within the society? Can the desired personality be created by the state or the group as it desires?

The answer is almost certainly *no*. But diverse personalities can exist within a variety of situations. There may be conditions in which one aspect of the personality may correlate with living within one culture or one state. The experiences in China suggest that relatively new approaches can be imposed with reasonable success. And the personalities of old China were no more alike than the personalities of the new China. At least some new values can be instilled by a systematic program designed to further such values. It comes to have an appearance of rightness and inevitability no matter what the alternatives may theoretically be. Acceptance need not be total; it merely needs to be sufficient. And coupled with all the other techniques available in totalitarian persuasion, the sufficient change in value structures may be small indeed.

EFFECTIVENESS

We need to address the question of the effectiveness of totalitarian persuasion. Is totalitarian rhetoric effective in the short run? Is it a viable procedure for the maintenance of a family, a group, an organized state for long periods of time? If the test is the ability to endure, states, groups, and families that function in a relatively totalitarian system are quite successful. Experience indicates that totalitarian entities can survive at least as long as more democratic states, groups, or families. Whether this success arises from the totalitarian approach is a much more difficult question. The use of totalitarian persuasion may not be the main cause or even a significant factor contributing to survival. To assume such inevitable causality is to commit a glaring post hoc fallacy.

In the short run totalitarian persuasion is highly effective. The persuasion efforts are one element of the success. To the degree that persuasive efforts give greater stability to the group, to the degree that such efforts stimulate productivity of the members, increase their pride in the group, create the conditions that permit basic human needs to be met more effectively than before, totalitarian persuasion is helpful to all concerned. Many argue that a totalitarian approach provides the opportunity for rapid and controlled response that leads people to sacrifice their own selfish desires for the betterment of others and for the betterment of those who are to follow. We may not be willing to save enough and invest enough that our children will have a better life. Totalitarians can mandate such actions.

The literature on small groups is replete with studies of various forms of leadership and ways in which members relate to one another. From topic to topic, group to group, and goal to goal the balance of relationships varies. At times a totalitarian leader and a group with a totalitarian leader accomplish more and express greater satisfaction with the results than a more democratically operated group does. But the nature of the task is an important consideration. Tasks that involve creativity, sharing of values, and a full, cooperative atmosphere may not be accomplished with as much success in a totalitarian climate.

To answer the question of effectiveness in any ultimate sense, we must raise questions of the nature of mankind and pose questions of value. Do people instinctively seek to choose for themselves, or do we seek survival and maximum security? If we could be assured that someone else will choose for us and make as good or better choices that we would make, should we gratefully accept? Is our desire for freedom only a product of socialization? Or does the infant's pressure for freedom from external restraint convey something of the essence of being human? Once the position on this value judgment of the proper image of humanity is made—and ultimately an agreement on some value is necessary to answer the question—the effectiveness of a totalitarian rhetoric is answered in at least one sense. Totalitarian persuasion does not fully respect the other (nor in some senses the self) in its efforts, and thus practice of such persuasion does not fully enhance the individual or best assist the individual in pursuit of her or his life plan.

Many limitations have been urged against totalitarian persuasion used in a totalitarian society. Some assert that it fails because it inevitably discards reality and confuses truth and falsehood. Others argue that the climate of restriction and the use of force and threats ultimately imprison too many members of the group or society. New ideas do not flourish when having them is too risky. Too strong a new talent may threaten the tyrant with an early demise. Too much time is spent adjusting to the totalitarian forces, and other alternatives cannot be pursued so forcefully or completely.

Changes in leadership are typically accompanied by paroxysms within the group or state. Radical shifts may unbalance the society. Stalin is hero. Stalin is villain. Can the human mind adjust its reality quite so quickly without some implicit questions arising about the new leadership? When the values and goals of one person become the goal for all, much that is good for the many will inevitably be lost.

BLENDING OF DEMOCRATIC AND TOTALITARIAN RHETORIC

This chapter began by apparently dichotomizing democratic and totalitarian persuasion. But the evolution of the chapter has brought many references to the blending of the two and to the idea that many techniques are used interchangeably.

We belong to many different groups. In any society some of these are largely democratic, some are largely totalitarian. Aristotle did not concern himself with the interaction among the slaves; he thought about the masters. Among the masters there was a sense of respect and mutual esteem. Among the slaves there must have been some sense of respect and mutual esteem. And there were areas in which slaves and free people did respect and value one another.

Use of propaganda, fallacious reasoning, distorted evidence, and deliberate falsification characterize all societies in part. Each of us has the power and at times uses it to coerce, to manipulate through fear, or to leave no meaningful choice to others. Sometimes we humiliate them further by making it clear they have no choice. But at other times we strive to prevent any sense of directing the choices another makes. In some areas of our life we welcome a decision made for us. But in other areas of our life we reject that decision for us even if it is the best one. All societies, all people blend totalitarian and democratic persuasion.

It seems reasonable that totalitarian persuasion is less dangerous when there are competing persuasion attempts. The lie has a greater chance of being detected when others are seeking to persuade to opposing views or to the same view on a different basis. People develop skill in sifting and winnowing the various goals and processes leading to those goals, but these skills must be developed by practice and by exemplification. Thus, access to other persuasive sources seems to mitigate some of the evils of totalitarian persuasion. Its very existence can help to keep us alert, to maintain an awareness of the tendency to be misled by others, either intentionally or accidentally.

SUMMARY

This chapter has sketched some items that contribute to an outline of a totalitarian theory of persuasion. The implications of the assumption that some will decide for many in terms of styles of leadership and in strategies employed were discussed.

The main assumption of a totalitarian rhetoric is that the one or the few should decide for the many. The support offered for this assumption may vary from survival of the fittest to the manifest burden for the wise to protect the unwise in the most noble of duties of man. Once made, this presupposition tends to other suppositions, particularly that ends can justify any means. Discarding the view that all should exercise choice gives to those making the choices the imperative of causing others to accept the choices made. Although force can be used, it cannot be used against every member of the society, for that would leave no society and no one to exert the force. So the more people who can be led to accept the choices made, the easier and the more profitable for those making the decision. Thus the totalitarian uses persuasion.

If in control or the agent of one in control, the persuader in a totalitarian system has some alternatives that other persuaders presumably do not have or should seek to avoid using: control of content and access to a communication; ability to manipulate content freely; the reinforcement of one point of view by any necessary combination of force, fear, reward, and punishment; and the creation of desired values to gain one's ends.

The effectiveness of totalitarian rhetoric cannot be fully assessed except in terms of value judgments. Also, each of us as persuader and as receiver participates in varying degrees in both types of persuasive streams. In many instances we prefer not having to choose so long as we might have the opportunity to do so if we wished. Perhaps that ability to choose if we wish to do so is the best workable distinction between a persuasion system labeled totalitarian and one labeled nontotalitarian.

DISCUSSION QUESTIONS AND PROJECTS

1. What sources and what examples might you use in the attempt to build a much more complete theory of totalitarian persuasion?

2. An interesting project could be to construct a persuasive message that is designed according to the principles of a democratic theory; then revise the message to make full use of techniques for a totalitarian theory.

3. If the messages constructed in project 2 were actually used, which would be more effective? Perhaps the class might try an experiment in which two comparable audiences are used, and each audience receives one democratic and one totalitarian version of two topics, and the other audience receives the matching messages in the different styles. What specific predictions could be made about the variety of responses?

4. Milgram conducted a series of experiments in which subjects were asked to engage in an experiment in learning. The subjects were asked to give increasing amounts of electrical shock to the learner who exhibited increasing amounts of pain, begged to be excused from the experiment, and then after a certain level of shock gave no reaction at all. In one experiment 62 percent of the experimental subjects (students themselves) gave the maximum shock possible—presumably 450 volts. Later experiments showed that as the learner was placed in closer proximity to the experimental subjects, they were less willing to give the heavier, apparently more intense, shocks. As the prestige of the experimenter conducting the study was increased, they were more willing to give shocks that apparently induced great pain. What are the implications of this for a theory of persuasion in terms of the democratic versus the totalitarian approach?

For further descriptions see Stanley Milgram, "Behavioral Study of Obedience," *Journal of Abnormal and Social Psychol-*

ogy 67 (1963): 371–78, and "Some Conditions of Obedience and Disobedience to Authority," in I. D. Steiner and Martin Fishbein, eds., *Current Studies in Social Psychology* (New York: Holt, Rinehart and Winston, 1965), pp. 243ff.

5. What is the responsibility of the agent within a system of totalitarian persuasion? The question of the guilt of many people in Nazi Germany highlighted the issue of the guilt of the individual who carries out orders and instructions. What responsibility does the agent of a totalitarian state carry? Knowing the data currently available, what responsibility does the advertising agency handling a cigarette account have? How similar are the two areas of responsibility?

6. Some questions of a philosophical and psychological nature that relate to a totalitarian rhetoric were raised. What additional questions do you think apply to this area?

7. As an individual or a class you might wish to try to sketch a different version of a theory of totalitarian rhetoric, or you might want to try to expand the version of a theory within some of the framework presented in this chapter.

8. To what degree does the use of violent confrontation, the use of body rhetoric in sit-ins, the use or the view that riots are means of communication necessary to attain one's ends fall within a totalitarian theory of rhetoric?

9. Is a totalitarian or a democratic rhetoric the more effective instrumentality in a society when massive discontent seems to be shaking the country? A totalitarian society could respond instantly and make the needed adjustments without waiting for public opinion to be won over to a view. Is the dichotomization of a totalitarian and a democratic rhetoric truly a very faulty view? Do all societies really practice a rather similar blend of the two and indeed need to alter from more of one then to more of the other for maximum progress to be made?

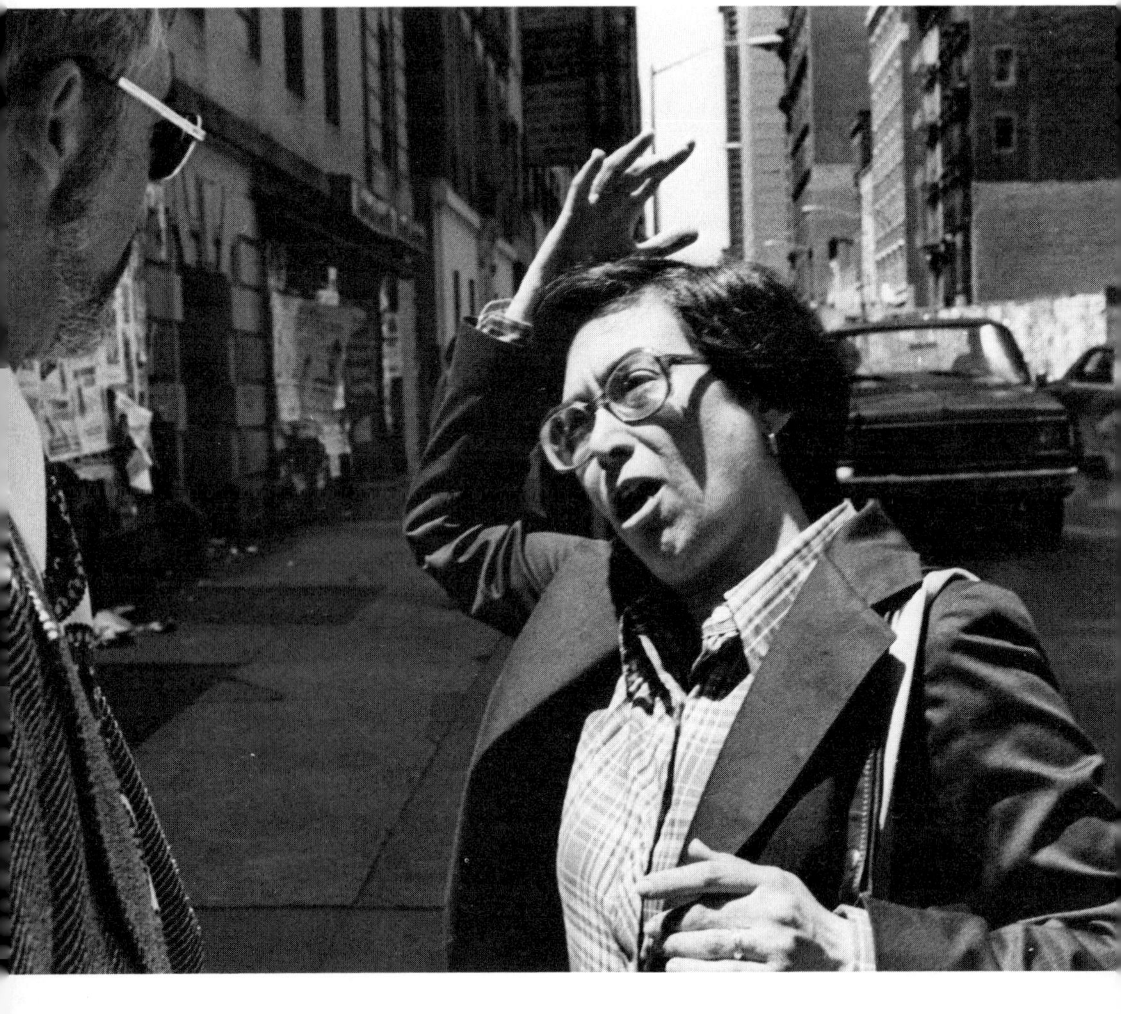

17 Evaluating Persuasion Effects

We are quite accustomed to giving and receiving evaluations of our communication efforts. College students certainly find their communication is subject to continual critical evaluation. Papers are returned with the notation that better organization would improve the communication of the thought. Essay examinations may receive low marks because the instructor was not sure you understood the opposing views on an issue. Speeches are criticized: "The delivery was great but you didn't say anything."

The development of better persuasion theory and practices depends upon further development of the ability to measure the contributions of the various elements in the process and the effects of the persuasion process as a whole and to evaluate the process critically. This section is concerned with questions that are related to the persuasion process but that reach significantly beyond it. In focusing upon problems of assessing elements in the persuasion process and its various effects, we are also concerned with making judgments about the means and ends of persuasion in terms that go beyond an easy measure of success or failure of a persuasive effort. We are concerned with making judgments about the quality of persuasion in terms of the value and impact of the process on society and on individuals.

There is no lack of people who are willing to offer their opinions about some aspect of the persuasion process. We lack individuals who are assigned the role of persuasion critic in the sense that we have music critics, drama critics, sportswriters, and political pundits. Anyone is free to assume the mantle of "persuasion critic at large." Most do this without much formal study of persuasion. One result of your work in this course and study of this book should be a greater skill and worth in being a persuasion critic.

General MacArthur's speech to the United States Congress on April 19, 1951, shortly after being relieved of his command has been popularly dubbed "Old Soldiers Never Die." Joseph W. Martin, Jr., Republican minority floor leader in the House, hailed it as a "masterpiece . . . possibly the great address of our times."[1] Karl Mundt saw it as "destined to become one of the classics of the English language." Richard Rovere said that it was "not a great deal better than the general run of public prose in the United States today. . . . I think not of history but of [a] second-rate historian as I read the speech. . . . He never came to grips with the issues."

None of these comments assesses the effectiveness of the speech in terms of a specific persuasion goal, however. Other critics who offered an analysis of the logical structure, the style, the delivery did not yield an assessment of its persuasiveness but rather of the qualities of the effort. The claims for long-term impact seem excessive. Do you know the content of the speech or the role which it played in history? Much of the criticism offered tells more about the biases or the hopes of the critic than about the judgments of the critic as to the reasons for the diverse responses to the speech and the worth of the effort.

By this time your class should have offered some excellent examples of the problems involved in measuring persuasion effectiveness. Some of my teachers advised that they were teaching how people should persuade and be persuaded, not how they are persuaded. I have graded more persuasion speeches, outlines, and compositions than I care to calculate. Now I have come to the point that I refuse to evaluate a persuasive effort unless I inform the individual that I can evaluate it only as it affects me or in terms of my persuasion theory, given some specific matrix of circumstances as to audience and setting.

Typically a student or speaker will ask, "Did I give a good speech? Was that good persuasion?" They appear discontent if my response is a series of questions such as: "A good speech for whom?" "Persuasive to whom?" "Under what conditions?" "In terms of what goals?"

Many of us have an image of what the communication and the ideal communicator might be. To the degree that a communication or communicator fits this stereotype, we tend to think of it as a good job. But

---

[1] This and succeeding comments are taken from Frederick W. Haberman, "General MacArthur's Speech: A Symposium of Critical Comment," *Quarterly Journal of Speech* 37 (1951): 321–31.

when measures of attitude shift are obtained, we are often surprised to discover that the person who did all the right things did not affect our attitudes and another person we thought less effective did shift our attitudes significantly. Although our perception of the first speaker as better and more effective is an important persuasion effect, we may be more interested in the shift of attitudes on the issue. Although both effects are important we should not confuse the two or assume that one is an accurate measure of the other.

The problems facing efforts at evaluation in the classroom suggest the difficulties that confront us in assessing persuasion in the whole range of persuasion settings. Furthermore, they suggest the difficulties of the critic and the researcher in the field or in the laboratory who attempt to assess persuasion effectiveness in order to enlarge understanding of the persuasion process.

COMPLEXITIES OF MEASUREMENT

Measurement is any systematic process of assigning numerals to things to indicate quantitative differences in one or more observable characteristics of those things. The person engaged in measurement is committed to the idea that anything that exists exists in some amount, and anything that exists in amounts can be measured. This faith commitment is ultimately valid. But to say that things can be measured is not to say that they have been measured as accurately, directly, or meaningfully as desired. Indeed, in some cases the errors of measurement may be almost as great as the variability of the things being measured.

The problems of measurement in the investigation of communication phenomena are complex. Obviously many things in the behavioral sciences cannot be measured in the same way and with the same precision as can certain objects in the physical sciences. To talk of no heat is feasible; to talk of no intelligence on the part of any living person is not. One can calibrate the length of syllables easily and precisely. Calibration of the degree of attitude change and the duration of such change or of a change in behavior is neither easy nor nearly as precise.

Deciding What to Measure

Whether in terms of effects or any other variable associated with persuasion, the same basic questions of deciding what to measure and how to measure it must be faced. The decisions of what to measure and how to measure it involve matters of human judgment. Different perceptions of the nature of the persuasion process or different models employed to represent the process may produce markedly different systems of measurement of the same effect or focus upon quite different effects.

Some effects or outcomes in the persuasion process can be measured. Initially the body of effects produced in the receivers—either intended or accidental receivers—seems most relevant. Effects could also be measured by the effects of the process upon the source, an area that has been largely neglected (as chapter 12 indicates). Does a source achieve catharsis or emotional release in attempting persuasion? Does access to the persuasion process and its utilization have implications for mental health, physical health, patterns of future behavior on the source? How much is the source controlled by the feedback she receives during the process compared to how much she controls the response of others?

Rather than becoming too involved in the gamut of measurement problems in relationship to the persuasion process, let us focus upon measuring effects on receivers. Since the ultimate goal of the persuasion process as viewed by the source is to achieve a desired change in behavior, we obviously would be interested in changes of behavior as a measurement of effect.

How does one measure a change of behavior? What might that change be? Behavior must take place to be observed and measured. One immediate problem is that a change in behavior may not be readily observable. Often the change desired may not occur immediately. For example, changes in a pattern of voting might be a good indication of the effectiveness of a campaign. But the voting day may be several weeks away. It may be difficult to isolate the votes of people who have received a given message from those who have not. Further, in a persuasion campaign so many factors and so many diverse stimuli are brought to bear upon the receivers that the effects of any portion of the total effort are impossible to isolate. It may be true that a candidate is elected, but she could be elected in spite of, not because of, the campaign.

Actions are the result of many factors. Quite significant changes can occur without being discernible in behavior. Presumably it is extremely important if a person has been made more resistant to counterpersuasive efforts. But such changes are difficult to measure in actions. A person may be much more strongly committed to the party. If he began to work for the party in a door-to-door leaflet campaign, this change in behavior could have great significance. But if the manifestation is a vote, his one vote is not stronger than his previous vote even if he pulls the lever of the voting machine more vigorously.

Because of the difficulty of measuring action and the problems of sorting out the desired effect from the many other elements relating to an action, persuasion measurements, both in the laboratory setting and in normal persuasion, often focus upon the processes that mediate between the persuasion effort and the resulting action. Assessment of attention, comprehension, or particularly the degree of acceptance or rejection of the proposition or ideas advanced by the persuader becomes the normal approach.

Of all the effects measures employed, the attempt to quantify a shift in attitude through a measure of change in opinion is by far the most common. This is seen in the public opinion polls assessing election campaigns. Commercial firms often engage in extensive product testing in trial areas, with test panels, or extensive opinion surveys. Public relations firms conduct extensive surveys that attempt to define the image a company holds for the public. Consumers may be asked to react to products —to supply adjectives that they would use to describe the product, for example.

Comprehension of the content of the communication has often been employed as a measure. This seems more relevant to learning and to expository communication since numerous studies suggest that comprehension is not causally related to persuasion effect. Attention has also been used as a measure. Some interesting studies have used eye contact, eye-blink rate, bodily movement, or other physiological changes as measures of attention. Unfortunately the relationship between attention and persuasiveness is not yet fully defined. Motivational researchers claim a high degree of success using measures such as eye-blinking rate as indications of persuasiveness.

We need to be sensitive to how limited a measure we are attempting. We may be interested in attitude toward the source, openness to future persuasive efforts on this topic, negative response to future persuasive efforts generally, effect of any shift on other attitudes or actions, consequences in different areas of the person's life such as spending money on one product that is urgently needed for some other purpose, and so forth. We need to be sensitive to the narrowness with which we typically estimate persuasion effects as well as the problem of obtaining accurate measures of the one or few narrow effects we do focus upon. The full range of persuasion effects from each attempt is of consequence for all of us, and we need to remind ourselves of this fact at every opportunity.

Operationalizing the Concept

Having decided what to measure (for example, change in action or change in attitude), we need to operationalize this proposed measurement. An operational definition is simply a description of the procedures involved in measuring the concept in question. How will a change in attitude be measured? Will several experts in the persuasion process observe the facial response of the audience and then estimate the persuasive effect? Will the subjects be asked to indicate what change they perceive themselves as having undergone? Will subjects be asked to fill out an extended opinion test before the communication and then complete an identical one afterward? Each of these procedures as implemented could constitute an operational definition. Each has some rather obvious limitations, however. But when we talk about the shift of opinion, what we mean is the change in scale value on the form, scale, or device used to quantify this change in opinion.

What the various positions or changes mean is not a question that can be answered by the measurement. The interpretation is the task of the user. Although statistical tests are often used for some purposes, we need to remember that a statistical difference may be of no practical difference and vice versa. We often get a rather accurate measurement or estimation but draw the wrong inference from it.

ESTIMATION OF INDIVIDUAL AND SOCIETAL EFFECTS

In most instances, the judgments of the effects of persuasion will be estimates that are formed by the persuader, receiver, or observer-critic. The validity of these estimates will vary according to how much the estimator is personally involved, how much the persons may seek to conceal effects, the many factors that make such estimation difficult in any situation, and the factors particular to the situation and variations among different individuals. Obviously too, the amount of previous experience, the knowledge of the persuasion process, and the acuity and sensitivity of the person making the estimate will affect the validity of the judgment.

The reliability (the consistency) of grading essay examinations may be extremely low or negative. Ruch found a median correlation of 0.59 of grades in two successive readings of essay examinations. In some instances the reversal in grading patterns was greater than would have occurred if the second set of grades were assigned by random chance. Different judges also yield different evaluations. The range of scores assigned to the same geometry examination by 115 different mathematics teachers went from 28 to 92.[2] And graders are presumably more motivated to derive accurate judgments than those offering casual assessments of

---

[2] Robert L. Ebel, *An Outline for a Course in the Construction and Use of Classroom Tests* (Iowa City, 1956), p. 36.

persuasion effects. Obtaining accurate estimates of persuasion effects is obviously a continuing problem.

Estimates in Normal Circumstances

Studies of the persuasion process may occur in the laboratory or in settings where it is possible to secure extensive and relatively precise measures of persuasion effects. Typically we are left with the problem of assessing effects on the basis of responses that occur in the normal communication setting.

Depending upon the setting, very good indexes of persuasion effect may be available. In the one-to-one and small-group settings, the interaction and direct interchange between the communicants permit direct questions about intention. Often the questions and responses of the receiver convey good indications of effect. People in these settings often interact over a period of time. The persuader has ample opportunity to assess the effectiveness of persuasion in terms of the action of the receiver. My wife has attempted for many years to get me to hang up my coat when I come home. She has almost daily evidence of the failure of her persuasive efforts. I have at least weekly demonstrations of my failure to convince her to abandon her efforts and accept me as I am in this respect.

Of course even in these settings the evaluator may lack knowledge of many relevant factors: the difficulty in the task faced, whether someone else would have initiated the persuasion if the persuader had not, what other effects may have occurred in addition to the change noted.

Many persuasion efforts are directed toward relatively immediate aims that can be measured. The insecure sales representative may worry that despite increasing commissions and sales, others might be doing a far better job with her territory. Yet she can compare her sales against the general pattern of others and come to some assessment. If she has a backlog of experience or some objective standards for comparison, a good estimate of her effectiveness may be formed. It is true, of course, that some companies lost in the glow of a rise in sales wake up one day to discover they have declined in proportion of the market by some 50 percent. Although sales are up, profits may be down, or the company may be in the red; if they had increased at the rate of other companies, they would have quadrupled profits. So the growth rate was in a sense negative: they were falling further and further behind. A valid assessment of effect must put the information in a total context.

Feedback is richly available in group and target audience situations, and there is even a degree of feedback in many mass media situations.

The problem of interpreting any feedback is important. An audience may be very attentive. They may indicate a great deal of impact. Or it may be that the audience has a tradition of giving close and careful attention; it may indicate that the audience is being entertained; it may indicate they are preparing the counterattack.

Feedback that is received is often atypical. Some few people in an audience always seem to stop by and congratulate the speaker on a fine speech. One person tells the pastor each Sunday, "That was the best sermon I have ever heard." Either the pastor glows with the realization he is improving each week, or he interprets the feedback as a nice pleasantry with no reference to effect. Attention, warmth of response, and degree of applause may indicate entertainment value, interest level, or any number of things that may not correlate with persuasiveness.

The mass media receive some delayed feedback. Letters of praise and indignation are sent to the station, the magazine, or newspaper. But the very fact these people did respond makes them atypical; the typical person does not respond. Although extensive attention is given to such feedback, its ultimate meaning is probably difficult to establish.

Direct observation of actions and interpretation of feedback are two methods of inferring effect. Judgments offered by others are a third source. Often relatively knowledgeable persons will offer evaluations of what succeeded, what failed. The members of a persuasion class and the instructor should develop particular sensitivities and abilities that enable them to function as critics and as estimators of effectiveness at a level far beyond that of the average person. Of course, the judgment of a friend may be biased—so may that of an enemy. "You were so right" often indicates I agree with you, not that you were persuasive. The Haberman article on the evaluation of MacArthur's speech shows that many of the critical comments had no relevance to estimation of persuasion—they simply expressed the critic's position in regard to MacArthur's firing and the interest in using MacArthur to advance the critic's own interests. Reports of observers, whether reporters or casual onlookers, may be valuable or meaningless. They are usually contradictory.

Perhaps the most valid means of estimating persuasion effect lies in the application of a sound understanding of persuasion theory to the information one can gain about response from the sources mentioned above. If one can observe a degree of warmth, unexpected questions, and interaction with a hostile audience that develops a noticeably less hostile tone, one can assume that some persuasion is taking place. This persuasion may relate more to acceptance of source than idea. Discovery that one's ideas are briefly summarized in the newspaper or a friend's mention that she heard about a speech you made suggest that the multistep flow is working. Knowledge of theory plus this information may well provide a relatively good estimate of the probable effect.

Extensive campaign efforts almost inevitably build in a series of measurements. This may involve public opinion surveys. In some instances the same individuals may be repeatedly surveyed at several stages to monitor the changing view. In other cases an entirely new sample may be drawn for each survey. The pattern of donations and the size of donations may be compared with those of previous years. During national elections the television stations identify certain key districts, and by checking for small deviations from previous patterns, they can predict the outcome with great accuracy on extremely small percentages of votes.

A company may attempt to check readership of its ads in various magazines by offering a premium or a "cents off" coupon, which carries an identification of the source. Thus, if three times as many coupons are returned from one magazine as another, the manager has some estimate of the audience being reached by magazines.

Estimation of Effects in Research

Research in communication phenomena is increasing and will probably increase exponentially with each passing decade. The researcher has techniques and procedures available that are not feasible in the typical persuasion setting.

The historian may be able to engage in an exceedingly detailed, minute examination of the nature of the audience, the situation, the elements in the communication itself. She has information added by the passage of time. The listeners at the Gettysburg dedication undoubtedly thought that Edward Everett's address would be one of the most remembered speeches of that era. Few gave much thought to the idea that Lincoln's "embarrassingly brief and awkwardly delivered remarks" would have any real impact. Time has given us a different perspective. The influence of the communication may be traced in later references, in impact on others. As new additions to persuasion theory provide greater insight into communication effects, the historian gains additional power to evaluate and judge the effects of communication.

The field researcher can develop sophisticated techniques of observation. Thus, voting behavior studies interview small groups of people in carefully planned patterns. Extensive in-depth interviews and projective instruments of various sorts may be used to extend the power of observation.

In some ways the most precise measurements of persuasion effects may be attempted in the laboratory. The growth in research and particularly the growth in the power of research efforts to generate useful findings and to provide more powerful tests of theory is directly related to improvement in measuring devices. These procedures will improve as more attention is given to the development of better measuring devices. As more people trained in sophisticated measurement techniques and the intricacies of research design focus upon communication as a major interest area, this process will be expedited.

Initially most measurements in the laboratory consisted of direct estimations of effect, either by so-called expert judges or by experimental subjects. Thus, a group of "experts," typically graduate students in speech, might read three speeches and identify the speeches as strong, medium, or weak in logical appeal but as similar in all other respects. Once a sufficient degree of consistency of judgment was reached, the speeches would be presented to an audience. Any difference in persuasiveness would then be attributed to the power of logic to persuade. What was logical to the judges, however, might not be perceived as logical by subjects who may differ significantly from the judges. Further, the differences in appeal might not be sufficient to yield a significant difference in effect—especially if the topic was not salient to the receivers.

Use of a typical measuring instrument for effect might consist of a check on a linear rating scale from one to ten relative to opinion on the major issue. One measure would be taken before the presentation, one after. Or a shift-of-opinion ballot might be employed. Before the presentation a subject checked a statement that he or she favored, opposed, or was neutral toward the proposal. After the presentation the subject checked whether he or she more strongly favored, was neutral, was unfavorable, or more unfavorable. All of these devices called for direct conscious perception and judgment on the part of those involved. Such consciousness need not correlate with actual change. Often the ratings were of the quality of the effort and not of persuasiveness.

Later devices have grown in sophistication. A typical experiment in the 1950s might involve administration of an opinion test of the Likert type, which presents many statements of attitude, and respondents check degree of agreement, disagreement, or neutrality. Second tests may utilize a somewhat different form of the instrument. Even if the same form is used, the number of responses is so numerous that it is impossible for a person to remember the responses given previously even if asked to duplicate them.

A wide variety of more sophisticated measuring instruments is available to researchers today, among them the semantic differential and Fishbein's scales that permit measures of intention to act and willingness to accept influence. Various methods of eliciting the personal constructs that people use to interpret their experiences hold additional promise for examination of factors related to change and evaluation of patterns of change with particular focus on the individual variations that contribute to persuasion effects.

Obviously we cannot build a persuasion theory solely through measurement. But advances in persuasion theory depend in part upon the development of different and better approaches to observation and measurement. Greater sophistication in measurement and in interpretation of the findings will be helpful in the refinement of persuasion theory.

PERSUASION CRITICISM

As participants in persuasion we need to function as effective critics—as people who attempt to understand persuasion and judge the process. As persuaders we seek improvement; as receivers we seek to understand so that we can select the best response. The final chapter focuses upon a strategy for the receiver to use in responding to the persuasion in the society and the persuasion directed at the receiver.

But persuasion is of significance to the society, the culture, and mankind generally. For centuries people have studied individual persuaders, campaigns, and social movements, as well as persuasion in special forms or situations such as presidential inaugurals, "disabling" speeches by British prime ministers, funeral orations, Fourth of July speeches, and summation speeches to the jury.

Analysis of persuasive efforts is not limited to the talk of ordinary conversation or specialized interaction. Much of what we ordinarily think of as fine art—poetry, fiction, belles lettres, art, drama, music—has been analyzed for persuasive method and effect. In this book I have tended to treat such artistic approaches as outside the scope of public affairs and daily interaction through speech and writing, which have been the focus. Those of you who have skill in the creation or appreciation of the arts will find many instances of persuasion to attempt or to study in the arts. For example, one student started from the premise that architecture makes a persuasive statement and also so structures the setting that various persuasive effects follow and then reviewed the architecture of various courtrooms to study the effect upon the interchanges in the trial.

The potential is there to analyze persuasion from many different perspectives, each of which has a contribution to make to full understanding of persuasion. The critic who ferrets out instances of persuasion in cases where we may not perceive the persuasive thrust performs an important function.

Criticism can help us to understand a person, group, society, or culture. Persuasion reveals a good deal about the individual persuader and the receivers as well. Analysis of appeals, subject matter, purposes, and strategies all provide insight about the times, the people, the intellectual currents that are taking place. The historian finds persuasive efforts a major force in determining history and records of persuasive interactions and analysis of these interactions of value in writing history. Since the message is a significant act by the persuader, we often use the message to get at the source—reconstructing motives, seeking to understand the source's conceptions and assumptions. Similar techniques give us insight into campaigns and movements although the range of materials must be broader and possibly less exhaustive. We can trace the history of an idea or a theme through persuasive discourse.

The critic can give us insights into moral and ethical issues generally and those linked to persuasion and the practice of persuasion at particular times and for particular individuals or groups. In our own time we can turn to the contemporary critic to provide insight about the moral and ethical issues being posed and those that we are neglecting. Such insight is essential as we seek to live in a healthier relationship with others and with ourselves.

The critic can often illumine the aesthetic dimensions of persuasive activities. Some persuasive speeches and essays live as great masterpieces of literature—sometimes for the originality or clarity of thought, sometimes for aesthetic reasons, often for a fusion of several excellences that unite in forming a masterpiece. We have a valuable heritage from the past. But we also rightly ask the critics (including ourselves) to point out possible masterpieces that have just come into being or are now coming to be recognized. Our daily exposure gives us a range from the awful through the mediocre and average to the good and occasionally the excellent. We can profit from being directed to that which may be superior. The sheer density of persuasion limits the chance for us to detect the superior.

Most of us are familiar with the statement that in communication we are interested in "who says what to whom, how, under what circumstances, and to what effect." The critic can help us to understand the "who," "what," "to whom," "how," "under what circumstances," and "to what effect." Most critics will not attempt to shed light on all of these factors, but assistance on any one is of value.

A critic is not merely a person who utters a hasty, impressionistic judgment. In some instances an educated, intelligent critic can offer immediate judgments, which we should respect. But she or he needs to develop an argument, a rationale that we may judge as a basis for accepting the criticism as of value. So we ask as a minimum that a critic take the time to analyze the subject chosen. The analysis should lead to a synthesis that gives us insights beyond that of the analysis. Ideally the critic offers us a judgment that culminates in the various critical activities. This judgment may tell us about the persuader, the audience, the effects and how and why they were achieved, and the reason certain effects were not achieved. The judgment may help us to understand policy, ethical or moral issues facing our society, or some other aspect of our society or culture. Your study of and interest in persuasion serves to increase your ability as such a critic.

SUMMARY

Estimation of persuasive effect is a very important element in the persuasion process. It is important to the source to perfect her or his skill as a persuader and to serve as a basis for succeeding persuasion efforts. The receiver may also seek some assessment of the persuasive effort on the receiver's attitudes and actions. Society in general is concerned with estimating public opinion or in seeing changes in social patterns. Commercial persuaders are interested in improving sales and in modifying images.

Measurement is difficult. Even general estimates as "pretty good" may be contradicted by the next observer who sees the same thing as "lousy." Precise measurements as to quantity of change or difference are obviously of greater difficulty to obtain although often more reliable and valid.

Response to persuasion efforts must often be inferred from limited feedback. Sometimes behavioral changes can be observed directly. Some people develop a high level of skill in estimating effect in given circumstances. A sound persuasion theory provides the best basis for interpreting what information is available.

Researchers are developing methods and instruments that provide both better quality and a greater quantity of data. While improved instruments are being developed to measure many aspects of the communication process, we need to develop more and better instruments. Improved measuring devices are not a sufficient basis for an improved persuasion theory, but they are a necessary factor in such a development.

We need more critical evaluation of persuasion in our society. Analysis of persuasive interactions is an effective approach to understanding much about an individual, group, society, or culture. In a sense we are likely to evaluate persuasion from the perspective of the persuader and the target of persuasion, but the implications of the persuasion process go beyond those identified with those roles. We and others need to function as persuasion critics to reveal the various characteristics of the persuasion process, including what it tells about our society and culture. We need to weigh the ethical issues revealed in persuasive discourse. We need to study persuasive practices so as to better understand our world and improve our ability to function within that world.

DISCUSSION QUESTIONS AND PROJECTS

1. What is the relationship between ratings of speaker effectiveness and persuasiveness in terms of attitude change? Should one expect the two to correlate? Why? Are there times when a communicator should be more interested in creating a change in the receivers' conception of his or her effectiveness rather than a change in attitude on the issues discussed?

2. An examination of famous speeches often demonstrates a clear difference between immediate reaction and delayed response. Which is the more valid measure of effect? What presuppositions underlie your response to that question? Is it a meaningful question?

3. What effects of the persuasion process other than those mentioned in this chapter might be of great interest? How can these effects be measured?

4. A review of various instruments used to measure persuasion effects could provide the basis of a lively discussion, an interesting series of reports, or a term project.

5. For one round of speeches the class might employ a series of different instruments to evaluate speeches. One day a shift-of-opinion ballot might be used; on another a semantic differential; a Likert type of instrument on a third. What are the strengths and weaknesses of the various instruments as measures of change in attitude?

6. Although you have not been given a detailed introduction to various methods of critical analysis, the theory you have studied indicates many ways in which the process of persuasion may be analyzed in whole or in part. As a class exercise, select one significant persuasive speech or campaign and have each person analyze it independently. When you share the analyses, you will see the complementariness of many of the analyses and illustrations of various approaches to criticism.

7. Read several of the analyses of persuasive discourse or cam-

paigns in recent journals such as the *Quarterly Journal of Speech* or the many collections of such analyses in books such as *The Kennedy-Nixon Debates*. Analyze the various critical approaches employed. Note the degree to which different approaches pose different, even unique, questions. What does this say about the value of having a variety of critics comment on the same material?

8. Select one or more examples of persuasion applied in one or more of the fine or applied arts. Discuss the degree to which the persuasive thrust complements the artistry and artistic dimensions of the piece. Discuss the degree to which the artistic dimension influences or determines the persuasive effect that may be achieved.

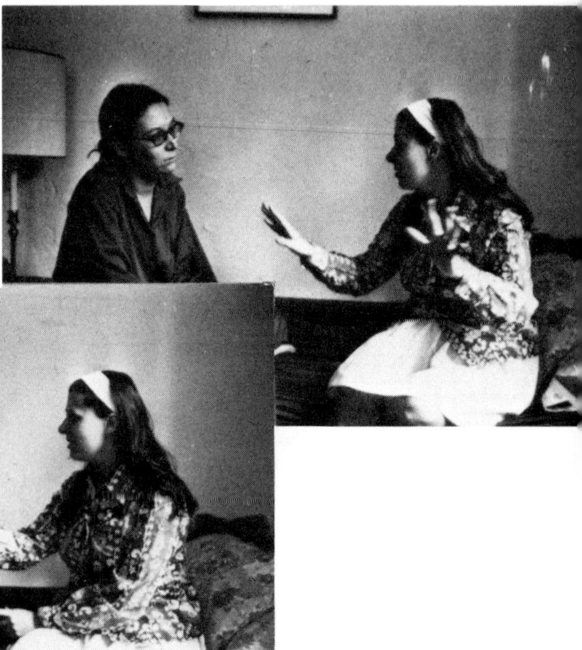
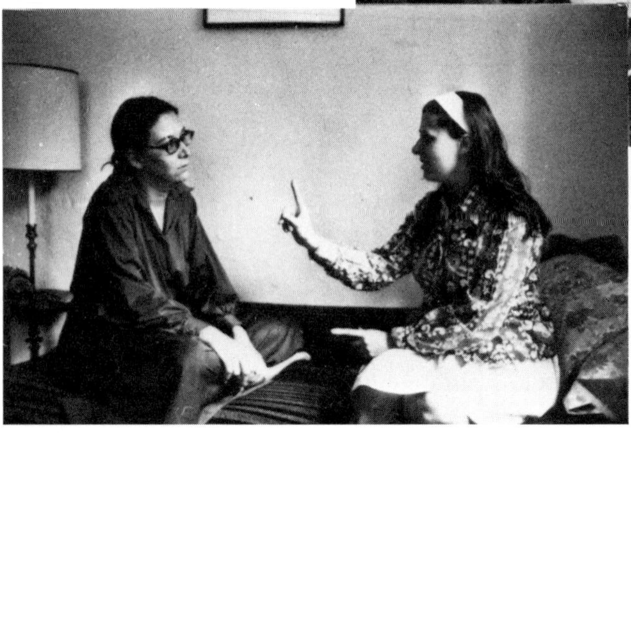

18 Creating a Response System to Persuasion

Despite the constant references to the persuasion process from the alternative viewpoints of source, receiver, and student of the persuasion process, I suspect that you and I have both approached this text and the persuasion process from the viewpoint of the persuader. Perhaps this is inevitable. The persuader usually is perceived as the active agent whereas the receiver is cast as the passive target. But clearly the receiver is not passive; he or she is very active. In many instances his actions determine whether he is even exposed to the persuasion stimuli. He may even ask the persuader to attempt persuasion. Nor is he powerless to reject the stimuli. Even in a totalitarian or brainwashing situation, some choice exists.

Although the receiver has a great deal of freedom in responding to external influences and controls, he possesses much less freedom in responding to his own internal influences and controls. Experiences in sensitivity training, T-groups, or being "told it like it is" suggest that a person does not perceive the self accurately. He may not recognize his own attitudes, values, and beliefs or see the ways in which they affect his actions and interactions with others. Each person is a prisoner because he serves as his own jailer. Perhaps the problem that the receiver faces in persuasion could be put more directly in a question: how much freedom does a receiver have in responding to the persuasion efforts of others?

When we function as persuaders we see others so caught in their attitudes and beliefs and the pattern of their actions that they cannot accept valid information or better, alternative courses of action. Clearly the same thing can and does happen when they function as persuaders and we function as receivers.

The obvious answer is that each person should be open to the possibility of change, but the application of this ideal poses many difficulties. Many factors make us resistant to such change. We cannot possibly give our attention to all the competing streams of persuasion, even on any one significant public issue; we could be overcome by the panoply of persuasion stimuli. Unless we choose among the alternatives, we would be simultaneously moving in three (if not thirty or three hundred) different directions. Often the alternatives are difficult to distinguish and the basis of choice among them is marginal.

Probably the majority of people never consciously face the problem of devising a means to be open to persuasion; they proceed as they go. To many people it would appear ridiculous for anyone to say that she wished to remain open to the possibility of being shifted to a new view even though she is convinced with reasonable certainty that her current view is right. Our world is filled with clichés that urge, "Be sure you are right and then go ahead."

To seek a system that ensures openness to persuasion seems the ideal of the ivory tower intellectual incapable of action or of trusting his judgment. But pragmatically, the arguments for just such a conscious decision far outweigh those against the decision.

THE GOAL: PUTTING PERSUASION TO WORK FOR THE RECEIVER

The persuader seeks to affect receivers in order to obtain the goal sought by the persuader. This is the typical view of persuasion. But the view can be reversed. The potential persuadee seeks to utilize the persuasive efforts of persuaders to achieve the goals that the receiver seeks.

Chapter 2 briefly described some ways in which the persuasion process can serve the receiver. The persuader may sound the alarm, provide information, cause us to test and alter our actions and beliefs, rouse us to action, including counterpersuasion. In doing these things the persuader, at least potentially, enables the receiver to attain her or his goals.

Stated most simply, the receiver—the intended persuadee—should attempt to use the persuasion process as a means to achieve the goals—personal, business, group, and societal—he sets for himself. The persuadee should use the persuasion efforts of others to serve himself, not necessarily in a selfish or narrow sense, but just as he employs the persuasion process as a persuader to achieve goals.

Analyzing how the persuasion process can work in this fashion means asking how to make the persuasion process work for the persuadee by examining the need for a planned response system.

Presumably we seek to make choices that maximize the probability of obtaining the goals we consciously and unconsciously identify as desirable for ourselves, for others with whom we interact, for society, and for humanity. There are many alternative poles in such choice making. We could act as if we are the sole basis for our choice. We would assume full responsibility and assume that we had sufficient resources and knowledge within ourselves. Thus, in effect, we need no one else to contribute to our choices; we would have the answer within ourselves. An alternative pole would be to assume that we have no basis for choice in ourselves. We must trust someone else to make our choices for us; we must find an authority. Neither of these two poles makes much sense, at least as a basis for action in all areas affecting us.

Other poles exist. We might assume that we are essentially powerless to control our destiny. Since we do not really make any choices, the whole question is irrelevant. We are already programmed, and so are all the outcomes. The opposite polar assumption that everything is totally within our control is also defeating.

Somewhere between these poles lies an assumption that we can make and meaningfully act upon our own decisions, but we need the actions and contributions of others to assist us in this process. Although some things are predestined and beyond our control, other things are not. We can determine to a degree our responses to the questions posed even if we cannot determine the questions to be posed. This leads to the view that people can act to utilize the matrix of forces, particularly the streams of persuasive communication, extant in the society to assist in reaching their goals.

Committing oneself to a system of response to persuasion efforts raises the issue of training in listening and reading as complementary to the areas of speaking and writing. Most of the attention to listening and reading has focused upon comprehension and retention. The desideratum has been that Johnny learns, remembers, retains, can use, and act upon what he has heard or read. Unfortunately, we too rarely ask what Johnny should not learn, should forget, should not use or act upon. The Institute for Propaganda Analysis began to identify a series of propaganda techniques and urge people to watch out for them. World War II and the need to practice many of these techniques contributed to a quieting of the campaign, however. English courses, courses in debate, logic, and critical thinking seek to alert us to the presence of slanted language, the emotional appeal, the incomplete syllogism. But they do not grapple fully with the problematic question of whether one should act or believe.

An emotional appeal may well be valid; slanted language may be necessary to rouse us from lethargy to needed action. Pictures of babies with flippers for arms are not without emotional as well as logical impact. And the former impact more than the latter led to banning thalidomide.

Clearly, then, development of a strategy of response involves more than listening and reading to maximize comprehension. And it involves more than simply identifying and arbitrarily acting or not acting on the basis of the logicality of the message or the absence of emotional appeal or slanted language.

The goal is to make the persuasion process work for the individual. The method is to create a system for responding to the massive amounts of ongoing persuasion extant in the society.

PLANNING THE RESPONSE SYSTEM

In order to plan a response system, one must identify the goals to which the system is intended to contribute. The key goal that I can identify is that a person should seek to become knowledgeable, even reasonably expert, in certain areas that are consciously identified as those in which she or he will seek special competencies. The range and interrelationship of these areas may help to determine the number of areas in which a person can seek special competency. Of course, the interests and commitments of a person help to determine these areas. Certain businessmen will center on areas particularly relevant to their work; others may become active in public affairs.

As a result of hobbies, personal interests, past experiences, abilities, and desires, a person inevitably develops certain areas of competence. Some people may know the earned run average of every major league team and most of the individual players. They may be able to discourse enthusiastically on the merits of a particular shortstop. Someone else may develop a palate that can distinguish the vintage of a wide variety of wines. People will value a particular competency quite differently. Each person must answer the question of whether a competency is of value to that person. To maintain a competency we must continue to acquire information and understanding in that area. And our areas of concern and competency may change; such change is one measure of remaining alive.

Immersion in an area of interest can be quite rewarding both for the sheer intrinsic pleasure on the part of the individual and for the contribution that can be made to others when they turn to the individual for help or guidance. But we cannot devote our lives only to certain areas of interest. We have to do those things that are essential to us. We have to eat, try to maintain our health, need the resources (financial and otherwise) that enable us to do more than just survive. So we must remain open to material relevant to these areas. In part we can do so effectively by a division of labor; we offer special competencies to others and thus help them; we draw on their special competencies to help ourselves.

Having identified the goal of developing special competency in selected areas of interest while remaining open to material about areas that can affect us, we can identify some components in a system of response to persuasion efforts. We must make the persuasion efforts of others offer us the maximum possible help at a reasonable cost in terms of time, money, effort, and so forth.

Strategy for Selecting among Persuasion Stimuli

We need to identify the sources that provide a range of information and persuasive material about the area(s) of interest. This includes people who share our interest and selection from among the many materials available in the mass media. Usually the latter involves printed material, especially material directed specifically at people with the same interest. Finally, direct observation and participation in the interest area is often highly feasible.

Let us assume I wish to become particularly versed on issues of local government. There is a wide range of possibilities available in the two communities of Champaign and Urbana: school boards, city councils, zoning commissions, liquor boards, streets and bridges commissions, mass transit board, assessment appeals boards, police and fire commissions and boards, many country boards, township boards, park boards, forest preservation boards, agriculture boards, county drain commissioners, the community college school board, the water conservation district commissioners, the soil conservation district, and about twenty-five other local groups that I located in the telephone directory. Obviously I cannot watch all these boards and groups myself. But the local newspaper helps. The League of Women Voters has watchers at most of these groups, and they report periodically to league members. I can become involved with people who share my interest in what is happening in local government, and between us we can be fairly sure we can do a reasonable job of coverage.

This extended illustration makes two points. First, even an apparently reasonable area of specialization turns out to be impossible to cover by oneself. Second, most of the people have no idea how many different groups exert a controlling influence over their lives at this local level. Every one of the groups mentioned uses my taxes for their own salaries and expenses and spends my taxes for projects that they approve. Sometimes these groups also decide what I can and cannot do in my own home or in the community.

Thus, the first step is to identify those people who are knowledgeable and interested in the same area or the relevant areas and meet them and also to find the media sources that will be helpful. The next step is to seek out alternative points of view. Particular magazines, groups, and individuals develop an approach, a frame of reference, and a point of view. To remain knowledgeable and to increase competency, one must have exposure to a full range of viewpoints. The person who is competent in an area knows the range of beliefs and the typical mistakes that people make. Even in an area one knows well, there is a need to check periodically to see what new information has developed or what old idea is back again with renewed vigor.

Some attention must also be given to areas outside the ones of special competency or interest. Many people are careful to read the daily newspaper headlines or subscribe to certain general interest magazines because these sources are likely to indicate areas of significant concern for many people. True, many were convinced that cigarettes were harmful to health long before there was much publicity about this issue in the mass media. The pressure built slowly with expressions of concern by a few sources and a few articles in limited circulation or scholarly journals. These articles in turn spurred others to concern, and gradually *Time,* the wire services, and newspapers picked up the story until the government finally acted to require warnings on packages and in advertising. Similar patterns occur with many other issues. Not all of our concerns will be touched upon by the media, but those that are likely to affect any large number of people will be, at least eventually.

Strategy for Reception

Many studies show that people filter material according to current attitudes, beliefs, actions. Because of habits, patterns of exposure, relatively constant reference groups, and limited potential for exposure to unique stimuli and interactions, we tend to be limited in the range of stimuli to which we are exposed. Some ways to alter this were suggested above. But this tendency exists also in comprehending and interpreting material in accordance with our established frames of reference. Clearly a strategy may be needed that will break this pattern. Although the items that follow are worded in terms of one stimulus, they apply to larger units of material as well.

1. An effort should be made to comprehend the material fully, especially material that contradicts our point of view. This process

of understanding should be separated somewhat consciously from the evaluation of the material. These processes normally occur almost simultaneously. When motivated to do so, we can distinguish the two processes.

2. The motivational structure *as well as* the logical structure of the material should be identified. What appeals are made? What motivations are offered to the receiver? What claims are made and what support is offered for them? This may involve extensive analysis including the labeling and identification of certain elements and perhaps the translation into less loaded language or supplying of missing items so as to grasp the total working of the persuasive stimulus.

3. The source for the material should be evaluated. Questions about the source's knowledgeableness, trustworthiness, involvement in the issue, and the biases and prejudices and the attitudes and values within which he or she operates are clearly basic to full understanding.

4. The presuppositions and the assumptions made should be noted. What values and ethical views are intrinsic to the material?

5. The new material should be compared with material already known. A decision may be reached to search out additional material, to take other steps as a prelude for later decision. (In effect, this is a decision about acceptance and action because other decisions are postponed and this decision is implemented.)

It is important to watch for relatively instantaneous responses that short-circuit the identification, interpretation, and weighing that is occurring. Awareness of one's own biases and commitments must be maintained.

Strategy for Determining Acceptance and/or Action

This stage of the process is most important because the effort to expose oneself to stimuli, the effort to extend comprehension significantly beyond mere understanding of what was manifest in the communication, is motivated by the desire to determine the acceptability of the persuasion stimulus and/or the action that should be taken.

Acceptance of a particular view is only one possible response to the mass of persuasion material available. In many instances little change will result. A persuasion stimulus may be fully in accord with one's current beliefs and actions, and the examination of a wide range of views may result in further confirmation of one's view. Much of the material may be discounted as valueless; it produces no change. But in some instances we may be moved to further investigation and possibly to some change in our present pattern of thinking. A decision may be made to act by communicating to others about the issues. In some instances one may be moved to counter directly some of the persuasion effort that is being mounted.

In a sense, this effort is valueless if one simply wants to know and does not want to affect the course of events in those areas in which he or she has been building this special competency. The key question at this juncture is "Have I reasons to believe, to act?" This question relates not only to information elements but also includes the ethical basis and the motivational basis from which a person acts. It relates not only to judgments concerning an issue or element but also to a larger context. How long can a researcher go on finding that a substance is producing cancer in animals or causing deformed or dead chicken embryos before she has cause to act? One runs risks of being hailed as savior or idiot. And both are real possibilities.

The agony of choice cannot be avoided. But again, as one trusts in a method to bring one to a stage where a decision can follow, so one may trust in a method or strategy to aid in this decision. Almost inevitably the strategy here will differ more from person to person and the weight given to the various questions will differ from case to case as well as person to person. But here are some questions that may be posed.

>1. Are the motivational forces sufficient to compel a decision? The persuasion directed at us contains a number of motivational efforts. Are these important enough to cause one to act? Further, although the motivational appeals offered may not be sufficient to produce action or acceptance, do I find some within myself that do operate with such an effect? A persuader may not offer the proper motivation to cause one to act. But this does not mean there are not valid forces working that should move one to action.
>
>2. Are the ethical questions related to the decision identified and assessed? The decision to act (or not to act) clearly has ethical implications for the self. And the ethical questions relative to the stream of ongoing persuasion have similar potential: should liars and cheats be allowed to dominate public discussion simply because others are not sure of the ultimate answers or do not want the risks of involvement?
>
>3. Are the evidence and reasoning available sufficient to produce a decision? Certainly the weighing of evidence and reasoning is important as a basis for decision and for action. Persuaders almost inevitably provide a wide variety of data and evidence and alternative chains of reasoning built from the same or different evidence and assumptions. These provide a rich source for the receiver to draw upon in reaching conclusions. We may well come to the same conclusions as many others but for quite different reasons.

Drawing upon these three identifiable areas of the ethical, motivational, evidential-reasoning factors, we must ask, "What do I believe? What is the best estimate of the truth that I can derive? Having derived this estimate, what imperatives do I face? Should I act? What should my action be?" Drawing upon this reserve of identified sources, we have presumably greater probability of integrating these forces in good reasons for belief and action. Such good reasons are not only the logical factors relative to the problem area.

ACCEPTING RESPONSIBILITY

This chapter has made an assumption about the nature of human responsibility: since people can make choices, we are responsible for as well as profited by optimal choices. Determination of what constitutes the optimal choices and how to make them is one aspect of our responsibility and an action basic to self-respect.

The matrix of competing persuasion efforts provides valuable assistance both in terms of information and in terms of motivational factors, ethical implications, alternative lines of interpretation; hence the variety of things that conduce to and contribute to a person's making decisions.

An individual cannot decide every one of the million things that could be decided in a day. Habit and past experiences mean that we do not perceive most of these as even involving choices. Yet any one of these can potentially become areas where we must make choices.

For most of us, giving our children baby food is not an issue. Yet, in late 1969 the concern about cyclamates being linked to cancer and a concern that monosodium glutamate, a salt that intensifies and improves flavor, may have harmful effects upon the brain, particularly in the developmental stages, did pose such an issue. Further, MSG is put into baby food primarily so that it will taste better to parents who are always condemning baby foods as tasting so terrible. Parents must accept the idea that they are responsible for giving the child these foods and yet know they are not the only ones accountable. Once the cry of alarm is sounded, responsibility is increased. Everyone is accountable as a citizen if federal regulatory agencies are not pressured to act. The responsibility cannot be left to the agencies even if they should act; others should act too. Cyclamates were banned in foods and beverages, including baby foods. In 1976 some baby food companies began to leave out additives such as MSG and sugar, but the market response will determine whether this adjustment is a success.

The strategy for response to persuasion efforts involves a willingness to accept responsibility for being an initiator of change as a persuader and for being an initiator of change in following through as a receiver. Each person provides an answer to that responsibility. Some find the responsibility impossible, meaningless, or simply one that they never perceive. But at what point can any of us ask the questions "Why didn't someone tell us? Why didn't somebody do something?"

Opinion leaders exist at every level of society. Different people may serve as opinion leaders on different issues. Anyone can be an opinion leader if she or he exposes herself or himself to information, including the persuasive efforts relative to that area of interest, becomes well informed, and interprets the information for and offers the best personal judgment to other people. In this sense everyone can be responsible to self and to others in at least some areas of significance.

We must maintain some perspective on our world. By far the greatest amount of the persuasive materials in our society has only limited relevance to us, and much of that relevance is indirect. Truthfully I do not care what company persuades you to buy an electric guitar or electric toothbrush. I am concerned if the products are dangerous to operate or if the sales techniques are so improper that you come to distrust any sales appeal.

With hundreds of products the only difference we are getting is the difference in our perception of the product. *Consumer Reports* indicates that hand soaps are about equal in getting our hands clean in most circumstances. They vary widely in color, scent, cost, brand name, and lots of other factors. Provided you can afford the difference in cost, how much difference does it make to you which one you buy? Choosing between the "skin you love to touch," being "really clean," and "wishing others did too" may worry you a moment. And in many senses it does make a difference because one company survives and another does not, and you do spend more or less money for the same performance. But there is no sense of an agony of decision.

Perhaps we need to use our sense of humor and maintain a degree of perspective. We need to sort out what really matters, what could matter, and what almost certainly doesn't matter. We also need to concentrate on things that hold greater importance for us. Doing this would almost certainly make most of the mass of persuasion rather irrelevant and highly manageable.

Finally, we need to appreciate the function of persuasion in our lives. We need to be educated, alert, watchful consumers of persuasion. An occasional slip in which we buy the worthless product or contribute to the charity that never spends any of its funds for its charitable purpose but uses the funds to pay the costs of raising the funds and the salaries of the fundraisers is probably good for us. Like other mistakes it reminds us to be careful to avoid a similar mistake. We are not dealing with "mere" persuasion; we are dealing with the choices in and of our lives individually and collectively.

SUMMARY

We are immersed in a complex matrix of persuasion stimuli. How can we structure our activity so that we are not buried by the sheer amount and variety of all this persuasion effort? To ignore external communication influences totally limits our own knowledge and the chance to profit from utilizing the efforts and thinking of others. To accept persuasion stimuli uncritically is quite stupid.

Recourse to the concept of developing areas of special concern that a person identifies and then developing a strategy in terms of attention, reception, and acceptance and/or action is one answer. Thus the persuasion efforts in society provide the receiver with a greater possibility of choice. To close off these stimuli is to limit choice.

Utilization of a strategy always demands some degree of effort. An individual must be motivated to put forth the energy involved in channeling attention, reception, and acceptance or action. If one seeks to accomplish certain goals and can identify his concern in developing competencies that relate to these goals, he may find a key to motivation in areas that will develop intrinsic interest for him.

In selecting material, the essential strategy is consciously to select communication sources that will give extensive and varied coverage relative to the areas of concern. In addition one seeks some awareness of sources that may sound the alarm concerning problems outside one's special interests. The reception process focuses upon going beyond mere comprehension of the various persuasion stimuli. Attention is given to supplying the missing ingredients by specifying the motivational structure, the ethical presuppositions, the logical and evidential (substantive) structure, and evaluating the source's interests and capabilities. The material is checked by what is "known" and by the sheer variety of sources.

In deciding upon acceptance and/or possible courses of action the individual must identify the relevant motivational, ethical, and substantive factors that bear upon the decision and seek an answer in terms of the interplay of these factors.

A person may accept responsibility both for serving as an active agent of change in areas where she seeks competency and as a responsive receiver in areas in which she has not sought special competency. Many do not perceive or do not accept the validity of this assumption of responsibility. But any one of us can assume this responsibility. We need not be an originator of ideas; we may be a powerful mediator of ideas instead.

If you will help me with some of this I'll help you with some of it in return. And you know what they say . . . two heads are better than one and several may be better than two in the effort to cope with the complexities of life.

DISCUSSION QUESTIONS AND PROJECTS

1. I committed myself to a value judgment on the nature of responsibility as a basis for developing a strategy for dealing with the mass of persuasion that exists in our society. Is it possible to develop a system or strategy without making a value judgment or operating from some ethical presupposition?

2. Research in listening shows that a person can improve listening retention quite markedly after a relatively short period of training. But over a period of time this ability in listening rapidly regresses to the original level. What implications do such research findings have for a person who is seeking to formulate and implement a system of response to the persuasion efforts that surround us?

3. To what degree is it possible for a person to separate the procedures involved in the fullest comprehension of the persuasive message and the procedures involved in judging the validity of the message?

4. Take a persuasive communication—perhaps one designed as "propaganda," perhaps one created in another project in this class. Identify the various propaganda devices in it. Does such identification assist you in determining the truth of the claims made?

5. Many people credit a sixth sense or an instinctive feeling as the best guide to accepting or rejecting a proposal or an idea. To what degree does such a view contradict the proposals set forth in this chapter? To what degree do many of the recommended procedures actually operate for most people but in a relatively habitual, unconscious way?

6. No attention was given to applying the suggested strategies to different areas. What differences might be involved in "shift-

CREATING A RESPONSE SYSTEM TO PERSUASION 413

ing to a new washday detergent that makes clothes whiter and brighter" versus shifting to a new viewpoint about the best way to study for exams?

7. Many people argue that the mass of the persuasive stimuli present in our society, perhaps 99 percent of it, is totally irrelevant to any one person. What is your attitude in terms of the relevance of the mass of persuasion stimuli to you as an individual?

Epilogue

To commit this book to the printer is a traumatic event for me. So much more could be said, so much more should be said and said more effectively that it is difficult to say *finis*. The attempt to develop a complete theory of invention based upon the theory of cognitive dissonance could occupy the space of this entire book. Of course, that would be a different book for a different audience and with a different purpose. Although realizing the inevitable limitations, one would always like to do what he does more effectively and to do more than he is able to do.

This book says much about my current view of society and my view of people. It is dangerous to say what one believes; it is so easy to be cut down by the chance remark of another. But time passes and one grows. What seems profound or at least useful today may seem trivial or simple-minded tomorrow. I will change, but this book will fix me at my present point in time for the reader. But I believe that a persuasion theory is inevitably grounded in a psychology of man and a philosophy or life view. It is not enough to report the data derived from all the experiments.

I hope that I have not tried to impress my values upon you. But I do hope the relationship of your theory of persuasion to your views and values, unconsciously as well as consciously held, has become manifest. If so, you too labor under the same burden that I have felt with increasing force as I have taught persuasion classes and as I have struggled with this book. I think it has been a good struggle for me to have had. I wish you a good struggle with the problems of persuasion, and not just for today.

Selected Bibliography

To keep the bibliography to a reasonable size, I have included only a limited number of works, largely books. Those cited are generally applicable to many aspects of the persuasion process rather than being limited to one area of interest. The few articles in the bibliography generally summarize a number of specific studies.

Many of the books included here were not cited in the text but are useful references. Some are important early contributions to persuasion theory and practice; others are recent works.

Although I have tried to provide a current list, new books and new studies date any bibliography by the time it is published. Continuous study of relevant journals provides a good means of keeping in touch with the latest research findings.

Adorno, T. W. et al. *The Authoritarian Personality.* New York: Harper and Row, 1950.

Aiken, Henry D., ed. *Hume's Moral and Political Philosophy.* New York: Hafner Publishing Co., 1972.

Alinsky, Saul. *Rules for Radicals.* New York: Random House, 1971.

Allport, Gordon W., and Postman, Leo. *The Psychology of Rumor.* New York: Holt, 1947.

Andersen, Kenneth E. *Introduction to Communication Theory and Practice.* Menlo Park: Cummings Publishing Co., 1972.

―――, and Clevenger, Theodore, Jr. "A Summary of Experimental Research in Ethos." *Speech Monographs* 30 (1963): 66–70.

Beighley, K. C. "A Summary of Experimental Studies Dealing with the Effect of Organization and of Skill of Speakers on Comprehension." *Journal of Communication* 2 (1952): 58–65.

418 SELECTED BIBLIOGRAPHY

Beisecker, Tom D., and Parson, Donn W., eds. *The Process of Social Influence: Readings in Persuasion.* Englewood Cliffs, N.J.: Prentice-Hall, 1972.

Berelson, Bernard R.; Lazarsfeld, Paul F.; and McPhee, William M. *Voting.* Chicago: University of Chicago Press, 1954.

Berelson, Bernard R., and Steiner, Gary A. *Human Behavior.* New York: Harcourt, Brace and World, 1964.

Berkowitz, Leonard, ed. *Advances in Experimental Social Psychology.* New York: Academic Press. 9 vols.

Berlo, David K. *The Process of Communication.* New York: Holt, Rinehart and Winston, 1960.

Bettinghaus, Erwin P. *Persuasive Communciation.* 2d ed. New York: Holt, Rinehart and Winston, 1973.

Birdwhistell, Ray L. *Kinesics and Context.* Philadelphia: University of Pennsylvania Press, 1970.

Black, Edwin. *Rhetorical Criticism: A Study in Method.* New York: Macmillan, 1965.

Brembeck, W. L., and Howell, W. S. *Persuasion.* 2d ed. Englewood Cliffs, N.J.: Prentice-Hall, 1976.

Brooks, Robert D., and Scheidel, Thomas M. "Speech as a Process: A Case Study." *Speech Monographs* 35 (1968): 1–7.

Brown, J. A. C. *Techniques of Persuasion.* Baltimore: Penguin Books, 1963.

Brown, Judson S. *The Motivation of Behavior.* New York: McGraw-Hill, 1961.

Brown, Roger. *Words and Things.* Glencoe, Ill.: The Free Press, 1958.

Bruner, Jerome S.; Goodnow, Jacqueline J.; and Austin, George. *A Study of Thinking.* New York: John Wiley and Sons, 1956.

Burke, Kenneth. *A Grammar of Motives.* New York: Prentice-Hall, 1945.

———. *A Rhetoric of Motives.* New York: Prentice-Hall, 1950.

Campbell, Angus; Converse, Phil E.; Miller, Warren E.; and Stokes, Donald E. *The American Voter.* New York: John Wiley and Sons, 1960.

Campbell, Donald T., and Stanley, Julian C. *Experimental and Quasi-Experimental Designs for Research.* Chicago: Rand McNally, 1963.

Chapanis, Natalia, and Chapanis, Alphonse. "Cognitive Dissonance: Five Years Later." *Psychology Bulletin* 61 (1964): 1–22.

Chein, Isidor. *The Science of Behavior and the Image of Man.* New York: Basic Books, 1972.

Cherry, Colin. *On Human Communication.* 2d ed. Cambridge: MIT Press, 1966.

Clevenger, Theodore, Jr. *Audience Analysis.* Indianapolis: Bobbs-Merrill, 1966.

———. "A Synthesis of Experimental Research in Stage Fright." *Quarterly Journal of Speech* 45 (1959): 134–145.

Cofer, Charles N., and Appley, Mortimer H. *Motivation: Theory and Research.* New York: John Wiley, 1964.

Cohen, Arthur R. *Attitude Change and Social Influence.* New York: Basic Books, 1964.

Cooper, Lane, trans. *The Rhetoric of Aristotle.* New York: Appleton-Century-Crofts, 1932.

———. *Theories of Style in Literature.* New York: Macmillan, 1922.
Cronkhite, Gary. *Persuasion.* Indianapolis: Bobbs-Merrill, 1969.

Dance, Frank E. X., ed. *Human Communication Theory.* New York: Holt, Rinehart and Winston, 1967.
Diggs, B. J. *The State, Justice and the Common Good.* Glenview, Ill.: Scott, Foresman, 1974.

Ellul, Jacques. *Propaganda: The Formation of Men's Attitudes.* Translated by Konrad Kellen and Jean Learner. New York: Vintage Books, 1973.

Fearnside, W. Ward, and Holther, William B. *Fallacy: The Counterfeit of Argument.* Englewood Cliffs, N.J.: Prentice-Hall, 1959.
Festinger, Leon. *A Theory of Cognitive Dissonance.* Stanford: Stanford University Press, 1962.
Fishbein, Martin, ed. *Readings in Attitude Theory and Measurement,* New York: John Wiley, 1967.
Fisher, Walter R., ed. *Rhetoric: A Tradition in Transition.* East Lansing: Michigan State University Press, 1974.
Fotheringham, Wallace C. *Perspectives on Persuasion.* Boston: Allyn and Bacon, 1966.

Goffman, Erving. *Interaction Ritual.* Garden City: Doubleday, 1967.

Hall, Edward T. *The Silent Language.* New York: Doubleday, Inc., 1959.
Heider, Fritz. *The Psychology of Interpersonal Relations.* New York: John Wiley, 1958.
Hennessy, Bernard C. *Public Opinion.* 3d ed. North Scituate, Mass.: Duxbury Press, 1975.
Hilgard, Ernest R., and Bower, Gordon H. *Theories of Learning.* 4th ed. Englewood Cliffs, N.J.: Prentice-Hall, 1975.
Himmelfarb, Samuel, and Eagly, Alice Hendrickson. *Readings in Attitude Change.* New York: John Wiley, 1974.
Hoffer, Eric. *The True Believer.* New York: Harper and Brothers, 1951.
Hovland, Carl I., et al. *Communication and Persuasion.* New Haven: Yale University Press, 1953.
Hovland, Carl, and Janis, Irving L. *Personality and Persuasibility.* New Haven: Yale University Press, 1959.
Hovland, Carl, and Mandell, Wallace. *The Order of Presentation in Persuasion.* New Haven: Yale University Press, 1957.
Hummel, William, and Huntress, Keith. *The Analysis of Propaganda.* New York: Dryden Press, 1949.

Insko, Chester A. *Theories of Attitude Change.* New York: Appleton-Century-Crofts, 1967.

Johannesen, Richard L. *Ethics in Human Communication.* Columbus, O.: Charles E. Merrill, 1975.

Johnson, Wendell. *Your Most Enchanted Listener.* New York: Harper and Brothers, 1956.

Karlins, Marvin, and Abelson, Herbert I. *Persuasion: How Opinions and Attitudes Are Changed.* 2d ed. New York: Springer, 1970.

Katz, Elihu. "The Two-Step Flow of Communication: An Up-to-Date Report on an Hypothesis." *Public Opinion Quarterly* 21 (Spring 1957): 61–78.

Kelly, George A. *The Psychology of Personal Constructs.* New York: Norton, 1955. 2 vols.

Kerlinger, Frederick N. *Foundations of Behavioral Research.* 2d. ed. New York: Holt, Rinehart and Winston, 1973.

Kiesler, Charles A.; Collins, Barry E.; and Miller, Norman. *Attitude Change.* New York: John Wiley, 1969.

Kiesler, Charles, and Kiesler, Sara B. *Conformity.* Reading, Mass.: Addison-Wesley, 1969.

Klapper, Joseph T. *The Effects of Mass Communication.* New York: The Free Press, 1960.

Knapp, Mark. *Nonverbal Communication in Human Interaction.* New York: Holt, Rinehart and Winston, 1971.

Korzybski, Alfred. *Science and Sanity.* Lancaster, Pa.: Science Press Printing Co., 1933.

Lang, Kurt, and Lang, Gladys Engel. *American Voting Behavior.* Glencoe, Ill.: The Free Press, 1959.

Larson, Charles U. *Persuasion: Reception and Responsibility.* Belmont, Calif.: Wadsworth Publishing Co., 1973.

Lazarsfeld, Paul F.; Berelson, Bernard; and Gaudet, Hazel. *The People's Choice.* New York: Columbia University Press, 1948.

LeBon, Gustave. *The Crowd.* London: Ernest Benn Ltd., 1898.

Lee, Irving J. *Language Habits in Human Affairs.* New York: Harper and Brothers, 1941.

Lomas, Charles W. *The Agitator in American Society.* Englewood Cliffs, N.J.: Prentice-Hall, 1968.

Lowenthal, Leo, and Guterman, Norbert. *Prophets of Deceit.* New York: Harper and Brothers, 1949.

McLuhan, Marshall. *The Gutenberg Galaxy.* Toronto: University of Toronto Press, 1962.

———. *Understanding Media.* 2d ed. New York: McGraw-Hill, 1964.

Martin, Howard H., and Andersen, Kenneth E. *Speech Communication: Analysis and Readings.* Boston: Allyn and Bacon, 1968.

Maslow, Abraham H. *Toward a Psychology of Being.* Princeton: D. Van Nostrand, 1962.

Merton, Robert K. *Mass Persuasion.* New York: Harper and Brothers, 1946.

SELECTED BIBLIOGRAPHY

Miller, George A. *Language and Communication.* New York: McGraw-Hill, 1951.
Miller, Gerald R., and Nilsen, Thomas R., eds. *Perspectives on Argumentation.* Chicago: Scott, Foresman, 1966.
Miller, Paul A. "The Process of Decision Making within the Context of Community Organization." *Rural Sociology* 17 (1952): 153–161.
Minnick, Wayne C. *The Art of Persuasion.* 2d ed. Boston: Houghton Mifflin, 1968.

Newcomb, Theodore M.; Turner, Ralph H.; and Converse, Philip E. *Social Psychology: The Study of Human Interaction.* New York: Holt, Rinehart and Winston, 1965.
Nichols, Marie. *Rhetoric and Criticism.* Baton Rouge: Louisiana State University Press, 1963.
Nichols, Ralph G., and Lewis, Thomas R. *Listening and Speaking.* Dubuque, I.: William C. Brown Company, 1954.

Osgood, Charles E.; Suci, George J.; and Tannenbaum, Percy. *The Measurement of Meaning.* Urbana: University of Illinois Press, 1957.

Packard, Vance. *The Hidden Persuaders.* New York: David McKay, 1957.
Pool, Ithiel de Sola, et al., eds. *Handbook of Communication.* Chicago: Rand McNally, 1973.

Rawls, John. *A Theory of Justice.* Cambridge: Belknap Press of Harvard University Press, 1971.
Rogers, Carl R. *Client-Centered Therapy.* Boston: Houghton Mifflin, 1951.
———. *On Becoming a Person.* Boston: Houghton Mifflin, 1961.
Rokeach, Milton. *Beliefs, Attitudes and Values.* San Francisco: Jossey-Bass, 1968.
———. *The Open and Closed Mind.* New York: Basic Books, 1960.
Rosenberg, Milton, and Hovland, Carl, eds. *Attitude Organization and Change.* New Haven: Yale University Press, 1960.
Rosnow, Ralph L., and Robinson, Edward J. *Experiments in Persuasion.* New York: Academic Press, 1967.
Ross, W. D., trans. "Nicomachean Ethics." In *Introduction to Aristotle.* Edited by Richard McKeon. New York: Modern Library, 1947.

Scheidel, Thomas M. *Persuasive Speaking.* Glenview, Ill.: Scott, Foresman, 1967.
———. "Sex and Persuasibility." *Speech Monographs* 30 (1963): 353–358.
Sherif, Carolyn W.; Sherif, Muzafer; and Nebergall, Roger. *Attitude and Attitude Change.* Philadelphia: W. B. Saunders, 1965.
Sherif, Muzafer, and Hovland, Carl. *Social Judgment.* New Haven: Yale University Press, 1961.
Simons, Herbert W. "Persuasion in Social Conflicts: A Critique of Prevailing Conceptions and a Framework for Future Research." *Speech Monographs* 39 (1972): 227–248.
———. *Persuasion: Understanding, Practice and Analysis.* Reading, Mass.: Addison-Wesley, 1976.

Smith, Alfred G., ed. *Communication and Culture.* New York: Holt, Rinehart and Winston, 1966.
Strunk, William, Jr. *The Elements of Style.* Revised by E. B. White. New York: Macmillan, 1959.

Thompson, Wayne N. *The Process of Persuasion.* New York: Harper and Row, 1975.
──────. *Quantitative Research in Public Address and Communication.* New York: Random House, 1967.
Thonssen, Lester; Baird, A. Craig, and Braden, Waldo W. *Speech Criticism.* 2d ed. New York: Ronald Press, 1970.
Toch, Hans. *The Social Psychology of Social Movements.* Indianapolis: Bobbs-Merrill, 1965.
Toulmin, Stephen, *The Uses of Argument.* New York: Cambridge University Press, 1958.
Triandis, Harry C. *Attitude and Attitude Change.* New York: John Wiley, 1971.

Vernon, M. D. *The Psychology of Perception.* Baltimore: Penguin Books, 1962.

Wallace, Karl, ed. *A History of Speech Education in America.* New York: Appleton-Century-Crofts, 1954.
Wiener, Norbert. *The Human Use of Human Beings: Cybernetics and Society.* Boston: Houghton Mifflin Co., 1950.
Wiseman, Gordon, and Barker, Larry L. *Speech—Interpersonal Communication.* San Francisco: Chandler Publishing, 1967.
Wright, Charles R. *Mass Communication.* New York: Random House, 1959.

Zajonc, Robert B. "The Concepts of Balance, Congruity and Dissonance." *Public Opinion Quarterly* 24 (1960): 280–296.
Zimbardo, Philip, and Ebbesen, Ebbe B. *Influencing Attitudes and Changing Behavior.* Reading, Mass.: Addison-Wesley, 1969.

Subject Index

Argumentation, 142–46 (see also Logical appeals)
Attention
 delivery and, 215–25
 factors, 109–10
 nature, 105–12
 perception and, 111–12
 persuasion and, 114–17, 172–73
 selectivity, 111–12
 style and, 198–201
Attitudes
 analysis of, 80–81, 88–93, 389
 behavior and, 53–57, 97–101
 measurement, 53–54, 88–93, 386–95
 nature, 49–54
 relationship to beliefs and values, 54–55
Audience analysis (see Receiver analysis)

Beliefs, 54–55 (see also Attitudes)
Bodily action, 215–20

Campaigns
 confrontation and, 328–33
 effectiveness, 324–28
 execution, 323–24
 function, 312–14
 multiple media use, 315–18
 nature, 309–14
 organization, 314–19
 planning, 319–23
 two-step (multi-step) flow, 318–19
Channel
 effects, 295–97
 interaction with situation-setting, 303–04
 mass media, 292–95
 nature, 15, 17, 287–95
 personal, 288–92
 strategy in use, 295–97
 types, 287–95 (see also Campaigns)
Choice, 3–4, 19–20, 27–30, 267–71, 349–50, 367–69, 401–11
Closed-mindedness, 94–95, 257
Cognitive balance models.
 cognitive consistency, 60–62, 275–77

423

SUBJECT INDEX

Cognitive balance models (*cont.*)
  cognitive dissonance, 63–64, 275–77
  congruity, 62–63, 275–77
Communication, 7–8, 10–14 (*see also* Persuasion)
Communication-binding context, 12–15, 18–19
Comprehension, 201–03 (*see also* Delivery, Language, Style)
Confrontation (*see* Campaigns, Choice, Ethics)
Construct theory, 28, 190, 241
Cultural effects
  on action, 218–20
  on attitudes, 50–53
  on language and style, 192–93
  on motivation, 57–60, 67–68

Decision-making via persuasion, 1–6
  alternatives, 33–35
  choice vs. force, 27–30, 33–39, 370–72, 375–77
  individual, 30–36
  societal, 36–39
  versus totalitarianism, 33–35, 367–81
Delivery (*see also* Bodily action, Nonverbal, Stage fright, Voice)
  effects, 223–28
  eye contact, 219–20
  nature, 211–12
  styles, 225–28
Demagogue, 371–72
Documentation, 149–50
Dogmatism, 94–95
Drive, 57–60

Effects, 385–98 (*see also* specific variables and Measurement)
Emotional appeals (*see* Motivational appeals)

Ethical appeals (*see also* Ethics, Ethos)
  extrinsic ethos, 253–54
  interactive effects, 252–62
  intrinsic ethos, 254–57
  nature, 252
Ethics
  approaches, 347–52
  code, 352–62, 379–80
  dilemmas, 342–46
  nature, 341–42
  relationship to choice, 3–4, 19–20, 27–30, 267–71, 349–50, 367–69, 401–11
  responsibility, 332–33, 341–42, 353–59
    receiver's, 355, 409–11
    two-hundred percent theory, 353–56
Ethos
  creation and change, 242–54, 257–58
  dimensions, 238–42
  effects, 254–62
  nature, 235–42
Evidence
  documentation of, 149–50
  nature, 143, 146
  presentational forms, 149–50, 158–62

Fear, 155–56, 370–72, 375–77
Feedback, 15, 85–88, 279–81, 390–98

Gender, 96–97

Humor, 196–98

Interest, 109–12 (*see also* Attention, Style)

SUBJECT INDEX

Language (see also Style)
  culture and, 192–93
  effects, 198–206
  learning and, 64–67
  nature, 187–89
Learning theory, 64–67
Logical appeals
  difficulty of isolation, 140–42, 162–65
  effect, 148–54
  form, 146–51
  motivation, 148–54
  nature, 140–46
  strategy in use, 151–54
  vs. motivational appeals, 154

Mass media (see also Channel)
  campaign use, 315–18
  kinds, 293–95
  nature, 292–97
  selective exposure, 300–02, 314–18
  situation-setting, 301–03
  two-step (multi-step) flow, 318–19
  vs. personal channels, 295–97
Meaning (see also Language, Style)
  culturally bound, 192–93
  nature, 9, 137–39, 189–92
  related to ethos, 258–61
  semantic differentiation, 189–192
Measurement
  attitude, 53–54, 88–93, 386–95
  complexity, 387–90
  estimation, 88–93, 387–90 (see also Receiver analysis)
  ethos, 236–42
  nature, 385–87
  problems, 385–89
  process, 389–95
  research procedures, 393–95
Message (see also Delivery, Organization, Style)
  matrix character, 138–39, 162–65
  nature, 15–17, 137–39
  preparation, 123–34
  purpose selection, 123–28
  role and function, 16–17, 123–24, 128–33
Model
  nature, 11
  of communication, 11–14
  of persuasion, 10–11, 15–19
Motivation
  attention, 114–17
  centrality, 47–49, 57
  interrelationships, 67–68, 162–65
  nature, 47–49
  self-persuasion, 271–77
  theories, 47–67
Motivational appeals
  approach-avoidance, 155–57 (see also Fear)
  audience-centered, 154–55, 162–65
  complexity, 140–42, 154–55, 162–65
  nature, 154–55
  strategy, 157–58

Negative persuasion, 100
Nonverbal communication, 212–25

Occasion (see Situation)
Organization
  body, 176–81
  conclusions, 177–78
  effects, 169–74
  introductions, 175–76
  patterns, 169–74
  process, 174–83
  strategy, 174–81
Outlining, 181–83

Persuadee (see Receiver and Receiver analysis)
Persuader
  decision to persuade, 30–35

SUBJECT INDEX

Persuader (cont.)
   effects of participation, 277–81
    (see also Self-persuasion)
   ethical responsibility, 354–55 (see
    also Ethics)
   nature, 15–16
Persuasibility, 93
Persuasion
   conscious intent problem, 7–9
   criticism and commentary, 395–97
   defined, 7–10
   goals
    general, 30–40
    specific purposes, 124–28
   nature, 3–19
   relationship to communication,
    3–19
   role and function (see also Choice,
    Ethics, Decision-making)
    means to choice, 3–4, 27–30,
     39–41
    persuadee, 30, 35–36, 401–11
    persuader, 30–35
    society, 36–39
   study, 19–21, 25–27
Persuasion model, 10–11, 15–19
Primacy vs. recency, 171–72
Proof
   interrelatedness, 162–65
   nature, 140–41
   types (see Ethical, Logical, and
    Motivational appeals)
Propaganda, 314 (see also Campaigns,
   Totalitarian persuasion)
Purposes of persuasion
   general, 30–41
   specific purpose, 124–28
    selection process, 124–27
    tests, 127–28

Reasoning forms, 146–48
Receiver
   classifications, 80–81, 88–97
   ethical responsibility, 355, 409–11

   nature, 15, 17–18
   persuasion's value to, 30, 35–36
   variability of response, 73–77,
    97–101
Receiver analysis
   process, 73, 80–101
   self as audience, 271–77
   stages, 80–88
   value, 73–80
   variables, 80–101
Referential groups, 50–52
Reinforcement
   learning, 64–67
   self-persuasion, 272–74
Repetition, 161, 173–74
Response prediction, 97–101
Response system for receivers
   function, 401–04
   strategy, 404–11

Saliency, 95–96
   attention, 110–11
   ethos, 250–53
   sex variable research, 96–97
Self-esteem, 93–94 (see also Choice,
   Ethics)
Self-persuasion
   action effects, 277–81
   significance, 267–71
   theories of, 271–77
Selective exposure (see also Situation)
   attention, 111–12
   avoidance, 401–06
   ethos, 253–56
Semantic differential, 62–63, 190–92
Setting (see Situation)
Situation
   analysis of
    process, 80–88
    value, 73–80
   effects, 225–28
   nature, 15, 17, 81
   relation to channel, 303–04
   types, 296–303

Sleeper effect, 261–62
Source (*see* Persuader)
Stage fright, 215–18, 278–81
Style (*see also* Language)
 effects, 198–206
 measurement, 195–96
 nature, 194–96
Suggestion, 112–14
 ethos, 253–57

Totalitarian persuasion
 blends in society, 379–80
 confrontation, 328–33
 effectiveness, 378–80
 nature, 367–69
 strategy, 372–78
 terrorism, 330
 totalitarian figures, 369–72
Toulminian structure, 144–46
Two-sided appeals, 148, 150–51
Two-step (multi-step) communication flow, 318–19

Values (*see also* Ethics)
 nature, 55
 totalitarian society, 367–69, 377–78
Voice
 effects, 220–28
 elements, 220–23

Author Index

Adorno, T. W., 94
Ajzen, I., 57
Allport, Gordon W., 50–53, 111, 223
Andersen, Kenneth E., 22, 156, 235, 239, 296
Andersen, Mary K., 327–52
Ardrey, Robert, 59
Aristotle, 140, 195, 238, 309, 343, 356

Baker, Virgil L., 350
Barker, Curtis, 375
Beighley, K. C., 170, 223
Bem, Daryl J., 276
Berelson, Bernard, 318, 325
Berkowitz, Leonard, 192
Berlo, David, 63, 172, 188, 239, 258
Bettinghaus, Erwin P., 63, 247
Bower, Gordon H., 65
Bowers, John W., 223
Brooks, Robert D., 251
Buffon, M. De, 194
Burke, Kenneth, 204–05

Campbell, Angus, 325

Cantril, Hadley, 223
Carpenter, Ronald H., 194–95, 199
Cathcart, Robert S., 149
Chein, Isidor, 19
Clark, W. K., 216–17
Clevenger, Theodore, Jr., 10, 217, 235
Cohen, Arthur R., 62, 171, 173
Colburn, C. William, 156
Conolley, Edward S., 277
Converse, Philip E., 10,. 325
Cooper, Lane, 140, 194, 195
Cotton, Jack C., 221

Darnell, Donald K., 170
Day, Dennis G., 350
DeQuincey, Thomas, 195
Diggs, B. J., 356ff
Dresser, William R., 150
Dunham, Robert E., 244

Ebel, Robert L., 390

Ehrensberger, Ray, 171
Eubanks, Ralph T., 350

Feshback, Seymour, 156
Festinger, Leon, 63–64
Fishbein, Martin, 56–57, 382
Freud, Sigmund, 59
Fromm, Erich, 377

Gaudet, Hazel, 318
Gerard, Harold B., 277
Gilkinson, Howard, 217
Goldstein, Michael J., 156
Goodman, Charles, 151
Gulley, Halbert, 63, 172

Haberman, Frederick W., 386
Haeffner, David, 156
Haiman, Franklyn S., 349
Hall, Edward T., 214, 219
Harrison, Randall, 212–13
Hartmann, George W., 149
Harvey, Ivan G., 244
Harwood, Kenneth E., 221–22
Heider, Fritz, 62
Heinberg, Paul, 224
Henrikson, Ernest, 217
Hewgill, Murray A., 156
Hildebrandt, Herbert W., 225–26
Hildreth, Richard, 249
Hilgard, Ernest R., 65
Hitler, Adolf, 368, 372
Hovland, Carl I., 91–93, 150–51, 171, 248, 262
Hume, David, 356, 360

Insko, Chester A., 60

Janis, Irving L., 93, 156, 248
Jersild, Arthur, 171, 173
Johnson, F. Craig, 23

Kant, Immanuel, 356, 360
Kelly, George A., 28, 190, 241
Kelly, Harold H., 248
Kelman, Herbert C., 262
King, Thomas R., 217
Klapper, Joseph, 325
Klare, George R., 23
Knower, Franklin H., 217
Korzybski, Alfred, 188
Kramer, Cheris, 197
Kumata, Hideya, 258

Lang, Gladys E., 325
Lang, Kurt, 325
Lazarsfeld, Paul F., 318, 325
Lee, Irving J., 188
Lefford, Arthur, 150
Lemert, James B., 239
Leventhal, Howard, 156
Lomas, Charles W., 369
Longinus, 195
Lorenz, Konrad, 59
Lumley, F. H., 221
Lumsdaine, Arthur A., 150–51
Lund, F. H., 171

McCroskey, James C., 150, 223, 240, 244, 255
McGuire, William J., 91, 173
McLuhan, Marshall, 225, 288, 290
McPhee, William N., 325

Markham, David, 239
Martin, Howard H., 22, 156, 296

AUTHOR INDEX

Maslow, Abraham H., 59–60
Mertz, Robert J., 239
Milgram, Stanley, 381–82
Miller, George A., 188
Miller, Gerald R., 140, 156
Miller, Warren E., 325
Morgan, J., 150
Morris, Desmond, 59
Morton, J., 150
Murchinson, C. A., 50

Nebergall, Roger, 91–93
Newcomb, Theodore M., 10, 62
Nichols, Ralph G., 171
Nilsen, Thomas R., 140, 351

Osgood, Charles, 52–53, 62–63, 190–92

Papageorgis, Demetrios, 91
Paulson, Stanley F., 149, 151
Petrie, Charles, 170
Pool, Ithiel DeSola, 212
Postman, Leo, 111
Powell, Frederic A., 94

Rawls, John, 356, 361
Ray, Jack, 140
Robinson, Edward J., 172
Rogers, Carl, 60
Rokeach, Milton, 52, 94–95, 257, 369, 377
Rosnow, Ralph L., 172
Ruechelle, Randall C., 162–63

Sapir, Edward, 192–93
Scheidel, Thomas, 96, 251
Schein, Edgar, 375
Schneier, Inge, 375
Scott, Robert L., 353
Sereno, Kenneth K., 258

Shanck, C., 151
Sheffield, Fred D., 150–51
Shenfield, Nathan, 150
Sherif, Carolyn, 91–93
Sherif, Muzafer, 91–93, 103
Skinner, B. F., 66
Spencer, Herbert H., 195
Steiner, I. D., 382
Stevens, Walter, 225–26
Stokes, Donald E., 325
Strunk, William, Jr., 201
Suci, George, 52–53, 62–63, 190–92

Tannenbaum, Percy, 52–53, 62–63, 190–92, 247
Terwilliger, Robert F., 156
Thistlewaite, Donald L., 150
Thompson, Ernest, 170
Thorndike, E. L., 66
Toulmin, Stephen, 144–46
Triandis, Harry C., 192
Turner, Ralph H., 10

Vernon, M. D., 111
Vohs, John L., 223

Wallace, Karl, 350
Walter, Otis M., Jr., 351
Weaver, Andrew T., 188
Weiss, Walter, 262
Whilhelmy, Roland D., 277
White, E. B., 201
Whorf, Benjamin, 192–93
Wieman, Henry, 351
Wright, Charles R., 292

Zavos, Harry, 140